AF804503

The New Europe at the Crossroads

PETER LANG
New York • Washington, D.C./Baltimore • Boston
Bern • Frankfurt am Main • Berlin • Vienna • Paris

The New Europe at the Crossroads

Edited by
Ursula E. Beitter

PETER LANG
New York • Washington, D.C./Baltimore • Boston
Bern • Frankfurt am Main • Berlin • Vienna • Paris

Library of Congress Cataloging-in-Publication Data

The new Europe at the crossroads / edited by Ursula E. Beitter.
p. cm.
Includes bibliographical references.
1. Europe—Civilization—20th century. 2. Multiculturalism—Europe.
3. Ethnicity—Europe. 4. Nationalism—Europe. I. Title.
D2009.B445 940.55—dc21 98-20813
ISBN 0-8204-3923-1

Die Deutsche Bibliothek-CIP-Einheitsaufnahme

The new Europe at the crossroads / ed. by Ursula E. Beitter.
–New York; Washington, D.C./Baltimore; Boston; Bern;
Frankfurt am Main; Berlin; Vienna; Paris: Lang.
ISBN 0-8204-3923-1

Cover design by James F. Brisson

The paper in this book meets the guidelines for permanence and durability
of the Committee on Production Guidelines for Book Longevity
of the Council of Library Resources.

© 1999 Peter Lang Publishing, Inc., New York

All rights reserved.
Reprint or reproduction, even partially, in all forms such as microfilm,
xerography, microfiche, microcard, and offset strictly prohibited.

Printed in the United States of America

Dedication

To my friends

Acknowledgments

I am very grateful for the support and constructive criticism of Dr. Heidi Burns. Also, I would like to thank Marion Wielgosz at Loyola for her skill, patience and technical support.

Contents

Preface

Background to the Conference "The New Europe at the Crossroads," held August 3–7, 1997 in York, England.

During the discussions with German authors at the Loyola College annual seminar on German literature in Berlin it became apparent that there was a genuine interest in such topics as multiculturalism, European identity, the role of the arts and classic education, not only in present day Germany, but in the Europe of the future as well.

To further shed light on these issues the Department of Modern Languages and Literatures at Loyola College in Maryland organized an interdisciplinary conference which took place on the campus of the College of Ripon/St. John in York, England. The purpose of the conference was to discuss how Europe's classical heritage, its traditions in education, in the arts, and in literature would serve a united Europe in the next millennium. Our call for papers was successful; scholars from the United States, Canada, Germany, Israel, Poland, Finland, Ukraine, Russia, Estonia, Holland, and Algeria answered the call and attended the conference to discuss issues that concerned the destiny of Europe in the 21st century.

Dr. Uwe Haus, in his capacity as chair of the Intercultural Group of the Society for the Study of European Ideas (ISSEI) disseminated information about the conference to colleagues in the arts and in the field of theatre. Dr. Haus also assisted in the selection of abstracts and chaired some of the sessions at the conference. The unique cooperation between Loyola College in Maryland, the Department of Modern Languages and Literatures, and the Intercultural Group of ISSEI proved instrumental to the success of the conference.

We would like to express our gratitude to Prof. Guy Stern, who delivered the key note address on Dr. Coudenhove-Kalergi and the roots of the pan-European movement. Prof. Stern's address provided the conference delegates with much appreciated background material on the ideological genesis of European unity.

The conference's success was also due to the support of Steven Watson, Principal Lecturer at the University of Scarborough, School of Management. Mr. Watson's introductory remarks about the city of York acquainted the conference delegates with the York's significant historical past. Mr. Watson was instrumental in having Rod Hills, Leader of the City Council of York, officially open the conference during our reception of St. Williams College. Mr. Hills spoke eloquently and passionately about York's historical legacy and about its growing importance to international business.

Of considerable worth were the contributions made by our colleagues from the former iron curtain countries. Their attendance involved clearing substantial bureaucratic hurdles and making financial sacrifices. For many of them, this was their first trip abroad since the fall of communism. The presençe of scholars from the East with their lively and passionate manner of disquisition, provided the conference with an intellectual and cultural breadth it would have lacked otherwise.

A number of the papers presented during the conference were selected for publication in this volume. I am grateful for the advice given me by Dr. Andre Colombat and Dr. Hanna Geldrich-Leffmann of the Department of Modern Languages and Literatures at Loyola. I am also indebted to Dr. Heidi Burns for assisting with the difficult selection and editing process.

Dr. Ursula E. Beitter

Introductory Remarks

Ursula Beitter

For politicians, economists, and global business the European Union became a reality on paper on Nov. 1, 1993. But judging by the still ongoing debates about what exactly constitutes a "European Union" and by the vehement opposition to it from grass roots elements in England, Scandinavia, France, and Germany, it is obvious that there is no accord on how to make this union a success, nor what it will eventually portent. For the most part the reservations expressed by the vox populi are being ignored in favor of speeches by heads of state who have staked their career on starting the euro. The average person in Europe remains skeptical about the alleged benefits of political union, not to mention a common currency. The grumblings of the Euroskeptics is not only heard on the streets of Germany, France, and Britain, they also form a very vocal group on the worldwide web. The chatroom for such diverse groups as Nei Til EU, June Movement, or European Union Follies and Myths make it quite clear that skepticism as well as opposition to a financially unified and politically integrated Europe is more prevalent than heads of state are willing to concede. Conboy's article in this volume, for example, informs us that the *Daily Express* launched a campaign which it called "Stop the Euro-Rot." Another paper, the *Sun*, referring to St. George's day, proclaimed: "Today is St. George's Day, when the people of England honour the knight who slew the dragon. St. George's deed is mythical, of course. But there is a very real dragon which threatens every single one of us throughout the United Kingdom. That beast is the European Union, an unelected body answerable to no one which aims to devour our national identity."

Even though the currency union is immanent, it might be worthwhile to review some of the changes that Europe has undergone since the idea of a united Europe was first conceived, to ascertain whether or not it might be prudent to re-consider the aims of a European Union. The century that will see the EU has little in common with the time in which the idea of a European union was born. Coudenhove-Kalergi's elite-humanist vision of a united Europe, the *Angst* of a guilt ridden nation (Germany) and its desire to sublimate its potential aggressiveness into the whole of a united Europe, the political power plays of the Cold War era, all had a part in forming the idea of a EU. Yet, in 1989, the political constellations were changed drastically with the fall of communism in East Germany and in the East bloc countries. This is not an appropriate forum to review the momentous changes wrought by the collapse of communism; suffice it to say that the politicians and engineers of the European Union have kept their eyes firmly fixed on the goals set for the EU during the Cold War era. In spite of the fact that the collapse of communism has brought fourth enormous changes in the political balance, not to mention the new migrations of peoples which are challenging societies in most of western Europe, a rethinking of the idea of European unity has not been a major factor in politics. As if on automatic pilot the politicians are pursuing a common currency and a united Europe; very few dare to consider that a united Europe might be an idea whose time has come, and gone —or that it is an ideal whose romantic essence of peoples living together without boundaries is constantly being mocked and challenged by the barbarous excesses we have been witnessing in the newly founded nations of the Balkans. Mr. Kohl, for example, has had two missions since he became chancellor: one, to work for the reunification of Germany, and the other, to arrange the political constellations in Europe in such a fashion as to prevent future wars. While the proponents of the idea of a united Europe (with Germany at the helm) are willing to pursue a political ideal that does not stress national identity (at least on paper), the excesses of nationalism and national pride are all too well alive in the fledgling countries that were born out of the former iron curtain countries. 1989 caught the West by surprise; a major oversight of the politicians has been to consider how the newly formed nations will relate to the West. Almost ten years after the fall of communism we are witnessing a belated debate over who will and who will not be permitted to become part of NATO. "Fortress Europe," might now have an entirely different meaning than the one it had when it was first coined. It no longer refers only to the apprehension of American big business that a united Europe might freeze out American businesses; it can also now be said that a united Europe is becoming a fortress against all the newcomers in politics and nationhood. Furthermore, since the idea of a united Europe first took shape, there are other changes in the world, most prominently, the idea and implementation of globalization, whose effects on national identity and European Union are not yet fully assessed.

It comes as no surprise that the speeches and visions of the defenders of a united Europe deal mostly with the purported economic benefits such a union would bring. Missing from the debate are serious explanations of how a common currency will benefit the average person; missing from the debate are ideas on how to deal with the recurring unrest in the former East-bloc countries, and, above all, missing are proposals on how to relate to the millions of Arabs and Turks in France and Germany, respectively, to the Caribbeans and Indians in the United Kingdom, not to mention the millions of peoples that have migrated to Germany and other EU countries, in order to flee the violence and religious persecution in their newly formed nations. But perhaps one expects too much of politicians to address questions that are less of a political and more of a human\societal nature. Certainly the answer given in Germany to the influx of refugees and asylum seekers was disappointing: the politicians decided that the way to deal with the influx of asylum seekers was to cut back on Germany's once liberal and generous asylum laws. In France the answer comes rather loudly in the form of votes cast for the New Right, intend on reducing the numbers of Arabs and Muslims in France.

In contrast to power brokers and politicians the delegates assembled in 1997 at the conference The New Europe at the Crossroads wrestled with questions of identity, nationhood, and multicultural relevancy. The main concerns of the majority of the delegates were not the economic ramifications of a united Europe, but how our "old" European heritage, our Judeo-Christian traditions would serve a multicultural Europe in the future. The main question that was raised repeatedly by professors from disciplines as diverse as Theatre/Arts and Philosophy to Literature was how do acknowledge and deal with the "Other" and what really constitutes cultural identity. Repeatedly the delegates not only discussed cultural but also national identity with conference delegates from Eastern Europe, who made it quite clear that the former East bloc countries are fervently seeking a post-Soviet identity. All too often, finding cultural and national identity seems to go hand in hand with religious orthodoxy and suspicion of foreigners and their ideas (see the contribution by Tereskinas in this volume).

While some zealously defended their pious illusions that the European Union would be able to realize its utopic vision of uniting diverse cultures, other delegates, of a more postmodern mind set articulated their skepticisms toward such an undertaking. Arnds' paper, discussing some German authors' views of multiculturalism, treats this question in detail: "If writers doubt the possibility of a union within one country (and Delius is not the only one), how then, one might ask, can such a union be accomplished between different nationalities, between different cultural origins?" Schindel, one of the authors cited in Arnds' paper comes to the conclusion "that a harmony between these different origins cannot be reached. The result can only be a fragmentation, a fragmented world" (Arnds). The author discussed by Arnds certainly concedes that the fascist tendencies of the eighties are still alive in the nineties, and Arnds is of the opinion "that fascism as an extreme version of intolerance toward the Other shakes the very foundation of the idea of a European Union." Images of the Other and national identity (and how it is maintained) also animate the paper of Conboy, who examines the dangerous and nationalistic role played by newspapers and tabloids in preserving, defining, or reconstructing Englishness. Conboy suggests that any "investigation into the future of Europe needs to explore the archive of nationalist discourse — what makes the site of Europe a potential concept? — and the contradictory role of nationalism within the archive."

Overcoming ignorance and the violent excesses of nationalism are also the topic of Egéa-Kuehne's paper. She points out that Derrida already wondered whether "the future (of Europe) will…escape monstrosity. For in the name of identity, be it cultural or not, the worst violences, those that we recognize all too well without yet having thought them through, the crimes of xenophobia, racisms, anti-Semitism, religious or nationalist fanaticism, are being unleashed, mixed up, with each other…with the very spirit of the promise." As already stated above the social, political, philosophical, and economic realities of the world have changed since the Cold War and the fall of communism. Egéa-Kuehne focuses on educators and intellectuals and their role in making Europe a more tolerant place to live. She quotes Derrida: "Intellectuals the world over have to re-think the meaning of 'old' paradigms, and develop new ones. For instance, what is the new model for a democratic society in the face of problems of homelessness, violence, fierce nationalism, virulent ethnocentrism, xenophobia, and exterminations?" For Egéa-Kuehne the answer to hatred of the Other is education. To the authors Ellis & Khan, addressing themselves to multicultural Britain, the answer lies more in accepting the identity of the Other, thus becoming "More unified while becoming more diverse." They indicate that the growing issue of racism was, to some extent, acknowledged at national and local levels through legislation and policy-making, but concede that the implications of the diversity of culture were far more problematic for government. Policies of assimilation, championed by politicians, are ultimately seen for what they were: unrealistic. Ultimately, so they seem to indicate, the parties involved embraced the catchword of "celebration of differences," all the time aware that "little was done to address the implications for citizenship of a multicultural society, or to effectively challenge the hegemony of the dominant culture." An outlook, which hesitantly contradicts the bold opening premise of the paper, that a society can be "more unified while becoming more diverse."

Time and time again, the discussions following the presentation of papers focused on what aspects of the past should be salvaged into our future. Or, to what extent the future could be liberated from the ballast of the past. Gould's presentation, drawing on the works of Derrida deftly combines questions to the past with deconstructionism and attempts to answer: "How can we set sail toward a newly new Europe without considering which histories are left behind, untold?" In other words, what should be repeated, what should not be repeated, taking into consideration the fact that when the Iron Curtain lifted in 1989 it "revealed a world that had not changed since 1939, a world rife with the same old nationalism and the same destructive inter-ethnic conflicts that remain at the heart of, say Bosnia." (Gould, quoting Robert Lafont). Gould comes to the sobering conclusion, that we live in a time that sees a "humanism in crisis. It can no longer guarantee the privileges of humanity that humanism, with its tradition of *belles lettres* and hermeneutic method, once promised." Khleif's contribution reiterates the fact that "the history of Greece is part of the European cultural heritage," and, at the same time, goes beyond the classical tradition to point out that there are other, less lofty aspects that have shaped the character of European identity: "The Crusades are part of European identity, of animosity against Arabs and Muslims, of vague feeling of revenge, of a desire to even the score." Khleif concludes his paper with references to racially motivated violence in our decade and ties it in with the theory that "identity needs a myth constructed about the 'Other,'" be it the Orient or Arabs in France or Turks in Germany. Maynard's paper also discusses fear and hatred of the "Other." Her presentation focuses not on the treatment of a particular ethnic or religious minority in a particular country — instead, she examines a common denominator in European countries — the young people. The next generation. She comes to the conclusion that a major problem of European identity are the symptoms of social pathologies manifested by many of the young: "disenfranchised young people, industrial decline, structural unemployment, violence, extremist or racist politics, and drug and/or alcohol abuse...as Europe approaches the millennium, the euphoria created by the end of the Cold War may be replaced by new anxieties about the continent's future involving xenophobia, neofascism, and various kinds of destructive (or self-destructive) behavior primarily by young people."

Cultural misunderstanding, understanding the "Other," was also the topic of Mensch's paper, who believes that the ideological conflicts of the Cold war have been replaced with the rise of cultural strife. Mensch uses a philosophical approach and simply investigates how we go about understanding different cultures. "What are the grounds and premises of such understanding? How does such understanding tie into the basic ethical theories that have marked the West?" Mensch calls for nothing less than the construction of a new paradigm, "one fundamentally different from that animating Western, scientific rationality." He suggests that we rethink what actually constitutes selfhood, which he believes is already implicit in the works of Plato, Kant, Freud and Darwin. Mensch's paper draws on the Western classic heritage and asks that we rethink ourselves vis-à-vis the "Other," that we admit others into our self-presence, which might then lead to meaningful changes in attitudes. Europe's classical heritage also plays an important part in the paper of O'Reilly, who seeks a solution to Europe's current cultural strife in the form of an enlightened humanist leader, such as Vaclav Havel. She believes that new times need new leaders and that Europe "should look to heirs of its humanistic tradition rather than to bureaucrats and technocrats to provide the leadership it needs in this difficult time of transition."

The majority of the papers are concerned with identity and difference, with attitudes towards the "Other" in European societies, and with the role of Europe's classical heritage during times of transition. Like Maynard's article, Pribic's paper makes clear that the "Other" does not necessarily have to be a stranger, from a foreign land. His article discusses the acrimonious debates and hateful accusations between the P.E.N. Club members of the former East-Germany, and the P.E.N. Club members of West Germany. The main bone of contention, up to 1997, was who was allowed to belong to the P.E.N. of the unified Germany, and who was to be excluded because he/she might have had communist leanings or have been too closely tied with the GDR-government and its secret service (the *Stasi*). Those of us who have been to Germany know that to this day, there still is a divide between East Germans and West Germans, a divide not only based on money and privilege, political background, and class, but a divide created by the fact that the citizens of each "former" Germany are obstinately determined to remain ignorant about each other, thus perpetuating old stereotypes. It is indeed sad that in a time of momentous transition — not only unification of Germany — but the creation of a common Europe, of globalization with its often negative economic effects of unemployment, the nation that spearheads the European movement is still divided against itself, and bickers over who is to be punished and stigmatized for not having opposed the regime of the GDR more vociferously. There is something almost comically, stereotypically German in this single-minded display of righteousness among the German intellectuals (Haus' article in this volume is an example of this attitude). Intellectually Germany is a house divided against itself, and the debate in the P.E.N. Clubs is but an example of this divide. At a time when Europe is about to be transformed Germany's intellectual leaders engage in internecine trench-warfare while the world they live in transforms itself. After almost nine years of bitter fighting, the disputing parties have agreed to a truce and to form a new P.E.N. club. The sad part is, that this logical step should have been taken much earlier. It is also sad that this bitter debate has consumed intellectual energies that might have been put to better use — such as, for example in helping to educate Germans about each other, to discuss the role, future, and contribution of Germany's many "foreign" citizens, and to keep an eye on the rise of German nationalism among Germany's unemployed youths.

During the discussions that followed each paper it became obvious that discussion of the "Other" always involved a discussion of the rise of nationalism. Be it in Germany — and much more so in France, where the presence of minorities has occasioned outbreaks of right-wing hostilities — the rise of nationalism is a very real factor in the societies of western Europe, but more so in the nations formed out of the former Eastern-bloc countries. Tereskinas' paper spares no words in describing the fact that the newly formed nations in the East use an anachronistic nationalism as a form of identity. "There is a united Europe, but the new nations emerging — and their nationalism form a threat to the new order." It seems to matter little to those countries, that this rhetoric was used by Hitler and is a rhetoric whose tragic consequences are still with us today in the Balkans. Tereskinas suggests that Lithuanians use old nationalistic rhetoric: "the rhetoric of archaic nationness," to "devalue all other identification," — and prevent identification with the West, which conservative Lithuanian intellectuals perceive as wildly capitalist, degenerate, und degrading. Tereskinas paper is disturbing because it implies that history is repeating itself in a very tragic fashion: while Europe is trying for political unity and harmony, new nations are finding their identity in old cliches, and unity in hatred. According to Tereskinas it is the intellectuals, conservatives, and right wingers, who have launched successful conspiracy theses in Lithuania, and are in search for an enemy. The enemy, so Tereskinas' interpretation of the Lithuanian press, is found in American liberals and Hollywood. Thus, forming a national identity can be accomplished only with searching for a scapegoat. It is disturbing that this rhetoric of blaming American liberals and Hollywood is reminiscent of the rhetoric used during Hitler's regime. And, as is the case in other western countries, one chooses the "Other as scapegoat." Tereskinas' paper is interesting for another reason: he points out that America's overwhelming presence in the electronic media, on television and in movies has made people think that

America colonizes Europe, that American culture will soon replace other, indigenous cultures, leading not to national cultures, but to "globalized cultural identies." The question as to whether such an identity could not be something positive considering the evils brought to us by a narrow identification with national values was not discussed at length but needs to be discussed. Senigaglia's paper also addresses the questions of identity and the "Other." Her paper sees the present-day confrontations between groups against a historical background. She contrasts the medieval world, which was "dominated by a central function of religion and by a hierarchical representation of reality, which were commonly accepted," to our "atomized society" in which individuals are seen as "particles." "At every corner we meet persons belonging to other cultures, religions, countries, who don't share our habits and rules. The result is that we live in a condition of permanent tension and contradiction.... This sense of indefinite dissatisfaction takes shape by means of an obstinate although implicit refusal of unity and homogeneity, often accompanied by an exaggerated will or desire to distinguish from the other."

Another approach to the question of identity was taken by Verthuy. The authors cited in her paper describe France as a nation that has a future in which differences "don't disappear nor merely coexist, they collaborate to create something new." The rise of the French right party is not much of concern to the authors whom she discusses. "The migrant writers are pointing the way towards a new France and a new Europe." A similar sentiment — that people share in a common experience but retain their own identity — is voiced in Everett's paper on the internationality of today's mega-musical operas.

It will not be possible to preview all the contributions in this volume, but it should be said that a unifying concern of the conference and of the papers was what of the past should be salvaged into the next millennium. As indicated earlier, this was an interdisciplinary and international gathering of scholars, and at one time or other, they raised the question whether or not the future can really be liberated from the negative aspects of our common past. And considering the strife in the Balkans and ethnic unrest in Europe, the answer was not always a resounding yes. And, still unanswered is the question of how to cope intelligently with a desire for national and ethnic identity in a century and society which will be made smaller by increased electronic communication and a globalized economic structure.

From the few papers introduced here it is clear that the conference's purpose "to investigate how Europe's classical tradition will serve it in the years to come," was a success. Not because it answered all the questions that concern our future and are usually not dealt with by politicians, but because it raised new ones and provided a forum in which to discuss them.

Introductory Remarks, II

Heinz-Uwe Haus

Without coming to terms with the past there will be no entering into the future. What animates such platitudes is not only disagreement about what happened in the past and what the past was, but uncertainty about whether the past really is past or whether it continues, albeit in different forms. During the conference "The New Europe at the Crossroads," some of the delegates articulated that people both desired and feared a retardation of change. Presently there are calls for a breather in European unification and for the increasingly reciprocal opening-up and cooperation among European countries and peoples. Many of the conference delegates thought that there is no alternative to further reforms in Central and Eastern Europe, and to a gradual continuation of European integration, and to the gradual inclusion of reformed post-Communist countries in the EU. Most of the delegates agreed that ideological concerns over the norms of identity is understandably entangled with the interests and agendas of the various nations. There was much discussion on what constitutes national identity, but there was agreement on at least one subject: that European identity is not homogeneous and probably would never be. Repeatedly the question was raised, to what extent the past (i.e., the old communist power apparatus), influenced the present, be it in the former East bloc countries or in the unified Germany. This particular issue animated the discussion in several sessions and many suggested that a solution could only be found when the Left discovered: "The sober prose of everyday democratic practice."[1]

Many of the conference participants saw the weakening of civil responsibility and solidarity as one of the principal threats to the process of democratization and unification in Europe. The future of its societies has been described again and again with three known catchwords: civil society, community, and Europe. The new concepts of "civil society" and "community" also take into account the events in Eastern Europe during the eighties. In a remarkable reversal of direction of influence, it is from there that the concept of "civil society" returned to the West-European debate, particularly among the Left. But in my opinion the short blossoming of the spontaneous civil society, separate from the state, as found in Prague, Warsaw or Budapest during the eighties, should not only receive positive appraisal, but should also be treated skeptically. Without wanting to devalue the close ties of natural community — everything that Eastern intellectuals like Vaclav Havel associated with the word "home" — I would rather call the ideal of the "heterogeneous" nation state which is to grow into the world society. I fully agree with Ralf Dahrendorf, that the German Left in particular, has failed "to understand the civilizing effect of the heterogeneous nation state."[2] I firmly believe that we have to be aware of the fact that there is still a Left misusing the concept of "civil society" as an antithesis to the concept of the liberal constitutional state. They are transforming the idea of a civil society into an ersatz ideology of the Left. I agree with Gerhard Wettig: "If a 'civil society' — as an essential prerequisite in the long term for the realization of Western value concepts, is to develop, only a national framework can provide the starting-point given the conditions which prevail in Eastern Europe. Under these circumstances, calling upon East European peoples to overcome their 'national restrictedness' would merely have a counterproductive impact. As experienced by the Western part of the continent in an earlier phase of history, the countries of Eastern Europe must go through the development of nationalism before they can work towards goals which lie further afield."[3] As evidenced by the many papers on "Identity" delivered during the conference, many delegates believe that the strongest challenge for Europe is currently being caused by the concepts of "nation" and "nationalism."

This international gathering of scholars repeatedly discussed the question of unity and identity. The economists that attended the conference focused on the crucial question as to whether the European nations would be able to form a political entity that could survive against global competition. They recommended, that the focus should be on minimum conditions for unification, all the time not forgetting that Europe's first priority must be an attempt to assist the post-Communist countries in every way possible while standing firm in international regional human rights requirements, demonstrating that it is in the latter's economic interest to meet all conditions for entry, especially human rights and legal-democratic requirements.

The conference and discussion did not answer all the questions on European identity in the next millennium, but it did make clear that how we formulate or represent the past shapes our understanding and views of the present.

Notes

[1] Tony Judt, *Political Management, in: The Challenge of Participatory Democracy*, Kyklos 5/1996, p. 17.

[2] Ralf Dahrendorf, in: *Policy Sciences*, p. 32.

[3] Gerhard Wettig, *Shifts Concerning the National Problems in Europe*, in: Aussenpolitik 1/1993, p. 70.

The Paradox of the European Union and Postmodern Literature in Germany and Austria

Peter Oliver Arnds

The idea of a European Union completely disagrees with the postmodern tendencies reflected in many literary texts. In this essay I want to demonstrate this paradox by means of three examples: one German novel, Friedrich Christian Delius's *Die Birnen von Ribbeck* (1991), and two Austrian novels, Robert Schindel's *Gebürtig* (1992), and *Selige Zeiten, brüchige Welt* (1991) by Robert Menasse. Whereas the European Union aspires to the utopian ideal of unity between diverse cultures, postmodern literature tends to do the opposite: it is often filled with a deep skepticism toward utopia, a historical pessimism, and it frequently fragments any sort of unity, whether between countries, between groups of people of different origins, or on the highly personal level of love relationships. In the following excursion through three literary examples I will show how they incorporate the possibility of a totalization process, which they then proceed to thwart. In each case the result is fragmentation rather unification. The idea of a European Union completely disagrees with the postmodern tendencies reflected in many literary texts. In this study I want to demonstrate this paradox by means of three examples: one German novel, Friedrich Christian Delius's *Die Birnen von Ribbeck* ("The Pears of Ribbeck," not translated) from 1991, written immediately after the German reunification, and two Austrian novels, Robert Schindel's *Gebürtig* (translated as *Born-Where* in Ariadne Press) from 1992, and *Selige Zeiten, brüchige Welt* ("Blissful Times, Fragmentary World," as yet untranslated) also from 1991 written by the Jewish Viennese writer Robert Menasse.

Whereas the European Union aspires to the utopian ideal of unity between diverse cultures, postmodern literature tends to do the opposite: it is often filled with a deep skepticism toward utopia, a historical pessimism, and it frequently fragments any sort of unity, whether between countries, between groups of people of different origins, or on the highly personal level of love relationships. As Paul Michael Lützeler and Jean-François Lyotard have shown among others, one of the central differences between modernism and postmodernism is the following: while the classical modern novel of such writers as Joyce, Gide, Kafka, Thomas Mann, Döblin, Musil, and Broch mourned the loss of totality that the realist novel of the nineteenth century still represented, "one central feature of the postmodern condition is the definitive acceptance of the impossibility to revive such a totality."[1]

In the following excursion through three literary examples I will show how they incorporate the possibility of a totalization process, which they then proceed to thwart. In each case the result is fragmentation rather unification.

I

My first example, Friedrich Christian Delius's *Die Birnen von Ribbeck* ("The pears of Ribbeck"), obviously implies a literary allusion to Theodor Fontane's equally named poem on aristocratic generosity and thriftiness. Delius's narrative takes place in the East German town of Ribbeck, visited shortly after reunification by a busload of West Germans, who want to celebrate the political event with the locals. They drink a lot of pear schnapps and plant a pear tree as a symbol of the union between east and west and the generosity of the westerners toward the easterners. One can hardly ignore the parallels with Fontane's poem, in which it was in the hands of the rich aristocrats whether they would generously let the poor children take some of their pears. In Delius's text, however, the westerners' generosity is muted by their very own gift, the pear tree, which yields only dry and sour pears. Moreover, they visit the village merely to get drunk, and are not interested in the complaints of the narrator, a Mecklenburg farmer. It is his complaints that fill the entire narrative in the form of a single seventy pages-long sentence. Since the farmer, who talks without much interruption, weaves in and out of the different time layers and his own associations, this is a spoken rather than an interior monologue. That it is a monologue and not a dialogue is important in the context of my discussion because the monologue reflects Delius's deep skepticism in the union of East and West Germany. A successful union would entail a dialogue between the parties to be united. What is expressed on a formal level, the difficulty of a union, is also reflected on the level of content. I want to elucidate this by way of three short examples from the text.

First, a union between east and west would mean a mutual approach, yet in this first step toward the union as it is presented in this text the western values are imposed on the eastern population. The West Germans are, in fact, depicted as colonizers. When the "Wessis' first arrive they gawk at the locals as if they were natives of a just discovered land ("bestaunt wurden [wir] wie Eingeborene" [9]).[2] They arrive with busses that are painted red, white and blue, i.e., in the colors of the tricolore, and the farmer reports how they occupy the village with their "herrischen" (7), their "imperative, domineering" vehicles. In addition to the gift of the pear tree they bring little trinkets like inflatable air balloons and pens, a gesture that is very reminiscent of the discovery of continents and the fact that discoverers like Christopher Columbus on first spotting the American natives gave them glass beads.

Second, the farmer is convinced that the union between east and west is merely a monetary union: "jetzt führt das Geld uns zusammen, Prost!" ("now the money leads us together, cheers!") (67). Ironically, he claims that he feels elevated by the harder currency but questions whether the new values can outweigh the dire consequences of the political union: can the fresh Tchibo coffee bean make up for the unemployment of the kids who leave school, do the bananas make up for the new and as yet unknown wave of crime, do the tasty chocolates make up for the plastic garbage mountains? Moreover, he feels that the East Germans have traded their storks (which for some reason have been feeling more at home in East Germany than in the west) as a symbol of the east for the symbol of the west, the coca cola can. At the same time he does not want to sing a eulogy on socialism, and is aware that the socialist party has suppressed him just as much as he thinks he will loose out under the new system. The historical developments have filled the farmer with a deeply rooted skepticism and have taught him that the changing political landscape does not necessarily entail changes for him and his fellow sufferers.

Third, the central image of the pear tree symbolizes that the union between east and west will not bear fruit. Intoxicated by the pear schnapps the farmer curses the westerners' gift: "aber kannst du mir sagen, weshalb ihr ausgerechnet eine Birne ausgesucht habt, die warme Lagen braucht, erst im Dezember reif wird und fade und trocken schmeckt, wenn die Früchte wachsen im dritten Jahr" ("but can you tell me why you have chosen a pear tree that needs warm locations, that does not ripen until December and tastes dry when it bears fruit in the third year") (63). This is reminiscent of the children in Fontane's poem who bewail the death of the old generous Ribbeck and the fact that they can no longer get any pears: "Das war nicht recht, ach sie kannten den alten Ribbeck schlecht, der neue freilich, der knausert und spart, hält Park und Birnbaum strenge verwahrt" ("That wasn't right, oh they did not know old Ribbeck well, the new one, of course, he's thrifty and mean, and keeps well-locked his park and the pear tree").

II

If writers doubt the possibility of a union within one country (and Delius is not the only one), how then, one might ask, can such a union be accomplished between different nationalities, between different cultural origins? This question is the central theme in the Austrian novel *Gebürtig* by Robert Schindel. Here the chasm lies mostly between Austrian Jews and Austrian non-Jews, the impossibility of their rapprochement, but also between Jews and Germans. A panopticum of characters illustrates again and again that the diverse *Gebürtigkeiten,* the *nationalities* (the term "nation" and "native" are linked to "being born," i.e., "gebürtig") cannot come to a mutual understanding and acceptance of one another. The German term *Gebürtigkeit* goes beyond the English concept of "nationality" in that it establishes boundaries between cultural identities rather than national ones. In this way the problem addressed in Schindel's novel, the irreconcilability of different group identities within one country, is similar to the unbridgeable gap between East and West Germans in Delius's text. However, another point of criticism in Schindel's novel, one that he shares with a large number of Austrian writers, is that their country is closed to the rest of the world, to the Other as anything foreign. Schindel's novel attempts to go against this by opening its terrain to various settings, which extend from Vienna to the Austrian province, from Venice to Hamburg, and even as far as New York City as the novel's multicultural utopia. Schindel renders his text multicultural also by introducing a multitude of characters of different origins. At the same time, however, the novel's conclusion is that a harmony between these different origins cannot be reached. The result can only be fragmentation, a fragmented world. In order to illustrate how the characters have a deep urge to unite but ultimately fail to do so I want to focus briefly on one narrative strand in the multistranded novel.

One of the characters is Emanuel Katz, a Viennese Jew and the author of a book within the book. He writes the story of Herrmann Gebirtig, a Holocaust victim who returns to Vienna from New York City to testify against an old Nazi bully. Emanuel has a weakness for tall blonde North German women, who are in mentality and appearance the very opposite of him who is short and dark. The novel presents Emanuel's love relationships as his attempts to unite with a complete counterpart, with what historically he should most despise. His friends in Vienna say that he wants to "blondify" himself through his North German valkyries. That his blondification ultimately fails becomes obvious in the scene when he visits the family of his girlfriend Käthe in the North German town of Bremen. Here he meets her brothers Hans and Holger, "eine Ansammlung semmelblonder Monster" ("a collection of monsters as blonde as wheatbread") (134), who are culturally perfectly insensitive.[3] They ask him, a banker by profession: "'Und wann werden Sie die Bank übernehmen?' fragte Holger und richtete seine klaren blauen Augen interessiert und ohne Anflug von Spott auf Emanuel. 'Gestern,' antwortete Katz. 'Meiner Sippe gehört jetzt schon das Bankwesen von Wien und das halbe von Unterhollabrunn.' Er lächelte." ("And when will you take over the entire bank?" attentively and without a trace of derision Holger directed his clear blue eyes at Emanuel. "Yesterday," answered Katz. "My mishpuche already owns most banks in Vienna and half of all the banks in Unterhollabrunn." He smiled.) (135). The provocations on the part of the North Germans keep piling up to the point that Katz gets completely exasperated with the whole family including his girlfriend Käthe. He ends up calling them a pack of Nazis and breaks up with her. Examples of this sort of tension between Austrians and Germans, Jews and non-Jews are legion in Schindel's novel. Schindel transposes a large amount of his criticism of Austrian fascism also into the Katz manuscript, which allows him to maintain an ironical distance. By disappearing behind the persona of Emanuel, Schindel's own voice is masked by the voice of a character. The distance thus achieved also results from the typically postmodern decentralization of time in the novel. The events involving Gebirtig are not only removed as a narrative level but also twice removed in time from Schindel's own writing: from the early nineties, through the time in which Katz writes his manuscript, 1983/84, to the time within the manuscript in 1981/82. Yet because of the constant interweaving of the past with the present the two can never be seen as isolated from one another. The result is that what Schindel denounces as a fascist tendency for the eighties contains the possibility of being still alive in the nineties. In the context of my discussion of the link between this type of literature and the European Union I want to emphasize that fascism as an extreme version of intolerance toward the Other shakes the very foundation of the idea of a European Union. In reading Katz's manuscript we follow Herrmann Gebirtig's changing emotions about Austria and primarily about Vienna. The development of his rapport with the city begins with his prejudices. When Lebensart, the character who is responsible for the still ongoing denazification of Austria, tries to talk him into coming to Vienna to testify against the former Nazi Egger, Gebirtig spills over with hatred for the "Austrian Nazis:' "'Soll ich daran schuld sein, wenn die österreichischen Nazis ihn nicht verurteilen?' 'Herr Gebirtig. Die Richter sind keine Nazis. Auch die Geschworenen nicht. Hoffentlich'" ("Is it my fault if the Austrian Nazis don't convict him?" "Mr. Gebirtig. The judges are not Nazis. Nor are the jury. I hope.") (121). What initially sounds like a prejudice, the fact that fascism in Austria may still be alive, takes on through Lebensart's reaction the color of a possible truth. In the one word "hoffentlich" (I hope) Lebensart, who has made it his "way of life" (hence the name) to hunt down Nazis, reveals that he secretly fears that Gebirtig's accusations may be true. This word becomes all the more daunting in its impact if we keep in mind that unlike Gebirtig, Lebensart has stayed in Austria and is therefore a keen witness of current events. Gebirtig's prejudice is directed not only against Vienna but also against rural life in Austria. Repeatedly throughout the novel Styria is identified with fascist tendencies: "Die Leute dort haben doch nie einen Hitler gebraucht. Die waren immer schon so" ("The people there have never needed a Hitler. They have always been like that.") (122). Vienna, on the other hand, Gebirtig labels as "die Welthauptstadt des Antisemitismus" ("the world capital of anti-Semitism") (208). His fears and prejudices that at first keep him from returning to Vienna function as a hyperbole that makes both the readers and characters, who may have become blunted to the presence of fascism nowadays, contemplate whether Gebirtig's reaction is not justified. When he does finally return to Vienna what initially seems to be a prejudice then slowly begins to reveal itself as the truth. The officials he encounters have such label names as Leibenfrost (Bodyfrost), Katzenbeißer (figuratively, the one who bites the author of the manuscript, Emanuel Katz, because the latter wants to expose Viennese anti-Semitism) and Kattelbach (Turdcreek), a potential speaker for Gebirtig's laudatio, whose record shows "bloß zwei judenfeindliche Passagen" ("only two anti-Semitic passages") (226). The city's fascism is also evoked by the appearance of the blackish-yellow German shepherd who keeps growling at Gebirtig as he walks through the streets of Vienna. The same mean dog occurs twice during Gebirtig's stay (298, 329) and we associate him clearly with fascism as we approach the end of the novel. In the epilogue's concentration camp setting we see a similar German shepherd among the Nazi oppressors (352). Yet the people Gebirtig encounters in the Vienna of the early eighties are not much better than their dogs. Those who were Nazis in the thirties and forties, like Hofstätter, the son of the former house principal, now try to justify their past crimes by calling themselves victims of those who were above them:

> "Den meisten ist es wirklich mies gegangen. Ihr habt das nicht so gemerkt, ich weiß. Da hat's der Hitler leicht gehabt.... Die oben machen immer, was sie wollen. Unsereiner hat alles auszulöffeln.... Sicher. Ich war ja damals für den Adolf. Aber das war nicht gegen euch persönlich" (306 and 307). ("Most of us have really suffered. You [the Jews] never noticed, I know. So Hitler had an easy time with us.... Those above always do what they like. And we have to suffer for it.... Sure. Back then I [Hofstätter] was for Adolf. But I was not against you personally [Gebirtig's family].")

Gebirtig forgives Hofstätter, shakes hands with him and in the course of his stay even develops an affection for Vienna. His original fear of it turns into the wish to stay and he wants to buy an apartment. "Viel hat sich verändert in Wien" ("Much has changed in Vienna") (307), he thinks, although now Lebensart shows more skepticism than before and warns him against staying, "Wien bleibt Wien" ("Vienna remains Vienna") (319), a view supported by such fine signals as the fact that the newspapers only cursorily mention Gebirtig's concentration camp years, of which he gives a lengthy description at the Egger trial. Along with Gebirtig, the reader is lulled into believing that all is fine under the blue Viennese skies until they hear the verdict of the trial. Despite Gebirtig's testimony Egger is set free. Immediately, Gebirtig's senses are sharpened again, and as we follow him through the streets of Vienna he sees the cold eyes of his former neighbor Mrs. Leitner, he becomes painfully aware of the people staring at him, he notices how Hofstätter hides behind the curtains rather than greeting him as he did only a few days earlier (328). The only one who is consistent in his reactions to Gebirtig is the mean German shepherd dog who never stops growling at him (329). His owner doffs his hat in an exaggerated manner and "alle hatten sie die Arme vor der Brust verschränkt" ("they all had their arms crossed over their chests") (329). Schindel's/Katz's narration becomes wonderfully measured on these last pages of the manuscript. Without telling us about Gebirtig's reaction to the outcome of the trial we are, however, fully aware of his emotions as he relinquishes all his plans concerning a permanent stay in Vienna, gets back on the plane and flies (flees) to New York. What was a prejudice at the beginning of the Gebirtig-strand sounds like a cliché outside of Emanuel's manuscript but is a truth within it: "Vienna remains Vienna."

At the end, the characters in Schindel's novel always fall back into their own *Gebürtigkeiten*, their own cultural identities. Relationships between Jews and non-Jews, Austrians and Germans break apart again, and the novel ends with such conclusions as "Jew remains Jew," or "Vienna remains Vienna." The novel's epilogue entitled "Verzweifelte," "the desperate ones," contains the enactment of a scene in a concentration camp for an American movie, in which one of the narrators and the editor of Emanuel's manuscript, the Jew Demant, plays the part of a prisoner. All prisoners run around barefoot in the snow and consequently get very cold feet. The image of cold feet and a heated head is a central one in this novel and expresses the coldness between the groups of different cultural and national origins, the irreconcilability of their differences, their cultural self-centeredness and intolerance of the Other. The last words of Demant may express a faint hope for the future: "Da denk ich mir, wann endlich warm werden die Füße, und Kopf bleibt wunderbar kühl, kann passieren, daß kommt nicht der Messias, sondern ein schönes Gefühl" ("I think to myself, when the feet finally get warm and the head stays wonderfully cool, it may happen, that not the Messiah will come, but a beautiful feeling") (353). This hope, however, gets crushed by the weight of pessimism that fills the entire novel.

III

The third and last example that I want to discuss is the novel *Selige Zeiten, brüchige Welt* (Blissful Times, Brittle [Fragmentary] World) by Robert Menasse, who, like Schindel, is a Jew from Vienna. The title of his novel unites the two sides of the paradox discussed here, the blissful times promised by the utopists who believe in the possibility of a unification of diverse cultures, and the brittle and fragmented world that such pessimists as the writers presented here hold against it. Of course, Austria in this text is merely one example of the cultural closedness it shares with many other European countries. In a travel guide on Great Britain, to give another example, under the category of Xenophobia one can read the following:

> Like many island peoples, the British, and especially the working classes, have a profound distrust of outsiders, perhaps equating them unconsciously with invaders. It is not by chance that it took them so long to agree, reluctantly, to help finance a tunnel beneath the English Channel. The writer Nancy Mitford expresses an extreme version of this narrow-mindedness: "Abroad is unutterably boring and foreigners are fiends." The actor Robert Morley was more circumspect: "The British tourist is always happy abroad so long as the natives are waiters.[4]

In his essay on Austrian identity, *Das Land ohne Eigenschaften* (The Land without Qualities, not translated), Robert Menasse has said: "'Österreichische Identität'—dieser Begriff hat etwas von einem dunklen und muffigen Zimmer, in dem man, wenn man aus irgendeinem Grund eintritt, sofort die Vorhänge beiseite schieben und das Fenster öffnen möchte, um etwas Luft und Licht hereinzulassen.

Doch wenn das Fenster keine Aussicht hat und sich der Raum daher nur wenig erhellen will?" ("Austrian identity—this term contains something of a dark and musty room, in which as soon as one enters one wants to pull aside the curtains and open the window to let in some air and light. But what if the window has no view and therefore not much light can enter?").[5] Throughout his work, Menasse has made it his main concern to provide Austria with such a room with a view, by which he hopes to achieve a double effect: the people inside will be able to enjoy the view of the world and will profit from the light and air that comes in, and, inversely, the world outside will be able to look into the room and, thanks to the light now inside, discern more clearly what is within. Menasse's novel *Selige Zeiten, brüchige Welt* is a good example of the extent to which a literary text wants to transcend its culturally determined boundaries. It is a text about the gestation of a philosophical text which at the same time is Menasse's very own sequel to the novel *Selige Zeiten, brüchige Welt*, called *Die Phänomenologie der Entgeisterung*, The Phenomenology of Despiritualization, published in 1995. The novel's protagonist Leo Singer, a Viennese Jew who is at home both in Austria and Brazil, unsuccessfully attempts throughout his life to write this thesis on Hegel's famous *Phenomenology of the Mind*. Leo and his girlfriend Judith Katz, herself a Jewish Brazilian of Austrian origin, are students in Vienna but end up in São Paulo, which used to be their parents' exile during the Nazi years. Here Leo manages to live comfortably thanks to the property he inherits from his parents. It is here also that Judith finally writes the Hegel text that Leo has always wanted to write. At the end of the novel Leo kills her in order to install himself as the author of the text she has written. *Die Phänomenologie der Entgeisterung* is hence a book produced within a book. Its theme is the regression of Hegel's evolution of thought to its disjunct beginnings and it has three authors: Menasse, its living author, Judith, its fictional author, and Leo, who makes himself its author by killing her.

With his novel *Selige Zeiten, brüchige Welt* Menasse attempts to open his country's windows primarily in two ways. On the one hand, the author widens the ethnic boundaries of his text by giving it multicultural characters and by locating the plot both in Vienna and São Paulo. On the other hand, the text wants to transcend strictly delineated cultural and chronological barriers through its intertextuality. The novel contains several subtexts of which Hegel's *Phänomenologie des Geistes*, one of the most difficult texts of western philosophy,[6] is the central structure-forming subtext. By creating a transcultural and densely intertextual text Menasse aims at a totalization of the world in his novel, an objective he shares with many of the realist writers in the nineteenth century. At the same time, however, he also fragments his fictional world. Hegel's principle of totality is the motivating force behind Menasse's attempt to transcend cultural boundaries. When asked for the links between Hegel and Brazil, Leo Singer answers that in his view Hegel's central category of totality implies that no country as only a small part within a whole can shut itself away from the world, which is that whole ("Ein Ort wäre nur ein kleiner Teil vom Ganzen.").[7] With the help of Hegel's philosophy, this book tries to annul qualitative differences that people make between countries. Brazil can easily be replaced by any country of the European Community to which any other E.C. country might consider itself superior. Hegel's notion of totality corresponds to the final stage in the development of the history of the mind, of *Geistesgeschichte*, which he called the Absolute Spirit. Hegel places his own philosophy at this peak of history, where in his eyes reason reigns supreme. Fredric Jameson has eloquently summarized what can be understood by this notion of the Absolute Spirit: it is "a space in which all contradictions are presumably annulled, the gap between subject and object abolished, and some ultimate and manifestly idealistic form of Identity is established."[8] The Selige Zeiten ("blissful times") in Menasse's title echoes this concept in all its idealism. It heralds the possibility of a world in which the gap between subject and object has been largely obliterated, in which the subject recognizes (Hegel's calls it "anerkennt") the Other and forms with it a synthesis, a world in which monocultural subjectivity is replaced by multicultural objectivity. The impossibility of such a world is suggested by the second half of the novel's title, brüchige Welt ("fragmentary world"), and especially by its sequel *Die Phänomenologie der Entgeisterung*. On a pragmatic level, the novel attempts to achieve some degree of objectification in that it exposes the reader to two cultures, Austria and Brazil. In all attempts at totalization and consequent objectification on a textual level, however, the novel fails, whether as a synthesis of the two places or of the two central characters, Leo and Judith. The failure of a Hegelian synthesis—note that this kind of synthesis is also the aim of the countries in the European Union—is, in Menasse's novel, entirely due to the anti-hero Leo. The novel is an Antibildungsroman in its best sense, that is, a deconstruction of the nineteenth-century ideal of the Bildungsroman in which the hero still came to a synthesis between himself and the world. The Bildungsromane following the example of Goethe's prototype *Wilhelm Meister* aspired to a balance at the end of the hero's formation between his personal egotistical aims and society's expectations of him, a resolution of what Hegel calls the conflict of the hero's poetry of the heart and its antagonistic prose of external conditions.[9] Menasse systematically deconstructs the blissful times of this traditional Bildungsroman-utopia of the nineteenth century. The realist novel in particular, with its aim of the character's successful integration into society, was an attempt to realize Hegel's concept of totality. By making use of a number of narrative categories typical of the Bildungsroman of the last century, Menasse tells us of the potentialities of those blissful times, were these not continuously thwarted by a world out of joint. That the world is indeed fragmented and that the individual's objectification is an illusion is his novel's sinister conclusion.

Leo achieves as little objectivity through exposure to two cultures as he does through love. Instead, he repeatedly comes to stand in front of mirrors (e.g., 97–98), a central image in this novel, and an activity that reveals his infantile admiration for himself, reflected but not recognized. In an evaluation of Freudian theories, Lacan has argued that the infant goes through a narcissistic mirror phase before it starts objectifying itself in the dialectic of an identification with the Other, which is the beginning of the subject's socialization.[10] Leo shares his mirror neurosis with Judith, who is constantly surrounded by mirrors (35). Their love is largely thwarted because according to Hegel love is a dialectic process that entails giving oneself up for the sake of the other. The loving subject loses itself in the beloved object, the thesis thus merging with an antithesis. The thesis finds its original identity obliterated but gains an altered and enriched identity through the experience of love. This new identity is the synthesis, which much like in Hegel's dialectics of history is located on a higher rung.[11] This ideal of the individual's objectification in a love relationship can be seen as corresponding to the rapprochement between different cultures. In either case the subject has to lose itself, step outside of itself to come closer to the Other. Whether the subject (Leo) has the possibility of being unified with the object as a foreign culture (Brazil) or as a lover (Judith), the success of such a unification would in both cases be a step towards the Hegelian ideal of totality. Yet in his fixation with himself, with his own reflection in the mirror and the Hegel text that he wants to write, Leo never unites with any other, neither Vienna, nor Brazil, nor Judith. None of these manages to alienate him from himself and his self-involved intellectual pursuit. The unbridgeable distance between Leo and Judith may be best rendered by an image which the protagonist describes in one of his early attempts at coming to grips with Hegel: he imagines himself in front of one mirror and Judith in front of another, with the two mirrors facing each other. The result of such positioning of mirrors is that both characters disappear in the infinitude of their own reflections, forever distancing themselves from one another (79–80).

Conclusion

My discussion of the three texts has shown how these authors toy with the notion of a unification process, a totalization of the world, which they then go on to fragment.[12] Particularly in view of rising fascism in Germany and Austria, opening windows becomes important in order to rid these counties of their ethnocentricity and to shape their self-understanding, since according to Hegel's dialectic one gets to know oneself better by getting to know the other.[13] The three texts, however, all end on a note of pessimism. In our age of egotistical interests, in which the individual is no longer willing to give up his/her subjectivity (hence the rise of fascism), the reconciliation between the poetry of the heart and the prose of circumstances to which the nineteenth-century Bildungsroman aspired has become a utopian ideal. This difficulty of an objectification between individuals as well as between individuals and their own cultural surroundings repeats itself between cultures, also between the cultures of the European Union. My three literary examples reflect their authors' doubts that in the nineties Germany and Austria have already transgressed Lacan's infantile stage of self-mirroring. The authors show these two countries still in a pre-socialization stage where, in the language of Hegel, neither country has begun objectifying itself in the dialectic of an identification with the Other as a foreign culture. In his recently published inaugural speech for the 1995 Bookfair at Frankfurt, Menasse expressed his own disillusionment:

> Es hat keinen Sinn, zu klagen oder zu verurteilen, wie es auch keinen Sinn hat, schön zu reden und auf etwas zu hoffen—eine schöne Utopie, wie zum Beispiel die, daß weltweit wirklich werden möge, was wir in dieser Woche auf dieser Messe erleben: ein friedliches und produktives Zusammensein von Menschen aller Nationen, Sprachen und Kulturen. (There is no use in complaining and condemning, as there is no use in fine words and in hoping for a beautiful utopia, like the one that we will see worldwide what we see at this fair this week: a peaceful and productive coexistence among the people of all nations, languages, and cultures.)[14]

For Menasse writing is like a loud chant in dark forests.[15] This chant carries with it the possibility of a depetrification of the conditions in such countries as Germany and Austria, yet how can he be heard from the middle of these dark forests? Windows can be opened but what if they have no view and therefore not much light can enter?

Notes

[1] Paul Michael Lützeler, "Von der Präsenz der Geschichte. Postmoderne Konstellationen in der Erzählliteratur der Gegenwart," *Neue Rundschau* 104/1 (1993): 95; my translation.

[2] Friedrich Christian Delius, *Die Birnen von Ribbeck* (Reinbeck: Rowohlt, 1991). All following quotations from this text are marked merely as page numbers in brackets.

[3] Robert Schindel, *Gebürtig* (Frankfurt am Main: Suhrkamp, 1992). All following quotations from this text are marked merely as page numbers in brackets.

[4] Roger Williams, ed., *Insight Guides: Great Britain* (Boston: Apa Houghton Mifflin, 1995) 110.

[5] Robert Menasse, *Das Land ohne Eigenschaften* (Frankfurt am Main: Suhrkamp, 1995) 7.

[6] Bertrand Russell, *A History of Western Philosophy* (New York: Simon & Schuster) 730.

[7] Robert Menasse, *Selige Zeiten, brüchige Welt* (Frankfurt: Suhrkamp, 1994) 160. All following quotations from this text are marked merely as page numbers in brackets.

[8] Fredric Jameson, *The Political Unconscious: Narrative as a Socially Symbolic Act* (Ithaca: Cornell UP, 1981) 50.

[9] Georg Wilhelm Friedrich Hegel, "Die Poesie," part 3 of *Vorlesungen über die Ästhetik,* (Stuttgart: Reclam, 1971) 177.

[10] See Jacques Lacan, *Écrits* (Paris: Éditions du Seuil, 1966) 94.

[11] This process is described very intelligibly in Wilhelm Weischedel, *Die philosophische Hintertreppe* (München: dtv, 1973) 213–14.

[12] Linda Hutcheon identifies this postmodern tendency for a number of novels. She calls it "the postmodern paradox of anti-totalizing totalization in…novels which structurally both install and subvert the teleology, closure, and causality of narrative, both historical and fictive." In: Linda Hutcheon, *The Politics of Postmodernism* (London/New York: Routledge, 1989) 63.

[13] See Robert Menasse, "Nützlicher Idiot Haider?" *Hysterien und andere historische Irrtümer* (Wien: Sonderzahl, 1996) 39: "Österreich droht neuerlich im Faschismus zu versinken" ["Austria threatens to drown in fascism these days"].

[14] Robert Menasse, "'Geschichte' war der größte historische Irrtum: Rede zur Eröffnung der 47. Frankfurter Buchmesse 1995," in *Hysterien und andere historische Irrtümer* (Wien: Sonderzahl, 1996) 33.

[15] Ibid., 36.

The Ethnic Origins of Readerships

Martin Conboy

This essay will examine the ways in which the national newspapers in Britain construct a discourse of national identity. In particular, it will inquire about the tradition which newspapers have evolved, that is, as articulators of a public interest in political affairs. In terms of the situation in contemporary Europe this essay will highlight how the British press, particularly the popular tabloid newspapers, far from conforming to liberal notions of a democratic media, are in fact exploiting their relationship with the discourse of nationalism to further the aim of a parochially oriented marketing strategy. This concept challenges the traditions of citizenship and participatory democracy within European discourses of the public sphere. The news media are able to articulate a tolerance for diversity and a plurality of opinion, while at the same time balancing this with their need to produce profits by targeting specific audiences within the nation. This is a central concern to the democratic traditions espoused in many discourses of the press and is key to how this develops in the context of the evolving political entity of Europe. Concerning this, Eric Hobsbawm wrote in the New Statesman and Society in 1992: "Historians are to nationalism what poppy-growers ... are to heroin-addicts: we supply the essential new material for the market."[1] Implicit in this statement is a loosened bond of intentionality. Poppy-growers do not deliberately create the addicts nor do historians construct nationalism as their primary objective. It is the contention of this essay that, in their paste and copy pastiche of national rhetoric and symbolism, national newspapers in Britain articulate aspects of the wider discursive formation of nationalism.

This essay examines the cultural and economic politics of the representation of Englishness in the British national press. These "nationals" have, through the very diversity of their registers — narrative, entertainment and metaphorical — a huge impact in fashioning the ways in which the nation is appellated.

The category of news itself has always been intrinsically linked to a sense of community and national specificity from pamphlets reporting the battle of Floddon and the flourishing of journals vying for the voice of the people of England during the Civil War to what Billig refers to as "news apartheid in the contemporary press."[2] In fact, it is possibly the only constant in the newspaper's claims to our loyalty — its national partisanship.

It is only comparatively recently that the press was able to consider itself as a Fourth Estate.[3] In Britain that particular historical moment soon passed into the more cautious assertion that the newspaper has its feet in economics and its head in politics. The institution and practice of the national press cannot simply be reduced to one ideal function. It is, in fact, located at a crossroads with routes marked responsibility, profit, entertainment and information. To retain its paradoxical coherence, it is permanently in the process of engaging simultaneously on all of these routes but may never stray too far down any of them. In its complex configuration, it is an excellent example of a vector of what Foucault may have identified as a discursive formation.

This location at a discursive crossroads has been made more problematic by the definition of these options evolving in the context of the nation state. One of the primary functions of the national newspaper, therefore, has been to define that nation and make good the connections with the nation's communal past. This sits uneasily with its claims to be a force for democracy and as an essential forum for the public sphere especially in an age when the sovereignty of the nation state is being eroded though globalizing pressures. From a Foucauldian perspective, such discontinuities provide the transformational potential which makes the newspaper such an agile agent of the discourse of nationalism.

Within a national, market economy the scope for differentiated appropriations of the discourse of the nation illustrate the alignment of the economic and the cultural, evident in the newspaper. Newspapers edit a selection of events which are identified as of interest to a particular readership. In terms of the nation, newspapers literally edit Britain, narrowing it down from a range of possible depictions. This composite must be one which will appeal to and feed into the readership's perception of the unity of the nation. Paradoxically, there will be convergence and divergence in the edited versions of the nation tailored to the inch for the intended customer/reader in different newspapers.

Newspapers, and particularly newspaper owners are keen to remind their readers of the democratic imperative which drives them. A recent example is Lord Rothmere reported in one of his own newspapers, the Daily Mail. On a trip to Hungary, speaking to the English Speaking Society in Budapest:

> One thing is sure. You cannot have a democracy today without freedom of speech and communication.…The old community of village was sustained by contact, mutual assistance and gossip.…It was evidence of people's interest in each other and caring for each other. That is dying — so newspapers and the electronic media must fill this important need.…Media in a free society must be commercial to survive. Its public responsibilities will always be subordinate to its need to meet the wages' bill and the need for profit.[4]

This makes explicit the linkage between profit and community in the newspaper industry yet, in the context of this discussion, it deflects attention from the national framework within which this democratic duty takes place. Likewise, canonical views of the press as Fourth Estate fail to account for the limitations of any public sphere based on the normative principles of the nation state with its logic of exclusion of outsiders. James Curran has stressed the role of the press in the "normative integration of British society" pointing out that, "There has been an extraordinary continuity in the symbols used in the popular press to de-legitimize radical or potentially deviant groups."[5]

The nation-state, as addressed and articulated in the national press can be regarded as a community based on imaginary bonds. Not just imaginary bonds between people who may never have met, as Anderson has expressed it,[6] but also imaginary bonds with a national past which supports and gives coherence to it. In reviewing Anderson's chief theses, Anthony Smith is keen to downplay the invented nature of nationalism or the imaginary role of the nation. Smith's analysis highlights the part played by ethnic tradition in the reconstruction of identities and the rise of nationalism and nations. "Typically, where the modern nation claims a distinctive ethnic past, as so often happens, 'invented traditions' turn out to be more akin to 'reconstruction' of aspects of that past. The latter acts as a constraint on 'invention.' Though the past can be 'read' in different ways, it is not any past, but rather the past of that particular community, with its distinctive patterns of events, personages and milieux."[7]

This is a fair exposition of the role of actually mediated memories and the continuity of symbolism required for any longevity in national identification but such continuity itself also needs re-constructing, refining for each generation, in terms of the specific conjuncture in which the new generation finds itself. What is gained and what is lost in the space between successive pedagogy and performance of the national rhetoric is the elusive substance of the discursive formation of the nation.

Here, it is useful to consider Foucault's suggestion that discourse is defined at its borders not by its interiority.[8] There is a field of conceptual compatibility which, as discourse, is demarcated by its field of incompatibility. This may assist investigation into the role that the newspaper plays in the discursive formation of nationalism and in the re-construction of continuity. The newspaper may not stray too far in one direction while using the compatibilities of nationalist discourse to promote its own economic and political self-interest. Incompatibility arises, for instance, when the rhetoric of exclusion rubs against the claim of the press to watchdog status on behalf of the public community as a whole. However, the newspaper retains its resilience as one of the most effective sites for this discourse of nationalism because of its location at a particularly dynamic/productive discursive crossroads.

This de-centered concentration allows an observer to concentrate on the exteriority of discourse, on the structuring within a particular institution rather than on the essence. It insists upon a focus on the reconfiguration in a specific time/place and on the power of that location in a specific time. It is an attempt to wrestle the discourse of nationalism away from the seductive power of essentialism. For in the examples that follow we will not see Bhabha's "scraps, patches and rags of daily life repeatedly turned into the signs of a national culture."[9] We see something much more grandiose — to invert Billig's phrase "grand memorable phrases rather than small words"[10] — a strategy of reconvening the symbols of the past as the unproblematic vehicles of present identity within the nation. "In the production of the nation as narration there is a split between the continuist, accumulative temporality of the pedagogical, and the repetitious, recursive strategy of the performative. It is through this process of splitting that the conceptual ambivalence of modern society becomes the site of writing the nation."[11]

The British national press is negotiating a place for a community in a globalized media landscape. This is chiefly driven by the economic reality that news is consumed locally although it may be owned by a global conglomerate. National identity in this scenario becomes a global media marketing ploy. Writing of the emergence of modern nationalism Smith claims:

> There is also a need, in such destabilizing circumstances, to mask the radicalism of social change with a veil of tradition and continuity with an assumed past, usually a national one. Certainly it is in the interests of ruling classes and sub-elites to foster such a sense of continuity in order to re-socialize uprooted populations and inculcate new values of order and hierarchy.[12]

This reveals that the discourse of nationalism that may be reactivated as a response to a very different set of challenges — those of accelerated globalization. Globalization is causing an erosion of power at the geographical site of national discourse. Yet, at the same time, as part of a wider resistance to the flattening pressures of the global, newspapers in Britain are pursuing a symbolic renegotiation of that terrain. The national newspaper paradoxically functions as a vehicle of the Other as news but is singularly unreceptive to the logic of globalization in its local (national) appeal.

Here is an opportunity to build upon Smith's analysis and add a Foucauldian gloss which will make it more apparent that the central concern is how these images are permitted to circulate and gather new meanings and messages in contemporary contexts. This does not make them any less constructed but it certainly takes the simplicity of agency away from what is a more complex and persuasive phenomenon. "The problem arises of knowing whether the unity of a discourse is based not so much on the permanence and uniqueness of an object as on the space in which various objects emerge and are continuously transformed."[13]

Foucault's observation on the unity of discourse can be applied as an interrogation of journalism's claims to generic coherence and reveal that the struggle is, paradoxically, to retain journalism's discursive heterogeneity. The effectiveness of newspapers lies not in internal coherence and continuity but in heterogeneity and discontinuity in performance. The relevance of this insight with regard to newspapers' relationship to the discourse of nationalism is clear:

> A discursive formation, then, does not play the role of a figure that arrests time and freezes it for decades or centuries; it determines a regularity proper to temporal processes; it presents the principle of articulation between a series of discursive events and other series of events, transformations, mutations, and processes. It is not an atemporal form, but a schema of correspondence between several temporal series.[14]

Smith's ethnic authenticity may be interpreted as what Foucault refers to as historical a priori. There is an eternalism of ethnic symbolism as if it has emerged apparently fully formed at the moment of the nation's birth. Is it possible to think a space that was Britain without it being populated by Shakespeare, John Bull, Britannia et al.. This is the specifically historical a priori knowledge that Foucault proposes as part of his analysis. Newspapers depend for their popular currency on the sophistication with which they adopt the archive's systematization of statements about the national community: the archive as " first the law of what can be said... also that which determines that all these things said do not accumulate endlessly in an amorphous mass, nor are they inscribed in an unbroken linearity, nor do they disappear at the mercy of chance external accidents."[15]

In the case of contemporary British nationalism what we are witnessing is a revision of nationhood; a return, in many sections of the press a lexical reconstruction of a certain "distinct ethnic past" and its effectiveness is ample illustration of how one of nationalism's strategies aligns with the economics of the popular press. If the persuasive deployment of the symbolism and rhetoric of nationhood is essential to the maintenance of control over other groups in a society then in the case of mediated national identities, it is coherence and fixity rather than dialogue and problematization which assist the cohesion of power elites. This aligns with the tendency to search for a more authentic past under the pressures of identity loss in the contemporary world. Writing of the conservation of identities against a tide of global forces, Robins and Morley have observed: "The driving imperative is to salvage centered, bounded and coherent identities ... it is about the maintenance of protective illusion, about the struggle for wholeness and coherence through continuity."[16]

Whatever the ethnic authenticity or "popular resonance," as Smith calls it, of these calls from the past, they are inextricably linked in their inappropriateness as representatives of a modern diverse citizenship. Stuart Hall has pointed out, "ethnicity, in the form of a culturally-contrasted sense of Englishness and a particularly closed, exclusive and regressive form of English national identity, is one of the core characteristics of British racism today."[17] It is what Anthias and Yuval-Davies refer to as "hegemonic 'Anglomorphic' ethnicity."[18]

In many quarters of the press a need to redefine national readerships is being articulated as a textual purification of the British nation. This is a dangerous notion to have at the heart of a notion of a public institution, yet it drives the logic of a press based on a market which is increasingly nationalistic.

The national newspaper in Britain is a hugely influential vehicle for narrating the nation. It has enormous institutional reach and has the flexibility to respond on a daily basis to the shifts of mood and the flow of information into the national community. In effect, newspapers renegotiate Englishness in Britain. The coherence of the British nation and the exact status of England within it, is extremely volatile. It is suffering locally as a result of its decline in status and power since the Second World War and globally from the generalized loss of national sovereignty implicit in the development of transport, technology and capitalist organization. Globally, a crisis in traditional relationships is driving attempts to reinterpret older modes of belonging such as nationalism, ethnicity, fundamentalism and even xenophobia into new paradigms. In such a crisis, loss of sovereignty and an increased awareness of difference is breathing new life into nationalism. As Raphael Samuel has observed, "The very uncertainties surrounding the idea of nationality may have served, paradoxically, to renew its popular appeal."[19] This is for the very good reason that if the nation-state wishes to retain its political authenticity it must retain its cultural attire for the sake of its credibility. In the press, the nation-state represents a market and a discourse of belonging. The crisis afflicts both nation and industry and one solution is a revision of England.

The following article was in the Daily Mail on April 23, 1996:

> "To be English in England today is almost a criminal offence. We have become a country in denial.... Richard Littlejohn asks why England is now a nation that dare not speak its name." He claims he was prompted by a dozen random guests at the Lord's Taverners' Spring Lunch not knowing when St George's Day was.

The newspapers' laments are accurate in that the patron saint of England is a forgotten irrelevance but it is they who attempt to (re)vitalize a tradition which they acknowledge as dead by injecting contemporary relevance into the symbolism, reworking rather than simply referencing an essence. Again this reinforces the exteriority of any definition of discourse located at the border where it becomes renegotiated in terms of a new historical context. Yet it also underlines the resilience of the discourse of nationalism and its felicitous association with the popular newspaper in Britain. The fact that the chief chroniclers of this alleged decline in national pride are the right-wing newspapers, The Daily Mail, The Daily Express and The Sun, indicates which forces attempt to make capital out of the recycling of this imagery. As Samuel has observed "Certainly a reinvigorated nationalism, albeit defensive rather than aggressive, has been not the least of Conservatism's popular appeals."[20]

Punning on its own version of telephone democracy, The Sun called on its readers to phone in their opinion on a variety of issues connected to the European Union:

> **“EU THE JURY**
> TODAY is St George’s Day, when the people of England honour the knight who slew a dragon.
> St George’s deed is mythical, of course. But there is a very real dragon which threatens every single one of us throughout the United Kingdom.
> That beast is the European Union, an unelected body answerable to no one which aims to devour our national identity.
> Britain’s role in Europe is the biggest issue this country has faced in the past 300 years.
>
> Sun - St George’s day.”[21]

The Daily Express launched a campaign which it called a “crusade” — Stop the Euro-Rot — on 23 April 1996, St George’s Day (also Shakespeare’s birthday). Columnist Derrick Hill’s piece is headlined, “By George, why the English must be more English.” — “It’s true, the English do not go a bundle on conspicuous nationalism and feelings of nationhood.” How can a nationalism so shy be so bombastic in its own defense? This apparent contradiction belies the important role the press plays in reconstructing Englishness. It exposes the part claiming to represent the whole which has the potential to undermine the solidarity of nationalism but at the same time characterizes the strategic imperative of the national newspaper, in its market mode, particularly in its popular format to define a national grouping. This synecdochal logic drives another element of the dynamic of national identification in the broader range of exclusion which it is able to call upon. Not just other nations but other groups of perceived outsiders can be marginalized by reference to a narrative of continuity and community. In the run up to the date we have an editorial in The Sun on 15 April

> “**By George**
> **Why does England care so little about its patron saint?**
> A St George’s Day parade in London has been canceled because the police said it would cause traffic jams.
> Can you imagine Dublin ignoring St Patrick’s Day, New York shunning July the Fourth or Paris banning Bastille Day?
> You can bet no one would have dared object to a march by militant gays.
> **St George will turn in his grave.”**

There is a certain irony in the revision of national identity in textual form through the medium of the newspaper. National newspaper ownership is far from co-terminous with nationality or residence in Britain as Murdoch, Black and Rothmere illustrate. Traditionally hostile to notions of increased European sovereignty, the entrepreneurial right in British politics are fully in favor of a deregulated free trade area of Europe to further their own economic ambitions. Such economic ambition is dressed up in traditionalist cultural clothes for the readers of the papers. As British newspapers are so clearly focused on national markets, at a time of diminishing newspaper readership, an increased appeal to the nation, whether as culturally or economically determined, certainly assists in enhancing its market appeal.

This is not the only irony in the textual renegotiation of national identity as part of global media empires. There is the intriguing juxtaposition of the advertisements and culture of transnational corporations, with their own images and symbolism flattening differences, and the vigorous nationalist campaigns in the editorial of the same newspapers. A glance at even the most vitriolically nationalist newspapers would reveal a host of advertisements for a whole range of identifiably non-British products and services. Yet the economic imperative of advertising does not disrupt the discourse of nationalism within the popular press illustrating once again the discontinuities and discursive flexibility which make such effective co-strategists.

Nationalist symbolism in its contemporary guise blurs sovereignty with heritage in staking a claim through the newspapers to our present identity. This conforms to wider patterns of the appropriation of nostalgia in Western societies. The eternal present of the newspaper meets the eternal past of the symbolic reservoir of the national memory inviting us to partake in a reinforced national present. The national newspaper, as discursive agent, owes its strength to the double articulation of communal experience of Benjamin's "empty homogenous time"[22] and the simultaneity of the essentialist, structuring device of national destiny. Such a thesis would confirm Barthes' observation that: "myth has the task of giving a historical intention a natural justification, and making contingency appear eternal."[23]

The historical intention is the renegotiation of the national at a time of threat and its legitimizing strategy is to pull on core symbols and reinject them with new meanings, in other words to re-historicise them. Billig writes that the sports pages echo the language of warfare and talks of the metaphors of weaponry in sports writing[24] but there is nothing banal or metaphorical in the political debate over the Beef Crisis. This was a hyperbolic intervention and they all joined in, even in condemnations of Euro-sceptic excess in the Guardian of 22 May 1996 where we find the language of combat and explicit reference to historical references to the Second World War:

"Major goes to war with Europe
CBI urges peace in our time
Sir Bryan Nicholson, president of the CBI, speaking last night"

From the aggressive reaction of the right wing tabloids to the reflection in the broadsheet Guardian on the importance of beef to notions of Englishness, the representation of the beef crisis in the press turned from health scare to a war of national defense. It is possible to reformulate the thesis proposed by Halliday, Jansen and Scheider, in the context of Eastern Europe - "crisis denotation as a way of identifying and especially targeting the foreign "other" necessary for maintaining the structures of power."[25] In terms of the European Union, press coverage suggests that it is an issue which lends itself to just that strategy and may be used as metaphor for deeper uncertainty about national sovereignty in globalized economic patterns. April saw campaigns to suit the policies of the papers. The Daily Express ran a week long campaign, "Stop the Euro-Rot." The Sun used Kitchener's famous First World War recruitment poster to run its referendum on a single European currency and offered chances to win Kitchener car stickers and badges of the campaign. The Daily Mirror ran a counter campaign to persuade readers of the benefits of EU membership. While the right wing press attempts to reactivate nationalist rhetoric in ways appropriate to the contemporary situation, the liberal press articulates its concerns over the crisis in its own terms. Crucially, both work within the confines of the homeland and give the impression that crises endanger the coherence of national identity.

Matthew Fort, food editor of the Guardian, illustrates this indicating that a sure way to a nationalist's intellect is through his stomach:

> Beef has a symbolic importance that far outweighs its dietary importance.
> Beef is one of the great unifying symbols of our culture.
> The Roast beef of Old England is a fetish, a household god, which has suddenly been revealed as being a Trojan Horse for our destruction. To have one of the mythic foundations of Our Island race so traduced and demeaned strikes at the very heart of our sense of identity.[26]

An excellent example of how the press, far from simply reporting national trends create and embroider upon themes created according to archival imperatives was the case of Geoff Hurst's ball from the football World Cup Final of 1966. The Sun and The Daily Mirror competed to find the ball and offered rewards for its recapture. It served as a burlesque illustration of the return to 1966 prefiguring the leitmotiv of Euro 96. Refashioning the characters in a drama all but forgotten by those under 40 enabled the papers to play an educational role in more than a civic, liberal sense: this was education in ethnic nationalism and its pantheon.

> Daily Mirror (27. April, 1996):
> "It's the moment all England has been waiting for."
> SAVED FOR THE NATION
> "We are proud to have returned this ultimate symbol of British sporting achievement to its rightful place. We are also extremely grateful to Richard Branson, our most dynamic entrepreneur, and Eurostar. The World Cup football is home where it belongs."
>
> Mirror Deputy Editor Brendon Parsons

The Sun 27. April, 1996 selects a few opinions from its readers about the affair. These reinforce what Barthes maintained about the potency of mythic discourse and its status as "depoliticized speech." Here we have common-sense, presented persuasively as vox pop within a cultural framework which is rearticulating a pastiche of German stereotypes as neutral, fun and unproblematic.

Laura Cunningham 19 "What do you expect from the Germans? They will try and sell their granny if they thought they could get away with it."

The Sun's front page on the day of the match with Germany 26. June, 1996 echoes the Falklands' campaign and the nationalistic reference to "our boys."

THE PAPER THAT GENUINELY SUPPORTS OUR BOYS

Printing words of the song "Three Lions on My Shirt," to support the team on its front page is indicative of the way newspapers can still be considered as an act of religious worship or at least the hymn book! These are some of the references by which certain imagery is kept in circulation and develops national significance at each mention.

On the eve of the Maastricht referendum in France 18. September, 1992 the Daily Star produced an historic double editorial. I quote selectively in order to illustrate a contrastive parodic potential to the revision of England in the light of historic alliances as represented in the tabloids:

> "The French and us have had a rough old history.
> Nous avons eu, avec les Français, une longue histoire mouvementée.
> France is a major player in the world league. It has a proud language, a proud history and a proud heritage. Just like us.
> La France joue un rôle primordial dans le monde. Elle est fière de sa langue, de son histoire, de son patrimonie. Tout comme nous.
> Alone in Europe, the French have the power to free us from its German-ruled chains.
> Seule la France en Europe a le pouvoir de nous libérer de ses fers allemands."

The segmentation of media markets added to an increasing global erosion of national political sovereignty cause deep problems for nation-states in how they articulate the political legitimacy of their structures. Such a crisis is expressed in the British national press in terms of a renegotiation of the symbolism of ethnic nationalism. Such nationalism is not however simply a matter of conforming to a selection of unproblematic ethnic memories. It is a profoundly textual affair and one embedded in the specific political and economic practices of the British press.

Conclusion

To return once again to Barthes: "What the world supplies to myth is an historical reality, defined, even if this goes back quite a while, by the way in which men have produced or used it; and what myth gives us in return is a natural image of this reality."[27] Newspapers remain just as influential at negotiating their role as myth-machines, especially when wedded to a rhetoric of ethnic authenticity. It is as if certain newspaper proprietors in Britain had gained privileged access to the poppy fields of history because of the specific relationship between the press and its public and its ability to function as an organ which renegotiates the discourse of nationalism between market and memory, politics and profit.

The practice and content of British newspapers with regards to national identity is supported and made possible through the broader discursive formation of nationalism. The discontinuities/contradictions of their cultural practices are harmonized through their economic imperatives. They are able to preach a revision of Englishness as a constituent of British identity, partly in response to the economic realities of news media even in a global environment, and partly in response to a heightened desire for stable identities. The success of the nation and the success of the medium are both bound up in nationalist discourse's attempts to restructure its hegemony. Globalization provides the programmatic underpinning for the reinvention of continuity in the newspaper press.

The implications for a Europe at the crossroads are twofold: first any investigation into the future of Europe needs to explore the archive of nationalist discourse — what makes the site of Europe a potential concept? — and the contradictory role of nationalism within that archive: second, to foreground the permanence of the location of the discourse of Europe at a crossroads. This is the sine qua non of the European experience rather than as a metaphor for a final choice of direction as a totalizing gesture. Within the paradox of the newspaper's narrative of belonging lies the problematic and the resolution of ethnic specificity in a plurality of narratives. It is in the plurality of registers within which the newspaper presents the complexities of the archive of national rhetoric, always defined at its borders, in contestation of its content, in reappraisal of its direction, that an appreciation may be gleaned of how we may highlight the contradictions in belonging which are inherent in the specific temporality of the discourses of Europe.

Notes

[1] Eric Hobsbawm, "Whose fault-line is it anyway?" *New Statesman and Society,* April 24 1992.

[2] Michael Billig, *Banal Nationalism,* (Sage, 1995) 118.

[3] George Boyce, "The Fourth Estate: the reappraisal of a concept" in *Newspaper History,* eds Boyce, Curran and Wingate (Sage, 1978).

[4] The Daily Mail, March 13 1996.

[5] James Curran,"The Press as an Agency of Social Control" in *Newspaper History,* eds Boyce, Curran, Wingate, (Sage, 1978) 74.

[6] Benedict Anderson, *Imagined Communities,* (Verso, 1987).

[7] Anthony Smith, "The Nation: Invented, Imagined, Reconstructed?" in *Reimagining the Nation,* M. Ringrose and A.J. Lerner eds, (Open University Press, 1993) 15.

[8] Michel Foucault, *The Archaeology of Knowledge,* (Tavistock, 1974) trans MA Sheridan-Smith.

[9] Homi Bhabha, "DissemiNation," in *Narration and Nation,* ed Homi Bhabha (Routledge, 1990) 297.

[10] Michael Billig, 93.

[11] Homi Bhabha, 279.

[12] Anthony Smith, 13.

[13] Michel Foucault, 32.

[14] Michel Foucault, 74.

[15] Michel Foucault, 129.

[16] D. Morley and K. Robins, *Spaces of Identity,* (Routledge, 1995) 122.

[17] Stuart Hall, "New Ethnicities," in Kobena Mercer, *Black Film, British Cinema,* ICA Document No 7, (Institute of Contemporary Arts, 1988) 29.

[18] F. Anthias and N. Yuval-Davies, *Racialized Boundaries,* (Routledge, 1993) 59.

[19] Raphael Samuel, "Introduction: Exciting to be English', in *Patriotism: The Making and Unmaking of British National Identity,* Vol 1 (Routledge, 1989) xxxiv.

[20] Raphael Samuel, xxxiv.

[21] The Sun, April 23 1996.

[22] Walter Benjamin, *Illuminations,* trans, Harry Zohn, (Fontana Press, 1992) 252–255.

[23] Roland Barthes, *Mythologies,* (Hill and Wang, 1972) 142–50.

[24] Michael Billig, 119–127.

[25] J. Halliday, S. Curry Jansen and J. Scheider, in *Media, Democracy and Crisis,* eds M. Raboy and B. Dagenais (Sage, 1992) 63–78.

[26] The Guardian, March 23 1996.

[27] Roland Barthes, 143.

The Challenge of Freedom in Eastern Europe: Derrida's Ethics of Affirmation and Educational Responsibility

Denise Egéa-Kuehne

Since the coming down of the Berlin wall in 1989, and the subsequent collapse of the communist block, central and Eastern European countries have been torn by racism and xenophobia, ethnic, cultural, and religious conflicts, and national and minority wars. Freedom for everyone in this "new" Europe is indeed a tremendous challenge, and in most cases education has been assigned the responsibility to overcome prejudice, racism, and ethnocentrism. How can one assume the singularly European heritage, and all that was "promised under the name of Europe,"[1] and *at the same time*, the necessity of questioning it, and of respecting the irreducible singularity, the uniqueness of the other. This essay argues that Derrida's ethics of affirmation can provide the paradigm to develop a greater awareness of the issues at stake, to aim for a better understanding of what they are, to articulate more clearly the problems, and to move toward a more responsive and responsible approach to knowledge and education.

> *the tremor that is shaking what are called Central and Eastern Europe* (see Annex) *under the very problematic terms* democratization, reunification, *entry into the* market economy, *access to political and economic liberalisms [t]his earthquake, which by definition knows no borders, is no doubt the immediate cause of [this] topic.* (original emphasis)[2]

Derrida pronounced these words during a colloquium on *European Cultural Identity* in May 1990 in Turin Italy. Following the collapse of the Soviet Empire, Central and Eastern European countries were then just emerging from years of communist control. Since then, "economic wars, national wars, minority wars, unleashing of racism and xenophobia, ethnic, cultural and religious conflicts have torn Europe,"[3] and the entire region of central and Eastern Europe has been in a continuous process of change, particularly the various education systems. Kozakiewicz's words still ring true: "to write today about the "present" state of education in these countries is like writing on the surface of a river."[4] Yet the title of this book, *The New Europe at the Crossroads*, raises two issues, both opened onto the future, and bearing a promise: (1) European identity as "new," as being renewed, or, in Derridean terms, still "to come;" and (2) the potential choices available for this "new" Europe, the "promise" (Derrida's term again) at the "crossroads." When addressing any issues about the "new" Europe, it is unavoidable to take into account Derrida's works[5] and his reflection on such questions as: "For what 'cultural identity' must we be responsible? And responsible before whom? Before what memory? For what promise?"[6]

The possibility of freedom, the promise of freedom for everyone in this "new" Europe, is indeed a tremendous challenge in countries where many diverse ethnic and racial groups live side by side, and where serious animosity and distrust are associated with a gulf separating these ethnic or racial minorities from one another, and from the mainstream native population. In most cases, education has been assigned the responsibility to overcome prejudice, racism, and ethnocentrism in multicultural countries, as schools have been expected to work toward the removal of barriers and boundaries. The challenge can be daunting, but the possibilities are immense. In any case, a heavy responsibility rests squarely on the shoulders of educators at all levels of the profession.

In an attempt to understand better what is at stake, after revisiting what Derrida has cautiously called the "deconstruction of the subject," this essay will emphasize the importance of the link he establishes with the concepts of human rights and democracy as related to the "other." The predominant role language plays in giving access to human rights and freedom, or in controlling them, will then be discussed, and the last part will suggest looking at Derrida's analysis of his notion of "double duty" in order to help educators respond to the challenge and responsibility of a seemingly impossible task.

Deconstruction of the Subject: An Affirmation of Otherness and Alterity

> *Deconstruction is ... an ethics of affirmation, it implies that you are attentive to otherness, to the alterity of the other, to something new and another.*[7]

The necessity of otherness and multiple voices in education has been strongly argued in recent scholarship,[8] especially in the context of Derrida's aporetic approach to academic responsibility.[9] Bernstein (1993) points out that the theme of otherness "has been at the very center of twentieth century Continental philosophy—especially German and French philosophy."[10] Though it has not appeared as a prominent concern in the twentieth century Anglo-American literature, that *is* changing, and McLaren (1991 showed that the role of schools in shaping students' identity is now one major issue in contemporary educational scholarship.)[11] An elaboration of the relationship between the self and the other is central to a postmodern critical pedagogy.[12] Theunissen (1984) also stressed the "powerful hold" of the question of the other, its essential place in ethics, and how deeply it reaches "into the foundations of philosophical thought."[13] He believes that it is inseparable "from the most primordial questions raised by modern thought,"[14] and of course from any educational considerations.

Critical pedagogy and curriculum theory have tried to include such areas of alterity as gender, race, and sexual orientation. For instance, in Gadamer's work the theme of alterity and elaboration of the relationship between the self and the other has been central. Like Derrida, he argues that only through encounter with the other, "the otherness of the other," can we further our understanding.

However, Derrida goes further than any of these authors, affirming that "identity *is* in fact constituted by the other [original emphasis]."[15]

> There is no culture or cultural identity without this difference *with itself*... This can be said, inversely or reciprocally, of all identity or all identification: There is no self-relation, no relation to oneself, no identification with oneself, without culture, but a culture of oneself *as* a culture *of* the other, a culture of the double genitive and of the *difference to oneself* [original emphasis].[16]

In a conversation with Montefiore, one of the 1992 Oxford Amnesty International Lecture Series, Derrida stresses that "if there is such a thing" as the deconstruction of the subject, it "can in no case amount to the dissolution of the subject." He reminds his Oxford audience that the word "deconstruction" has erroneously been understood by some to designate "simply a negative project which undermines everything and doesn't leave anything in place." Derrida is adamant: "we have to reject this." For him, deconstruction has never meant dissolution, since deconstructing in the sense he uses it does not mean to "destroy," or "dissolve,"or "cancel the legitimacy of what you are deconstructing." What it would amount to ("if there is such a thing") is a "historical," "genealogical" analysis of the formation of the subject, of the "different layers which have built" the concept of subject. Derrida reiterates that "every concept has its own history, and the concept of subject has a very, very long, heavy, complex history."[17]

Retracing the history of the concept of subject is beyond the scope of this essay. However, it can be noted that in the Oxford Amnesty International Lecture, Montefiore stresses that he refers to the subject "in terms of liberal tradition,"[18] which has considered human beings as the subject of what they are doing, thinking, saying. He also indicates that "subject" is a problematic term. Among other determinants, Derrida emphasizes that the word "subject" is not used the same way in the Anglo-American tradition as it is in the Continental (German, French) philosophical discourse. Therefore a "translation" is necessary, not just from one language to the other, but "in *all* possible idioms" since "deconstructing the subject means being aware of those historical components."[19] It entails looking back all the way to the Aristotelian tradition where the subject was already considered "*the* center of an identity" (Derrida's emphasis), "something identical to itself ... [which] cannot be divided, can be counted as one."[20] According to Derrida then:

> when you deconstruct the subject, you underline all the assumptions, the hidden assumptions which are implied in the philosophical, or the ethical, or the juridical, or the political use of the concept of subject .... [D]econstruction of the subject is first, among other things, the genealogical analysis of the trajectory through which the concept has been built, used, legitimized.[21]

Derrida acknowledges concurring with Husserl's position when he writes "the other as alter ego signifies the other as other, irreducible to *my* ego, precisely because it is an ego, because it has the form of an ego [original emphasis]."[22] However, Derrida's point differs from Husserl's in that he does not follow the logic of *Aufhebung*, he does not entertain the possibility of a reconciliation of the opposites. Quite the contrary. And that is where Derrida's ethical argument is evident, in the "double duty," the aporias he describes and discusses in *The Other Heading*, and to which we will return at the end of this essay. This is where we see the ethical aspects of Derrida's deconstruction of the subject, where it "conditions the *respect* for the other *as what it is* [original emphasis]."[23]

Human Rights and Democracy: A Promise

> *Deconstruction of the subject ... a move toward strengthening an appreciation of the importance of protecting human freedom.*[24]

Respect of the other is an essential component of human rights, where the "other" can also be "I," and "I" the "other."[25] It is essential that there be a genuine desire to at least be willing to actually *listen*, to actually try to understand what is different, what is other, *and* be understood as what is different, what is other. Courage is necessary, the courage to let go of one's own assumptions, presuppositions, certitudes, for dialogical communication to occur. Concurring with Levinas, Derrida declares that "the other is the other only if his alterity is absolutely irreducible, that is, infinitely irreducible."[26] However, he disagrees with Levinas to the extent that he does not believe that "to make the other an alter ego ... is to neutralize its absolute alterity;" quite the opposite; "if the other [were] not recognized as ego, its entire alterity would collapse."[27] Derrida adds that "[w]ithout this acknowledgment, which is not a knowledge, or let us say without this 'letting-be' of an existent (Other) as something existing outside me in the essence of what it is (first in its alterity), *no ethics would be possible* [emphasis added]."[28] Furthermore, "[w]ithout this, no letting-be would be possible, and first of all, the letting-be of respect and of the ethical commandment addressing itself to freedom."[29]

In this context, in Derrida's view, the concept of the subject is tightly linked to that of human rights. For it is in the process of the constitution of human rights, "of the constant battle to improve our understanding, perhaps to ... enrich our concepts of what constitutes human rights" that the concept of subject is being discussed. In his conversation with Derrida on the deconstruction of the subject, Montefiore concludes that indeed, for Derrida, deconstruction of the subject means "taking into account all the determinations ... and trying to *improve* the concept of the human subject." Montefiore understands that Derrida does not see the deconstruction of the subject as a threat to human rights, but quite the contrary, "as a move toward strengthening an appreciation of the importance of protecting human freedom."[30]

Derrida describes human rights as "a set of concepts, laws, requirements which were not given in nature, from the beginning." He recognizes that they are the result—yet always in the making—of a "long, long conquest, a long battle, to formulate" what they "are or should be." This concept of human rights itself has a history, a genealogy; it was not bestowed once and for all, be it labor rights, economic rights, women rights, children rights, and so on. In his conversation with Montefiore, Derrida evokes that history, and some of the variations on the Declaration of Human Rights. Many versions of similar declarations were crafted through the centuries, through many a socio-political storm, each determining a more specifically formal concept of human rights, thus determining what the subject is, i.e., "is the child a subject? is a woman a subject? is a non-European a subject?" Montefiore stresses the close interwoven nature of human rights and the concept of the human subject itself when he comments on what he calls Derrida's "continual understanding of the subject." Based on the close link Derrida establishes between the concept of the subject and the concept of human rights, Montefiore sees "the enrichment of one's understanding of human rights" as amounting to "an enrichment, an ongoing transformation of the concept of the human subject itself."[31]

Obviously, Derrida sees "the very concept of human rights [as having] an essential link to an ideal of democracy." However, his reference is not to democracy "as we know it," as determined by Western societies. In *Specters of Marx* (1993), Derrida makes it clear that the social, political, philosophical, and economic dimensions of our world have changed, are still changing, and that intellectuals the world over have to re-think the meaning of "old" paradigms, and develop new ones. For instance, what is the new model for a democratic society in the face of problems of homelessness, violence, fierce nationalisms, virulent ethnocentrism, xenophobia, and exterminations? For Derrida, the future holds a promise, for "at the core of the idea of democracy, there is a promise," that of the "ideal of democracy." It entails "some openness to the future, and the openness to the future and the openness to the other imply that we don't simply reconstruct," as suggested by Montefiore. That is "why, when referring to ... democracy, you have to speak of democracy today ... democracy-to-come,"[32] and experienced as always possible. It does not mean a democracy which will realize itself only in a future time, nor a "regulatory idea in the Kantian sense, nor a utopia."[33]

By "democracy-to-come," Derrida refers to the very concept of democracy "as the concept of a promise" which can manifest itself only where there is disruption and upheaval, when there exists a gap between the present state of democracies and the ideal of democracy. Thus the apparent failure of democracy is "*a priori* and by definition" characteristic "of *all* democracies, including the oldest and most stable."[34] In fact, it is in this very gap that democracy is being shaped,

> between an infinite promise (always untenable because it at least calls for an infinite respect of the infinite singularity and the infinite alterity of the other as much as for the calculable, subjectable equalities among these anonymous singularities) and the specific, necessary, but necessarily ill fitting forms which must measure themselves against that promise.[35]

In this gap must be preserved heterogeneity, "as the only chance of an affirmed, or rather re-affirmed future."[36] Without this gap, without this disjunction, democracy may simply believe, in all good conscience, that it has succeeded, that "its duty is accomplished," and therefore "miss its chance for the future, for the promise or the call … (in other words, for its very possibility)."[37]

Inherent to that notion of democracy, there is the necessity to be "vigilant" when discussing such idioms, and to look critically at "the best intentioned of European projects, those which are quite apparently and explicitly pluralistic, democratic, and tolerant."[38] Within their supposedly clearly understood meaning, and despite the best intentions to remain true to their "spirit," lurks the danger of wanting to "impose the homogeneity of a medium, of discursive norms and models."[39] For instance, talking about Europe, Derrida wonders whether

> the future will … escape monstrosity. [For] in the name of identity, be it cultural or not, the worst violences, those that we recognize all too well without yet having thought them through, the crimes of xenophobia, racism, anti-Semitism, religious or nationalist fanaticism, are being unleashed, mixed up, mixed up with each other, but also, and there is nothing fortuitous in this, mixed in with the breath, with the respiration, with the very "spirit" of the promise.[40]

Derrida has discussed at length his concern about "the problem of the access … of people who until now had no access to human rights—children, women …."[41] This is in part why Derrida's texts are especially significant when discussing the consequences of exclusion due to the hierarchies prevailing in the so-called history of the West.[42] He has denounced "violence, inequality, exclusions, hunger, and therefore economic oppression" as having never before "affected so many human beings, in the history of this planet and humanity,"[43] and he has pointed to the limits of any institutional discourse on democracy. Derrida's profound understanding, from experience, is at the root of some most perceptive descriptions of the dynamics of exclusion, discrimination, and exile, and he calls on us "never to neglect this macroscopic evidence made of innumerable singular tragedies."[44] A discussion of questions of exclusion and privilege, hegemony and access to language, knowledge and educational institutions, can be traced throughout his writings, conferences, and seminars. In addition, these questions are the specific focus of the texts he gathered in *Du droit à la philosophie* (1990).[45] In these texts, Derrida explores the conditions of access to philosophy, to the "proper" discourse, to language, to instruction, research, publication, and to the "legitimacy" of philosophy and education. He asks: Who has a right of access to philosophy, education, language? Who holds their power or privilege? Where does the responsibility lie, to whom, for whom?

The Affirmation of Language: A Matter of Responsibility

> *It concerns an irreducible experience of language, that which* links *it to the* liaison*, to commitment, to the command or to the promise.*[46]

Throughout history, whether in Europe or in North America, examples abound showing how one group can compromise or restrict language rights in an attempt to gain control of the political and economic fate of a nation. In the U.S., the current agenda of organizations promoting the legislation of English as the official language (i.e., *U.S. English, English First*), provides a vivid example of hegemonic language planning, and of its consequences for education.[47] While these groups present themselves as advocating legislation for the sake of "preserving bonds," and "promoting opportunities,"[48] their action in fact aims at restricting language rights, thus limiting access to education, and impeding socio-economic participation. Phillipson (1992)investigated the use of languages and the hegemonic principles behind the promotion of a particular language (English in that case).[49] Since language is constitutive of reality,[50] it can be, and has been used in Eastern Europe, as a mechanism of ideological control, to manipulate and shape the thinking and values of various groups (see Annex). Phillipson (1992) argues that "the monolingual approach legitimates the ignoring of local languages and the cultural universe that these languages mediate."[51] Through language control, access to content education can be denied, and as a consequence, language minorities may be excluded from access to the languages, education, and information needed to be socially and economically engaged. In the U.S., where this approach is reflected in the actions of "English only" groups and in educational policies, one can see where efforts declared to be promoting national unity in fact "break up, marginalize, shut off, deny access, and disconnect," all things Derrida denounces as a return to "old forms of religious fanaticism, nationalism, and racism."[52] Aronowitz (1989) describes how schools can function "to strip away what belongs to the student," and how those who succeed in the institution sometimes "do so at the cost of their ethnicity, race and sex, all of which are stripped away."[53]

In addition, the media play a major role through the press, television, telecommunications, and all "unprecedented techno-social structures."[54] While they can provide minorities with access to channels of information, and possibly with a means of expression (via phone, internet, or some television programs), they may not provide them with access to institutional life and government, or institutional representation. They may, to a certain extent, alleviate some errors and injustices, but this so-called democratization does not provide minorities with legitimate representation. "It never represents without filtering or screening ... a 'public opinion'."[55] Therefore, it is essential to remain vigilant and denounce censorship and its effects, under any guise, and "to fight against accumulation, concentration, and monopoly; in short, against all quantitative phenomena which might marginalize or reduce to silence anything which cannot be measured on their scale."[56] Through these techno-social structures, a struggle over cultural hegemony is taking place, "through the established and traditionally dominant powers of certain idioms, of certain culture industries."[57] For the existence of a cultural capital of European culture "always concerns language, not only the predominance of a national language, tongue, or idiom, but the predominance of a concept of the tongue or of language, a certain idea of the idiom which is being put to work."[58] Through major political events—say the fall of the Berlin wall and the demise of the Communist block—but sometimes less blatantly, our perception of the balance of ideologies, and of the traditional concepts (i.e., democracy) can be changed, and we may be forced to "reconsider all the relationships between State and nation, individuals and the citizen, the private and the public, and so on."[59]

In his conversation with Montefiore, Derrida reminds us that any time we take on the issue of human rights, the problem of language needs to be addressed. For "if there are human rights, which means universally valid human rights, they should be accessible, understandable to everyone, whatever language they understand or speak."[60] Derrida discusses the importance of the affirmation of language and its link to responsibility as "the 'I am addressing you, and I commit myself, in this language here, listen how I speak in my language, me, and you can speak to me in your language; we must hear each other, we must get along' [*nous devons nous entendre*]."[61] In a new Europe, it is necessary more than ever to consider this affirmation of language, and the problem of idioms and translation, in order to avoid "both the nationalistic tensions of linguistic differences, and the violent hegemonization of languages through the neutrality of a translating medium which would *claim* to be transparent, metalinguistic, and universal [emphasis added]."[62] Throughout his works, Derrida has discussed questions of language, idiom, and translation. He has analyzed and used the "polysemy [which] gathers the homonyms and derivations at play in the lexical roots"[63] of language, and which render it sometimes untranslatable. He has described with a remarkable awareness and sensitivity the problems of the uniqueness of a discourse which can convey "a speech act ... possible only in the idiom of [one's] own language."[64] But the dilemma is that while it is necessary to respect minorities, differences, singularities, idioms, and languages, it is at the same time imperative to respect also "the universality of formal law, the desire for translation, agreement and univocity, the law of the majority, opposition to racism, nationalism, and xenophobia."[65]

The Experience and Experiment of the Possibility of the Impossible: Education's "Double Duty"

> *That is not easy. It is even impossible to conceive of a responsibility which consists in being responsible* for *two laws, or which consists in responding to two injunctions. But there is no responsibility which is not the experience and the experiment of the impossible.*[66]

This double injunction, this paradox of universality, is a challenge to all educators to take an ethical stance, and develop an ability to mediate differences and boundaries, exclusions and violence, hierarchies and borders, whether they are concerned with language, ethnicity, race, gender, and so on, or ideas. How can one respond *to*, respond *for*, be responsible *to and for* two imperatives? For example, how can one respond both to the necessity of respecting the voice of the other, the idiom of the other, the heterogeneity which welcomes the other, *and* at the same time to the necessity of a universal formal law? How can one satisfy to the conflicting imperatives of "neither monopoly, nor dispersion"?[67] How can one choose between two equally imperative injunctions? And why, points out Derrida, is it so important that we should *not* have to choose? In *The Other Heading* (1992), Derrida describes dilemmas and paradoxes present everywhere in the new Europe, and gives examples of aporias. They are characteristic of the challenge educators have to face the world over, in countries where diverse ethnic and racial groups have to live side by side:

1. It is necessary to "make ourselves the guardians of an idea of Europe, of a difference of Europe," but it is also necessary to open Europe to the difference, to "that which is not, never was, and never will be Europe."

2. It is necessary to welcome "foreigners," but also "to recognize and accept [and respect] their alterity."

3. It is necessary to criticize "('in both theory and practice,' and relentlessly) a totalitarian dogmatism which, under the pretense of putting an end to capital, destroyed democracy and the European heritage," but also "a religion of capital which institutes its dogmatism under new guises, which we must also learn to identify."

4. It is necessary to cultivate "the virtue of such critique, of the critical idea, the critical tradition," but also to submit it to a "deconstructive genealogy," "beyond critique and questioning."

5. It is necessary to assume the uniquely European heritage of an idea of democracy, while also "recognizing that this idea is … never simply given … but rather something which remains to be thought and *to come* [*à venir*] [original emphasis]."

6. It is necessary to respect "differences, idioms, minorities, singularities, but also the universality of formal law, the desire for translation, agreement, univocity, the law of the majority, opposition to racism, nationalism, and xenophobia."

7. It is necessary to tolerate and respect "all that is not placed under the authority of reason … different forms of faith" but also "thoughts which, while attempting to think reason and the history of reason, necessarily exceed its order, without becoming … irrational … acknowledging [the] limits" of the ideal of Enlightenment (Derrida's text in quotation marks).[68]

These double injunctions, contradictions, aporias, are, according to Derrida, the essence of responsibility.[69] Derrida has described and discussed extensively and in most of his texts how these dilemmas are inherent to the concept of responsibility, are in fact *the very condition* of its possibility. For "at a certain point, the promise and the decision, that is to say the responsibility, owe their possibility to the test of undecidability which will always remain their condition."[70] He stresses repeatedly that, if there is an easy decision to make, there is, in fact, no decision to be made, therefore, no responsibility to be taken, only a set of rules to follow, or a program to implement.

Derrida links this concept—this condition of possibility as being dependent on the simultaneous necessity of a condition of impossibility—to a notion of "messianism," to the experience of the promise. It is by opening a space for the affirmation of this promise, of the "messianic and emancipatory promise," of the impossible event as a promise, that it will preserve its capital of possibilities, of dynamic ideal in-the-making, to-come. There is danger in settling for an easy consensus, for "transparency," since while "claiming to speak in the name of intelligibility, good sense, common sense, or [supposedly] the democratic ethic, this discourse tends, by means of these very things, and as if naturally, to discredit anything which complicates this model."[71] As soon as we settle for a common space, we turn all possibilities into a program or into an "onto-theological or teleo-eschatological scheme."[72] Derrida defines responsibility as "a certain experience and experiment of the possibility of the impossible: the testing of the aporia from which one may invent the only possible invention, the impossible invention."[73] He also shows how closely related aporia, responsibility, and ethics are, declaring:

"ethics, politics and responsibility, *if there are any*, will only ever have begun with the experience and the experiment of the aporia."[74]

As educators, it may be easy to be attracted by the lure of making everything understandable and accessible to all, removing all sources of possible contention, attempting to "neutralize" education "through a translating medium which would *claim* to be transparent, metalinguistic, and universal."[75] We saw that under the pretense of "pleading for transparency … for the univocity of democratic discussion, for communication in public space, for 'communicative action'," such a simplifying discourse in fact "tends to impose" a thinking model through a language model, a model which "coincide[s] with certain institutional powers."[76] In *Du droit à la philosophie*, Derrida has questioned these institutional powers, and thoroughly discussed our responsibilities as educators.[77] Yet he encourages us to be cautious and vigilant, and not reject everything, for he warns "we must be suspicious of *both* repetitive memory *and* the completely other of the absolutely new."[78] He also offers the educational profession the example of an institution—The International College of Philosophy—whose goal is "never to be univocal, neutral, or transparent," but an "exemplary place for questioning the forms, structures, and institutions of education and communication—including the university."[79]

Conclusion

Through Derrida's texts, this essay explored the links among the concepts of subject as affirmation of otherness and alterity, and human rights and democracy as related to the other. It pointed to the role language plays in gaining access to human rights and freedom, and the responsibility facing education in re-evaluating, re-considering, and re-interpreting its position along the double-duty continuum described by Derrida.

As educators, not only must we refuse to settle for easy consensus, to simplify, to neutralize, or to translate; we must also accept and assume the responsibility to "think, speak, and act" within aporetic situations, under the double contradictory imperatives of a continuum of double duty. Most of all, we must engage students in a quest for knowledge which should take them way beyond the boundaries of their immediate socio-politico-cultural context in space and in time. We must encourage them to take risks in learning and discovering the other, the unknown, while building a greater sense of responsibility. "The alternative," writes Grant, "which we can guess at from what is going on [at the time of his writing] in the streets of Sarajevo, the mountains of Karabakh, and … numerous spots the world over, is terrible to contemplate."[80]

Notes

[1] J. Derrida, (1992) *The Other Heading*. Pascale-Anne Brault & Michael B. Nass, Trans. Bloomington and Indianapolis: Indiana University Press, p. 76. Translation slightly modified throughout quotations.

[2] Ibid., p. 19.

[3] J. Derrida, (1993) *Spectres de* Marx Paris: Editions Galilée page references in French edition), p. 134 Translation Egéa-Kuehne throughout quotations.

[4] M. Kozakiewicz, (1994) The difficult Road to Educational Pluralism in Central and Eastern Europe *European Education 26*(3) pp. 25–35.

[5] Although a discussion of questions of exclusion and privilege, hegemony and access to language, knowledge and educational institutions, can be traced throughout Derrida's writings, conferences, and seminars, this essay will limit its references essentially to *The Other Heading*, *Specters of Marx*, *Du droit à la philosophie* and the 1992 Oxford Amnesty International Lecture.

[6] *Other Heading*, p. 13.

[7] J. Derrida, & A. Montefiore, (1996) *Jacques Derrida* 1992 Oxford Amnesty Lectures Princeton, NJ: Films for the Humanities & Sciences Text of video tape transcribed by Egéa-Kuehne, unpublished, no page numbers available.

[8] Here and throughout this essay, "otherness" does not simply refer to a blanket label, but includes what one anonymous reviewer (another paper) once called "myriad specifics of different interrelationships encountered within educational settings" (communication January 24, 1996) It also refers to the "other" as being both "you" and "I," and to "otherness" within ourselves, such as described by Susan Griffin ("The Way of All Ideologies," in N.O. Keohane, M.Z. Rosaldo, and B.C. Gelpi, Eds *Feminist Theory: A Critique of Ideology* Chicago: University of Chicago Press, 1982), and to otherness within same-name groups.

[9] D. Egéa-Kuehne, (1996) Neutrality in Education and Derrida's Call for Double Duty In *Philosophy of Education 1996* Urbana, IL: University of Illinois.

[10] R.J. Bernstein, (1993) The New Constellation: The Ethical-Political Horizons of Modernity /Postmodernity Cambridge, MA: The MIT Press, p. 67.

[11] P. McLaren, (1991) Decentering Culture: Postmodernism, Resistance, and Critical Pedagogy In N Wyner (Ed.), *Current Perspectives on the Culture of Schools* (pp. 231–257) Boston, MA: Brookline Books.

[12] P. McLaren, & R. Hammer, (1989) Critical Pedagogy and the Postmodern Challenge: Toward a Critical Postmodernist Pedagogy of Liberation *Educational Foundations*, pp. 29–62.

[13] M. Theunissen, (1984) *The Other*, Trans Christopher Macann Cambridge, MA: MIT Press, p. 1.

[14] Ibid.

[15] M.B. Nass, (Trans.) (1992) Introduction In J. Derrida, *The Other Heading* Bloomington & Indianapolis: Indiana University Press, p. xlvi.

[16] *Other Heading*, pp. 9–10.
[17] Oxford Lecture.
[18] Ibid.
[19] Ibid.
[20] Ibid.
[21] Ibid.
[22] Ibid.
[23] J. Derrida, (1978) Violence and Metaphysics: An Essay on the Thought of Emmanuel Levinas In *Writing and Difference* Trans A Bass Chicago: University of Chicago Press, p. 78.
[24] Montefiore in the Oxford Lecture.
[25] See Note 8.
[26] *Writing and Difference*, p. 104.
[27] Ibid., p. 125.
[28] Ibid., p. 138.
[29] Ibid.
[30] All quotes in the preceding paragraph from the Oxford Lecture.
[31] All quotes in this paragraph from the Oxford Lecture.
[32] All preceding quotes in paragraph from the Oxford Lecture.
[33] *Specters of Marx*, p. 110.
[34] Ibid.
[35] Ibid., p. 111.
[36] *Other Heading*, p. 68
[37] *Specters of Marx*, p. 56.
[38] *Other Heading*, p. 54.
[39] Ibid and Egéa-Kuehne, Neutrality in Education.
[40] *Other Heading*, p. 6.
[41] Oxford Lecture.
[42] D. Egéa-Kuehne, "Derrida and the Challenge of Education in a Multicultural Society," Unpublished paper, American Educational Research Association, San Diego, CA, (1998).
[43] *Specters of Marx*, p. 141.
[44] Ibid.
[45] J. Derrida, (1990) *Du droit à la philosophie* Paris: Editions Galilée.
[46] *Other Heading*, p. 60.
[47] Egéa-Kuehne, Neutrality in Education.
[48] U.S. English (1995) *Towards a united America* Brochure Washington, DC: U.S English.
[49] R. Phillipson, (1992) *Linguistic Imperialism* Oxford, England: Oxford University Press.
[50] A. Cicourel, (1985) Text and Discourse *Annual Review of Anthropology, 14*, 159–185 Also, Foucault, M (1979) *The Archeology of Knowledge* New York: Pantheon.

[51] Phillipson, *Linguistic Imperialism*, p. 254.
[52] *Other Heading*, p. 43.
[53] S. Aronowitz, (1989) Working-class Identity and Celluloid Fantasy In H. Giroux & R. Simon (Eds.), *Popular Culture: Schooling and Everyday Life* Granby, MA: Bergin & Garvey, p. 200.
[54] *Other Heading*, p. 57.
[55] Ibid., p. 98.
[56] Ibid., p. 99.
[57] Ibid., p. 37.
[58] Ibid., pp. 46–47.
[59] *Specters of Marx*, p. 120.
[60] Oxford Lecture.
[61] *Other Heading*, p. 61.
[62] Ibid., p. 58 Also, Egéa-Kuehne, Neutrality in Education.
[63] *Other Heading*, p. 60.
[64] Ibid.
[65] Ibid., p. 78.
[66] Ibid., pp. 44–45.
[67] Ibid., p. 41.
[68] Ibid., pp. 76–78.
[69] D. Egéa-Kuehne, (1995) Deconstruction Revisited and Derrida's Call for Academic Responsibility *Educational Theory 45*(3),
[70] *Specters of Marx*, p. 126.
[71] *Other Heading*, p. 55 Also Egéa-Kuehne, Deconstruction Revisited and Derrida's Call for Responsibility; and Neutrality in Education.
[72] *Specters of Marx*, p. 126.
[73] *Other Heading*, p. 41.
[74] Ibid.
[75] Ibid., p. 58.
[76] Ibid., p. 55.
[77] Egéa-Kuehne, Deconstruction Revisited and Derrida's Call for Academic Responsibility.
[78] *Other Heading*, p. 19.
[79] *Du droit à la philosophie*, p. xlix.
[80] N. Grant, (1995) Language, Culture, and the Curriculum Among European Minority and Peripheral Peoples *European Education 27*(3) 5–13 p. 13.

Multiculturalism and the Islamic Challenge

Patricia Ellis and Zafar Khan[*]

As the millennium approaches, Europe can be characterized as becoming more unified while at the same time encompassing greater diversity than ever before. The original economic alliances of the European Union have developed into a movement for a European identity based on shared cultural understandings. The assumption is of a common classical heritage that all citizens can draw upon. However this is to ignore the demographic impact of European colonial histories and the ramifications of the economic and political policies of the past four decades. Europe is now home to a growing number of groups of non-European origin who are committed to retaining key aspects of their own cultural heritage. In this article, the authors assess the politics of multiculturalism in the situation where European ideological and cultural hegemony is challenged by minorities of non-European origin. They seek to demonstrate, in theory and in practice, the eurocentric assumptions underlying the concepts of multiculturalism and how these are being confronted by the growing Muslim presence in Europe. The case study is that of Muslim settlement in Britain and the issue of education, as this particularly highlights the contradictions to be found in the concept of multiculturalism as employed by public authorities. This analysis is important for discussions on the future of European culture, because the Muslim challenge to cultural hegemony is not confined to Britain but is a growing source of tension across Europe.

Muslim Settlement in Britain

Throughout its history, Britain has been the recipient of waves of people speaking other languages and bringing with them other cultures. Some came as conquerors, such as the Normans and the Danes, some came as political refugees, such as the Huguenots and the Jews of Eastern Europe. Others came as economic migrants such as the Irish. Those who conquered left the imprint of their culture and language on the early development of British society. Those who came subsequently as political or economic refugees prior to the present century were, in the main, gradually assimilated into the mainstream culture and life. By the middle of this century there was a widely held belief in the homogeneity of a British culture that was, in reality, one dominated by English culture.

Belief in the superiority of English language and culture was a driving force in the maintenance of the British Empire. It was during this period that, for the first time, British people in any great number were exposed to non-European cultures and languages. The operation of this vast empire not only took members of the ruling class out to the colonies but also those of the middle and working classes. To retain control in this situation, it was seen as important that British people did not "go native." So it was that belief in the superiority of European and particularly British culture was reinforced, while emphasizing the inferior "otherness" of the inhabitants of the colonies.

In 1947 the British Raj ended, and the break-up of the empire began. However with the economic prosperity of the 1950s and 1960s, British people renewed their contact with the inhabitants of the former colonies when they entered as economic migrants to fill the jobs that British people no longer wished to do. Two major assumptions were made at the time about these migrants. The first was that they would in the main return to their homelands after a few years work, and therefore could be regarded as "visitors" in relation to the cultural norms of the "host" society, and not expected to adapt during their temporary sojourn. For those who, from the outset, were not transient, it was assumed that they would quickly be assimilated into the dominant culture. These assumptions had to be revisited by the early 1970s. This was the period when it became clear that most migrants were now, in reality, making the decision to settle, as their spouses and children joined them in large numbers. The homogeneity of British culture was now under question. This was particularly the case with the development of large and concentrated communities of South Asian origins. Unlike those from the Caribbean and Africa, the main languages of communication were not English. The religions were not Christian based, and the cultures were those of the "Orient." British politics was split in its reactions to these developments.

The growing issue of racism was, to some extent, acknowledged at national and local levels through legislation and policy making. However the implications of the diversity of culture were far more problematic for government. Many politicians still assumed a policy of assimilation as the response to the changes. It was at the local authority level, in those areas of high ethnic minority group settlement, that there was a recognition that their populations were multicultural. Policies of assimilation were now seen to be unrealistic, with services needing to reflect this changing demography. Community work and education were the two services with the most overt policy moves toward multiculturalism. "Celebration of difference" became a catch phrase, and it was felt that teaching children about the various religious festivals, foods, and dress would lead to greater understanding between communities. Little was done to address the implications for citizenship of a multicultural society, or to effectively challenge the hegemony of the dominant culture. Minority cultures and their associated religions assumed increasing importance within Britain as the populations grew more quickly that the white majority. Geographical concentration facilitated community actions. Faith based activities expanded whether associated with Caribbean based Christian churches (shunned by many of the established mainstream Christian churches), Hindu

Temples, Sikh Gurdwaras or Islamic Mosques. By the mid 1990s, out of all the minority community faiths, Islam has become the vehicle by which British society is being most severely challenged over its notions of multiculturalism.

The Politics of Culture

Islam, over many centuries, has posed a major challenge to European ideas and political operation. It is seen by many, in the late twentieth century, as the greatest threat to the West. Whilst these perceptions were initially nurtured during confrontational encounters with Muslim countries in the period of the Crusades and the Ottoman expansion, they were developed in their most significant form during the colonial expansion of Britain and France in the 19th century. As Said has so powerfully argued in his identification of the phenomenon of "Orientalism," in Europe "the Orient was ... one of its deepest and most recurring images of the Other. ... the Orient has helped to define Europe (or the West) as its contrasting image, idea, personality, experience."[1] This body of theory developed over 150 years, and underpinned British and French colonialism in North Africa, the Middle East, and India. It was important in supporting a major component of European culture, the idea of European identity as a superior one in comparison with all the non-European peoples and cultures. Significantly, Said demonstrates that there developed the idea of the "good" and "bad" Orient, and the latter is attached to "parts of North Africa and Islam everywhere."[2] The impact of the experience of the Orient on European ideas of cultural superiority have important ramifications not only in present day Europe, but also in the USA, and in the identity of the "West."

Europe is a mix of nations, and associated cultures, as clearly can be witnessed by some of the debates within the European Union. However, there is an overarching monoculture of the West to which all subscribe. This twentieth century monocultural notion of the West is heavily influenced by the ideas of the USA. Goldberg argues that this emanated from a drive from the USA to establish, within its own boundaries, a cultural reflection of the Christian Europe of the past. Within the USA, this modeling was then hardened into an idea which, throughout this century, informed "political institutions and institutional politics." This included immigration, with its "ethnoracialized demarcation. ... [and this] monocultural ethnoracial Eurovision had become cemented into the US as hegemonic intellectual ideology and institutional practice."[3] So the Orientalism of the European colonial empires became incorporated into the American cultural landscape. As the world economic system succumbed to American dominance, then this White Western monoculture not only defined the core of US identity but also that of Europe, and the other countries that subscribed to membership of the "West." As Goldberg points out, on an international level, acceptance of Western culture is seen as proof of its "universalism." However, in reality, it is a reflection of the hegemony of the dominant ideology, and not a proof of some essential characteristic of the ideology.

For groups in the US, acceptance into that society meant assimilation to these core cultural values. The exception was where groups were seen as impossible to assimilate, and were therefore marginalized. The USA, however, has been the centre of some of the most publicized and violent confrontations with those who see themselves as having been marginalized. "Multiculturalism and commitments to cultural diversity emerged out of this conflictual history of resistance, accommodation, integration and transformation."[4] Many academics and politicians have looked to the experiences of the USA for the development of the idea of and the practice of multiculturalism. However, the reality is that this multiculturalism, as a political position, assumes multiple and, at times, paradoxical forms both for those challenging and those making policy. This multiplicity of form is exemplified in one of the significant off-shoots from the "integration oriented" Black Civil Rights movement: the growing support for the Nation of Islam movement which, under the leadership of Farrakhan, tends toward separation.

A critique of multiculturalism, as it has emerged in its various forms, is that it can create a force for the real articulation of difference as a basis for progress, or constrain groups into entrenched boundaries with no flexibility for development, or be a glib public relations exercise which pays only lip service to cultural distinction. Many Muslims in Britain would place the British government position in this latter category. Whatever particularities are examined, Goldberg believes that "the emergence of contemporary multiculturalisms, then, is to be understood in relation to the twentieth century dominance of monoculturalism."[5] It is in this situation that Muslims settled in the West find themselves.

Not all countries in the West, which have a mixture of cultural groups living within their boundaries, have accepted a political position of multiculturalism. France is an important example of this. The French state's position has to be seen within the context of the French republican model of integration which is that: "one of the guiding principles of political incorporation and participation in France since the time of the French revolution has been the suppression and non-recognition of culturally or ethnically-based identities in the public sphere."[6] This rejection by the French state of multiculturalism does not mean, though, that this position is accepted by all its citizens. Many conflicts have been seen, in recent years, between the French state and Muslims from North Africa in relation to the education system. The move for identity based on community and ethnicity is the new challenge in French society today.

The politics of multiculturalism has become particularly significant in the 1990s for Muslims across Western Europe as they attempt to establish their identity as Muslims in the monocultural West. It involves not only challenges to the hegemony of the majority culture, but also to prevailing ideas of citizenship. This is happening at a time when there are already challenges to the operation of the nation-state with the concept of a European citizenry high on the agenda of the European Union. In Britain, this is exemplified by the contrast between the recent speeches of a Conservative Member of Parliament and the Queen. In his well-publicized speeches, Norman Tebbitt, at the 1997 Conservative Party Conference, attacked the notion of multiculturalism, identifying it as being a destructive force within the nation-state. The Queen, in her 1997 visit to Pakistan, praised the contribution of British Muslims to the development of modern, multi-faith, multi-ethnic Britain. Multiculturalism, as an idea in Britain, is an area of political contestation.

Recent developments in theory within social sciences have been used by academics to examine the politics of multiculturalism, and the experiences of those participating in these events. However it is clear that approaches, such as post-modernism and post-colonialism, can in turn be as problematic as they are illuminating. A serious criticism, directly relevant to this essay, is that much of the work in these fields still implicitly "centres" the West. As Sayyid says of postmodernism, it "can be seen as a recasting of the relationship between the West at the centre and the periphery. It is the contrast of the 'politics of difference' at the centre using a Western definition of difference with the 'politics of authenticity' at the periphery."[7] This is echoed by Kahn's critique of the assumptions of postcolonialism, that it is supportive of multiculturalism because of its apparent pluralism. However, as Kahn argues, the view of a non-power laden discourse is to miss how power is introduced into postcolonial discourse. As he says:

> first by establishing specific criteria — the ability to 'bracket' one's own cultural values and/or the possession of a particular cultural identity — as prerequisites for the creators of interpretation, hence empowering some and not others as capable of authenticity; and second, by introducing culture as Said has reminded us a concept inevitably saturated with power, once again into the equation (this time the cultural identity of the author).[8]

He supports Said's position which is to see the new sensitivities of the contemporary "cross cultural" dialogue in postcolonialism as an attempt by the former colonizers to again take the power away from the colonized, precipitated by the "emergence of an identity politics amongst those previously denied a voice by orientalism."[9] These criticisms of postmodernism and postcolonialism are particularly apposite when considering the often negative way in which the actions of Muslims in the West are portrayed by academics.

A more specific criticism of the postmodernist approach is with the defining of the "politics of contestation" in terms of self-definition and representation under the heading of "politics of recognition."[10] This can overshadow mobilization around material resources and political power. Within the literature, the rejection of the grand theoretical meganarratives has, on the one hand, fueled the multiculturalism drives, but on the other hand, emptied them of political action. Politics is seen as a "signifying activity" through which identities are created rather than as a mobilization of power.[11]

For leading Muslim activists in Britain, the content of these critiques would strike a chord in relation to their experiences of interacting, not only with government spokespeople, but also with academic commentators and "liberal thinkers." In particular, the apparent sensitivities to cross-cultural issues which in reality still center on the Western discourse and are denigratory of others' cultural practices. This was particularly evidenced in John Patten's open letter to "leading British Muslims" following the Rushdie affair.[12] The tone was patronizing, with the inclusion of the obligatory phrases that are used to display a supposed sensitivity, in this case to Muslim values, while basically telling the British Muslims that they needed to change in order to fit into British society. There was no suggestion that British society should make any changes in order to accommodate this broadening of the cultural and religious base. The idea of amending the Blasphemy Law was rejected, with the clear implication that Muslims hadn't understood the ramifications of their request. A strong message was that the communities should stop looking back to their place of origin as in the view of government this was hindering their incorporation into British society. This latter point is one which fails to recognize that, for British Muslims, most of their concerns are situated in the present contexts of their metropolitan experiences.

The position of the authors, in evaluating the experience and implications of Muslim activists challenging British notions of multiculturalism, can be best described by Goldberg's model of politics. In this model, he identifies politics as a contestational (co)defining of the common conditions of a human collective which can assume three interrelated forms:

1. politics of cultural contestation, in which symbols are the form by which conditions and concerns are articulated; this can be seen as the politics of representation;

2. politics of the state apparatus, where the struggle is over the distribution of institutionalized power and its material effects;

3. politics of local mobilization and social movements, around material resources, powers and opportunities outside of the state apparatus.[13]

The Islamic Challenge

For many years in Britain, Muslims have been challenging the hegemony of the state and its cultural domination, particularly in education. The contestational nature of the challenge from Muslims has been operating in all three forms of the model of politics outlined above. The importance of the education arena is clear. For the state, education is important, because it is here that future citizens are socialized into British values and culture, and trained to support the needs of the economy. For parents, it is here that children gain the skills to progress and achieve within the society, fulfil their potential, and gain an understanding of morality within the broader framework of society.

Islamophobia, with its antecedents in the Orientalism identified by Said, has not diminished with time, but permeates throughout the environment into which Muslims have settled in the West. Willy Claes, whilst heading NATO, in 1993 declared that Islam had replaced communism as the greatest threat to the West. Yet Western governments vie with each other for lucrative arms contacts with various Muslim regimes, irrespective of the potential changes in regional and international balances of power, while simultaneoulsy condemning many of these regimes for their style of operation. Terrorism, around the world, is assumed by people at all levels of Western societies to be Islamically based, and this mind set was exemplified in the initial assumptions that Islamic terrorism was the cause of the Oklahoma bombing. This made life very difficult for local Muslims until evidence emerged that it was the work of White American, right-wing extremists.

Islamophobia is well entrenched in Britain, with "Islamophobia assumed to be natural and unproblematic," as the current Runneymede Trust commission is finding.[14] This is not a phenomenon restricted to those individuals and organizations traditionally seen as xenophobic and right-wing. Roy Jenkins, a "liberal" and senior statesman, has said: "In retrospect we might have been more cautious about allowing the creation in the fifties of such substantial Muslim communities here."[15] Islamophobia is not just about Islam being "perceived as implacably threatening" and "Islam's adherents using their faith mainly for political or military advantage," it is also about Muslim culture being seen as monolithic, unchanging and intolerant, and wholly different from other cultures.[16] The implications of this range of features of Islamophobia forms the basis of the Runneymede Trust Commission's work at present.

While Muslim families and communities were in the process of settlement and initial development in Britain, their political focus was on the setting up of mosques, the availability of *halal* meat in schools, and the right to wear appropriate Muslim dress. These issues fit the concept of the politics of cultural contestation, as these were very much symbolic of a Muslim presence at a local level rather than challenging state hegemony. Local mobilization was achieved by appealing to people's Islamic sensibilities. In most local authorities, with sizeable Muslim populations, concessions were made relatively quickly, and easily because they had already begun to accept a working policy of multiculturalism. The issue of Islamic dress in school in France, however, has not been easily conceded, and has gone from local level to the supreme court level, which is consistent with the French position on multiculturalism.

For British Muslim activists, food and dress, while significant, are very superficial in terms of challenging the dominant ideology, and exposing the hollowness of the operation of multiculturalism. Patten's response was much more indicative of the reality of the government's position, and in particular toward Muslim communities. But what does the state fear? Duncan Macpherson drew parallels with the settlement of the Irish Catholic communities: "Like the Muslims now, the Irish then were seen as dirty, superstitious, and disloyal. They spoke in an alien tongue and owed allegiance to a foreign religion that seemed to aim at a global theocracy."[17] He perhaps should have added, that with the rise of the IRA and its activities, they were also associated en mass in the public mind with terrorism as are Muslims. The concept of state loyalty is significant. Muslims are part of the worldwide *ummah* (the Muslim world wide community), and therefore look outside of Britain for an important aspect of their life beliefs. They are also likely to qualify their state loyalty, as a reaction to the British state's attitudes towards them, and the Muslim world. For any Western state, this makes Muslims potentially less easy to control as they are less bound up with the state's beliefs and actions than many other citizens. Although the British state is nominally secular, it is strongly based on Christianity, and Christian beliefs, and Muslims have mounted the first serious challenge to this Christian hegemony in state operations. While the activities during the Salman Rushdie affair directly affected the state, the pressure over education for Muslim children drives much more clearly and consistently to the heart of the notion of multiculturalism, and the reality of its operation at the state level. This is the "politics of the state apparatus where the struggle is over the distribution of institutionalized power."

Social scientists have, in the main, found it difficult to categorize this struggle over education in language that coincides with that of the Muslims because this does not emanate from within the Western paradigm. Although there are references to the politics of authenticity, this does not move the debates much further forward. For those who see this as a period of late modernity, social class is not as useful an analytical tool as might be expected because there is not a traditional form of "class consciousness/class solidarity," nor is there a racialized solidarity as such. The basis of solidarity is religion, which is not a phenomenon presently encountered on this scale in other sections of the population on the British mainland.

While questions over education have been raised for several decades by Muslims, it is only now, in the 1990s, that these have become as assertive, as consistent, well publicized, and widely supported within the communities. Why now? Three major factors: the first full generation of Muslim pupils have now completed their education in British schools; applications for Muslim schools to receive voluntary aided funding have been turned down by government; and, major changes to the RE curriculum, and, worship provision have been introduced by government.

A major worry, in Muslim communities, is that British state education has failed Muslim pupils. An editorial in *Al-Madaris,* the journal of the Association of Muslim Schools, reminds Muslims of this as a reason why they should consider Muslim schools: "...Muslims are in the vanguard of under-achievement. Muslim children are as likely as anyone else to be on the exclusion lists these days."[18] The Muslim Educational Trust, in their report presented to Gillian Shephard as Secretary of State for Education, draw to her attention that British policy is that "all children are entitled to the highest educational standards." They then point out that, because of their location in the inner cities: "Muslims in particular are disadvantaged as they live predominantly in such areas. Moreover Muslim children do not see their faith community well represented in the teaching profession and so lack role models with whom they can identify."[19]

In the same report, the issue of funding of Muslim schools by the state is tackled. "The educational concepts and aspirations of Muslims are not unlike those of Jews and Christians. Religious value oriented education is common to these faith communities.... Muslim and many non-Muslims feel that Muslim schools have not received equal treatment compared with Christian and Jewish Schools." The support of non-Muslims was exampled in a speech by Tim Brighouse, the Chief Education Officer for Birmingham, in December 1996, when he called for: "official acknowledgment of the injustice of the law and the state system which allows Anglican, Catholic and Jewish schools to be funded by the state but hasn't found a way to allow Muslim schools to have similar status."[20] At the same occasion, Yusuf Islam, the chair of the Association of Muslim Schools (AMS), pointed out that: "the liberalism of Britain's democracy actually highlighted its hypocrisy. How can a liberal society *force* people to integrate if 'liberalism' is to be maintained? ... we want to integrate but on our terms."[21] An assessment by Dwyer and Meyer, of the arguments surrounding the failure of the application for funding of the Islamia School, quoted one of the reasons put forward by Brent Council for its opposition "that an Islamic school was contrary to their policy of multi-cultural education." The authors concluded that: "it is clear that the decision-making process for the Islamia School was influenced by particular ideological constructions which operated to militate against the legislative precedent of granting state-funding to Islamic schools." The article then proceeds to demonstrate how the ideological construction of "Muslims" is embedded in the decision-making process. The debates have centred around the concept of "integration" which is a concept that is central to ideas of multiculturalism and yet as they say it is rarely defined.[22] Muslims have stressed that, for those who wish to use them, separate schools, recognized by the state, are a way of integrating (but not assimilating) Islamic schools more closely within the official educational establishment of this country, and that not only the Muslim community but also the wider national culture of education would benefit.[23] Other arguments used against the Islamic schools movement are that they do not meet the various requirements of the system. However in terms of the National Curriculum, many Islamic Schools have a good record of achievement, as can be seen from the "League Tables" published in 1996,[24] and serious work is being undertaken in INSET groups to adapt the curriculum appropriately for the schools. The Education Reform Act 1988 placed a responsibility on schools "to provide a broad and balanced curriculum which promotes the spiritual, moral, cultural, mental and physical development of pupils at school; and prepare each pupil for the opportunities, responsibilities and experiences of adult life." Muslims argue that, as with other "denominational" schools, they are well placed to meet these responsibilities. This question of lack of state funding of Muslim schools, (there were 54 in operation by the end of 1996), is a significant challenge to the reality of multiculturalism in Britain.

The third challenge concerns the nature of Religious Education (RE) in schools and collective worship. In January 1996, Muslim parents in Batley, West Yorkshire, withdrew 1500 children from RE. AMS reported that: "local Islamic scholars were consulted and agreed that sending Muslim children to RE lessons wherein Christianity predominates and Islam is likely to be taught by a non-Muslim is unacceptable."[25] This reaction has to be viewed in the context of the new model syllabuses introduced by the School Curriculum and Assessment Authority (SCAA) as a result of amendments to the 1993 Education Act. These state that "the relative content devoted to Christianity should predominate." Not only Muslim groups, but other faith groups and professionals, have objected to what is seen as a shift in emphasis from an educational to an evangelical role. As other Muslim commentators have said "It is important, therefore, to ensure that future generations have a religious education which enables them to understand, rather than fear, the beliefs and values of other fellow citizens."[26]

Debates Within the Muslim Communities

The issue of Muslim or Islamic schools is symptomatic of a wider turmoil in the Muslim communities. This turmoil centres around the question of how to maintain an identity as Muslims while at the same time integrating into the wider society. For the migrant generation, they did not experience this issue when growing up. They then lived in Muslim societies which, by their monocultural nature, supported the development of an identity as a Muslim, irrespective of the position of the family. However for those developing their identity while growing up as part of a minority Muslim community in a non-Muslim society, they cannot look to the state to support this process. This raises issues for the whole family and community. Participation in state education means participation in a system which is primarily about socialization into the British way of life. That is about culture, preparation for citizenship and membership of the nation-state, and, social engineering to meet the needs of the economy. These first two produce conflicts, in particular, for Muslims. The dominant cultural values are not the same as those of Muslims, but to fight against this socialization is likely to result in a derogatory labeling as "backward and non progressive," and an exclusion from social participation in British society. To question the status of the nation-state, which is a concept inherently alien to Islam as it is based on the notion of the community of Muslims (the *Ummah*), or to question the negative attitudes towards Muslim states, is to be labeled as disloyal which raises questions over fitness for political participation in British society. Preparation for economic life does not appear to be evenly distributed, with Muslims over represented in poorer paid work and unemployment. Many in the majority population assume that this reflects lack of commitment to education, and a wish to "sponge" off the state rather than have a full economic participation in the society.

Debates around these issues have been going on within the Muslim communities in Britain for many years. They cover several areas:

- determining the real position of a community within a plural society, and the degree of choice that is available;
- understanding the stage of development of the communities, and therefore their future prospects;
- identifying the moral values that are key for underpinning the development of the communities, and how they should be best acquired;
- compensating for the overall poor results of the generation who have now gone through the state education system, and assessing the implications for succeeding generations;
- realizing and articulating the impact of Islamophobia on community, and individual development;
- dealing with an education system that reflects the aspirations, needs, and values, of the majority population.

In the 1990s, sections of the Muslim population have an agenda which they would define as social, cultural, and religious, in aim rather than political. However, any action that challenges hegemony, particularly of the state, is by definition political. For Muslims, analyzing their options as British citizens, the stark alternatives can be: accommodation to the system, and therefore a forfeiting of a Muslim identity in the public arena or, rejection of the system with very restricted participation. There is evidence of both these options being taken. It would appear that, in reality, multiculturalism, as practiced, is not allowing full participation and acceptance in British society for those who value a Muslim identity. Those who choose to pursue careers as professionals or politicians are forced into accommodation which involves the suppression of their Muslim identity in order to succeed. Being a Muslim then becomes an aspect of life which is confined to the domestic and community environment. For others Muslim identity is more important than acceptance into the wider community, and they adopt an instrumental approach to work. It is an alienation from the system which results in parallel working, interacting only as far as necessary with the system. There is evidence that this is happening to some extent among the young British born and educated generation who are disillusioned with their experience of multiculturalism. There is a third option which is to join the system to change it from within. However the reality is that the system is too strong and well entrenched to succumb to the onslaught of a minority.

Conclusion

Multiculturalism can be seen, in its most complete form, as being a commitment to cultural diversity, with the "real articulation of difference" as a basis for progress. It is about integration that recognizes and works with diversity as a positive feature of that society. This stands in opposition to monoculturalism, which is an overarching feature of the West in the late twentieth century. Yet, it is the case, as the result of post war settlement, that the leading countries of the West have increasing cultural diversity within their societies, associated with past colonial and economic policies. If one accepts Said's thesis of orientalism as still holding sway in the West, then it is Muslims as a group who are going to present potentially the most difficulties for the West as they represent the "other," the "contrasting image." It is not surprising therefore to find that, in Britain, as in other Western European countries, the biggest stumbling blocks for the state in the social and economic integration of groups are with Muslims. As the personification of the "other," Muslims present the biggest challenge to the commitment of the state to the acceptance of multiculturalism, with its legitimation and celebration of diversity of culture. The challenge is to the hegemony of majority culture and assumptions of universality.

For Muslims, personal and community identity is intertwined with religious belief. Islam integrates the social, political, and economic aspects of life into religious life, so that the concept of separate public and private domains for religious activity does not apply. Therefore for Muslims, their religious beliefs are potentially involved with all levels of the activities of the community and the state. In Britain, this has been evidenced through the nature of the major conflicts between Muslims and the state, which have challenged the operation of the Foreign Office, the Home Office, and the Department of Education, as well as the activities of local government. Is it possible for Muslims to be fully integrated within British society? The apparent coherence and underlying "homogeneity" of British society is a difficulty that Muslims in particular face with their identity intertwined with a religion and culture regarded by many as alien. The erosion of the beliefs and values inherent in and integral to their identity may well be a price that is too high to pay for many Muslims. Education is the key to social and economic integration for future generations, and so it is in this arena that the strongest stands are now being taken, and where the reality of commitment, on both sides, to models of multiculturalism is most revealingly under the spotlight.

All the evidence suggests that the overwhelming majority of Muslims in Britain wish to progress within pluralist British society, and participate as full citizens, while maintaining their identity as Muslims. The high levels of participation in local and national elections are an example of a commitment to participation. However, full social, economic, and political participation is dependent upon an approach to multiculturalism that, in reality, reflects the multicultural nature of current British society. Given the particular demographic characteristics of the

Muslim ethnic minority groups, the proportion of the population from these groups will continue to rise for the foreseeable future. This places an urgency on government to replace the superficiality of present multicultural approaches with a real commitment to acknowledging pluralism as the basis for the future. Such a commitment needs major campaigns to deal with the corrosive impact of entrenched Islamophobia on moves toward such integration. Perhaps the Islamic challenge will come to be seen as the pivotal pressure which brought about a meaningful reevaluation of British policies which, in the long term, benefits all citizens.

Notes

* Patricia Ellis is an Honorary Research Fellow at the Centre for the study of Globalization, Eurocentricity, Marginality (CGEM) at the University of Manchester and is former Director of the Centre for Ethnic Studies at the University of Luton. Zafar Khan is a Senior Lecturer in South Asian Studies and Community Relations in the Department of Social Studies at the University of Luton.

[1] E. Said, *Orientalism* (Harmondsworth, UK: Penguin, paperback edition, 1991), pp. 1–2.

[2] Said, *Orientalism*, p. 99.

[3] D.T. Goldberg, "Introduction: Multicultural Conditions" in D.T. Goldberg (ed) *Multiculturalism: a critical reader* (Oxford: Blackwell Publishers, 1994), p. 4.

[4] Goldberg, "Multicultural conditions," p. 7.

[5] Goldberg, "Multicultural conditions," p. 11.

[6] D. Blatt, "Towards a Multi-Cultural Political Model in France? The Limits of Immigrant Collective Action, 1968–94" *Nationalism & Ethnic Politics* 1 (1995), p. 156.

[7] B. Sayyid, "Sign O'Times: Kaffirs and Infidels Fighting the Ninth Crusade" in E. Laclau (ed.) *The Making of Political Identities* (London: Verso, 1994).

[8] J. Kahn, *Culture, Multiculture, Postculture* (London: Sage Publ., 1995), p. 9.

[9] see, Kahn, p. 13.

[10] C. Taylor, "Politics of Recognition" in D.T. Goldberg (ed) *Multiculturalism: a critical reader* (Oxford: Blackwell Publishers, 1994).

[11] see, Goldberg for a full exploration of this point.

[12] J. Patten, "Letter of 4 July 1989 from Mr. John Patten, Minister of State at the Home Office, to a number of leading British Muslims" Appendix D, *Law, Blasphemy and the Multi—Faith Society* (London: Commission for Racial Equality, 1989).

[13] Goldberg, "Multicultural conditions," p. 29.

[14] Runneymede Trust Commission on British Muslims and Islamophobia *Islamophobia: Its features and dangers* (London: Runneymede Trust, 1997), p. 8.

[15] quoted in major report in the Independent "Muslims in Britain," A. Brown & P. Vallely "Pride and prejudice" *Independent* (section two) (5 December 1995), p. 2.

[16] Runneymede Trust Commission, p. 8.

[17] quoted in the above report.

[18] Editor "Islamic Education: balanced and broadly based" *Al-Madaris* (Winter 1996/7), p. 6.

[19] Muslim Educational Trust *Education in Multi-Faith Britain : meeting the needs of Muslims* (London: Muslim Educational Trust, 1995), p. 2.

[20] Association of Muslim Schools "Local Authorities cooperation sought" *Al-Madaris* (Winter 1996/7), p. 1.

[21] as previous reference.

[22] C. Dwyer and A. Meyer, "The institutionalisation of Islam in The Netherlands and in the UK: the case of Islamic schools" *New Community* 21(1) (1994), pp. 37–54.

[23] R. Shah-Kazemi. "Islamic Schools: enriching the culture of education" *Dialogue* (March 1997), p. 7.

[24] Editor "Muslim Schools GCSE Results 1996" *Al-Madaris* (Winter 1996/7), p. 2.

[25] Association of Muslim Schools "News" *Al-Madaris* (Spring 1996), p. 2.

[26] K. Knight & U. Hegedus "Religious education in context" *Dialogue* (April 1994), p. 8.

The Mega-Musical as Transcultural Phenomenon

William A. Everett

Nineteenth-century European opera was both national and international in terms of language, subject matter, and musical style. The contemporary mega-musical, exemplified by works such as *Les Miserables* and *The Phantom of the Opera*, continues these traditions. These recent works parallel political changes on the European continent: national identity is maintained and promulgated within a broader multi-national context. A critic proclaimed, after attending the theater:

> Screaming unisons everywhere, and all the melodies of that peculiar style the parallel whereof is rope-dancing.... The unfortunate man [the composer] is incapable of real melody—his arias are such as a man born deaf would compose by calculation of the distances of musical notes and the intervals between them.[1]

And another wrote, after seeing a different work:

> Those who were present at the performance ... were little prepared for the revolting effects produced by musically illustrating the torture and murder scenes.... The alliance of a pure art with scenes so essentially brutal and demoralizing ... produced a feeling of nausea. There may be some who will find entertainment in this sensation, but all true lovers of the gentle art must deplore with myself its being so prostituted. What has music to do with a lustful man chasing a defenseless woman or the dying kicks of a murdered scoundrel? It seemed an odd form of amusement to put before a presumably refined and cultured audience.[2]

Although these reviews may sound as if they refer to contemporary musical theater, they are in fact reactions to nineteenth-century Italian opera. The first is a response from 1850 to Giuseppe Verdi's *Macbeth*, while the second, from 1900, offers a description of Giacomo Puccini's *Tosca*. Critics of nineteenth-century Italian opera and twentieth-century musical theater share many common concerns about musical inferiority and inappropriate plots in works from their respective genres. Striking parallels between nineteenth-century Italian opera and late twentieth-century musical theater only begin here: the two genres have a great deal in common. Audience popularity, the language of performance, set and costume design, the very concept of nineteenth-century Romanticism, with its emphases on the big and the supernatural in particular, and the genre's ability to convey socio-political messages are but a few of the areas which become manifest in both nineteenth-century Italian opera and twentieth-century musical theater. Modern mega-musicals such as *Les Miserables* and *The Phantom of the Opera* continue many of these operatic conventions of the nineteenth century and reinterpret them for twentieth-century audiences.

Just as Italian opera dominated the nineteenth-century musical stage, as we shall see, the so-called "mega-musical," represented by works such as *Les Miserables* and *The Phantom of the Opera*, controls many aspects of today's popular musical theater. In the past century, musical selections from the latest Italian opera were available in local music shops, and excerpts from current operas could be heard outside of the opera house in performances by local organizations (bands, choruses) or as background music in various settings. Today, sheet music sales account for a great deal of revenue from a West End or Broadway show, and recordings significantly increase their popularity.

During the nineteenth century, it was not just opera, but more specifically *Italian* opera, which dominated the musical theater scene. Works by composers such as Verdi and Puccini enjoyed tremendous fame throughout Europe. Most often, but not always, they were performed in the Italian language, regardless of the vernacular of the country of performance, for the Italian language suggested a kind of sophistication. Italian opera was the international style of musical theater which audiences saw and heard in opera houses throughout Europe, from Great Britain and Scandinavia in the north to Italy and the southern parts of the Austro-Hungarian Empire in the south.

The issue of language was paramount during the nineteenth century, as it is today. Should opera be sung in its original language or in the vernacular of the country of performance? No definitive answer to this question, as central to nineteenth-century Italian opera as it is to the contemporary mega-musical, exists. Two historical examples will have to suffice for the moment as demonstrations of the complexity of this issue: the "Querelle des Bouffons" in eighteenth-century Paris and the 1896 season at Covent Garden in London.

Between 1752 and 1754 in Paris, a debate which became known as the "Querelle des Bouffons" (War of the Buffoons) arose after a performance of an Italian comic opera, Pergolesi's *La serva padrona*, by a travelling troupe in 1752. The central issue of the quarrel regarded the preferred language for opera: French or Italian. Over sixty letters and pamphlets appeared during the ensuing three years. Composers, writers, and philosophers all expressed strong opinions about the respective merits of the French and Italian languages for singing. At the end, neither side could claim a decisive victory. Then, as today, a clear-cut answer to this perennial question could not be found.

A century later in London, the issue of language had an engrossing display at the Royal Opera House, Covent Garden. During the 1896 season, the company staged three operas by Richard Wagner (1813–83), a German. Wagner wrote each of the operas with a German libretto, but audiences at Covent Garden heard

Wagner's music sung in three different languages that season: *Die Meistersinger* in Italian, *Tristan und Isolde* in German, and *Die Walküre* and *Tannhäuser* in French. Although there are reasons for the choices of these particular languages (a treatment of which is beyond the scope of this discussion), English is not among them. Some level of anti-vernacular attitudes towards language existed in nineteenth-century London opera circles.

The preference for foreign-language opera productions in nineteenth-century London is perhaps best reflected in the realm of Italian opera. Nineteenth-century Britain had a tremendous fascination with Italy and things Italian. This is reflected in literature (E. M. Forster's novels *Where Angels Fear to Tread* and *A Room with a View*, for example), the visual arts (the Pre-Raphaelite movement), and music (Italian opera). The Royal Italian Opera, which gave performances at Her Majesty's Theater, was a mainstay of the musical scene from as early as 1842. As a sign of its strength, in 1847, the company commissioned Giuseppe Verdi to write *I masnadieri* (The Bandits), and Verdi traveled to London for the ill-fated opera's premiere. The company was still in existence when the present-day building for Her Majesty's Theatre opened in 1897 as Her Majesty's Theatre for Italian Opera. We shall return to the significance of this particular venue later.

The prominence of Italian opera in London was such that one Italian opera company in the city was not enough; for in 1847, the same year as Verdi's visit to London, a second enterprise, also using the name Royal Italian Opera, began to offer performances at Covent Garden. The only language sung on stage by this company for over fifty years was Italian. This resulted in performances of Meyerbeer's French opera *Les Huguenots* as *Gli Ugonotti* in 1848 and Balfe's English-language *The Bohemian Girl* as *La zingara* in 1858. It was not until 1889 that the Royal Italian Opera began to offer productions in languages other than Italian. As their linguistic preferences became more liberal, the company changed its name in 1892 to the Royal Opera, the appellation it retains to the present day.

While Italian opera dominated the scene not only in London but also throughout Europe, a number of distinctive national styles emerged within European opera, each in its own language. Central to this discussion is French opera, although composers in Germany, Russia, Czech lands, Britain, and other nations were making important strides toward their own individual voices in the operatic realm. But it was Italian opera against which composers, critics, and audiences generally defined these other styles. Even in countries where Italian opera was not the exclusive type of musical theater entertainment, its essence and influence were nonetheless quite evident.

French opera is of particular importance in this discussion, for the modern "mega-musical" has its roots in the genre. In nineteenth-century France, a variety of styles existed within the realm of opera.[3] Central to the present discussion is grand opera. The operative word in grand opera was "grand." Huge choruses, stages filled with people and sets, and a true "bigger than life" concept were all central to the genre and were fundamental to its immense popularity. A serious plot, often on a historical subject, provided the means through which the composer, librettist, director, set designer, and choreographer could realize their grandiose ideas on stage.[4] Grand opera was sung throughout, and was intended to be a stage spectacle. Set design and costumes were of tremendous importance, and audiences expected extraordinary special effects on stage. The visual was as important as the musical. A production of Giacomo Meyerbeer's *Le prophete* in 1849 even included a roller-skating sequence(!),[5] predating Andrew Lloyd Webber's *Starlight Express* by more than 140 years.[6] Supernatural elements often played into the plot, thus allowing for astonishing staging possibilities. The Cloister Scene in act 3 of Meyerbeer's *Robert le Diable* (1831), for example, included phantom nuns rising from their graves.

The ballet was one of the most important components of French grand opera. French opera, it should be noted, has its roots in the dance. During the nineteenth century, Parisian opera audiences demanded a ballet at the beginning of the second act. The ballet had to be at this point in the evening so that members of the prestigious Jockey Club, who would arrive late so as to be seen, would not miss it.

In what ways has today's musical theater continued the legacies of its predecessors in the last century? In terms of the mega-musical of the late twentieth century, how have nineteenth-century traditions, principally those of Italian and French opera, been continued and developed? To explore these questions, we shall look at two of the most successful musicals of the late twentieth century, *Les Miserables* (1985) by Claude-Michel Schoenberg and Alain Boublil and *The Phantom of the Opera* (1986) by Sir Andrew Lloyd Webber and Tim Rice. Both works come under the relatively pseudo-scientific designation of "mega-musical." Perhaps a viable, though long-winded, working definition for a mega-musical is as follows:

> a musical-theater work conceived and realized on a large scale in terms of staging, set design, choreography, and overall dramatic plan. A mega-musical contains a high percentage of music (as opposed to spoken dialogue), and is marketed with the intent of reaching a broad audience and achieving "popular" status through a long profit-making run in London and/or New York in addition to other productions, either "resident" or "touring," along with financially-successful cast recordings and other merchandise. (definition mine)

The immensely popular *Les Miserables*, the creation of two Frenchmen, began life as an "arena version" at the Palais des Sports in Paris on 18 September 1980. British producer Cameron Mackintosh, whose vision transformed the French work into a truly international phenomenon, heard the recording of the production and subsequently took on the task of overseeing the show's metamorphosis into its present form.[7]

The English-language result, a collaboration between Mackintosh and the Royal Shakespeare Company and first performed at London's Barbican Theatre on 8 October 1985, was a huge success. The show was an international enterprise—a French foundation with a British realization. *Les Miserables* transferred to the Palace Theatre in London's West End on 4 December 1985, and since that time, has continued to draw packed houses. Central to this topic, the show has been produced throughout the world to great popular and critical acclaim. Its description as "the world's most popular musical" is certainly not to be taken lightly. Within two years of the show's London success came performances in Hungary and Iceland in the vernacular languages of those countries. In the years which followed, productions opened in Norway, Austria, Poland, Sweden, the Netherlands, France, Germany, the Czech Republic, Spain, Denmark, and Finland, each in the vernacular. Furthermore, recordings of the show have appeared in English, Hungarian, German, Swedish, Dutch, French, Czech, Danish, and Spanish.

Whereas Italian opera was usually performed in Italian during the nineteenth-century, *Les Miserables* today is generally heard in the vernacular. This important distinction allows for immediate accessibility of the libretto by European audiences regardless of their native languages. What is perhaps even more significant in this regard is that today English is widely spoken throughout Europe (certainly to a much greater degree than Italian was in the last century), and audiences *could* understand *Les Miserables* in an English-language production. It is a testament to the internationalism of the genre and of the show itself that producers choose to translate the show into vernacular languages rather than to employ the *lingua franca* of English.

Les Miserables shares with Italian opera of the last century a truly multi-national popularity, as we have seen. Its structure and *ethos*, though, are much closer to that of French grand opera. Here, two strands of national identity from the nineteenth century intertwine in the twentieth.

The most obvious parallel between *Les Miserables* and French grand opera is that both contain continuous music; they are sung from beginning to end. *Les Miserables* also exhibits other characteristics of its ancestral genre. In addition to solo songs (arias) and duets, the show includes huge choral numbers, such as "Do You Hear the People Sing?," designed to create a stirring effect upon the audience. The large-scale nature of the production is another obvious comparison; the staging for *Les Miserables* includes set pieces and scenery which become characters in and of themselves. The barricade that emerges on stage to dramatic musical under-scoring is central to the show, as is the otherworldly use of direct overhead light when a character dies or re-appears as a ghost. The work is serious in its overall tone; Victor Hugo's novel provides a solid dramatic base, although it had to be severely abridged and adapted for musical treatment.

An important parallel between nineteenth-century French grand opera and *Les Miserables* concerns the socio-political message inherent in Hugo's novel. One of the most politically important operas of the nineteenth century was Auber's *La muette de Portici* (The Mute Girl of Portici; 1828). Revolutionary ideas in this opera influenced a popular uprising in Brussels in 1830 which ultimately resulted in Belgian independence. The opera itself thus became a symbol for revolutionary ideas and ideals. This was not the end of its popularity, however, for by 1882, it had been performed 505 times in Paris alone, and, like *Les Miserables*, received performances in several European languages all over the continent.

La muette de Portici is important in another way to this discussion, for many consider it to be the first grand opera. The new genre was born with the first performance of *La muette de Portici* in Paris on 29 February 1828. The first grand opera, therefore, has a performance history with many parallels to its modern-day descendent—both are works which have been performed in translation and both have resonances with contemporary political situations.

The socio-political message of justice and freedom from oppression in *Les Miserables*, considered in such numbers as "Do You Hear the People Sing?" "One Day More," and "Empty Chairs at Empty Tables," is an integral part of the show. Edward Behr describes the implications of the musical in Eastern European productions:

> The Hungarian version of *Les Miserables* was probably—of all the foreign versions currently playing around the world—the most emotional, and certainly the most moving. To the Hungarian people, the barricades have very special, symbolic connotations: they cannot but recall the tragic 1956 Budapest uprising, crushed by Soviet tanks. The same emotional atmosphere marked the opening of the Polish version of "Les Mis" at the Muzyczny Theatre in Gdynia in June 1989 and the premiere of the Czech version in Prague's Vinorhady Theatre three years later.[8]

So, we come full circle with *Les Miserables*: just as in the last century with *La muette de Portici*, today there is a wildly popular musical with ideas of revolution and social reform performed in the vernacular languages of people throughout Europe. The musical theater continues to be relevant to political situations in both the nineteenth and twentieth centuries.

Les Miserables, the creation of two Frenchmen, represents a revival of the French grand opera tradition. Accordingly, *The Phantom of the Opera*, the creation of two Englishmen, a homage to the same genre. Based on the novel by Gaston Leroux and set at the Paris Opera, the supernatural tale of a singer is told in grandiose style, with interpolations of specially created operas and even the obligatory ballet. Several musical numbers in the show are in a style which is much more operatic than is typical for a West End musical.

Scenes from three different imaginary operas appear in *The Phantom of the Opera*: *Hannibal* by Chalumeau, *Il Muto* by Albrizzio, and *Don Juan Triumphant* by the Phantom himself. By including these operas, Lloyd Webber pays tribute to aspects of the French tradition. *Hannibal* is a grand opera, complete with a scenic elephant, while *Il Muto* recalls an earlier style of Italian opera, the opera buffa—a genre which would have been known to French audiences. *Don Juan Triumphant* is a decidedly modern work which heightens the dramatic effect of the libretto.

Hannibal ably demonstrates many of the conventions of French grand opera. The story is one of heroism based on actual historical events: Hannibal and his army are returning to Carthage to save the city from the Roman invasion under Scipio. Huge sets, including the afore-mentioned elephant, and lavish costumes provide the audience with a taste of grand opera.

Il Muto, by contrast, is a farcical opera buffa in which the Countess is having an affair with Serafino, her page boy, and disguises him as her chambermaid to hide him from her jealous husband. It was this very type of opera, even with a mute character, which instigated the afore-mentioned "Querelle des Bouffons" in mid-eighteenth-century Paris. Conventions such as the disguising of a male youth as a female were popular in eighteenth-century Italian opera, and are perhaps best known from Mozart's *Le nozze di Figaro* (The Marriage of Figaro; 1786), where Susanna and the Countess disguise the page boy Cherubino.

The third opera introduced into *The Phantom of the Opera* is the title character's *magnum opus*, *Don Juan Triumphant*. The Phantom himself assumes the title role in this "show within a show." The Phantom and Christine, the heroine, sing their duet, "Point of No Return," in the context of the opera. Lloyd Webber said of *Don Juan Triumphant*, which does not appear in Leroux's novel:

> I decided that if we adapted the plot to include a performance of an opera specially composed for Christine by the Phantom, we could not only introduce a far more modern musical ingredient in the score, but could contrive a situation where the Phantom was not only unmasked in front of many characters, but on the stage of his opera house, in his own opera, in what was supposed to be his night of triumph.[9]

In *The Phantom of the Opera*, Lloyd Webber pays homage not only to French grand opera but also to the operas of Wolfgang Amadeus Mozart (1756–91). Mozart's operas, whether of the Italian or German varieties, are among the finest works ever written for the musical stage; some would even argue *the* finest. In *Il muto*, Lloyd Webber pays homage to *Le nozze di Figaro* by basing his scene on Mozart's disguising of Cherubino as a young girl in act 2. In *Don Juan Triumphant*, Lloyd Webber honors *Don Giovanni* (1787). *Don Juan Triumphant* and *Don Giovanni* are versions of the same tale, but the similarity in this case goes further. The only scene from *Don Juan Triumphant* we see is the banquet scene, the setting for which is that of the well-known penultimate scene in *Don Giovanni*. Thus, reworkings of two of the most famous scenes from Mozart operas appear in Lloyd Webber's tribute to the opera world.

In addition to the operas themselves, the dance, so integral to the French concept of opera, is likewise a crucial part of *The Phantom of the Opera*. Our first image of Christine Daae, the heroine, is in a line of ballet dancers reminiscent of a Degas painting. The costuming of the dancers throughout the musical maintains this initial image of the ballet. "Masquerade," the New Year's Eve celebration which opens the second act with a wide array of spectacular and unusual costumes, would not have disappointed Parisian audiences a century ago. In order to heighten the already impressive effect, costumed dummies appear alongside live actors on the huge staircase, filling the stage with glamorous visual delights.

Further references to several operatic conventions are also present in *The Phantom of the Opera*. The lavish sets and special effects point directly toward French grand opera. Among the most memorable stage moments are the ascent of the great chandelier as it rises over the stalls at the beginning of the first act, only to come crashing down just before the interval, the ever-descending ramps to the Phantom's lair, the boat ride across the fog-enveloped underground lake lit by candelabra, the emergence of the Phantom from behind the headstone of the proscenium arch, lowered mid-way, and, at the end of the show, the Phantom's mysterious disappearance.

Similarly, stereotypical depictions of Italian singers accentuate comic aspects of the opera world. The prima donna, Carlotta Guidicelli, is as self-centered as one can imagine, and enjoys having her adorers sing her praises in the paean "Prima Donna." Carlotta's jealously of Christine is evident throughout the show, and her "croaking" in *Il Muto*, the result of the Phantom's curse, is crushing. Likewise, Signor Piangi encompasses all the cliches associated with an Italian tenor of the last century—the huge ego and the inability to sing "new" music, namely the whole-tone scale in *Don Juan Triumphant*. His inability to sing something which does not fall naturally, despite coaching, reenforces the attitude that tenors, especially Italian ones, are in love with their own voices and can sing only in *bel canto* style.

Furthermore, Lloyd Webber and Rice pay homage to nineteenth-century opera and important aspects of the entire romantic age through the inclusion of supernatural elements. The cemetery scene in *Phantom*, when Christine is visiting her father's tomb, is reminiscent of the afore-mentioned cloister scene in Meyerbeer's *Robert le Diable*. Supernatural characters are a mainstay of the German operatic tradition, a heritage which we cannot explore in greater detail due to time restraints. Suffice it to say that *Zauberopern* (magic operas) were popular in the eighteenth century, the most famous of which today is Mozart's *Die Zauberflöte* (The Magic Flute, 1791). Supernatural characters and their effects upon mortals are evident in Carl Maria von Weber's *Der Freischütz* (first performed in 1821) and many of the music-dramas of Richard Wagner, including *Tristan und Isolde* (first performed in 1865) and *Der Ring des Nibelungen* (first performed in 1876). The Phantom, therefore, continues this tradition of a person with magical or supernatural abilities influencing ordinary humans.

Finally, extramusical elements reflect the internationalism of *The Phantom of the Opera*. The show plays in London at Her Majesty's Theatre, a house chosen specifically by Lloyd Webber because of its somewhat similar appearance to the Paris Opera House. But the connection of *Phantom* with nineteenth-century opera goes beyond this, for, as was mentioned earlier, when the present Her Majesty's Theatre opened in 1897, its full name was Her Majesty's Theatre for Italian Opera. A house intended for performances of the international musical theater of the last century fulfills the same purpose today. French, Italian, and English elements coalesce in performances of *Phantom* in this far from arbitrary choice of venue.

Could works such as *Les Miserables* and *The Phantom of the Opera* be reflective of the "New Europe," the theme of this conference? The works certainly are international in their concept, for they draw upon a variety of national traditions. The same music is performed in each production—a universal, while the language is the vernacular—a specific. Does this not reflect at least in part European identity, common elements with specific distinctions? The coming together of a variety of traditions, each of which maintains its specific identity, is also evident. These ingredients are not disenfranchised partisans in a potpourri of national identities, but rather are significant components of a multi-faceted, yet unified, musical work. Inspiration for and creation of the works take place on a multi-national level, as do performances. Just as Italian opera influenced the entire realm of European opera in the last century, the mega-musical motivates European musical theater in this century. Hardly a composer can write a work for the musical theater without being compared to either Andrew Lloyd Webber or Claude-Michel Schoenberg.

The historic tenth-anniversary concert of *Les Miserables* which took place in the Royal Albert Hall on 8 October 1995 provides a fitting conclusion to this essay and the questions it raises. After a performance which included principals from all over the world (not just Europe) and almost all of the some two hundred and sixty veterans from *Les Mis* productions in London, a surprise grand encore took place.[10] Seventeen actors who had played the lead character Jean Valjean processed into the hall to sing the anthem "Do You Hear the People Sing?," each in his native tongue. Issues of language, socio-political messages, and the operatic heritage of the mega-musical all come to the fore in this powerful display of the national within the universal.

Conclusion

The modern mega-musical continues and redefines many of the norms associated with nineteenth-century European opera. The question of language, subject matter (references to socio-political situations), and musical style are but a few of the commonalities between these two traditions. Two of the most popular mega-musicals, *Les Miserables* and *The Phantom of the Opera*, look back to the nineteenth-century operatic heritage: *Les Miserables* through the re-creation of French grand opera, and *The Phantom of the Opera* as a homage to French and Italian operatic styles. The international popularity of works such as these attests to their significance as a unifying force in the cultural development of the "New Europe"—a group of nations which, though sharing common interests, each maintains its own identity.

Notes

[1] George Templeton Strong's Diary, 28 April 1850, quoted in Nicolas Slonimsky, *Lexicon of Musical Invective* (New York: Coleman-Ross Co., 1952), p. 218.

[2] Unidentified London newspaper, 13 July 1900, quoted in Slonimsky, p. 135.

[3] Other sub-genres in French opera contrasted with grand opera, each with its own characteristics. Opera comique was generally lighter in concept, and included spoken dialogue. Earlier examples of the genre were almost farcical in their plots, while later ones have more sophisticated libretti. Somewhere between grand opera and opera comique was opera lyrique, which may or may not have had spoken dialogue, but lacked the pretentiousness of grand opera. Jacques Offenbach developed a tradition called opera bouffe, which in effect was a parody of other styles and serious traditions.

[4] Many of Cecil B. DeMille's films, such as *The Ten Commandments* (1956), exemplify this same concept.

[5] George Perry, *The Complete Phantom of the Opera* (London: Pavilion Books, 1987), p. 11.

[6] All the characters in *Starlight Express* are on roller skates, and the theater is transformed into a roller-skating arena, with actors skating on platforms among the audience.

[7] Edward Behr, *Les Miserables, History in the Making* (London: Pavilion Books, 1996), p. 7.

[8] Behr, p. 148.

[9] Perry, p. 70.

[10] Behr, p. 154.

Redefining the Status of France and of the French Language within the European Union

Françoise Ghillebaert

Tout d'abord un pays doit charmer par son nom.
Sans quoi vous ne serez jamais d'intelligence avec lui.
Vous, Francis, aimez l'Ile-de-France.
A votre joli nom son beau nom se fiancé
et votre art et vous-même ajoutez à ses dons.
(Paul Fort, "Les Beaux Noms," 1909)

As the European Union evolves, France is redefining itself in its new role as Union member and potential leader. This article looks at the emerging role of France in the European Union, as it is reflected in the feelings of the French about themselves and in the attitude toward France of not only another key Union member, Germany, but also of its influential ally, the United States. Since the French language has long been a reflection of the French culture itself, we will also look at the position of the French language in the world of the twenty-first century. As final talks on the implementation of the Economic and Monetary Union, the last link in the consolidation of the European Union, are under way, attention focuses on France and on its role in the formation of the Union. France draws particular attention from Germany and the United States because stability in Europe cannot prevail without good relationships between these three countries. On this matter, Steven Philip Kramer writes:

> France possesses political institutions and a political class well suited to playing a global role. But France's capacity to play this role requires a continuing Franco-German partnership as well as cooperation between Europe and the United States.[1]

Since the death of former socialist president François Mitterrand, political changes have occurred in France which have affected the relationships between France and Germany, and between France and the United States. The advent of Jacques Chirac's Gaullist government has both pleased and worried Helmut Kohl.[2] The chancellor is concerned about the continuation of the talks on the Monetary Union planned for January 1999. In addition, the new cohabitation, the third in the past two decades, this time between a right-wing president and the socialist prime minister Lionel Jospin has caused concern in both the United States and Germany. What is at stake are the terms of the political and economic structure of the

European Union as they have been delineated by the late French president and in the Maastricht Treaty. As France's political structure continues to oscillate, American and German leaders wonder whether the shaping of the European Union will run its course as planned. In addition, France is experiencing internal economic and political problems. As a result, an atmosphere of "malaise" pervades France and spreads to its relationship with the United States and Germany. In order to determine the causes and effects of this "malaise," and the extent to which it affects the prestige of France and of the French language, we propose to make a brief review of some of the literature which addresses these concerns.

In many current writings on French politics and French studies, the word "malaise" comes up as a leitmotiv, as if France was suffering from a chronic disease. Fortunately, the word "malaise" evokes by definition a temporary problem and there is hope that the situation will improve. As Kramer says: "Post-war French society and its political class have shown nothing if not resilience. This is not a country in decline."[3]

Historically, France has always been one of the leaders of Europe. The success of Europe, which has recovered from two devastating wars and whose excellence Paul Valéry recalls in "La Crise de l'Esprit,"[4] has rested essentially on the joint efforts of France and Germany. The role of France as leader is constantly undermined from within, however, and this in turn makes its partners dubious of French society's ability to function at its full potential.

Kramer highlights the problems which have affected the French nation in the post-cold war era. He states that French voters have lost "faith in the ability of democratic parties to solve basic economic problems."[5] As a result, "a pervasive malaise"[6] has developed in France which focuses on the economic weaknesses of the country and on its problems with immigration. This "malaise" has been exploited by the far-right and has propelled Jean-Marie Le Pen's political party, the "Front National," into national prominence. In addition, according to Kramer, "the debate over Maastricht allowed the Front National to tie its fears about loss of French identity to anxieties about European integration."[7] The fear of the loss of national identity is a legitimate one shared by all the nations in the Union. Eric Izraelewicz writes in *Le Monde* that "The difficulty which the Europeans must face is therefore to imagine a new culture — a European culture — which would take into account national cultures."[8] The difficult task for each nation will be to be part of Europe and yet keep its cultural identity; for the French, to "move towards Europe without dismantling France," says Lionel Jospin.[9]

This sense of political "malaise" is not new to France. It has been discussed by several authors, Marie-France Toinet, David Cameron, Gérard Mermet and Alain Peyrefitte, to name but a few. Marie-France Toinet recalls that "according to historian and sociologist Pierre Rosanvallon, French politics has been in crisis for two centuries!"[10] She reassures the reader, however, that the situation in France is not a crisis in the sense that analysts like Maier and Huntington give to the word, that is to say a disabling of the structures of the country. It is instead linked to an identity crisis which the French are experiencing because France is no longer the sole decision maker for its private affairs. This identity crisis reveals itself in "electoral volatility" which, according to Toinet, is "an indication that the French electorate [...] believes there are political alternatives to the status quo within the general political framework."[11] The French way of dealing with its discontent over public affairs, however, worries the United States. David R. Cameron claims that the reason behind the "malaise" lies in the difficulty for France of maintaining a healthy economy and strong employment while at the same time "honor[ing] the various commitments to Europe agreed [to] by [the] predecessors" [to Chirac's government].[12] Gérard Mermet, author and specialist in the analysis of social change in French society writes in *Francoscopie 1997* of "a new trouble in France: the "misérabilisme."[13]

If the tarnished aura of France today is due to the murky image that it projects in political, economic, and social situations, the root of the problem may very well lie in the archaic traits of French society, which Alain Peyrefitte outlined as early as 1976 in *The Trouble with France*.[14] In the up-dated 1986 version of his book, Peyrefitte puts the blame for the "French malaise" not only on the socialist administration of the past decade but also on the archaic administration that he, as then head of the Ministry of Information, found as far back as 1962, and on the stubbornness with which the French refuse to learn new technological methods.

The very reluctance to change which gives French society charm and stability also renders technical advance difficult. Peyrefitte points out the problems brought on by this national characteristic. He writes:

> In order to meet international competition, private companies have to use Anglo-American techniques and an imported vocabulary: "engineering" and "leasing," [...]. No purpose is served in being indignant at this invasion of *franglais;* it only translates our mental weaknesses. We will remain awkward in *têtes-à-têtes* with others and with reality until we set ourselves to learn these techniques systematically. Anglo-Saxon man is trained from childhood for real life. The French will think abstractly as long as they are taught mechanical theory through formulas without ever having to install a piston or dismount a carburetor.[15]

Indeed, the French, while masters at theorizing, seem to lack the desire to use new technology. Over a decade after Peyrefitte's remarks, Jacques Chirac proved to the world that the computer revolution had not yet reached French leadership when, at the opening of the new "Bibliothèque Nationale" in Paris, the president of France was puzzled by the function of a computer mouse. His response to this most common of computer gadgets illustrates the lack of interest the French show for certain types of technology. Ironically, the French attitude toward modern technology is in part due to the popularity of a French technological marvel, the Minitel, as Mermet notes:

> The use of home computers is developing more slowly in France than in Northern European countries, and of course than in the United States or Japan. The real growth spurt occurred in 1994; over 20% of households were equipped by the end of 1995, that is double the number of 10 years before. The spread of home computers has probably paradoxically been slowed down by the lead taken in telematics, with the Minitel, with which 26% of households are equipped. […], France is the first country in the world as far as the use of phone services is concerned. This may be why the French have not rushed yet on to the Internet which requires other types of equipment and which does not appear to be a true competitor to the Minitel in regards to services.[16]

According to Mermet, a 1988 survey by the Eurostat agency[17] showed the largest number of families possessing a computer to be found in the Netherlands, with Americans coming in second. No information was given concerning France. Although the French do not lack ideas in matter of technology, (the creation of the Minitel attests to their inventiveness) the recent progress in computer technology and telecommunications has not yet reached many sectors of the French society.

Certain French companies show a similar reluctance to adopt new technology, despite Lionel Jospin's exhortations.[18] Like Mermet, Frédéric Filloux explains that, as a consequence of its "technological and economic performance," the Minitel "stunted the growth of the Internet in France."[19] He writes: "no sector that has tasted the financial success of 'kiosque'[20] is willing to venture onto uncertain territory such as the Internet."[21] Although communication between companies and their consumers would be more efficient and cheaper through the Internet and the use of Web pages, big companies like the SNCF still prefer to advertise through the Minitel despite the cost to consumers. Numerous other companies, however, take a more modern approach and reach out to the public through Web pages.

Radio France is a striking example of this more modern approach. While in the 1960's, as Alain Peyrefitte noted, it was impossible to tune in to a French radio program from anywhere in the world outside of France or francophone countries, today's French radio broadcasting makes a breakthrough on the Internet, Filloux writes:

> Today, there's not a country in the world […] that's inaccessible to the major French radio stations: Radio France (comprising Radio-France International, France Inter and France Info), RTL and Europe 1.
> "We were amazed to discover that our site gets regular hits from Indonesia, and even from a little out-of-the-way town in Japan where there's a surprisingly high number of French speakers," says Jacques-Gabriel Mariotti (founder of Medianet).[22]

Because of the software Real audio, the user does not have to wait for the complete downloading of a file to read it. This software allows French radio broadcasting to reach the French community in the United States and the rest of the world. "Users can retrieve any program aired within the previous 24 hours," says Filloux. Outside of France, French radio on the Internet will quickly supersede the traditional ways of catching air waves or receiving recorded radio programs, while allowing a higher sound quality. This service will greatly favor the diffusion of the French language around the world, and will satisfy even the expert internauts. The Internet has also become a means by which the French Cultural Services and the French Embassy can distribute current information about any topic related to French society and Francophony.

One of the primary goals of the French Ministry of Culture is to promote the use of French in the world.[23] Philippe Douste-Blazy, Minister of Culture, outlined the three principal linguistic objectives of the Ministry in a talk given to the Cabinet in March, 1996, at the International Day of Francophony:

- to consolidate the presence and influence of French as the language of the Republic
- to maintain the role of French as a language for international communication
- to promote multilingualism

To fulfill the first objective, a new decree aimed at encouraging the enrichment of French through the adoption of new terms in economics, sciences, and technology was adopted on August 4, 1994. According to Pierre Oudart, this decree, known as the "Loi Toubon" has made necessary "the renewal of a system to coin new words in order to enrich the French language."[24] Oudart further writes that on July 9, 1996, the *Journal Officiel* published a new decree outlining how this linguistic enrichment is to take place. From now on, specialized commissions within a given office will communicate new terms to the general committee on terminology ("la commission générale de terminologie") headed by Mr. Gabriel de Broglie. The new terms will then be submitted to the *Académie française* for approval before they are finally published in the *Journal Officiel.* Once this procedure is complete, the secretary of each commission will be able to make the new lexicon available on the Internet and readily accessible to translators and technical writers. The promptness of the availability of the new material will allow for immediate feedback and comments from users before a term is definitively established. As Pierre Oudart writes "the experiments in cooperative terminological work done on the Internet by the general French language delegation showed that Francophones have a great interest for that subject."[25] An interest also evidenced by the fact that, since March 1996, the general French language delegation offers the use of new words used in technology, free of charge, from the server of the Ministry of Culture.

In order to maintain the role of French as a language for international communication, the second objective of the Ministry of Culture, the "loi Toubon" plans to set up a system of translation for conferences which take place on French soil. Action will also be taken to assure the position of French as an official language, equal to English, in the Olympic Games. The status of French has not always been respected at the Olympic Games, and the National Olympic and French Sports Committee was created in June 1994 to ensure the effective use of French during the Olympic Games of Atlanta in July 1996. This committee organized the translation of necessary documents about the games into French and the training of volunteers in charge of the reception in French.

Finally, in order to preserve cultural and linguistic diversity within the Union, the third objective of the Ministry of Culture, France has taken part in a series of initiatives aimed at encouraging linguistic pluralism. On March 31, 1995, for example, the European Union Council issued a resolution aimed at improving the quality and diversity of the training and teaching of languages in member States.

As for the use of foreign languages on the Internet, the Ministry of Culture will support the development of software and word processing packages which respect the diacritic marks and other lexical particularities of French, and the development of tools such as lexicons and electronic grammars. These resources are poorly structured in Europe, and the European Commission has pushed for the creation of an association with headquarters in Paris to collect, evaluate, and distribute such resources for the languages of the Union.

The French are active in promoting the spread of their language. The time has passed when Alain Peyrefitte could lament the linguistic conservatism of his compatriots. The French are following the linguistic evolution called for by the use of new technology. It is remarkable that the *Académie française* backs their efforts, yet such support is essential at a time when the French language is invading the Internet. Websites in French are indeed growing steadily, and Thierry Lunati, inventor of the "Francophone research engine Lokace"[26] (Internet plus), gives a valuable account of the presence of French on the Internet:

> We think that there exist today about 20 000 Websites in French: 58% in France, 20% in Quebec, 8% in Belgium, 6% in Switzerland, 8% in other Francophone or non-Francophone countries. These figures are on the rise, about 1500 sites in French are created each month. We believe that the Francophone Web space makes up about 1,5% to 2% of the Web.
> There are about twice as many pages in French as in German, although there are more sites in Germany which leads one to believe that the Germans are creating a lot more sites in English. The number of pages in Spanish is a lot lower and four fifth of them are in Mexico.
> It is most likely that the number of pages in English represents close to 85% of the entire existing pages.

> [...] we estimate that we will go over 1 200 000 pages in French before the end of 1996 and that we will have 4 million pages at our disposal by the end of 1997.
> All these figures must be taken with great precaution because they change extremely quickly.[27]

Although these figures are promising, it can be argued that the influence of French through the Internet is limited to the Francophone and francophile internauts and their teachers. Since they are largely outnumbered by speakers of English and Spanish, the effort of the French government to encourage the growth of Web resources does not have as their purpose the unrealistic aim of reversing this situation but instead simply to reach French language supporters, hoping that this number will grow.

The Internet and multimedia supplement the traditional methods of learning a language: with a book or a stay in the country. In the past, many students interested in the French language came to France to learn it. As far back as 1325, students came from Scotland, Ireland, and Sweden to study French or to perfect their acquired knowledge, writes André Reboullet.[28] They even came from neighboring provinces such as Brittany or Strasbourg because, although French had been the official national language since the Ordinance of Villers-Cotterêts in 1539, many regions had maintained their dialects. Today, as in the past, a stay in the country is still undeniably valuable. But new technology makes it possible to reach out to the large number of learners who cannot afford a stay abroad with the offer of an interactive and exciting learning experience enhanced by audio-visual tools. Learning, teaching, informing, and communicating through the Internet may very well be the answer to the stagnating enrollment in French classes.

Measures are also being taken to modernize teaching methods at the school and university level using media resources. Conscious of the inefficiency of learning languages in large classes, French universities have organized language learning resource centers which allow students greater freedom of use. The centers offer a large variety of video and televised documents, language laboratories, written works, software, and conversation workshops.

The actions taken by the French Ministry of Culture are a sign of a concerned government, and as Mermet writes: "to be aware of the new trouble with France is to contribute to its cure."[29] Despite current efforts to support the language, however, French studies are on the decline in both the United States and Germany. Studies show that enrollment in French classes at secondary schools and post-secondary institutions in the United States is steadily declining. In 1991, 61% of high school students chose Spanish over French, says Michel Gueldry,[30] and in the state of New York the number of college students studying French has lowered by half against an increase in the number of students taking Spanish. It is clear that French is losing the privileged status that it possessed in the 1980's. A possible reason may be the recent growth of economic ties between the United States and

Central and South America. The proximity of the United States to Spanish-speaking countries is another strong incentive for American students to learn and practice Spanish. American students seem to find it less attractive to study the language of a distant country like France. Although French is thriving in Quebec and surviving in Louisiana despite the constant threat of English encroachment, French presence in America is generally giving way to the Hispanic culture.

The situation of French in Germany is somewhat similar. The *Hamburg Agreement* between the governments of the German Länder[31] excluded French as a first foreign language in the schools, says Ernst Ulrich Grosse.[32] "Only about 10% of all pupils in the old federal states learn French, while figures for the new states are currently at only 4.1%."[33] At the university level, however, Grosse indicates that a "center for research on France has [...] been established at the Mainz university library" and that "the study of romance languages has intensified at universities in the east of Germany."[34] However, the Germans' interest in languages has turned toward the languages of eastern countries since the unification of the two Germanies. In addition, the instruction of what Grosse calls "partner languages," that is to say French and German, "in both lands is suffering due to the *overwhelming preponderance of English*."[35]

In contrast to the decline of interest in French on the part of France's close partners, Greece, a more distant partner, is seeing a renewal of interest in French. Didier Kunz is proud to announce the good news in *Le Monde*: "The French language is alive again in Greece."[36] Two new publications in French: "La Tribune hellénique" and "Athèmes"[37] have appeared on the market. According to Kunz's article, the publisher of "La Tribune hellénique" sees it as "an answer from the Francophone world to the English invasion."[38] The prime objective of the publication is to inform the French-speaking community living in Greece about their adopted country's political, economic, and social systems. "Athèmes," on the other hand, is a cultural publication whose purpose is to inform the French community about Greece by organizing cultural talks between French and Greek artists around a theme.

As far as TV broadcasting is concerned, Grosse predicts that the market in the European Union will be dominated by the "control of satellites, extensive cable networks and a sufficient number of terrestrial frequencies, and through alliances with the large publishing and movie companies [...] originating from Germany."[39] However, the French channel *Canal Plus* "expanded to Spain, Belgium and Germany," he says.[40] In America, broadcasting of TV5 in French will begin in December, says Christian Rioux.[41]

The resources available for teaching French or for using the language as an instrument of communication and research are thus abundant; the next important task will be to increase the public's awareness of the opportunities available to those with a knowledge of French. To this end, the University of Limbourg in Northeastern Belgium, has launched a French contest called "le concours Tour Eiffel" to motivate young speakers of Flemish to learn French, writes Willy

Clijsters.[42] The strong participation in the contest (over 4, 600 students in 1995) attests to the success of the undertaking. The program had already shown good results in the Netherlands where it began in 1994 and finds support from Flemish universities in Belgium, the *Talenacademie* in Maastricht, and various associations of teachers of French. The contest consists of 300 multiple choice questions which cover four categories (general French studies, business French, arts and culture and technical and professional areas) and an oral examination.[43] Emphasis is on the communicative approach, says Clijsters, and the prizes are as attractive as those of a sweepstakes. Apart from receiving the "Tour Eiffel" award, the best performers (the top 5% of the participants) receive prizes commensurate with the quality of their performances: a trip to Quebec or France, books, and money. In addition, the contest is in itself a useful teaching tool. An interactive CD-ROM has been created based on the questions given in previous exams and has been made available to schools in Belgium. Teachers use the results of the participants to evaluate their own teaching. As Clijsters stresses in his article, the "Tour Eiffel" contest has reached several objectives: "To motivate, to have fun, to compete, another way to learn."[44]

Conclusion

Peyrefitte and the media painted a rather pessimistic view of France. According to Peyrefitte "Because France's weaknesses are profoundly French, they are imperceptible to the French."[45] A study of the situation, however, shows that the French government and educators are awakening to the twenty-first century. They are taking measures to catch up with modern technology in order to keep Francophony and the French language alive. As Gérard Mermet says "The situation is a lot less dramatic than is rumored in France."[46] France is still among the most developed countries in the world, and a recent survey conducted by Eurostat and other survey agencies shows that partners in the European Union place France in first position as the best country in which to live.[47] There is therefore an inconsistency between the way the French feel about France and the perception that others have of it which can be explained by the tendency of the French media to give a grim portrait of the social situation in France, and the age-old distrust of the French for their own state institutions.

Today multiculturalism is overcoming linguistic imperialism, and the Internet contributes to the weaving of an extensive web of international relations and cultural exchanges. "One can no longer talk about the hegemony of the French language but rather of the cohabitation of French with other languages," writes Albert Valdman,[48] President of the American Association of Teachers of French. French is still a universal language, and will continue to play an important role throughout the world of the future.

Notes

[1] Steven Philip Kramer, *Does France Still Count?* (Washington: Washington Papers, 1994) 5.

[2] See Laurent Cohen-Tanugi, "Europe. Les vraies Priorités,"*Le Monde* 13 juin 1997, 13.

[3] Steven Philip Kramer, "France and the New Germany," *German Issues* 11 (1993): 23.

[4] Paul Valéry, *Variété*. "La Crise de l'esprit". 2 (Paris: Gallimard, 1919).

[5] Kramer, *Does France Still Count*? 74.

[6] Kramer 74.

[7] Kramer 77.

[8] Translated from Eric Izraelewicz, "L'Union des Quinze, un choc des cultures." *Le Monde* 12 juin 1997, 18.

[9] Izraelewicz 18.

[10] Marie-France Toinet, "The Limits of Malaise in France." *Chirac's Challenge. Liberalization, Europeanization, and Malaise in France*. Eds. John T.S. Keeler and Martin A. Schain, (New York: St. Martin's Press, 1996) 279.

[11] Toinet 282.

[12] David R. Cameron, "National Interest, the Dilemmas of European Integration, and Malaise." *Chirac's Challenge. Liberalization, Europeanization, and Malaise in France*. Eds. John T.S. Keeler and Martin A. Schain, (New York: St. Martin's Press, 1996) 370.

[13] Translated from Gérard Mermet, *Francoscopie 1997* (Paris: Larousse, 1996) 7. The word "misérabilisme" is coined on the French word "misérable"(= wretched).

[14] Alain Peyrefitte, *The Trouble with France* (New York: New York UP) 1986.

[15] Peyrefitte 258–9.

[16] Translated from *Francoscopie 97* 23.

[17] *Francoscopie 97* 23.

[18] See "Télématique" in *Challenges* octobre 1997, 42.

[19] Filloux 42:37.

[20] 'Kiosque' is a payment system by the users of the Minitel to the servicers.

[21] Filloux 42: 37.

[22] Frédéric Filloux. "Getting with the Program. Old-Fashioned Radio is the Talk of the Net." *France Magazine* 41 (1997): 37.

[23] The following discussion is based on information given on the Internet by the French Ministry of Culture. "Une Politique pour l'emploi de la langue française." June 19, 1997. Online Posting. Internet. Mistral.culture.fr/culture/dglf/com-min/fich-00-16.htm. June 19, 1997.

[24] Translated from Pierre Oudart. "En Français. Internet et Multimédia." *Le Français dans le Monde* 284 (1996): 34–5.

[25] Oudart 34.
[26] Translated from Thierry Lunati. "Internet en Français: état des lieux." *Le Français dans le Monde* 284 (1996): 34.
[27] Lunati 34.
[28] André Reboullet. "Le Français langue étrangère en France. Perspectives historiques." *Le Français dans le Monde* 279 (1996): 98–101.
[29] *Francoscopie 97* 7.
[30] Michel Gueldry. "La France contemporaine: pourquoi l'étudier et comment l'enseigner?" *The French Review* 69.4 (1996): 583–94.
[31] "Länder" are an administrative division of land in Germany.
[32] Ernst Ulrich Grosse, and Heinz-Helmut Lüger. *Understanding France in Comparison with Germany* (Berne: Peter Lang, 1994) 355.
[33] Grosse 362.
[34] Grosse 362.
[35] Grosse 356.
[36] Didier Kunz, "Le Français, de nouveau langue vivante en Grèce," *Le Monde* 10 juin 1977, 31.
[37] A pun formed on the name of the Greek capital "Athènes" and the French word for "themes".
[38] Translated from Kunz's article.
[39] Grosse 300.
[40] Grosse 300.
[41] Christian Rioux. "TV5 s'attaque aux Etats-Unis." *Le Devoir* 9 octobre 1997, B7.
[42] Willy Clijsters. "Sensibiliser au français. Objectif Tour Eiffel." *Le Français dans le Monde* 281 (1996): 40.
[43] Clijsters 40.
[44] Translated from Clijsters 40.
[45] Peyrefitte 5.
[46] Translated from Jacques Pécheur. "La France, ce malade imaginaire… Entretien avec Gérard Mermet." *Le Français dans le Monde* 287 (1997): 4–5
[47] *Francoscopie 1997* 38–9.
[48] Albert Valdman. "Letter from the President." *AATF. National Bulletin*. 22.4 (1997): 1–4.

A Newly New Europe Waking after the Holocaust

Evlyn Gould

Reconsidering the influence of the Greek philosophical tradition in the shaping of a newly new Europe, this essay highlights the work of two postmodern European Jewish philosophers, Emmanuel Levinas and his student, Jacques Derrida, who seek to reinsert into that tradition the history and contribution of the Jews of Europe and of their literary practice called "Midrash." By demonstrating the potential usefulness of a counterpoint to the Greek ideals of teleological rationalism, economic gradualism, and enlightened discovery, these Jewish perspectives pose an array of unanswerable questions or philosophical double-binds, in the style of the *midrash*, in order to illustrate the importance of critical thinking and of detailed textual analysis in the formation of ethical response and responsibility among postmodern Europeans and to create forums for the irresolute realities of public life in Europe today.

The European Jewish philosopher Emmanuel Levinas invites us to think about a new Europe waking after the Holocaust. He initiates this invitation in an essay titled, "The Bible and the Greeks," by considering the events of the Holocaust to be the cultural endpoint of the Greek experiment.[1] Levinas situates this experiment at the root of a modern Europe whose very history "is the permanent temptation of an ideological rationalism and of experiments carried out through the rigor of deduction, administration and violence" (135). To awaken us to the enrootedness of this mode of history, Levinas calls us back to the Bible and to its power to interrupt the perseverance of human self-interest (133). This power to invert and to interrupt the course of being for the sake of being may be understood as a waking with at least three symbolic resonances: the waking that follows upon the death of loved ones lost to the Holocaust; the waking of a new dawn which is "always a new calling" (135); and in a light cast by the work of his celebrated student, Jacques Derrida, the waking of a vessel as it moves through the sea. As metaphors for ways of thinking about a newly new Europe, these wakings provide a working definition of a new Europe at the crossroads.

The first waking refers to the continued mourning for loved ones that persists in Europe today as we discover whose money is buried in Swiss banks, or what happened to French anti-Semitism in the silence following the fall of Vichy France, or whether Germany is a victim of Hitler just like the Jews, if differently. We are all survivors of the Holocaust, Levinas seems to suggest, especially as we stand readied to respond to a new calling for Europe today. Without diminishing the real trauma of those who truly survived the events of the Holocaust, Levinas compels us to look back at the history of European culture and the progress of Western civilization from the point of view of the Holocaust, or more recently, from that of Stalin's Gulag. We are all responsible for thinking about what brought Western humanism to that rigor of rationalism, of deduction, and of violence; we are all still waking to a "spirituality whose future is unknown." The looking back is, in any case, a way of compelling the waking.

The second sense of waking refers to that something unique afoot in Europe today, a new design for a post-nation-state Europe put in motion as a project of economic gradualism. With the express ideological intent of insuring peace, economic prosperity, and some kind of dual citizenship, this project echoes the promise of many an old new Europe dating, at the very least, from the time of the Roman Empire.[2] As the project graduates beyond economics to political, social, cultural, and even religious questions, what will be newly new in a Europe waking up to the future of those past new Europes? How can we do adequate service to our memories of Europe and, at the same time, move beyond them into a newly new European design?

Third and finally, this waking supposes a navigational sense as in the wake of a vessel setting out on a new voyage of discovery. This sense of waking complements the first two in a piece titled, "The Other Heading," by the student, Derrida.[3] In the wake trailing behind the inevitability of today's economic heading, Derrida wonders, which are the other headings that this Europe would or should not repeat? How can we set sail toward a newly new Europe without considering which histories are left behind, untold? Who trails behind history's unfolding of a singular destiny, in other words, behind the impetus toward teleological purpose a Eurocentric gradualism with Greek roots imagines? To put this less cryptically—though these difficult questions are part of the point— implicit in the work of these European Jewish philosophers, Levinas and Derrida, is the notion that we must reconsider the project of economic gradualism shaping today's new Europe from the perspective of its utopian endpoint or *telos*: the promise of cultural unity and the idea of a greater European identity.

Reacting to this multitude of questions, some scholars would accuse Derrida of veiling real events behind philosophical double-talk and real progress behind cultural "double-binds"—looking forward, we must always look back. This accusation is staked out primarily by American Jewish detractors of deconstruction, notably Deborah Lipstadt, David Hirsch, and Jeffrey Mehlman, who see in deconstruction a direct link to Holocaust denial.[4] I would like to suggest, on the other hand, that by reading Levinas between the lines of Derrida's elusive queries about Europe today, his deconstructive analysis may also reinsert a Jewish perspective back into the traditions of European humanism. It is true that unlike his teacher, Levinas, Derrida never foregrounds the biblical roots of his inquiry into Europe today, nor does he name the Holocaust in this discussion of Europe. I would argue, however, that by inviting us to read in his musings about Europe the presence of his absent teacher Levinas, Derrida's double-talk attempts rather to represent a thought process that precedes nomination and that, in so doing, figures a mode of critical thinking that counters Europe's new project of economic gradualism with an image of the mental confusions engendered by the very idea of waking after the Holocaust. These cultural double-binds invert and interrupt a process with a motive of its own.

To the extent that Levinas and Derrida propose conundrums and unanswerable questions to talk about today's Europe at the crossroads, our three wakings can be associated with three evocative and topical themes: the question of ethical response and responsibility; the question of history and the memory of history; the forging of community among new Europeans today. But to the extent that these themes concern an earthy rather than purely metaphysical yearning, I would like to consider them via the remarks of one Sigmund Sobolewski, prisoner 88 from Auschwitz, and in the name of the some 200 who perished for every single survivor of the camp.

Sigmund Sobolewski is a Polish Catholic survivor of Auschwitz, interned because his father was an officer in the Polish army. Though his concerns are not related directly to the work of these European Jewish philosophers, his remarks help contextualize in current affairs, the pressures of their philosophical conundrums and of their postmodern double binds. On the first theme of ethical response and responsibility in the waking of Holocaust mourning, Sobolewski is unwavering, enjoining us to think about our responsibilities as survivors of the camps. Specifically, he is focused on the Catholic community in Poland today that still resides in an insulated Catholic nationalism. In recalling their own victimization as part of their national heritage, Catholic Poles continue nonetheless to teach an ideology of anti-Semitism to school children visiting the camp. Sobolewski asks them to denounce their anti-Semitic teachings and, with them, those aspects of their Christianity responsible for the horrors and untruths. But he also asks them to return to their Bible and to find there a culture of tolerance and love for the future. To denounce and to tolerate, Sobolewski asks them to think a double bind.

Though Sobolewski has no answers for the questions raised by a tradition of Polish Catholic nationalism, his question is tremendously resonant since, at the advent of our postmodern world, when the Iron Curtain was raised, it was raised in an atmosphere of perestroika and glasnost—of openness, of sharing, and of the tolerance Sobolewski seeks. But as the French critic Robert Lafont has suggested, when the Curtain was raised in 1989, it revealed a world that had not changed since 1939, a world rife with the same old nationalisms and the same destructive inter-ethnic conflicts that remain at the heart of, say, Bosnia.[5] So our modern history haunts our postmodern world—looking forward, we do also look back. And to ask Levinas's question slightly differently: what happens to the history of the progress of western European civilization if we look back at it from the endpoint that is Bosnia? Or, as Levinas puts it in "The Bible and the Greeks," what "would not render human responsibility—always my responsibility—a senseless notion" (135)?

To insert new meaning into the prospect of human responsibility, Levinas's first answer is that the progress of Western civilization has failed. Despite all of the astoundingly beautiful and important artistic, legal, social, and philosophical innovations that fill our Humanities survey courses, its humanism is in crisis. It can no longer guarantee the privileges of humanity that humanism, with its tradition of *belles-lettres* and hermeneutic method, once promised.[6] In a Europe built on the design of Christian values and a Christian tradition of ideonic readings of ancient biblical texts, its humanism has lost its Jewish roots, so to speak.[7] As he states in *Difficult Freedom*, speaking of "Judeo-Christian Friendship:" "The presence of the Jews reminds conformists of every kind that everything is not for the best in the best of all possible worlds" (202). In this passage, we may read the failures of the rationalism of the Greek experiment into Levinas's gesture to its 18th-century reawakening in Voltaire's enlightened garden.

His second response appears to be a way out of the stalemate of Eurocentric critique: that a specifically Jewish thinking reinserted back into the story of Europe and into the history of Western philosophy may help us to reconsider where Europe went wrong. One way of understanding the Jewish thinking that Levinas solicits may be to assume that it refers to the *Midrash*, a mode of rabbinic exegesis focused on close re-readings of the Hebrew Holy Scriptures. Resulting in an ongoing form of debate or questioning based on the constant posing of questions and answers and questions about potential allusions in the text, it is a practice of midrash that Jews pursue in their continual re-interpretation of their *Torah*. This idea of midrash is one entrance into the thinking and the reading of those others who inhabit the forgotten soul of a monotheistic Europe. As Geoffrey Hartman has suggested in another context, however, it is this other kind of thinking, of reading, and of learning that echoes in the more popularized writing of Jacques Derrida and in his notion of the postmodern "double bind."[8]

As an example of a modern midrash at work in Derrida's thinking about today's Europe, let us look at what is said and unsaid in the following passage from "The Other Heading" written in 1989. Derrida writes:

> Europe today, in the *today* that Valéry writes in capital letters, is at a moment in its history (*if* it has one, one that is *one,* identifiable), in the history of its culture (if it can ever identify itself as one, as the same, and can be responsible for itself, answer for itself, in a memory of itself), when the question of the heading seems unavoidable. Whatever the answer may be, the question remains. I would even say that this is necessary: the question should remain, even beyond all answers. No one today in fact thinks of avoiding such a question, and not only because of what has started, or rather has accelerated, these past few months in the east or at the center of Europe (16–17).

The initial italics of a repeated *today* carry with them the resonance of Paul Valéry's remarks of 1939 in *The Freedom of Spirit* that have occasioned this modern midrash. Reading them, Derrida like Lafont, evokes parallels between a Europe on the eve of Hitler's new Europe and a new Europe at the crossroads in the today of 1989.[9] Is there one history that begins and ends today? Or as Jean-Francois Lyotard writes, "is an end always a conceptual start?" And is that history the story of one European culture, Valéry's notion of an exemplary point and purpose from which Europe leads the world today?

More importantly, in the parenthetical remarks that interrupt the writing of any one continuous sentence, the absent center of textual allusion so common to midrashic readings of scripture takes a place. I would even argue that the very otherness of European cultural uniqueness at question in the parenthetical disruptions of the passage recalls the parenthetical status of the "Jewish question" between 1939 and 1989. It is the fate of the Jews that is both left unsaid and revisited in the unknown something that has accelerated at the east or in the center of Europe. As infamous representatives of the European tendency to define a cultural identity in opposition to its others, the memory of the Jews haunts both the new animosities and destructive nationalisms that lead to that heart of Europe that is Bosnia, as well as the tolerance and the sharing, the reuniting of a divided Germany also at the heart of Europe. If we want to move forward, Derrida suggests, we must always look back to the past; if we talk about culture, we must wonder what or who has been left out, and for whom, in the name of what ideological purpose.

In the question that always remains, we can read a warning in the admonition to reconsider how we think and teach about Europe. But there is also a kind of hopefulness in the unavoidability of the posing of the question and in the inevitability of heading forward while purposefully looking back.

Derrida continues:

> This question is also very old, as old as the history of Europe, but the experience of the *other heading* or of the other *of* the heading presents itself in an absolutely new way, not new "as always" [*comme toujours*] but newly new. And what if Europe were this: the opening onto a history for which the changing of the heading, the relation to the other heading or to the other of the heading, were experienced as always possible? an opening and a nonexclusion for which Europe would in some way be responsible? for which Europe would *be*, in a constitutive way, this very responsibility? as if the very concept of responsibility were responsible, right up to its emancipation, for a European birth certificate.(17)

Conceptually and stylistically, Europe's uncertain future unfolds in a post-modern double bind. More precisely, in the repeated question marks of non-exclusion, Europe moves forward, but we are compelled to pause. The closure of a Europe new "as always" opens onto one that is "always possible," but the inability to name the newly exemplary renders a sense of stalemate produced by this kind of self-centered critical response. If there is a way out of the double-talk, it lies in the potentiality of the other headings only a reader can decide to think. That is, reading the exclusion of the Jews and of Europe's others into the textual hesitations that give us pause, we understand that those very hesitations beckon to a third party; they address a new reader equally capable of filling pauses. This addressee is a version of what Levinas refers to as the face of an unknown and unique stranger whose very presence requires us to step out of the self-consciousness of a purely philosophical world ("Bible," 134), a third party, a new reader who joins me in my silent dialogue with the writer. Put otherwise, the stylistic ticks of Derrida's passage—parentheses, italics, question marks, and elusive headings—carve a way out of the double-talk, in the very potentiality of the other headings only another reader can think. They also give me license to muse about what Hartman calls an "originary supplement" to the midrashic call to think anew, in this case, the absent teacher, Levinas.

But in situating a group of old Europeans, Levinas and the Jews, in the absent center of new European animosities and hopes, the idea of a European birth certificate resounds loudly, at the end, in a silent evocation of today's immigrants, migrants, and post-colonials, the new nomads, Europe's new others, who may or may not play a role in a new European economy. This absent center further condemns the very unaccountability of European history itself as the past becomes a parenthetical space of hesitation open to a multitude of unique and individual accounts. How can we be responsible to all of the possible accounts—those other headings—when our writing of history tends to singularize them and force the past into a pattern of continuity? In the fervor of our effort to head out toward the possibility of the newly new, how does the singularity of history alter and revise the memories other telling might recall?

This brings me back to Sobolewski and to his fear that memories of the Holocaust are being buried or revised not by deconstructive criticism, but by the very monuments we erect to it. I am not referring to revisionism as such, but to the fact that the museum that Auschwitz has become presents itself in ways that alter what Sobolewski saw. Specifically, Sobolewski is concerned with inaccuracies regarding medical experiments performed on Jewish women—inaccuracies printed in a brochure distributed regularly to tourists and visitors to the camp. Then there is the active burying of history: the shopping mall that would be erected outside the gates of Auschwitz where soil tests reveal that the earth is composed of 50% human ash. And beyond the absent memories of Auschwitz sealed over in concrete, other camps, Ravensbruck and Sachsenhausen camps, are collapsing due to disrepair and the cutting of federal funding, while a certain Berlin citizens' initiative provided by Helmut Kohl's government offers a 12 million dollar budget and five acres of prime Berlin real estate (worth about $140 million) to build a new monument to the Holocaust.[10] As the actual "lieux de mémoire"—the settings of our memories— disappear, the monument re-memorializes their history in order to move beyond them.[11]

In re-memorializing the Holocaust, this monument serves an important political agenda. It plays what Jane Kramer has called a "politics of memory" to come to terms with "Germany's unmasterable past."[12] Helping Germans to see themselves as victims, like the Jews, of Hitler's violent aggression, the monument would fulfill their duty to remember while satisfying their need to forget (Kramer 48–49). It gives Germany a chance to head forward, but it does so by creating a history that alters memories. This too, Levinas argues, is a fundamental aspect of Europe: "an obsession with the definitive… with an order to be established on universal but abstract rules…the permanent temptation of an ideological rationalism…." ("The Bible," 135). But what does it mean to head forward in Germany, today, or in Europe today, by re-memorializing and retelling history, if the heading at stake in rationalizing the past is based on political and ideological agendas?

One answer may be that ideology helps people to feel as if they belong to a culture of shared values. It helps build senses of community which, as Benedict Anderson describes them, are largely "imagined."[13] This brings me to Sobolewski's third point about political ideologies and the cultural products that serve them. What is it, Sobolewski asks, that allowed an elite and well-educated group of SS officers to forge themselves an imagined community untouched by the laws of humanity? The answer provided by Sobolewski was that a huge machine of cultural propaganda helped them to define an identity in opposition to a conception of the Jews as infectious vermin to be tortured, gassed, and burned. But the power of such cultural propaganda provides an important warning for us today when we think about what it is that will make Europeans think of themselves as part of a larger Euro-community. What is it that will encourage Romanians, Germans, Frenchman, Hungarians, Turks, and so forth to imagine themselves belonging to a greater European identity?

Anderson's *Imagined Communities* helps devise the answer by suggesting, in the context of rising nationalisms and allegiance to them, that one's sense of belonging to a community that extends beyond personal, religious, ethnic, or local particularities is an imaginary effect nurtured by print capitalism. His is a very forceful argument of course because the rise of the press paralleled the rise of nationalism in dramatic ways. But with today's unprecedented agreement among European nations to forego some measure of national political autonomy, how does this idea of nationalism as an "imagined community" relate to a newly new Europe?

If we translate Anderson's "imagined community" into Noam Chomsky's idea of *Manufacturing Consent*—the idea that a culture of shared values is precisely what the American media foster—we can also translate the image of print capitalism into what Derrida imagines to be a large tentacular media brain at work in Brussels today. Focusing on the media hype surrounding the Réunion of 1989, France's controversial celebration of the bicentennial of the French Revolution,

Derrida has in mind the frightening capacity of the media to turn the ideals of liberty, democracy, and human rights into an illusion of liberty, democracy, and human rights (54–58). Creating illusions paid for by business interests that support a newly re-united Europe—a reunion—the media centralize, standardize, and homogenize European opinion. The attitudes of Europe's marginalized—the Arabs, the Turks, the Africans—are not actually represented in the media, Derrida argues, they are merely re-presented by them, packaged into media sound bites in the name of public debate.

This explains the feeling of stalemate in that passage we read; it explains why Derrida seems to put the brakes on the project of economic gradualism that is the New Europe. Returning briefly to that citation, however, we can once again emphasize those stylistic ticks—the marks of the letter that hesitate and pause—the hopeful gestures toward the "newly new," the "always possible," the "opening and non-exclusion." These stylistic gestures force us to stop and to re-read, to give pause and to think critically. They further invite us to reply by posing an array of unanswerable double-binds or questions—questions whose answers pose questions in the style of the midrash—because critical thinking forms the very basis of ethical response and responsibility.

As a paradigm for that thinking that reinserts the Bible into the Greeks, the example of Derrida's prose portrays critical thinking as another of Europe's most fundamental legacies. Indeed in the face of a pop-market culture of shared values and consent manufactured via reactions to Eurodisney, to MTV videos, to Bennetton ads, or to the concerts of U2, this thinking creates forums for the actual, thorny and uncomfortable, heated and irresolute realities of public life. If we are to build community in Europe, Derrida muses, it is only through uncomfortable encounters with complete strangers whose values we do not share. It is only by responding to what Levinas calls the "face of the other" inscribed in those earthy commandments to the Jews forgotten in the progress of European history:

> "You shall not murder."
> "Neither shall you commit adultery."
> "Neither shall you desire your neighbor's house, or field, or male or female slave, or ox or donkey, or anything that belongs to your neighbor." Etc.

These are the commandments that invert the enrootedness of being for the sake of being.

> These words the LORD spoke with a loud voice to your whole assembly at the mountain, out of the fire, the cloud, and the thick darkness, and he added no more. He wrote them on two stone tablets, and gave them to me.

The Lord gives commandments that necessitate awareness of a larger human community and with them, the Jews are figured as the recipients of human responsibility. But the Lord also delivers to us, as newly new, a difficult text to read.

Conclusion

Through a demonstration of the contributions of the two postmodern European Jewish philosophers, Levinas and Derrida, this discussion has sought to link their heady, philosophical reconsideration of three aspects of the Greek tradition to everyday public realities at work in the post-modern European imagination. From questions wrought by Holocaust collaboration to attempts to rememorialize and to move beyond that bloody history, to the pop-culture manufacturing of public consent about European cultural identity in the wake of that "Jewish" burden, this reconsideration examines vital concerns that form a crossroads for new Europeans today. Insisting that the desire to build a greater European "community" must not give way to the easier political choice of forging a federated Europe, a European "union," by neglecting European philosophical traditions, this demonstration asks us to give pause, in the midst of a historical moment of symbolic waking, to issues that would interrupt the persuasive gradualism of a purely economic design.

Notes

[1] "The Bible and the Greeks," *In the time of the Nations* (Bloomington: Indiana University Press, 1994) 134–135.

[2] I am indebted to a lecture by John Nicols a historian at the University of Oregon for a lecture on the Romans that took these three promises as its starting point. The lecture was delivered in the context of a unique interdisciplinary course developed on campus by the European faculty titled, "The Idea of Europe." On further similarities between the Roman Empire and today's Europe, see also Antoine Winckler, "L'Empire revient," and Maurice Sartre, "L'Empire romain comme modèle," *Commentaire* 57.15 (Printemps 1992): 17–22, 27–35.

[3] "The Other Heading: Memories, Responses, and Responsibilities," *The Other Heading: Reflections on Today's Europe*, trans., Pascale-Anne Brault and Michael B. Nass (Bloomington: Indiana University Press, 1992).

[4] For an overview of this antagonism toward deconstruction, toward Paul de Man but also Derrida, see Elaine Marks, *Marrano as Metaphor: The Jewish Presence in French Writing* (New York: Columbia University Press, 1996) 13–20.

[5] Robert Lafont, *Nous, peuple européen* (Paris: Editions Kimé, 1991) 5.

[6] "Antihumanism and Education," *Difficult Freedom*, trans., Sean Hand (Baltimore: Johns Hopkins University Press, 1990) 281.

[7] See Joseph Dan "Midrash and the Dawn of Kabbalah" on the question of Christians reading un-original texts, that is, scriptures already translated, and on the university and church leaders who have a tradition of searching for one true single meaning in those scriptures. In *Midrash and Literature*, eds., Geoffrey H. Hartman and Sanford Budick (New Haven and London: Yale University Press, 1986) 128–130.

[8] Hartman makes a specific link to Derrida in the introduction to *Midrash and Literature*, but this is a reference to a piece of biblical exegesis by Derrida contained in the volume and titled, "Shibboleth" (307–47). See the introduction to *Midrash and Literature*, x–xi.

[9] Derrida's essay presents itself as a anti-Eurocentric reading of Paul Valéry's *The Freedom of Spirit*, but it is occasioned by the event in France known as the "Réunion" (*The Other Heading*, 8), a major media event celebrating the bicentennial of the French Revolution in the name of a re-united Germany and a newly united Europe. The parallel between 1939 and 1989 is not purely, then, of Derrida's making.

[10] Jane Kramer, "Letter from Germany: The Politics of Memory," *The New Yorker* (August 14, 1995) 48–65.

[11] I have borrowed this French expression from Pierre Nora who traces just these kinds of settings in his magisterial *Lieux de Mémoire*. The many volumes of this original study are reduced in an English translation to one volume translated by

Lawrence D. Kritzman and titled, *Realms of Memory* (New York: Columbia University Press, 1996).

[12] Charles S. Maier, *The Unmasterable Past: History, Holocaust, and German National Identity* (Cambridge and London: Harvard University Press, 1988).

[13] *Imagined Communities*, 1983, reprint (London: Verso, 1993) 1–7, 37–46.

Cultural and Political Challenges: The Dialectics of European Identity

Heinz-Uwe Haus

This essay summarizes some of the factors that can be viewed as obstacles to European identity. The author focuses in particular on the Communist legacy in the now united Germany and raises the question to what extent and how long the Communist nomenclatura will continue to influence and impede the process of European integration.

If we talk about identity, we can not forget, why the people said "no" to communism. First, because of its cynical conception of human rights. Rights were granted to individuals by the state in exchange for loyal social behavior. Such an understanding and practice was meant to justify the state's cruel control of the destinies of the people in the name of revolutionary ideals. The regime "graciously" granted to people what it had first ruthlessly deprived them of. Second, the Central and Eastern European revolution was directed against the communist "command economy." Third, the revolution pulled down the central pillar in political structure of socialist society: the permanent and unconditional monopoly of power held by the Communist Party and its government. The Marxist-Leninist party acted as authentic interpreter and implementor of the monolithic will of the people. Such understanding was not only the pillar of communist totalitarism, but was one of the main (though not the only) cause of the crisis of these societies, and the central obstacle in overcoming that crisis. What was happening in Central and Eastern Europe was a victory for the people in their struggle for freedom and for the implication of fundamental human rights.

It was by no means inevitable that these developments would unfold in a linear fashion in the direction of free democracy, with a sound economic basis, which is a precondition for genuine stability. The reforms are irreversible. But the outcome of the ongoing process is still uncertain, even when the people involved know exactly what the ultimate goal they are working toward is. My notes attempt to shed some light on the subliminal contradictions between the intended results and the unintended consequences of the measures taken.

One most destructive challenge for the creation of the new societal order is the "old boy's network" of party cadres in Culture, Economy and Administration, which was not really abolished but has been "redirected." "As a result of ideological targets, political loyalties, varied favors or extortionist commitment, the single-party system established long-term personal ties and dependencies on a large scale. The links extended into the most remote corners of society and above all of the apparatus of state, where the Communist nomenclature generally existed beneath the headquarters level."[1] What is more, a major enzyme for its cohesion and loyalty towards the political system was its opposition to the Federal Republic of Germany, which represented a permanent challenge.

It was against this background that the last Communist government in East-Berlin after mid-November 1989 achieved on a substantial scale to cover up the destruction of the State Security Service ("Stasi") files incriminating the Communist regime against the opposition of the population and enabled to transfer considerable assets to Stasi members, which not only gave the recipients financial benefits but which also, in many instances, safeguarded positions of social power.

Ferdinand Kroh's analysis for eastern Germany in 1992 is representative to the East in general: "Wherever they can, former communist power elites are taking hold of the 'economic foundation' by buying profitable companies and handing over the remaining mass of firms to the taxpayer. At the same time, like-minded comrades at the 'intellectual superstructure' level are not only ensuring that no public fuss is made about these activities, but also that the tremendous reconstruction attempts by the new democratic state and by the free and western-oriented market forces are presented as perfidious action against the people. The success of such power retention strategies by those who ruined the GDR under their rule impedes and jeopardizes the process of reconstruction in eastern Germany."[2] This leads to questions which still remain unanswered today: " To what ends will the forces trained in Communist conspiracy, strategy and tactics exert their influence? Is financial gratification the only aim? Will the Communist forces be willing to accept compromise, and to demonstrate loyal cooperation, as observed among the former elites in other revolutions, or can a different code of behavior be expected in the case of the Communists?"[3] The persistent re-naming of the revolution to "re-direction"/"change" ("Wende") by that forces, is an eloquent reflection of the longstanding efforts for legitimization which was practiced by representatives of the old regimes and which would not have been possible without the "Toleranz" of the citizens' movement.

In the Fall of 1989, the need for theories existed, which, — freed from the East-West conflict — questioned the origin of the identity crisis, searched for criteria of new social ethics and demanded viable political ideas. "In general, these groups reflected political currents of thought whose political goals and hopes were associated with the continued existence of the GDR with a reformed socialist-style system. Reforms were the main aspects. The revolution was a result, not the aim, of activities during the take-off phase."[4] The revolutionary ambitions during this phase before 9 October 1989 were in large hindered by the different national self-awareness in West Germany. As Wettig summarizes: "Following the ideological revolution of the West German Left in 1968, there was often a conviction in the corresponding circles that the Germans should never again become a nation in view of their past national guilt. They had discredited themselves once and for all through their former national ambitions and had to expiate their guilt by renouncing not only a nation-state but also a national identity. Many leftists also took the view that the Germans should never again be allowed to exercise far-reaching decision-making powers. In some left-wing circles, therefore, the elimination of German nature became an undisputed postulate. Adding to the foreign policy goal on integration, those who held such views also postulated the domestic policy goal of creating a 'multicultural society.' An overlaying of German nature through alien components was regarded and encouraged by such circles as progress toward greater humanization. The envisaged de-nationalization of the Federal Republic of Germany was perceived as the prelude to the Europe- and worldwide elimination of 'national-narrow-mindedness' in general. Notions of this kind explained why some left-wing German intellectuals failed to understand and to accept the unification of their native country in 1989/90."[5] It was during this culmination phase of the revolution, which lasted about six months, from October 9, 1989 to March 18, 1990, that the German masses in the East insisted on the termination of the division of the country. It was their pressure "from below" which formed the policy and created history.

It is clearly evident that the reunified Germany has irrevocably become part of the West and that the dissolution of the Soviet empire could not change this in the least: it had not created the "Russian option." The only realistic question was where would the eastern frontiers of Atlantic civilization run in the future? But what exactly is European identity? "To me, all those nations are European which were exposed during the course of their history to the three-fold influence of Athens, Rome and Jerusalem," Paul Valery declared in a famous lecture he gave in the Twenties.[6] Today we would without hesitation also mention Celtic, Germanic as well as Slav roots, while the influence of the Arabic countries should not be ignored, either. And in this connection, would it be wrong to refer to the scientific and liberal approach, or to Romanticism and Socialism?

Precisely which Western values are basic to democracy? Inevitably the focus falls on the set of values loosely called "individualism," however vague and even slightly pejorative the term may sound. Western democracy has been founded on a specific understanding of the individual as an autonomous being. This understanding means that the individual has a capacity for freedom, for realizing himself in the course of his actions, and that he has inherent rights over and against the demands of any community to which he may belong.

It is not very difficult to trace the source of these notions in the convergence of two cultural streams: the first originating in biblical religion, with Protestantism playing a decisive role in its application to political democracy; the second rooted in the Hellenistic view of man, transmitted to modernity via the Renaissance and the Enlightenment, and applied to the invention of democratic institutions by the French revolution and its successors.

But just as democracy is an idea that manifests itself in concrete institutions and social processes, so the autonomous individual is not only an idea but a lived experience. Actual human beings must feel themselves to be autonomous, to be free or aspiring to freedom, to have inherent rights.

Experiences through which these ideas and values become plausible in actual life are necessary. The fact that Western individualism has been challenged from within Western culture, notably by Marxism, complicates the situation. The unusual assumptions of Western individualism become sharply evident as soon as one compares them with what is taken for granted in the great majority of non-Western cultures, in all parts of the world, and indeed in the traditional substrata of Western societies as well, as in the remaining peasant cultures of southern Europe.

As Peter L. Berger states, "democracy is not a "luxury of the rich," as has been argued; the rich, with or without democracy, usually manage to take care of themselves."[7] If democracy is indeed a political structure to safeguard the rights and liberties of the individual, it also happens to offer the most plausible structure for the protection of traditional values.

The state is not the only threat to traditional values. Other modern institutions and processes — the forces of the market and of technology, modern urban life, mass communications — create their own threat.

The history of the European Union as an institutional mechanism of democracy shows that it not only allows but creates breathing space to traditional values and institutions. Only the democracy fosters pluralism and coexistence between modernized and more traditional sectors of society.

But what is essential to all this, democracy is the most practical method for safeguarding those "mediating structures" that are, themselves, the matrix of democracy.

Mediating structures are institutions that both give shape to peoples' private identities and also help them relate to the large structures of a modern society. These institutions exist both in highly modern and in less developed societies, and they are very important in both. The most important of these are the family, organized religion and the structures of local community.

Others are such innovations as cooperatives, labor unions and other associations to protect or promote particular interests. Virtually everywhere, people have a strong interest in these institutions, because their most precious values and self-identifications are closely bound to them.

As we all have experienced in the past, totalitarian states, by their very nature, can not tolerate even the relative independence of such institutions; these must be leveled, controlled and integrated into the all-embracing policy. Six years after the "velvet revolution" the situation in the former communist states asks for a spirited westernization of public life.

The lack of a more thoroughgoing democratic component within the all-European framework has meant that "there has been little discussion during more recent times about the meaning and the purpose of the EU,"[8] as Prince points out. European integration was a product of an early post-war desire: "to preempt any recurrence of the kind of nationalist eruptions that precipitated the Second World

War. This desire was melted together with the promise of prosperity for all to create the political and economic conditions that would reduce the likelihood of war. As a process of this post-war need for security and reassurance, the EU today is confronted by the fact that it no longer possesses the Wert an sich (self evident value) it once did; its appeal to a so-called post-materialist culture, spoiled by the expectation of prosperity and peace, has ebbed."[9] As the transparency of the European policy-making structures grows dimmer and the number of members grows larger, the greater will the need to renew public commitment to the idea of Europe become for the cultures.

It is not so much the diversity of the sources of European cultural identity which is challenging, but rather the influence that such sources brought to bear on the principle of unity, that unity which is subliminally linked with this identity. Jacob Burckhardt formulated this as follows:

> If, in largely intellectual matters, we do not feel we belong to this or that people, no longer to this or that country, but feel that our allegiance is to Western culture, then this is because the world was once Roman and all-embracing and the whole culture of antiquity has devolved upon us.[10]

A multifarious cultural identity has developed from this melting pot over the centuries and continues to flourish to the present day. And the great wealth of our continent is found precisely here. Far from preserving unchanged what has been attained, by fearfully retiring into a cultural shell, this multifarious cultural identity constitutes a factor of living and original synthesis that is constantly renewing itself. This kind of identity consequently emerges as the precondition for individual progress, group progress and the progress of nations. This identity stimulates and establishes a community of interest, mobilizes inner reserves for action, and provides creative adjustment from necessary changes.

Denis de Rougement emphasized this, as follows: "Each one of our cultures has to refind its personality, because fruitful dialogue is possible only between partners who are quite different and who know what they want, or who they are, or who at least passionately wish to fathom it. Nevertheless, none of our cultures, which have been personified this way, is an end in itself. Culture means just the totality of the means that are made available to people; they depend on culture in order to approach truth."[11]

Diversity — in values, in communication, in religion, in technology, in everything from politics to poetry — begins to replace uniformity. New institutions, from self-help groups and political splinter organizations to transnational agencies, spring up in the rubble of the democratization. The Western societies are "demassified" as Alvin Toffler predicted for the eighties. The political, economical, and communication networks and bonds since the 1989 revolution develop into a global civilization on cross-nation and non-state base. It was Peter Brook who reminded us a year before the wall came down about these irresistible directions:

"The valid truth is the truth of the moment. When many influences interact, through their converging rays, through their friction, a new view can emerge, fresh, surprising. (…) even within a single culture, each individual is conditioned by an ever-wider mixture of global influences. As cultures intermingle (…), the audience is brought together before precise, yet universal truths."[12]

It is this challenge which enables a mutual respect of nations, their progressive cooperation, and their integration with the aim of a common management of problems. But the structure of current relations in Europe and the nature of their resultant problems can only be properly understood against the background of the historic changes brought about by the end of the Cold War. Overcoming the factors of uncertainty which existed for decades and establishing a reliable and sustainable union between East and West does appear to be a real possibility. The challenge for culture today is how to use its anticipatory abilities. The dialectics of European identity shape the emerging outlines of the future.

Conclusion

Using the Left in the united Germany and the former East bloc countries as an example this essay attempted to show that the potential for a democratic European identity is being impeded by the still effective Communist power apparatus and the influence of the new Left.

Notes

[1] Vaclav Havel, in: Skyline Democracy, Kyklos Nicosia 1990, p. 2.

[2] Ferdinand Kroh, "Cliques and Old Boy Networks": Power Detention Strategies of the Former East German Elite, in: Aussenpolitik, 2/1992, p. 147.

[3] ibid., p. 150 Cf. Benno Zanetti, Der Weg zur deutschen Einheit, Muenchen 1991 and Ehrhart Neubert, Eine protestantische Revolution, Berlin 1990.

[4] Helga Schubert at a forum discussion of the Adenauer Foundation, Magdeburg, 07. February 1993 (tape).

[5] Wolfgang Schuller, ibid.

[6] Paul Valery, in: Europäische Stimmen, Bonn 1963., p. 7.

[7] Peter L. Berger, in: Dialogue, 2/1984, p. 8.

[8] K. Michael Prince, Germany, Europe and the Dilemma of Democratic Legitimation, in: Aussenpolitik, 1/1995, p. 14.

[9] ibid.

[10] Jacon Burckhardt, Europaeisches Gut, Wien 1936, p. 12.

[11] Denis de Rougement, in: Europaeische Stimmen, Berlin 1990, p. 32.

[12] Peter Brook, World Theatre Day Message - March 27, 1988, flyer, US-Center of ITI.

Ancient Greece, Post-Modern Autochthony: Hellenism and the Ideology of Europe[1]

Dirk t. D. Held

The New Europe is presented with a dilemma of inclusion: where does Europe end and begin, who is truly European, and what if any political ideals are distinctively European? For example, the European Union debate over the admission of Turkey focuses on whether that country recognizes an array of rights which European governments hold to be universal in scope, and whose observation has been made a standard of entry. This essay argues that Hellenism, a concept constructed in 18th century Europe, has produced a symbolic unity: By drawing on the prestige of Greece as the founder of European democracy, it has become a critical component in the identity of the New Europe. Nonetheless, this essay questions whether the fragility of what is ultimately an ideological foundation is adequate to the challenge of articulating European identity when the symbolic capital amassed in universalist ideals is corrupted by particularist centrifugies of ethnic, religious and nationalist interests, most notably on Europe's eastern borders.

Europe has always exceeded geography. Like the concept of Western civilization, "Europe" designates history and philosophy as much as it does geography. Indeed its geographical fundamentals today are essentially identical to those that existed in antiquity, but the historical, political, and social discourses written onto its geography —and the truths emanating from those discourses— have varied immensely. *Verum factum* says Vico: truth is what is made. The truths that comprise Europe have been constructed and reconstructed, simultaneously generating truths about its neighbors. Europe has been deeply valorized as a concept at least since the time of Herodotus[2] and remains so today. The need to engage now with "The *New* Europe," most assuredly a problematic entity, is but another indication of this.

The conceptual meaning of Europe derives from the historical and cultural continuum that is imagined to reach back from the Europe of today, through post-Reformation and medieval Europe, all the way to the culture and institutions of classical Greece and Rome.[3] This Europe is a rhetorical construct, an "imagining," the product of discursive history. But it is a problematic product, for as J.G.A. Pocock had recently written, "Europe today is a contested notion."[4] This is the result of the multiple imaginings, the diverse construals of what Europe is and what Europe ought to be. Because of this multiformity, the notion is afflicted by instability and indeterminacy not only in respect to the territory it denotes, obviously most insecure on the margins, but to its semantic valuations as well, within and between the nation-states that comprise it. It is hardly unreasonable to ask what the unities are that constitute Europe. Indeed the urgency of the question "What is it to be a European?" has accelerated at the very time when a clear answer seems ever more elusive. This is notably so at the margins or, in the case of immigrant groups it involves people from the margins and sometimes outside them altogether.

This is not the occasion for detailed argument regarding the political and cultural articulation of Europe throughout its history. I shall look merely at some ways by which the Enlightenment articulated Europe's modernity—then too, there was a "new Europe"— paying particular attention to how the Enlightenment developed and deployed Hellenism towards this end. I will then touch on the ideological potency of the residual, thin current of Hellenism in contemporary debates over what constitutes Europe and European identity, along with the unresolved tensions these conceptualizations present.

II

In 1980, a minister from the Foreign Office reportedly characterized Greek entry into the EC as "fitting repayment by the Europe of today of the cultural and political debt that we all owe to a Greek heritage almost three thousand years old," and French President Giscard d'Estaing spoke of France as the daughter of Classical Greece and welcomed the modern country into the Community as a sister.[5] These two statements express not only the ideology of Hellenism but equally, confidence in the grand narrative of European progress so accelerated by the Enlightenment. Now as all good postmodernists know, grand narratives are scarcely *à la mode*, but are instead met with disdain. Nonetheless, according to this narrative of European progress, ancient Greece is the origin of democracy and individual freedom, and its idealization as a society characterized by the pursuit of reason still attracts, despite inroads made upon this heavily fortified monument of rationality by Nietzsche, E.R. Dodds, and others.

Greece is designated the birthplace of "Europe." This "rhetoric of aboriginality"[6] is significant for two reasons. The first is that it assumes the passivity of ancient Greece's simpler civilization in contrast to modern Europe's individualistic and modern originality.[7] Secondly, it certifies autochthony for Europe and European values, and in so doing it procures legitimization for the ideology of Europe while it purifies it from the taint of pollution by outsiders. Autochthony, you will recall, is the quality of a people sprung from their native soil, whose origination in their own land means they are untainted by non-indigenous blood, a quality greatly prized by the ancient Greeks and frequently proclaimed by the Athenians. Not for the last time would commonality of blood and origin be given as a reason to resist the Asiatic other, as Herodotus does at VIII.44 in a passage promoting "Athens as the natural home of culture as well as of political leadership"[8] and the natural defender of Hellas against the Persians.

How did it happen that Greece became the birthplace of Europe, since Greece had not been so highly regarded prior to the Enlightenment? Contributing factors are readily found. The 18th century was of course the first true age of archaeology, and for the first time in centuries Western Europeans could travel to Greece and see first hand what were then mostly ruins, decrepit and ill regarded by ruling Turks and native Greeks alike. And they wrote extensively about their travels. Most importantly, these phenomena were concurrent with an emerging sense that a major "historical discontinuity" had transpired, a "'revolution' in human thought" (as well as political revolution) which opened up new rational powers. There was a sense that this was a time of an "origination in history, a beginning not bounded or conditioned by tradition or religious authority, finally free and independent, and so fully self-conscious about its own possibility."[9]

There is not space to do more than mention the political values of ancient Greece to which the French philosophes appealed in their struggle against monarchy: these include freedom, democracy, and justice. I will turn instead to the interest in establishing a secular society and its rationalization through a variety of universalist values. The realization of this begins not in the realm of politics but in science. Mary Louise Pratt has eloquently described the development of what she terms "European planetary consciousness" which was inspired by European scientific expeditions throughout the world as well as by the systematization of nature envisioned in the comprehensive classificatory scheme of Linnaeus' *Systema Naturae*. Thus "through the descriptive apparatus of natural history" Europeans could construct "global scale meaning." She goes on to claim that "this new planetary consciousness" served as "a basic element in constructing modern Eurocentrism."[10] It did so because in the shape of the transnational goals of European science it held out the possibility of epistemological transcendence that reduced local knowledge to an inferior and untrustworthy entity, all the while waving the standard of universal and unprejudiced science.

What is the relation to Greece? Greece's imputed aboriginality set it outside of modern historical time.[11] There it became an inhabitant of mythic time and accordingly subject to mythologizing discourses. Moreover, like other ideals, Greece acquired transcendent stature. Secular civilization was marked by diversity, and had come to be defined through distinctive national traditions for which Greece could be used to provide a "transcendent unity." Secular civilization embraced "the internal diversity of the European peoples" demanded by a European ideology which saw "political divisions as a sign of robust health, and [the resultant] squabbles as the free expression of individuality refined through constant competition."[12] For the 18th century, Greece symbolized a new beginning in a way that Roman culture could not. The isolation of Greece under Turkish rule provided a discontinuity concomitant with the Enlightenment's perception of a radical break with the past. This contrasted to the continuity of Rome's cultural influence,[13] additionally burdened by an undesirable association with the Church. The rediscovery of Greece in the 18th century offered a way to posit a single origin for all European civilization which transcended nationalist quarrels[14] even as it allowed for the political complexity—an ineradicable feature of modernity—that spawned these quarrels. Greece, as it was constructed in the Enlightenment, symbolized the universalized intellectual goals, the devotion to reason, and the political institutions and values we today refer to as the Enlightenment Project.

III

There necessarily will be inconsistencies between universal ideals and particular instantiations, but the case of Hellenism is so "highly idealized...[that it came to embody] a tradition of historical theory...that...dehistoricized and universalized itself."[15] The modern country of Greece provides a good example of the confrontation of abstract European ideals with the more raucous and less tractable realities of a nation's political and cultural life, and so reveals the inevitable tensions between abstractions and experience. Indeed, the "powerful reserve of the imagination"[16] which Greece gave Europe in the 18th century, insistently confronts lived experience at the personal and political level on an almost daily basis in modern Greece, and an extensive literature documents this strain. The untidiness of historical events, political processes, and individual's unpredictable responses all chafe against the imposition of homogeneity and the discourse of national unity.[17]

Moving to the larger canvas of Europe as a whole, an analogous situation can be discerned. Identity, of individuals and nations alike, is perceived primarily as local and territorialized. Even in today's international and transnational age, nationalism and ethnicity continue to play a powerful role. To use Clifford Geertz's well-known term, the values and identities by which individuals measure themselves are of the "thick" variety, packed with rich, local associations and meanings, particularist, and frequently linked to some ethnic identity. By contrast, European sanctioned rights are universalized, abstract, and cosmopolitan. To a considerable degree they reflect ideals first promulgated as universal during the Enlightenment. To the extent that they do so, they bear the legacy of Hellenism which retains its ideological potency as demonstrated in the quotes earlier in paper. Europe's commonalities are proclaimed to be democracy, justice, freedom of the individual, and participation in government as a citizen, all identified with ideals constructed from Hellenic antiquity. Fulfillment of these goals is set as the criterion for inclusion in Europe, as we see for example in the debate over Turkey's full incorporation into the European community of nations.

Numerous complications arise when these universalized, Hellenic ideals are pressed onto the cluttered political landscape. We must acknowledge the reality described by Tony Judt in his recent book *A Grand Illusion? A Essay on Europe.* in which there is "a 'Europe of the mind,' of human rights, of the free movement of goods, ideas, and persons, of ever-greater cooperation and unity." He goes on however to call this a "hyper-real Europe, more European than the continent itself, an inward and future projection of all the higher values of the ancient civilization but shorn of the darker qualities."[18] He himself darkly comments that "Just as an obsession with 'growth' has left a moral vacuum at the heart of some modern nations, so the abstract, materialist quality of the idea of Europe is proving insufficient to legitimate its own institutions and retain popular confidence."[19] In other words, however much Hellenic ideals underwrite this "hyper-real" Europe, it is a form of Hellenism that is too "thin" (the other member of the Geertzian dyad) to serve as more than an ideological charade. We are left with only a thin morality of the sort vigorously critiqued by such contemporary moral philosophers as Bernard Williams.

It is also striking that someone so closely associated with post-modernism and deconstruction as Jacques Derrida should himself be enchanted by the siren song of European hyper-reality, be drawn to what most will acknowledge as the legacy of Enlightenment universalism. I am speaking here of his attachment to the value of justice, of which Richard Rorty, himself an exponent of irony, contingency, and particularity, remarked that it was the single thing about which one should not be ironic. Rorty says of Derrida and justice "The thought of justice, the thought of what Derrida sometimes calls 'the democracy that is to come' haunts Europe." This is the reason, continues Rorty, why Eurocentrism remains attractive."[20]

The question which hangs over the new Europe is whether the thin morality of justice, the legacy and contrivance of a now thin Hellenism, can carry the day amidst localized disputes, often bitterly contested between groups proclaiming strong ethnic identities that are seemingly impervious to universalist goals. What ideological force will any universally recognized political and moral values have in the post-modern world of fragmented national identities? Yet if we lack a grounding in some set of universal values, are we limited to a brute pragmatism which cannot generate justification beyond the self-interest of contending communities?

The challenge faced by Europe today is to integrate the multiple histories and consequently multiple truths of post-modernism. The "thick" local identities must be constructively related to the "thin" universalisms of justice, equality, and freedom for all. Only thus will the abstract discourses that have constructed the concept of Europe find dialogue with the particularist identities of nationalisms and ethnicities. The greatest challenge is to construct this dialogue with being goaded by "the fear of the Turk" and the demonization of some non-European Other.

Conclusion

The essay has argued that the concept of Hellenism was a product of the European Enlightenment, when it served the important ideological function of establishing a birthplace for modern Europe and its new political ideals. Since Greece lacked political and economic power, and was not a rival to European powers of the day, its function as the origin of European civilization was able to transcend nationalist quarrels. Greece today retains the ideological potency granted it in the Enlightenment, but its very embodiment of "hyper-real" European values now threatens its legitimating value. The question pressing upon the New European order is how to enact an identity built on universalist claims of justice under conditions of localized strife and allegiances.

Notes

[1] I am indebted to Prof. Michael Herzfeld's invitation to participate in the NEH/SSRC research seminar at Harvard University in 1993 on European Identity and its Intellectual Roots for stimulating my thinking about this topic.

[2] Francois Hartog, *The Mirror of Herodotus*. Berkeley: University of California Press, 1988, pp. 30–33.

[3] Silvia Federici, "The God that Never Failed: The Origins and Crises of Western Civilization." in Silvia Federici, ed., *Enduring Western Civilization. The Construction of the Concept of Western Civilization and Its "Others."* Westport CT: Praeger, 1995, p. 70.

[4] J.G.A. Pocock, "What Do We Mean by Europe?" *The Wilson Quarterly* 21 (1997), p. 12.

[5] Richard Clogg, *London Review of Books* 18 Aug 1994, p. 22.

[6] Michael Herzfeld, *Anthropology through the looking-glass. Critical ethnography in the margins of Europe*. Cambridge: Cambridge University Press, 1987, p. 25.

[7] Herzfeld, p. 57.

[8] Sarah Morris, *Daidalos and the Origins of Greek Art*. Princeton: Princeton University Press, 1992, p. 329.

[9] Robert B. Pippin, *Modernism as a Philosophical Problem*. Cambridge MA: Basil Blackwell, 1991, p. 47.

[10] Mary Louise Pratt, *Imperial Eyes. Travel Writing and Transculturation*. New York: Routledge, 1992, pp. 27–29.

[11] Herzfeld, p. 54.

[12] Herzfeld, p. 77.

[13] Frank Turner, "Why the Greeks and not the Romans in Victorian Britain?" *Rediscovering Hellenism. The Hellenic Inheritance and the English Imagination*. ed. G.W. Clarke. Cambridge: Cambridge University Press, 1989 , p. 61.

[14] Mary Beard and John Henderson, *Classics: A Very Short Introduction*. Oxford: Oxford University Press, 1995, p. 13.

[15] Herzfeld, p. 93.

[16] Artemis Leontis, *Topographies of Hellenism. Mapping the Homeland*. Ithaca: Cornell University Press, 1995, p. 75.

[17] Herzfeld, p. 30.

[18] Tony Judt, *A Grand Illusion? An Essay on Europe*. New York: Hill & Wang, 1997, pp. 3–4.

[19] Judt, p. 117.

[20] Richard Rorty, "A Spectre is Haunting the Intellectuals" *European Journal of Philosophy* 3 (1995), p. 291.

Homeland and Heterotopia
The Place of the Stranger in Multiculturalism

Machiel Karskens

In the Netherlands multiculturalism today has become fashionable as a fresh label for all things related to ethnic groups. It is a substitute for "allochthonous," which replaced "ethnic minority," which again substituted "foreign laborer." However, multiculturalism is used especially to refer to the programme of integration of immigrants and refugees into the "colourful melting pot" of Dutch culture. In my opinion this euphemistic usage of multiculturalism rather than "social integration" is an unashamed perversion of the genuine challenge of multiculturalism. In this essay I will defend the thesis that this challenge is exercised as a critique on the dominant culture by the *strangeness* of other cultural groups. In my argumentation I will focus on a single — albeit not the only — crucial aspect of the strangeness of other cultures, i.e., their connection with a — real or imagined — homeland abroad. I will restrict my discussion to a philosophical, that is to say conceptual, analysis of the meaning and function of the notions of "stranger" and "homeland" in multiculturalism. I will not engage in any empirical description of foreign homelands, how they are actually used by cultural group now, and in their actual role in the dominant culture.

1. What is multiculturalism?

In most academic literature the notion of "multiculturalism" is analyzed by following a set of distinctions desegregating three types or dimensions: a) multination states, b) polyethnicity (Raz 1995: 310; Kymlicka 1995: 30); and c) (cultural) minorities (Joppke 1996).

a. Defining the situation of a multination state, a confederation or an empire, multiculturalism refers to a geographical partitioning of different cultures within a single (political) unity or system. Broadly speaking this has been the historical situation in Western and Central Europe since the time of the Roman and the Holy Roman Empire, and it will probably be again the situation in the European Community of the third millennium. Multinationalism was and still is also the internal situation of most nation-states composing the actual European community, notwithstanding the processes of cultural and political homogenization engendered by the emergence of centralized nation-states between 1850 and 1950. Kymlicka discusses this type of multiculturalism from the viewpoint of group-specific rights, which, in his case, are mainly the self-government rights of indigenous peoples in Canada (Kymlicka 1995: 27). In Europe questions of regional autonomy, separatist movements, and special status for (cultural, linguistic, or religious) minorities can be found in every country.

b. Polyethnicity is a more difficult notion; it is used mostly to describe the situation of today's immigrant groups in urbanized western societies and states. Often, these immigrants have come from former colonies, confronting the dominant culture with its own (neo-)colonialist attitudes (Joppke 1996: 452). In other cases they have come from foreign regions with different cultural or religious traditions, challenging the western universalist claims of liberal freedom, rule of law, and democracy. In contrast with the phenomena of a multination state, confederation or empire, one point is clear: these ethnic groups are not actually living in different provinces, but they are using the same public places, institutions, and services within the same geographical or local space. Locally, they live together with the dominant groups, mostly in modern cities, but they remain clearly differentiated or even segregated from each other as different ethnic cultures or communities. Obviously, a crucial role in this type of multiculturalism is played by the notion of "ethnie." I will use the definition given by Anthony Smith (1994: 189): "a named unit of population with myths [I prefer to use the more neutral notion of "discourses"] of common ancestry, shared memories and culture, an association with a home-land and sentiment of social solidarity." In the same line Kymlicka defines a culture, nation or people as "an intergenerational community, more or less institutionally complete, occupying a given territory or homeland, sharing a distinct language and history" (Kymlicka 1995: 19). I will mainly focus on the role of the *homeland*, mentioned in both definitions, which is an extension of the definition of ethnicity by descent alone.[1] I will try to show that homeland is a constitutive factor in ethnic multiculturalism.

Kymlicka discusses this type of multiculturalism from the perspective of group-specific measures or "polyethnic rights," without paying any further attention here to the role of the homeland. Furthermore, he includes in this category religious groups as well. I believe this would weaken the specificity of ethnic groups, especially the role of their homeland; or, reversely, it raises questions about the intrinsic bond between religion and ethnie, and thus between religion and some sort of religious homeland.

c. In this article I will not discuss the third type of multiculturalism, which is the cultural diversity of lifestyle groups, subcultures, and minorities. The latter notion specifically refers to the historically, socio-economically or politically disadvantaged, excluded or discriminated groups or classes within a society, culture or political community (Joppke 1996: 450–452). Their problems and interests are sharply distinguished by Kymlicka as "representation rights," from the (legal) problems involving polyethnicity (Kymlicka 1995: 19, 31). These cultural (sub)groups can be clearly distinguished from the other two types of multiculturalism because they don't need to be per se intergenerational[2] and — which is my particular point — they do not refer to a (foreign) homeland. I insist on this distinction in order to disentangle — and save — the strangeness of an ethnic culture from its reduction to socio-economic, cultural, and political suppression, exclusion and disadvantage. However, ethnic problems, and the struggle to overcome them, are of course mostly intermingled with these other suppressive processes, and they share with them common strategies and tactical considerations (for example, social identity formation, emancipation, and affirmative action).

> My questions about the role of the homeland may now be phrased as a paradox of ethnic multiculturalism or polyethnicity. In ethnic multiculturalist society, different ethnic groups really live together in the same local space, although at the same time they seem to live elsewhere in different homelands. What does it mean to live in different homelands? In my opinion "homeland" is not just a metaphor here. Homeland does not only refer to or represent foreign places elsewhere, it also exists here in the present reality. How can that be? I will explain this paradox with the help of two propositions. The first is that any notion of stranger or foreigner involves bilocation (section 2), and the second is that a culture or society always constitutes foreign places within its own cultural space, the so-called "heterotopias" (section 3).

2. The place of a stranger

"Space" and "place" will be used in a realistic sense here, describing how they are actually experienced in social interaction and social practice. Real space cannot be reduced to the "bifocal vision that traditionally views space as either a mental construct or a physical form" (Soja 1989: 18). Rather, it is the landscape or empirical geographical space of the earth, on the one hand, and the actually embodied and occupied space, i.e., the place of the social actors, on the other. Geographical spaces are, of course, transformed, modeled and marked by a variety of human and natural (inter)actions and processes, including the ideas, knowledge and beliefs of the social actors. Therefore, geographical space will always be social space or locality, i.e., "a two- (or more) dimensional place, an area within which multiple and diverse social and natural events and processes take place" (Smith & Katz 1993: 67). However, a social space also remains a given, real, physical space, which should be distinguished both from the metaphorical use of space as a purely social or political sphere and from theories arguing that social space is a full product of human activities and imaginations.[3] My insistence on this point is polemic: I react against those political theories — geopolitics being the great exception — which neglect physical or local conditions. The conceptual reason for this seems to be the prevalence of time over space in our modern view of man and society as being primarily historical beings and events.

If we start from such a realistic concept of social space, we can describe an experience of fundamental difference between myself and the other simply as the evidence *that he or she is always located in another place*. This is due to the physical bodily existence both of myself and the others. Since I am an individual body and never a free-floating spirit, other persons must be elsewhere in relation to my bodily position, which is here, and vice versa. The implication for social interaction is that this original difference in location will always entail a fundamental asymmetry between human beings in their knowledge, experience, evaluations, and (inter)actions, notwithstanding the mutual similarities, common information and communication. It was this point which was used by the phenomenologist Edmund Husserl in his analysis of our experience of strangeness (*Fremderfahrung*); among others he described the other person as a stranger, i.e., "an ego now coexisting in the mode There" (Husserl 1931: 119).

I believe this local difference is an essential — although not exhaustive — element of the definition of a stranger as being "someone coexisting in another place." But it is also a rather general definition, stating in fact that any other person may be called a stranger. Some further analysis is needed to discriminate between acquaintances or friends, on the one hand, and our common notion of strangers or foreigners, on the other.

First of all, we can make a distinction between the inalienable portion of space which is actually occupied by an individual — from now on referred to as *bodily place* — and the organized social space or location within which a bodily place is situated — called *local space*. People move and act in local space, where they are involved in a great many social and natural events and processes. Paradoxically, local space is both the lived space of orientation organized from the perspective of a bodily place and the pre-existing room in which the individual and other beings are given. Thus, local space can be characterized as an area that is occupied and organized by a contingent set of bodily places.

Someone's (bodily) place is located somewhere in local space, and at the same time *moveable* in that space. Therefore, an individual's location in space need not be a fixed place in order to be his bodily place. The portion of local space with which an individual completely coincides, i.e., his bodily-place, is actually although *not necessarily* occupied space. All other places related to an individual in a very intimate way are never inextricably bound up with him, and, particularly, they are never inaccessible to other ones. This holds true even for one's residence or home, for one's property, and for the homeland, being either one's native ground or the national territory that is occupied and governed by the political body of a nation-state. Moreover, all things and persons need space in order to move or act, and the presupposition is that local space provides room for them. Local space, therefore, is also a specific condition for the actions and movements of persons and things.

I am using the awkward notion of "bodily place" merely to underline that the (inter)actions between individuals entail a set of spatial characteristics, such as: the non-identity of bodily place and local space as a precondition for interaction; the bodily place as a genuine part of some specific local space; and the presence in the same space of other bodily places. A bodily place, therefore, is always directly related to other places sharing with them a common space of action. However, none of them can be completely reduced to the place of the other. And each of them will qualify in a unique way the local space in which it is located together with the others. In this respect, I would argue that a common local space will always be *organized asymmetrically*.

Now, the difference between friends or acquaintances and strangers may be described as a difference in location and in spatial relations. Strangers exist and act in a local space which is differently and asymmetrically organized, both from my perspective and location *and* from their perspectives and location. However, it can be one and the same local space. The notion of *homeland* may be introduced here to explain the asymmetry. If his homeland can be locally identified with the actual local space, then the individual will be at home. If his homeland is somehow situated in another (local) space while he or she is present in the actual local space, then the individual will be a stranger. If this homeland can be identified with a real, existing foreign country elsewhere in another local space, then the stranger is a foreigner. The point is that, at the same time, both local spaces somehow coincide. If this common space is viewed as a common meeting ground and space of (inter)action, then the other appears socially as an acquaintance and politically as a fellow citizen. In this way I may consider my Turkish neighbor both as a foreigner and an acquaintance.

We may now give a more strict characterization of strangers or foreigners as people who are located in a homeland in *another* local space, while at the same time being present in our local space. It is this bilocation of the stranger which is at stake in the multiculturalist conditions of ethnic plurality of western societies today.

3. Heterotopias and homelands

In the previous section I suggested an interpretation of the notion of stranger or foreigner and of his homeland from the perspective of the individual's spatial experience and his position (bodily place) in local space. I concluded with the assumption that in conditions of multiculturalism the characteristics and experiences of the individual can be transposed into those of a group or culture, the ethnie. In this section I will draw on Michel Foucault to propose a more functional or structural analysis of the role of a foreign homeland in a dominant culture, society or state.

Foucault repeatedly criticized the above mentioned prevalence of time and historical thinking in modern political theory, which ignored the role of space. He called it "bergsonism."[4] In his theory of disciplinary power exposed in *Discipline and Punish* (1975) he actually paid some attention to the political significance of organizing physical space and bodily place, but he did not develop this point.[5] I will restrict myself here to some of his ideas exposed as early as 1967 in his essay called *Des espaces autres* (DEA),[6] which I will apply to the case of a foreign homeland in order to defend my thesis that a foreign homeland can be present in our local space. Foucault himself has not mentioned the case of strangers or foreigners and their homelands.

In his introductory remarks in DEA Foucault introduced the notion *emplacement* for local space. In his view emplacement involves a modern political conception of space including demographic questions about human stocks and their circulations, which contrast with the infinite, extended and homogeneous space of the mechanist worldview and with the hierarchically ordered space of localizations in the Middle Ages (DEA 753). Local space or emplacement organizes and models the actions and processes of the individuals and determines them from outside. It is formally defined as the relations of vicinity between points or elements while actually being a given set of (spatial) relations within a culture or society (DEA 753). As a result of its external determinations, an emplacement is in itself a heterogeneous space; in fact we live within sets of relations which define different and irreducible emplacements (DEA 755).

The rest of the essay is devoted to a special kind of emplacement, called "heterotopia." A *heterotopia* is a *real existing* local space or emplacement — as opposed to a utopia — which is organized and designed with the aim of contesting and inverting existing emplacements of a culture or society (DEA 655–656). Foucault outlines six principles of a heterotopia:

1) *Every culture constitutes heterotopias*. Foucault illustrates this by giving examples of liminal or sacred places in "primitive cultures," and of deviancy places in modern society, such as asylums, prisons et cetera (DEA 756–757). In my opinion the foreign country or homeland should be seen as another example of heterotopia. This does not seem to be right since a foreign homeland is by definition situated outside our own social space, which is our state or homeland. Still, I would like to argue that, in politics and in social life, both the idea and the effective existence of some outside local space always are required in order to demarcate and to model one's own local space. This can be seen as a case of the so called "permanent constitutive outside," as Derrida has shown us, an exterior to the community that makes its existence possible" (Mouffe 1993: 114). In other words: politics without a worldview that includes the places and functions of other foreign countries is impossible. Moreover, foreign countries always are somehow present inside the existing local space, for example as embassies, national houses, military bases, et cetera. But, most of all, they are present through the presence of foreigners within a given society, as immigrants, merchants, travelers, tourists, refugees, and so on.

2) A society may *transform already existing heterotopias*, which shows that heterotopias have very specific functions in a given society. Foucault gives the example of the different locations and different meanings of the graveyard in pre-modern as against modern western cities (DEA 757–758). I would like to add that, in political history and theory, the continuous transformation of foreign countries or external local spaces is a leitmotif. Other countries are treated and imagined as barbarian wilderness, as hostile soil, friendly nations, the promised Land, and so

on. In the actual situation of multiculturalism, this is the kind of transformation in the notion of a foreign country that is now going on. The foreign country, which is claimed to be the homeland of an ethnie, is no longer exclusively another sovereign nation-state, but it can be a mixture of birthplace, motherland, another state, another cultural local space, and even another religious local space.

3) Heterotopias may *juxtapose different and incompatible locations* (*emplacements*) in one and the same place. Foucault cites the examples of the theatre and cinema in our modern society and the gardens in ancient Oriental societies representing the cosmos (DEA 758–759). It is my proposition that the place of a stranger, who has settled himself as an immigrant in modern urban society, is described by the same principle. The stranger is present in local space here while at the same place and time she or he organizes, is part of, and is perceived by others as belonging to a different and other emplacement. How this bilocation may be achieved was partly explained already in section 2. However, the real presence of a foreign homeland instead of its symbolic representation by an individual is not yet fully explained. Its real presence is explicitly stated by the principle that a heterotopia is a real, existing place, but it will not be fully explained until the fifth and sixth principle has been considered.

4) Heterotopias are often *linked to some division of (heterogeneous) time*. This is illustrated by Foucault with the infinite time accumulation in galleries and libraries and with transient time emplacements such as fairgrounds and holiday villages (DEA 759–760). In political theory, the historical narrative of the birth of a nation and the national timescale are essential elements in the legitimation of (the origins of) law and constitution, and particularly in legitimizing the occupation and demarcation of the actual territory of a homeland against any claims of other countries or peoples.[7]

5) A heterotopia presupposes a *system of opening and closing* (*fermeture*) through which it is accessible and at the same time isolated. In this context Foucault discusses the special emplacements of purification (bathhouses) associated with rituals of entrance and a few illusionary openings which are in fact exclusions, such as the guestrooms at South American farms or the motel in the USA (DEA 760–761). In fact, what he describes here is the general function of borders or boundaries, which is not only typical of local spaces or emplacements, but also of any processes of real and conceptual demarcation or differentiation. Any category, set or group needs borders in order to specify itself, i.e., to differentiate itself from other ones. In doing so, it specifies and organizes the residence, entrance, and departure of its members and of outsiders.

The point is that a border is in itself a system whose opening may also function as a lock, and vice versa. As a spatial system, a border is a set of rules specifying the opening or closure of the relations of vicinity between given points or elements — for example, bodily places — in space. Thus they mark out an emplacement or local space. It is this principle which underlies the third principle that incompatible emplacements may be juxtaposed *in the same space* because a border may trigger relations of access and of inaccessibility anywhere in space. In this way the real presence of a foreign homeland may be explained. It is present here as a *hetero*topia, i.e., as a space from outside (*espace du dehors*), which exists and operates here in precisely the same way as another local space elsewhere, as will be explained by the sixth principle.

I have explained the ontological conditions of this bilocation of a foreign homeland in section 2 by using the notion of bodily places, their coexistence within local space, and their asymmetrical organization of the same local space. Now this bilocation is explained by different sets of functional relationships of access and closure between spatial elements in the same space.

6) A heterotopia has a *critical function*, which may be situated somewhere between illusion and compensation. In this respect a heterotopia mostly resembles a utopia, but it is opposed to a utopia as it is also a *real other* space. Examples are the whorehouses, being an illusionary critique inside the existing local space, and the colony, being a compensatory critique outside that space, and finally the boat as a piece of space that is literally floating between local spaces (DEA 761–762). It is the example of the colony as a settlement in some other local space far from the original local space, that corroborates my point that a foreign homeland can be in fact a heterotopia, despite its external location. On the other hand, the sixth principle shows a second important characteristic involved in the notion of strangers and their reference to a homeland elsewhere. This is the critical, compensative function of the notion of strangeness that can only be effectuated by some *negative* interaction that creates or shows incompatibility. In other words, the *meaning* of the other as a stranger or foreigner, and of his homeland as *foreign*, will always be connected with some *negative* discourse and action inside the local space of a culture, society or state. And, finally, it is the border effectuated as a spatial system of closing and opening which is this negative interaction effectively working in space. Discursive practices and real organization of space are interwoven here into a genuine system of power/knowledge (*pouvoir/savoir*), as Foucault called it.

4. Conclusion: Homeland as a Critical Heterotopia in Multiculturalism

Concluding I would like to suggest that it is the negative — critical — function, mentioned by Foucault as the sixth principle, which is at stake in a genuine multiculturalist society. When people belonging to different ethnic groups rightly refer to other places as their homeland, they actually perform some kind of social and political negation, which is in itself a fully political action. In my view this negation consists first of all in the *intrinsic negative force* which is always entailed by the notions of location and "being home" and their necessary spatial embodiments. This negative force is partly descriptive as far as it refers to the "here - there" differences between my (our) position, and your (their) position. And it is a moral, evaluative negation which is essential in the assessment of that position as either a home or a dislocation.

The notion of *bodily place* which was introduced in section 2, may now be used to elucidate the intrinsic negative and critical force of the foreign homeland. After all, the notion of bodily place accounts for the basic fact that the strangeness of another individual is related to his local position elsewhere. It connects the ideas of mutual interaction within the same local space with the asymmetric organization of that space by different actors. What is validated from the inside by the members of a particular culture cannot be observed and valued by other people but from the perspective of the outsider. And at that very moment local difference is at stake. But neither this asymmetry nor this local difference will ever justify any claims of a culture or group to definite and fixed location.

Moreover, the notion of bodily place may elucidate the problem of the embodiment of a culture. It is a fact that, in geographical space, cultures and ethnies are embodied in particular locations: their homeland, capital towns, sacred places and so on, which will become uniquely qualified by their culture. All cultures deal with these places in their social imagination *as if* they are fixed and inalienable bodily places of that culture. Individual members of the culture, in their turn, will define their own place and identity using that particular homeland. However, the obvious fact that bodily place is mobile and can never be described definitively by giving its actual location accounts for the mobility and omnipresence of homelands which are characteristic of multicultural interactions. After all, a culture is embodied most directly by its individual members; when they qualify their position by using their homeland, they embody it directly and actualize it as a heterotopia in the local space in which they are living.

It is my conclusion, therefore, that a core problem of multiculturalism can be described as a paradox: the cultural space of an ethnie entails some special location as its homeland, whereas the culture cannot be more than its actual embodiment by its members in the space in which they are living. The proposition that a homeland is a heterotopia may solve this paradox. However, this solution does not alleviate the challenge of multiculturalism, which is not meeting with other persons through common understanding, but accepting their strangeness and inaccessibility which are involved when they present a foreign homeland in our local space.

This way, part of the challenge of multiculturalism may now be explained as the critical negation involved in the function of the homeland as a heterotopia. This negation, however, should not be misunderstood; it is *not* the constitutive and excluding political negation between friend and enemy to which, for example, Chantal Mouffe refers by quoting Carl Schmitt when she says: "a fully inclusive political community can never be achieved since, as Schmitt tells us, in order to construct a 'we' it must be distinguished from a 'them', and that means establishing a frontier, defining an 'enemy'" (Mouffe 1993: 114).

Multiculturalism is indeed the rejection of this idea of "a fully inclusive political community." It questions, and thereby develops, the "frontier" of a political community by introducing relations to other homelands which are really present *in* the political community itself, and which are not inherently inimical. In doing so the critical negation involved in the foreign homeland as a heterotopia confronts all theories about strangers that use exclusion — or being the other side of the coin, inclusion — as the major social reaction to strangers and foreigners. According to these theories, the strangeness of others will always be a full product or effect of the rejecting actions by (the people of) the dominant culture. Yet, I would like to insist that the system of power/knowledge of the foreign homeland as a heterotopia does not entail that the immigrant and his homeland simply are products of our excluding imaginations and actions. It is that both are given facts in themselves which makes multiculturalism into more than an (imaginary) process of (reciprocal) exclusion or inclusion. From this point of view, immigrants and ethnic groups, and their foreign homelands, are the real ambivalent counterparts of our social and political identities, dreams, and fears.

Notes

[1] See, for example, Brian Barry's definition and discussion of ethnicity in "Self-Government Revisited," in *The Nature of Political Theory*, ed. David Miller & Larry Siedentop (Oxford: Clarendon, 1983), 133–135; or George DeVos, "Ethnic Pluralism" in *Ethnic Identity. Creation, Conflict and Accommodation*, ed. Lola Romanucci-Ross and George A. De Vos (London: Altamira, 1995 (third edition)), 28: "ethnicity, as defined here, is primarily a sense of belonging to a particular ancestry and origin and of sharing a specific religion or language."

[2] I will not go here into a discussion of the intergenerational or even hereditary causes of poverty.

[3] For example, see the use of "metatopical space" by Charles Taylor, "Modernity and the Rise of the Public Sphere," in *The Tanner Lectures on Human Values, 14* (Salt Lake City: Univ. of Utah Press, 1993); see also the phenomenological approach of spatiality in Hannah Arendt's use of "space of appearance" and in her description of the ancient Greek *polis* which "is not the city state in its physical location; it is the organization of the people as it arises out of acting and speaking together, ... no matter where they happen to be" (*The Human Condition*, Chicago 1958, 198). As to the place of strangers, see the phenomenological analysis by Bernard Waldenfels, *Der Stachel des Fremden* (Frankfurt a. M.: Suhrkamp, 1990). For a marxist, socio-economic theory of space, see, for example, Henri Lefebvre, *The Production of Space* (Oxford: Blackwell, 1991), and for a radical analysis see Ernest Laclau's argument that "politics and space are antinomic terms. Politics only exists insofar as the spatial eludes us" in *New reflections on The Revolution of Our Time* (London: Verso 1990), 68.

[4] Michel Foucault, "L'Oeuil du Pouvoir" in *Dits et écrits* III, ed. François Ewald and Daniel Defert (Paris: Gallimard, 1995), 192–193) and "La scène de la philosophie" (ibid., p. 576).

[5] See note 4, and further *Dits et écrits* III: 516. Foucault is frequently reluctant to further develop his ideas about space, see his discussion with some geographers (o.c. III: 32–33, 94) and architects (o.c. IV: 270 ff.). See a general presentation of Foucault's ideas on space and knowledge/power by Edward Soja under the heading "the ambivalent spatiality of Michel Foucault" in *Postmodern Geographies* (London: Verso, 1989), 16–21.

[6] This essay, originally written in 1967, was not published until 1986; see *Dits et Ecrits* IV, 752–762. References to this article will be included in the text with the initials DEA, page numbers refer to *Dits et Ecrits*, volume IV.

[7] On the (onto)logical connection between law (nomos) and settlement, see Carl Schmitt, *Der Nomos der Erde* (Köln: Greven, 1950), and Gilles Deleuze and Felix Guattari, *Mille Plateaux* (Paris: Minuit, 1980) ch. 12 and 13.

The Idea of Europe and Its "Others"

Bud B. Khleif

The purpose of this essay is to explore certain facets of the idea of Europe, namely, the forging of European identity on the basis of colonialism and notions about non-Europe, the Other. This is done within a socio-historical context, briefly and roughly starting with Ancient Greece as heritage and ending with ethnic disturbances in some parts of present-day Europe that label themselves "non-immigration countries."

The working hypothesis for this essay is that to understand the idea of Europe, one has to anchor it in some assumptions about the social construction of hierarchy, of hegemony, particularly through ideological stability, and that hegemony itself is never permanent or complete, a stage of siege between rulers and the ruled. Control of what was known in Roman times as Plebeians (*Plebs*) through control of the symbolic system and some material rewards (e.g., SPQR — "Senatus Populusque Romanus," that is, inclusion of "we, the people" in the SPQR motto; "panem et circenses," bread and entertainment to distract the "people"); of peasants or "commoners" in Medieval Times, e.g., through the Church's monopoly on salvation; of the working class in 19th-century Britain, e.g., through a doctrine of race supremacy and Acts of Parliament for some economic concessions — all to prevent what is known in modern times as "class conflict" (cf. Gran, 1996:13), and in the gracious language of the American Founding Fathers as ensuring "domestic tranquility," seems to be a *sine qua non* for consolidation of the state and expansionism beyond its borders. In other words, creation of an enemy, an alien, an underclass or under-caste beyond the state's borders seems to be a crucial element for its stability, for its Pax Romana or Pax Britannica.

What Is "The Idea Of Europe"?

The idea of Europe is a collective notion that European identity is superior to that of any non-European peoples or cultures,[2] an identity of racial and cultural supremacy, in its full version constructed particularly in the 19th century during the age of Empire, but still informing social relations in and outside Europe itself.

To understand the idea of Europe, one has to ponder the unity of opposites, of self and others, namely, that Europe's identity is embedded in its putative opposites, that the Other is crucial to defining the self (cf. C. P. Cavafy's poem, "Waiting for the Barbarians," that ends with the two verses, "And now what will become of us without Barbarians? — / Those people were some sort of a solution,"[3]

Let us look at some socio-linguistic aspects of the idea of Europe:

Self vs. The Other (the majority of the world's periphery)

1. (a) Greeks
   (a) Barbarians
   (b) Europe (for the Greeks)
   (b) Asia

2. (a) Christendom
   (a) Islam (Shakespeare Medieval and Early used "Turks" to Modern-Europe) refer to all Muslims)
   (b) The Old World
   (b) The New World (the colonizing English dubbed the Irish and American Indians, respectively, as "Old World Barbarians and New World Savages"

3. (a) The Occident
   (a) The Orient
   (b) The West
   (b) The East (Near, Middle, and Far, the Non-West in a recent book by Samuel P. Huntington of Harvard, simply dubbed "The Rest").

4. (a) The First World
   (a) The Third World (including the Fourth World, one without natural resources; before the collapse of the Soviet Union, also the Second World)
   (b) Developed Countries
   (b) Developing Countries (at first, called "Underdeveloped")
   (c) The North
   (c) The South current designation

What do we conclude from the above? That "privileging" the self is done at the expense of the other, that the other is a variant of the self, a deliberately unacknowledged variant perhaps.

The Myth-Charter of Europe

Obviously, the Europe we are talking about is North-West Europe in particular, especially Britain, France, the Low Countries, later on joined by Germany in further formulation of race theories. In other words, the idea of Europe, understood as an all-permeating ideology worldwide, is "essentialized," that is, made equivalent to Plato's theory of forms, an invariant essence. But as Gran (1996 9–12) argues, if Europeanness is a standard, then how European is Italy, Russia, or Albania? For some, they are *in*, but not totally *of* "Europe"[4]

What, then, is the legacy of Greece, that has served as part of the ideology of distinct Europeanness? Europeanness starts with two versions of a myth, concocted by the Ancient Greeks:

(a) The goddess Europa is abducted from her *Asiatic* homeland by Zeus, disguised as a bull. In Crete, she is impregnated by her divine abductor. The myth emphasizes Greece's Asiatic lineage (cf. descent, property rights, territorial claims) and particularity or distinctiveness. As Hentsch (1992:6) emphasizes, the history of Greece is part of the European cultural heritage: Modern Europe has appropriated ancient Greece, as to both its accomplishments and enmities.
(b) The other version of the myth is found in the opening paragraphs of Herodotus's history, namely the theory that the wars between Greeks and Persians are the "manifestation of a secular antagonism between Asia and Europe"[5]

What is sociologically interesting about this so-called theory is its nesting in gender and identity politics: Phoenician traders kidnap a Greek king's daughter ("they started it!"); Greeks from Crete retaliate by carrying off the Princess Europa from her home in Tyre in Phoenicianland (note the name "Europa" as a Phoenician, i.e., Northern Canaanite, Semitic name). This is followed by aggression from the Greek side, the ravishing of Medea by the Argonauts. The Asiatic response finally is the rape of Helen by Paris, the alleged cause of the Trojan Wars (Bury, 1958:52). That is to say that the antagonism of Europe and Asia has to do with issues of honor and shame, or protecting women and avenging insults. That for the ancient world, and perhaps for the modern one, made sense, was readily understandable. As Herodotus himself comments, the Trojan Wars solidified the enmity between Greece and Persia, Europe and Asia (Herodotus, in Finley, 1963:30–31). The theory became a world view, a unifying ideology.

II

Europe Spills Into Asia: The Crusades, Or European "Jihad"

According to Toynbee (1957:230–231), "four stigmata" have been used by Europeans to *brand* others — those of "Heathen," "Barbarian," "Native," and, finally, "Racially Inferior." *Heathens*, or non-Christians, could cross the line by conversion; *barbarians*, by learning the language and customs of the masters; *natives*, eventually by intermarriage or economic endeavor. There is, however, no easy escape from "racial inferiority" or race as social boundary, a European emphasis that was elaborated especially after "discovery" of, that is, military and colonial expeditions into, the New World (cf. Khleif, 1996).

Toynbee's "four stigmata" are reflected in the work of Robert Redfield, the American anthropologist. According to him, there are three historic principles of discrimination, somewhat sequential in their development: religion, language (or culture), and race; race being the latest, the post-Columbus one (there is no word for race in ancient Greek). Obviously, these three boundary markers may operate separately or in combination. Religion and language (language as the key to culture) as the older boundary-markers can be transcended, but not race, the latter being a distinct legacy of European colonialism in the post–1492 era.

For the ancient world, the Mediterranean was the center of civilization. Those who controlled the trade routes from the Eastern Mediterranean into Europe — the trade in silk, gems, pearls, spices — were envied, a lucrative target (cf. the opening verses of Milton's *Paradise Lost*, Book II, about the "gorgeous East" and its riches). Under the guise of religion, the masses of Europe were mobilized by the Pope and by secular rulers, Islam for Europeans already fashioned out as the enemy of Christianity, the Anti-Christ. Muslims were the external undercaste to Europe's poor.

What is known as the Crusades (1096–1291 A.D.) consists of seven expeditions, including even one known as the Children's Crusade, that is, successive waves of invasion. European armies communicated among themselves through a variant dialect of Occitanian (cf. Provençal), hence the expression "lingua franca," metaphorically used thereafter.

Two Crusades, that is, invasions or military expeditions, are worthy of mention: the Fourth Crusade (1202–1204) and the Sixth (1248–1254). The Fourth Crusade was directed not only against Muslims but principally against the citadel of Eastern-rite Christianity, Byzantium. "It is fair to say that Byzantium's most zealous tormentors lay in the Christian West, not the Islamic East. In 1204, the walls of Constantinople… fell…. There followed three days of pillage and massacre, of book-burning and heresy hunting, on an unprecedented scale. 'Even the Saracens are merciful and kind,' declared a Byzantine writer, in comparison with those 'who bear the cross of Christ on their shoulders'" (Meyer, *New York Sunday Times*, 3/30/97).

What has the Fourth Crusade to do with the Idea of Europe? First, that religion continues to be a traditional segment of that idea — even today, among the titles of the King or Queen of England is "Defender of the Faith"; secondly, that the European faith is Western Christianity, not the Eastern one. Even today, regarding the *Gastarbeiter* or *Mindenheden*, when it comes to an ethno-religious undercaste in Germany, Netherlands, or Belgium, Greeks as Greek-Orthodox are not considered Christianly equal, just a bit more accepted than Muslim Moroccans or Turks.

The Sixth Crusade, led by Louis IX, King of France, called St. Louis perhaps for his Christian zeal, attempted to establish a beachhead in Egypt as part of controlling the Egyptian-European trade, but that Crusade ended in defeat (Holt, 1986:82–83). Religion, of course, often masks material interests.

The Crusades are part of European identity, of animosity against Arabs and Muslims, of vague feelings of revenge, of a desire to even the score. An illustration suffices (Kabbani, 1986:5): In 1920, when the French occupied Syria, it is said that as soon as General Gouraud entered Damascus, he went straightaway to the tomb of Saladin, the Muslim commander who had defeated Europeans in the Third Crusade, and, pounding with his swagger-stick on the tomb, gloatingly announced, "*Nous revoilà, Saladin*!" (*We are here, we have returned, Saladin*!). The European Jihad continues: In the words of the publisher of Karen Armstrong's book on the Crusades (1991), "Nearly nine hundred years later, the consequences of the epoch-making call to arms resound almost nightly on news bulletins around the world." As Ernest Barker opines, "Crusade is a magic word and magic words are magnets" (1949:52), attractive of old, glamorous associations.

The Crusades were the first European attempt to establish Asian colonies and control the trade routes to Europe. The second attempt was Columbus's expedition to India, to circumvent the old trade routes and go directly to the source of gems, silk, and yes, pepper.

III

Post–1492 European Colonialism

With the Protestant Reformation and the Catholic Counter-Reformation, that is, with the split of Western Christianity into hostile camps, the designation of *Christendom* for Europe, or even "Holy Roman Empire," was no longer serviceable; hence, the name Europe was activated again. From the end of the 15th century to about the end of the 19th century, Europe spilled out into the New World and many areas of the Old World, establishing colonies, fashioning out nation-state ideologies for control of internal masses as well as external, colonial ones.

Here, we draw upon certain notions of Gran's as a useful way for interpreting some aspects of the ascendancy of Europe and develop these notions further. For Gran (1996:7, 337, 343), the supreme preoccupation of the nation-state is disguising class conflict within its borders, that is, hiding from the masses what they share in common, namely, their oppression by government-backed class forces, deflecting their attention so that they may find some solace and pride in belonging to a privileged race or gender. The masses accept their position in the class structure because at least they are not at the bottom of society.

In Britain, the technique for "buying off the working class for a generation or two" (Gran, 1996:8), was a mixture of an ideology of racial superiority and some welfare-state concessions. This way, Britain could maintain her empire (one-fourth of the globe, where the sun, from east to west, never set). "Hegemony works when most of the population has a stake in...continuation of at least a part of the dominant set of ideas and practices" (Gran, 1996:7).

In addition to social construction of an undercaste, internal or external, political elites of the European nation-state also constructed what Gran calls "buffer races" (1996:348), what is known in sociology as "middleman minorities," such as Indians in Kenya and elsewhere, who helped the stability of the British Empire for a long time (cf. Ignatiev's book, *How the Irish Became White*, that is, from despised Celts by Britain, to part of the upper color-caste in the U.S. upon their immigration).

But what is important at the height of the European colonial enterprise particularly in the 19th century is the construction of race as an insurmountable, impermeable boundary. The important point is this: Whereas, according to Toynbee, the conquering Ottomans showed the usual arrogance and haughtiness of the conqueror, unlike European colonists, they never stooped further downward to attribute human nullity to their subjects as "inferior races" (Toynbee, 1957: 230–231). Are Easterners a bit more civilized?

It can be said that race prejudice was developed and promoted historically among Europeans with the rise of capitalism and rationalism as instruments of imperialism, and vice versa. In his magisterial study, *Race: The History of an Idea in the West* (1996), Hannaford reviews the work of Linnaeus and Blumenbach as earlier classifiers of the human races and goes on to discuss in detail the work of Renan (1823–1892), particularly his concept of the "bond of blood" in writing about the Celts (Renan himself was of Breton, i.e., Celtic background, hence his praise of the Celts), and the work of Gobineau (1816–1882) on the inequality of races, Gobineau who says that the "racial question overshadows all other problems of history, that it holds the key to them all" (Hannaford, 1996:251, 264). In addition, Hannaford discusses German and British refinements of racial theories, writers who asserted that for the 19th century it was not class struggle that was the crucial concept, the engine of change in history, but "race struggle." It is no wonder that race, as a preoccupation and predilection within the Idea of Europe, leads a modern historian to assert that "bourgeois democracy is a *hegemony based on rule by race*" (Gran, 1996:13, emphasis added).

We can go back to the proceedings of an international congress held almost on the eve of World-War I in London, a congress on inter-racial problems, in which famous academicians and statesmen took part: Franz Boas; Ferdinand Toennies; W.E.B. DuBois; L.L. Zamenhoff, the father of Esperanto; D.S. Margoliouth, the Orientalist; and, among others, Sir Charles Bruce, G.C.M.G., former Governor of Mauritius, author of "The Broad Stone of Empire" (Spiller, 1911). One paper, in particular, draws one's attention, that of Sir Charles Bruce, entitled "The Modern Conscience in Relation to the Treatment of Dependent Peoples and Communities" (in Spiller, 1911:279–292). In it we find, in thumbnail sketch, an important aspect of the Idea of Europe, Imperial Europe, that is. Sir Charles propounds what he calls the "theory of monopoly of capacity, inherent in a trinity of race, creed, and colour, peculiar to the West" (Bruce in Spiller, 1911:288), a "*monopoly of the capacity of self-government*, based on an indivisible interrelation between European descent, Christianity, and the so-called white colour" (1911:292, emphasis added). In all fairness, we should add that Sir Charles called for transcendence of this Western theory in his paper, in his call for harmony ending his paper with a sort of hymn: "God's in the Occident/God's in the Orient" (1911:292) — God unites East and West.

Accusing colonials of lack of capacity for self-government (i.e., "they ought to be governed by us"), is a familiar colonial refrain, part of the hegemony of Europe. Quoth Arthur James Balfour, of Colonial Office fame, in a speech before the House of Commons on June 13, 1910, that is, almost around the time the aforementioned international conference on interracial problems was held in London in 1911:

> "First of all, look at the facts of the case. Western nations, as soon as they emerge into history, show the beginnings of those *capacities for self-government*.... You may look through the whole of history of...what is called, broadly speaking, the East, and *you never find traces of self government*" (cited in Said, 978:32–33, emphasis added — "capacity" must have been a popular word at the time).

By the turn of the 20th century, Europe had become the "Occident"; the rest of the world, the "Orient"; later on, simplified as the "West" vs. the "East."

IV

The Special Case Of "Orientalism" in European Identity

Here, in passing, we merely single out the ground-breaking volume by Said (*Orientalism*, 1978) and briefly allude to a sort of myth Europeans have concocted about the Orient. Kabbani defines this myth, in part, as "projection of evil onto a faraway culture," where Islam is seen as the negation of Christianity and the Islamic world as Anti-Europe (Kabbani, 1986:5). The Orient is made to be "the Other, the opposite, the enemy, the foil," a vehicle for self-dramatization and assertion of differentness (Kabbani, 1986:10, 11). In her examination of European travel narratives about the Arab-Islamic world, Kabbani includes titillating chapters, for example, about the "Lewd Saracen" and the Turkish Seraglio and its odalisques (cf. the famous painting in the Louvre by A.D. Ingres, the nude entitled "La Grande Odalisque"). The Orient is heavily feminized by male writers and painters in Europe.

Orientalism is part of feelings of innate superiority of Europe, of the Idea of Europe, part of an on-going Western hegemony.

V

Inside The Whale in Modern Times: Islam And Afro-Asia within Europe

Because of labor shortages in Western Europe during the post-World-War-II era of economic boom — roughly 1955–1973 — contract workers, known as *Gastarbeiter* (literally, "Guest Workers," although they were paying guests) were imported. These *Gastarbeiter*, many of them Muslims from Morocco, Algeria, and Turkey, have stayed on, bringing in their families, comprising distinct ethno-religious communities in various cities in Germany, France, Belgium, and the Netherlands. Although they had been actively recruited and welcomed with open arms (I have seen old newspaper clippings showing flags and drums and hospitality committees welcoming *Gastarbeiters* outside train stations, e.g., in Tilburg, Netherlands, upon their arrival), they are now resented and used as scapegoats to explain away the post–1973 economic slump.

Currently, there are virulent anti-immigrant sentiments in Western Europe, exploited by xenophobic political parties, e.g., the National Front of LePen in France, Vlaams Blok in Belgium, and the Neo-Nazis in Germany. Not only Muslim *Gastarbeiter* or *Mindenheden* (Dutch for "Minorities") are persecuted, but also asylum seekers from Africa and other parts of the world.

What accounts for anti-foreign, anti-Muslim, anti-immigrant, and anti-Gastarbeiter sentiments and activities in the post–1975 era of economic downturn? Perhaps the following:

(a) The pressures of globalization have undermined the state's ability to provide economic and psychological security. These same pressures have led to transfer of low-skilled, labor intensive jobs from Western Europe into Third-World areas of low labor-costs. The undesirable, low-prestige jobs have become, if ever available, the lot of immigrants. Older members of the workforce have become resentful (Hossay, 1996:345, 347).

(b) High unemployment is coupled with proliferation of irregular, part-time, marginal jobs. Both middle-aged workers who had known better times, and young, unskilled, less-educated youth entering the labor force are resentful, frustrated with the status quo, angry at political corruption and the inability of politicians to improve the economic situation. This places the state's legitimacy in question.

(c) Members of the lower middle class perceive their socio-economic situation as deteriorating, using immigrants to account for their loss. It is a case of downward displacement of aggression against an already identifiable undercaste. For example, Flemish shopkeepers, pushed out of the local market by the supermarkets of a globalized economy ("Wal-marted"), blame the immigrants as being both unfair competitors and illegitimate residents (Hossay, 1996:355).

(d) Quoth Karl Dillen, a leader of the Vlaams Blok, the Flemish xenophobic, right-wing coalition: "It is easy to assimilate and integrate one foreigner, but not a million of them, because *differences in lifestyle, culture, and religion* are so enormous that confrontation, not integration, will be the upshot.... Let us defuse this time bomb. *It has nothing to do with racism*" (*La Libre Belgique*, 12 November 1991 — cited in Hossey, 1996:355, emphasis added).

(e) In Western Europe, in constructing Islam and immigrants as the enemy, in the rise of xenophobia throughout supposedly civilized countries, there is now a new rhetoric, a type of *neo-racism*, the emphasis of which is not on biological heredity or skin color, but on "*cultural differences*" that are thought to be insurmountable, on the incompatibility of life-styles and traditions, on the desirability of cultural homogeneity (Hossay, 1996:354). The nation-state, of course, has never been mono-ethnic, mono-lingual, or mono-religious: "immigrants," "races," and "cultures" are not givens; they are deliberately constructed under socio-economic conditions and manipulated as boundary markers for structuring collective inclusion and exclusion.

In the words of Will Hutton, columnist for the *Manchester Guardian Weekly* (2/7/93), "Europe's new tribalism could infect us all.... Europe's tribes are coming back, bewildered by unemployment, atomisation, and sense of loss of control," living amidst "disintegrating assumptions and irreconcilable tensions." *The notion of the outsider, the barbarian, the Other, is always accompanied by its twin, ethnic purity*. The notion and twin work both internally and externally in ever-expanding contexts. Are the countries of south-east Europe "unambiguously 'European'?" Hutton asks. Is Europe attempting to draw limits to its geography? According to the French philosopher, Bernard-Henri Levy, who took part in the World Economic Forum at Davos, "*Europe feels that its border implicitly stops somewhere around the limits of Catholic Europe* — certainly before the complexities of the Balkans" (Hutton, *Manchester Guardian Weekly*, 2/7/93, page 8, emphasis added). These issues of definition of self and others, of internal and external outsiders, currently preoccupy Europe; they are part and parcel of the Idea of Europe, of what Peter L. Berger calls "alternations," that is, the constant review and editing of experiences and identity.

Attacks on "internal foreigners," particularly segments of the ethnic and racial undercaste or underclass in Britain, for example, have tripled since 1988. In 1996, according to a human-rights group based in London, called Human Rights Watch, there were more than 12,000 racial incidents, three times the figure for 1988 (Associated Press Brief, *The New Hampshire*, 5/13/97, page 9).

In 1992 and 1993, in a wave of attacks by suspected Neo-Nazis, several hostels for Third-World asylum seekers were set ablaze, burning alive a number of foreigners, e.g., in Eberswalde in eastern Germany and in Dolgenbrodt. However, not only skinheads and other fringe elements of society were involved: The town elders in Dolgenbrodt, according to confessions of those arrested, seem to have backed the Neo-Nazi torching of an immigrants' hostel in their village. In the words of William Drozdiak, columnist for the *Washington Post* (part of *Guardian Weekly*, 2/23/97, page 17; emphasis added):

> Rather than shame, the villagers of Dolgenbrodt have expressed anger and dismay towards state authorities who, they say, made a stupid decision to base foreigners in their midst — and *thus compelled them to take drastic measures to protect their community* from an invasion of Third World refugees.

In other words, it is the fault of foreigners for being in Dolgenbrodt in the first place; they are the cause of bringing out the worst in the natives, so-to-speak!

Growing racial intolerance, not only extreme xenophobic hatred, is also shown in regulations passed by state authorities. For example, in January, 1997, Germany passed regulations that require immigrants' children who are under 16 years of age — although, in the words of the *Frankfurter Rundschau* newspaper, they "know no other homeland but Germany, who speak only German, and whose future is here" — to obtain residence permits, that is, they "need regularly to ask for official permission to live in Germany" (Traynor, *Guarding Weekly*, 1/26/ 97, page 7). The irony of it all is that these regulations against German-born children of immigrants coincided with launching *1997 as Europe's year of anti-racism*! Seemingly not to be outdone, about the same time, the British Government unfortunately vetoed a worthy plan, "a plan to establish a European Union centre to monitor racism and xenophobia throughout the Union" (Palmer, *Guardian Weekly*, 2/2/97, page 10).

France also shares in racial discrimination against non-Europeans in its midst. In a national poll taken in November, 1995, quoted by the National Commission on the Rights of Man, 40% of respondents said that they were "slightly" or "considerably" racist. In a TV show in 1995, Superman, Spiderman, and Batman were dressed up and presented as Muslim thieves, producers of the show being taken to court thereafter. The mayor of Montformeil refused to admit the children of immigrants to the local school system. The principal of the Paul Painlevé School in Lyon established two segregated tracks within his school — one for the real French ("les petits Français de souche"); another, for the rest. All these items are reported by Boudes and Ulrich, in the weekly magazine, *Evenement*, 4–10 April, 1996, p. 25.

Within the Idea of Europe, the engine of change in history, of social movements to restructure hegemony, is, according to some writers, not class conflict, or blatantly race conflict any more; it is culture conflict.

VI

Conclusion

In this essay, we anchored the Idea of Europe in discussion of the stratificational tension of the nation-state, its "established and outsiders," "shearers and shorn," rulers and ruled, and the necessity of distracting the "shorn," the ruled, from understanding the workings of hegemony and exploitation, even their own victimization. We tied this to the ascendancy of Europe as a colonial power, to its charter-myth acquired through appropriation of Ancient Greece as heritage, and particularly its "argument of blood" or "race" as legitimation for its colonial, and even postcolonial, hegemony. Nowadays it seems, race is partly masked as "culture," "cultural differences" being made to account for irreconcilable arrangements, e.g., integration of immigrants and asylum seekers into the citizenship structure of Western-European countries.

Is Europe unique in its proclivity for scapegoating and dreaming-up of persecutable "foreigners"? Certainly not, but it should be acknowledged that Europe has contributed to a sort of unbridgeable chasm between self and others, namely race theories and racism, something infecting the whole world beyond the divisiveness of language and religion.

Obviously, we have painted with a broad brush. What is needed is some specific case studies, e.g., regarding "ethnic cleansing" in various parts of Europe, a sequel to 1932–1945 racist events in Europe. To what extent can racism be confronted and combatted? To what extent can we stop making the culture of the Other so dehumanized and Satanized as to make the Other fit to be genocidable? As Hutton (1993) states, the new tribalism of Europe is doubly divisive: it inhibits the international collaboration necessary for increasing the economic growth rate and encourages protectionism. Along with economic and monetary unity, a human-rights unity is called for: establishment of a European Union center to streamline the legalities of immigration and treatment of immigrants, to promote an equitable policy and enforcement measures throughout the Union.

In view of its great achievements in many fields of endeavor, what do we ask of Europe? Perhaps three things: That it face its own history; that it live up to its ideals; and that it acknowledge its kinship with the colonized Other, whether internally or externally cornered.

References

Armstrong, Karen 1991 Holy War: The Crusades and Their Impact on Today's World. New York: Anchor Books, Doubleday.

Associated-Press Brief 1997 "Racial Incidents in Britain Triple since '88." The New Hampshire, 13 May 1997, p. 9.

Barker, Ernest 1949 "The Crusades." pp. 40–77 in Arnold, Sir Thomas, and Guillaume, Alfred (eds.), The Legacy of Islam. Oxford, England Oxford University Press.

Boudes, Richard, and Ulrich, Claire 1996 "Racistes? Non, Français." Evenement, 4–10 April 1996, p. 25.

Bury, J.B. 1958 The Ancient Greek Historians. New York: Dover Publications.

Cavafy, C.P. 1972 Selected Poems. Princeton, NJ: Princeton University Press.

Drozdiak, William 1997 "Bonn Probes Depths of Racial Passions." The Washington Post Section of the Manchester Guardian Weekly, 156(8):17, 23 February 1997.

Dubbelman, J.E., and Tanja, J. (eds.) 1987 Vreemd Gespuis (Dutch for "Foreign Scum"). Amsterdam, Netherlands: Anne Frank Stichting (Anne Frank Foundation).

Finley, M.I. (ed.) 1963 The Portable Greek Historians: The Essence of Herodotus, Thucydides, Xenophon, Polybius. New York: The Viking Press.

Gran, Peter 1996 Beyond Euro-Centrism: A New View of Modern World History. Syracuse, NY: Syracuse University Press.

Hannaford, Ivan 1996 Race: The History of an Idea in the West. Washington, DC: Woodrow Wilson Center Press.

Hentsch, Thierry 1992 Imagining the Middle East. Translated by Fred A. Reed. Montreal and New York: Black Rose Press.

Holt, P. M. 1986 The Age of the Crusades: The Near East from the Eleventh-Century to 1517. London and New York: Longman.

Hossay, Patrick 1996 "'Our People First!': Understanding the Resonance of the *Vlaams Blok's* Xenophobic Programme." Social Identities, 2(3):343–364, 1996.

Hutton, Will 1993 "Europe's New Tribalism Could Infect Us All." Manchester Guardian Weekly, 148(6):8, 7 February 1993.

Kabbanai, Rana 1986 Europe's Myth of the Orient. Bloomington, IN: Indiana University Press.

Khleif, Bud B. 1994 "Problems of Multi-Culturalism and Multi-Lingualism in Self Labelled 'Non-Immigration' Countries: Some Observations on the Myth of Ethno-Religious and Ethno-Linguistic Singularity of the European Nation-State." Duisburg, Germany: Paper No. 258, Applied and Interdisciplinary Papers. University of Duisburg.

Khleif Bud B. 1996 "Some Observations on Ethno-Religious and Racial Issues in Parts of the European Union: Stigmata of Differentiation within the Nation-

State." Paper read at the First European Urban and Regional Studies Conference, Entitled "A Changing Europe in a Changing World: Urban and Regional Issues," session on Europe's frontiers, Crossmead Conference Centre, University of Exeter, Exeter, England, 13 April, 1996, Mimeo., 35 pp.

Meyer, Karl E. 1997 "The West's Debt to Byzantium: A Cultural Lesson in a Gorgeous Mosaic." (In part, a review of a paper by Samuel P. Huntington published in *Foreign Affairs*, entitled "The Clash of Civilizations.") New York Sunday Times, 30 March 1997.

Palmer, John 1997 "Major Vetoes Racism Fight." Manchester Guardian Weekly 156(5):10, 2 February 1997.

Said, Edward W. 1978 Orientalism. New York: Pantheon Books, Random House.

Spiller, G. (ed.) 1911 & Inter-Racial Problems: Papers from the First 1970 Universal Races Congress Held in London in 1911. New York: The Citadel Press.

Toynbee, Arnold J. 1957 A Study of History: Abridgment of Volumes 7–10. New York: Oxford University Press.

Traynor, Ian 1997 "Germany Cracks Down on 'Foreigners'." Manchester Guardian Weekly, 156(4):7, 26 January 1997.

The Challenge of Freedom in Eastern Europe: an Evaluation of the Legacy of 1989

David W. Lovell

The focus of this essay is on the revolutionary and emancipatory character of the events of 1989 in Eastern Europe, on the dynamics of freedom revealed by those events, and on the challenges to freedom inherent within them. They were revolutionary events in the core sense of redefining the proper sphere of government. 1989 was an affirmation of freedom against paternalism; it represented a natural alliance between two dynamics, anti-Soviet and anti-communist. Once the "double rejective" task of the revolution was complete, these two dynamics began to diverge as the space created for freedom filled with the competing demands of nationalism and civil society. There are many challenges to building freedom in Eastern Europe today, many of them associated with overcoming the economic and social dislocation inherited from communism and developing the institutions and attitudes required for a civil society. But while these tasks are important, they are confronted above all by the attractions of a tribal nationalism which threatens the entire project of creating an open society.

This essay asserts that the events of 1989 in Eastern Europe were both revolutionary and emancipatory. It argues that the dynamic of freedom had two elements—the demands of nationalism and of civil society against the common enemy of Soviet-backed communism—but that their alliance soon dissolved into competition. The primary challenge to freedom in Eastern Europe consists in resolving the tension between nationalism and civil society. The key is a substantial rise in prosperity, but the market brings its own problems, and its ability to deliver long-term social benefits depends on its relationship with the state.

1. The contest for "freedom"

The events of 1989 in Eastern Europe brought about the end of an era. They embodied the hopes for freedom, prosperity and national independence of populations long subject to Soviet domination. They signaled an easing of international tensions. And they were proclaimed the ideological victory of capitalism over communism. These events, and this "victory," were largely unexpected. For nearly seventy years, the initiative and the advantage seemed to lie with communism. Its economic record widely impressed; its claim to historical inevitability was often tacitly (even if reluctantly) accepted; and the credentials and motivations of its opponents were suspected.

Against communism, the West constructed military alliances in the name of freedom. Yet the military strategy contributed to a global nuclear deadlock and fear of annihilation. And "freedom" was by no means a trump card in this contest. Western freedoms were criticized as narrow and formal in a largely successful attempt to diminish their achievements. The Western story of freedom—given dramatic emphasis by the building of the Berlin Wall, and reinforced by the accounts of defectors, such as Victor Kravchenko's *I Chose Freedom*[1]—was discounted as ideological trimming. Capitalism's material successes after the Second World War were believed variously to be exceptional, unstable, and ephemeral.

Such an appreciation of the contest between capitalism and communism altered vastly during the 1980s. In some respects, the change in perspective is breathtaking. Western fears of a Soviet military threat, for example, are now widely seen as grossly exaggerated (and self-serving). The problems of the command economy are now regarded as self-evident and ultimately fatal. "Capitalism," a term once shunned even by market supporters, is now respectable.

The story of freedom in Eastern Europe, however, is much more complex and less certain than ideological hubris would suggest. The demand for "civil society" was an attempt to achieve freedom conceived not as proclamations of human and civil rights, which communism offered in abundance, but as the development of social and political bases on which such freedoms could be delimited and guaranteed. The demand for national independence saw freedom as the development of national institutions and solidarity. It is the potential for these conceptions to diverge and conflict—something not apparent in the euphoria of 1989—that I want to emphasize.

Whatever the differences between Eastern European states and revolutions,[2] after 1989 to a greater or lesser extent, the united rejection of Soviet domination and communism began to fracture. In some cases, people wanted the freedom of the market with the security that had been provided by the state. But more importantly, nationalism and civil society fell apart. Resolving that conflict is the key to the challenge of freedom in Eastern Europe.

2. The revolution of 1989

Our image of revolution has been powerfully shaped by the events of 1789, 1848, 1917 and 1949. We expect manifestoes, drama, and violence. We anticipate disappointments, failures, and recriminations. Yet little of this traditional image was recognizable in 1989. The events of 1989 were largely peaceful; they have not devoured their children. Indeed, there was little evidence of dedicated leadership, except perhaps in Poland. If we try to discern a change in the social location of political power, our investigation would not be conclusive. Yet this was clearly no coup. How should we respond to these difficulties? Hobsbawm argues that using the word "revolution" about these events is "apposite, but misleading"[3] because there was a collapse rather than an overthrow. Crampton agrees that communism "abdicated."[4] Timothy Garton Ash described 1989 as less than a revolution, but more than a reform, and coined the term "refolution."[5]

"Revolution," I would insist by contrast, is chiefly concerned with both the extent and rapidity of change, not the method. Its proper focus is the basis of a government's legitimacy, as Close also argues: all other use of the term is metaphor.[6] In this respect, 1989 was unequivocally a revolution. The normative basis of government—how it went about its business, and the scope and content of that business—fundamentally shifted.

It is worth examining some of the purported peculiarities of 1989. That the revolution was unexpected is quite true. Of course, there were few who did not see basic problems in Soviet-type systems: economic irrationalism; ideological exhaustion; and an underdeveloped institutional structure. In the short-term, too, there were many serious challenges. *That* the collapse of communism occurred is surprising only to communist ideologues; but its timing was a surprise to us all. Why, then, did it collapse when it did? The initiative of communist leaderships constitutes the second peculiarity. Archie Brown focuses on the "Gorbachev factor." Leaderships lost their beliefs, not so much in Marxism (which had long been a formality), but "in what they were doing."[7] Furthermore, Dahrendorf noted that the Eastern European revolutions were not made in the name of new ideas but—where they appealed to ideas—in the name of existing ideas, many of which had been debased by communism.[8]

Notwithstanding these peculiarities, 1989 exemplifies Lenin's acute observation that a revolution can triumph only when "the '*lower classes' do not want* the old way, and when the 'upper classes' *cannot carry on in the old way*."[9] Lenin's analysis directs us to a dual process: the protracted decline of communism and the response of the communist elite; and the rising expectations of the people, especially the younger generation. Crampton saw the latter as crucial,[10] and Berend noted the attraction of the young to "the enticing Western lifestyle: the music, freedom and affluence."[11]

1989 was the culmination of a protracted decline in three respects: economic, political, and ideological. The problems of communism are encapsulated by two pieces of evidence: first, the increasing use of the term "nomenklatura" to describe the ruling apparatus, and to suggest not bureaucratic rationality but corruption and privilege; second, the recognition by communists, from the mid-1960s, that the economy was in need of major changes. Only in trying to confront these problems did their extent and systemic nature became apparent to all.

State socialism had set itself the task of "catching up" with the economic conditions of the West, as a prelude to surpassing them. This mimicry put socialism at a constant disadvantage, especially when the West moved its economic goal posts. Central planners, reduced to setting industrial targets by incremental creep (for want of useful economic information), were unable to understand or follow the West's move to a post-industrial society.

Most commentators agree that it was the increasing integration of socialist economies into the West in the 1970s, partly in an attempt to bridge the technological gap, which exposed their difficulties and their comparative disadvantages. In the 1960s, two-thirds of the international trade of the socialist states was within their own sector.[12] When oil prices increased over the 1970s by something of the order of 15 times, the structural problems of socialist economies were obscured by a windfall of oil export dollars, and by the availability of large, low-interest loans. By the early 1980s, however, interest rates had risen and Eastern Europe entered a "crisis of indebtedness."[13] Poland, Yugoslavia and Bulgaria became technically insolvent.[14] Eastern Europe tried an export offensive, exhausting its reserves. Romania, by extraordinary efforts in cutting into living standards, paid back its debt by 1989; thus, electricity consumption in 1985 was 20% of the 1979 level.[15]

Communism had staked its reputation on its ability to deliver a better material outcome than capitalism. The length of time it took to expose the follies of central planning is a testimony to the natural and human resources available to the Soviet bloc (squandered and abused), to the stubbornness of will of these regimes, and to the lifeline of Western loans in the 1970s.

The revolutions were largely peaceful because of the demoralization of the ruling, communist elites (bereft of ideological righteousness and Soviet stiffening), and their calculation that they could benefit in the new society. As Gellner put it, "Never was a sinking ship abandoned with such alacrity and unanimity, never was an experiment condemned so conclusively."[16] The bureaucrats turned to consider their advantage. The skills which had elevated many of them to prominence would still be required. It seems that the managers of the old system have indeed begun to prosper under the new. The cultural elites which played such an important role in the mass mobilizations of 1989 had little stomach to become a new political elite, or to fix accounts with the old. The "bulk of administrators remained in office" and "the nomenclatura class—excluded from top political positions— continued to work in leading posts in the economy,"[17] sometimes solidifying their positions by manager buy-ins.

The "negative" character of the events of 1989 stand out. The absence of dedicated revolutionaries, of revolutionary programs, and the relative absence of violence belie the profound nature of the changes which 1989 ushered in. Holmes has dubbed 1989 a "double rejective" revolution: a rejection of Soviet domination and communism.[18] The absence of political freedoms and the economic hardships of communism were repugnant. In sum, the revolution of 1989 was a rejection of paternalism, and an affirmation of freedom.

3. The dynamics of freedom in 1989

The normative shift in 1989 centres on a rejection of paternalism, Soviet and communist. The identification of Soviet domination and communism was so strong that the demands of nationalism and civil society merged. But if the anti-Soviet dynamic was unambiguous, the anti-communist dynamic was rather more complex. While 1989 has even been seen as primarily a response to falling living standards—Eastern Europeans having negotiated a "social contract" to trade off freedom for material benefits[19]—such an interpretation does a grave disservice to both 1989 and their previous attempts to gain freedom, in 1953, 1956, 1968 and 1981. It is understandable that Eastern Europeans would accommodate to their regimes; nor should we doubt that prosperity was one of their key hopes in 1989. But the thrust of 1989 was for freedom, not renegotiating a contract for satisfied slavery.

Eastern Europe was socialist because socialism was imposed upon it by the Soviet Union after the Second World War; because, as Fowkes put it, "Stalin wished it."[20] The Soviets saw Eastern Europe as a defensive military barrier between themselves and the West. They formalized the relationship in the "Brezhnev Doctrine" which allowed only limited sovereignty to the socialist countries.

Eastern Europeans chafed under communism in large measure because they detested subordination to Russian chauvinism. The Soviets may have extracted economic resources from Eastern Europe under terms highly favorable to them, but—more importantly—their massed military presence in Eastern Europe affronted local populations, and their refusal to concede (or even confront) instances of Soviet suppression of Eastern Europe denied the latter's history and identity. The revolutions were a reaffirmation of Eastern Europe's histories, of a remembering that had been denied by the Soviets: the Katyn massacres, the Nazi-Soviet pact, the mass burials in Kuropaty forest, among others.[21]

The "Brezhnev Doctrine" was effectively abandoned by Soviet leader Mikhail Gorbachev by the middle of 1988. On the seventieth anniversary of the Bolshevik Revolution he had explained that "unity does not mean uniformity… There is no model of socialism to be imitated by all."[22] In 1989, he publicly declared that the Soviets would not use military force to compel socialism in Eastern Europe, and soon thereafter the regimes began to collapse.

J.F. Brown saw 1989 as a "surge to freedom": freedom from Soviet domination.[23] In writing of Czechoslovakia, Hungary and Poland, Wandycz argues that a good part of their history "has been filled with the struggle for freedom. Oppression came from outside."[24]

But the removal of Soviet domination offered little in the way of a positive program for reconstruction. The social legacy—or damage—of communism had to be addressed. In 1989, "freedom had a bitter taste and the price that needed to be paid seemed exorbitant. Economically ruined, socially dislocated, corrupted, and demoralized by forty-odd years of communist rule, the peoples of East Central Europe discovered that such things as liberty, pluralism, and democracy were not a panacea but were conditions essential for building a new reality."[25] National freedom, therefore, was only a beginning, an opportunity. "Freedom," Dahrendorf explained, "does not just happen, it has to be created."[26] The work of reconstruction found its rubric in "civil society."

We should not wonder at the absence of "freedom" on the historical banner of 1989, and in its stead the inscription "civil society." Whatever the genuine philosophical differences over the concept, "freedom" had been the subject of an ideological debate which had often been simply dishonest, had conflated freedom with other values, such as social justice, and had characterized restraint (whether justified or not) as liberty. "Freedom" had become a mere slogan. Vaclav Havel explained, instead, that he wanted a republic which served the individual—not a republic which subordinated the human to it. The re-assertion of humanity was an important element of this revolution; it does not lend itself easily to slogans.

The demand for the demotion of government to a servant of the individual and the community struck at the very heart of communism. Communism's criticisms of the "negative liberties" of bourgeois society were often well aimed, and its notion of freedom as self-determination may be cogent. But it tried to create a free society by abolishing the distinction between public and private spheres of life (a division which Marx had seen as characterizing, and fundamentally flawing, the liberty of bourgeois society). Self-determination became paternalism because the ideal of a rational, truly free and spontaneously cooperating society—which animated all of Marx's work—was seen by him not as a moral ideal but as immanent in history; it was an empirical problem, not a moral one. What began as a doctrine of freedom became a doctrine of authority—the authority of the state or party that claimed to speak on behalf of the "real" or "higher" self. 1989 was a rejection of this whole line of reasoning. The very success of communism in industrializing backward economies only led to the demands to establish the "bourgeois" distinction between public and private life.

Marx had envisaged a rational society, in which man would be self-determined, co-operating rationally and spontaneously with his fellows, mastering nature and social life instead of being mastered by them. Kolakowski argued that "there is no reason to expect that this dream can ever come true except in the cruel form of despotism."[27] Thus did 1989 represent a protest against dehumanization, with humanity dependent on the recognition and re-establishment of the distinction between public and private.

4. Freedom and security

Communism built its all-encompassing state on terror. Once it had disposed of its political enemies, it offered its citizens a type of security: if they accepted the goals of communism (or at least did not oppose them), they would be housed, fed, educated, and employed. Yet in so far as this can be considered a "contract," it was not equally advantageous to both parties. It was a contract citizens refused on pain of death; it gave them no guarantees; and the exchange it promised had no agreed or enforceable rules. In most contexts, such a "contract" would be allowed its real name: extortion. The sense of material security provided by the years of economic growth in Eastern Europe blunted the reality of this extortion, and the longevity of authoritarian government created routines which gave the appearance of guarantees. The citizens of Eastern Europe gave a type of consent to this situation which—in terms used by John Locke—was "tacit" or presumed rather than "explicit,"[28] and which many critics of Locke see as providing an inadequate basis for the obligations presumed to flow from it.[29]

Whether it was from fear, tacit consent, or merely habit, Eastern Europeans came to an accommodation with their regimes. It was not always an easy accommodation, as periodic Soviet invasions attest. Nevertheless, some thought they discerned the development of a greater concern among ordinary people for preservation and security than for freedom. Havel tells us that the citizens of Eastern Europe were concerned largely to live "a relatively tranquil life"[30]—even though this constituted a type of self-betrayal.

Dissidents feared that passivity meant contentment. This was perhaps most clearly expressed in Russia. Alexander Zinoviev declared that there really was a "new Soviet man": not the hero of socialist imaginings, but a man at ease in a corrupt and inefficient system.[31] Afanassiev argued that "Our system has generated a category of individuals supported by society, and more interested in taking than in giving ... *Homo sovieticus* ... is both ballast and brake. On the one hand, he is opposed to reform, on the other he constitutes the base of support for the existing system."[32]

The relations between freedom and security in modern political thought and practice are complex. Freedom is one of the central political values of our times, and arguably the core value of—though it is understood differently in—both liberalism and socialism. Freedom is variously conceived as the essence of being human, or as fundamental to human flourishing. How much (or how little) content is poured into "being human" makes an enormous difference to the practical and institutional consequences of these views of freedom. Few of us disagree on the value of freedom up until this practical point (even if we might agree with John Gray that we cannot rationally privilege freedom as the pre-eminent value).[33] In socialism, however, freedom is generally seen as a consequence of material security, and is sometimes even equated with security. Such a view, which has its origins in Marx's works, has allocated a much larger role to the state than liberalism finds comfortable.

Marx gave the proletariat a philosophical license to pursue its material interests as the emancipation of humanity by declaring it to be the "universal class."[34] Marx came to socialism in the name of rationality, freedom and self-determination, but never explored what the realm of freedom was,[35] apart from its abundance. Socialism subsequently lost its emancipatory inspiration to the drudgery of everyday, material questions, and socialism in power was obsessed with economic organization. Taken together with the critique of formal freedoms, it is not surprising that freedom and security were ideologically conflated. This became a liability—added to others—when socialist states could not ensure the material security of their citizens, which was increasingly the case from the 1970s.

Security is clearly an important concern for the citizens of any state. And concerns about the reduction of personal responsibility in the face of state paternalism have strong echoes even in the West. But the relative quiet of Eastern Europeans need not be interpreted as a sacrifice of freedom for security. As Kavan put it, the silence of Eastern Europeans was "the silence of disagreement."[36] In the first place, the nature of an authoritarian regime means that attempts at freedom—when the time is not right—produce only a rather pointless martyrdom, and may invite more intense repression. Timing is therefore crucial. In the second place—and even more importantly—the nature of communist authoritarianism and its attempted unification of civil and political life mean that freedom begins as a personal, low-level reassertion of one's authenticity.[37] Communism made ordinary people into dissidents, by frustrating their desires to live their own lives, to have their own memories, to make real choices.

While security was, and remains, important to Eastern Europeans, their desire to live a free life—to "live within the truth," in Havel's words—was transformed from individual acts of defiance into a ground swell. The demands for freedom were elemental. They were embodied in individual lives, not proclaimed in political manifestoes. Politics, after all, was discredited.

Despite the changes since 1989—indeed, because of them—many Eastern Europeans continue to expect the social entitlements of the old regime. Surveys of their attitudes towards postcommunism suggest that there is much about their present condition that they do not enjoy.[38] Rising prices and unemployment, and falling GDP have been the rule, whether or not the new regimes adopted gradualism or "cold shower" capitalism.[39] It may be that mistakes have been made in the new systems, or that these economies will take time to work through the economic legacies they inherited, or that even wider exposure to Western economies will produce greater shocks. Whatever the case, there are great political dangers in the short term if the economy fails to improve. Eastern Europeans may look, as they already have, to communists and their successors for economic solutions.

Nostalgia may distort memories of communist inequalities,[40] and sharpen an appreciation of the insecurities of the open society. The desire for security is constantly in tension with the desire for freedom, even in established open societies. But nostalgia cannot erase the fundamental conflict between communism and freedom which came to a showdown in 1989.

5. The requirements of civil society

The notion of "civil society" drew from opposition perspectives within Eastern Europe, which had attempted to use Marxism against communism itself. It has become almost a cliche since 1989. Yet it remains more helpful than concepts such as "democratisation" in explaining the core of the revolution.

Civil society distilled the demand for a non-political realm. It controverted the notion of freedom as a perfectly unified human community which had inspired Marx, and which had found its practical expression in the attempted crushing of all private associations and the hypertrophy of the state.

Marx's critique must be reconsidered in almost every aspect. There is no doubt, for example, that civil society is characterized by formal equality and substantive inequality, and that it encourages the pursuit of individual self-interest. But Marx's assumption that these phenomena give rise to psychic injury and the destruction of all social bonds is unsustainable.[41] Civil society signifies a different type of society, one in which the potential rewards—in material and associational terms—are as real as the uncertainties and hazards. It should not be forgotten that the certainties of the *Gemeinschaft*, often idealized by communitarians, were enforced by religion, status, and immobility.

In clarifying the contemporary role for, and attractiveness of, civil society Gellner argued that it is not just a sphere separate from the state, but requires a certain sort of society. In addition to markets and other social institutions which can counterbalance (but not subvert) the state's roles in maintaining order and arbitrating competing demands, civil society requires that individuals are not subjugated to social sub-groups and rituals. It thus requires an open society. But building such a society is neither easy nor quick, partly because it needs—even more than economic and ideological pluralism—the attitudes and habits appropriate to getting the best from them.

Civil society, therefore, is not just an empty space created by the absence of the state. It denotes certain sorts of social relationships. Historically, these have developed in commercial societies. If they are driven by self-interest, they are also characterized by a high level of trust and civility between people who are effectively strangers to each other, but must cooperate in exchanges. The individual of civil society is not the atomized monad of Marxian critique. The social bond of trust, of course, is not automatic. It is tempered by scepticism, and needs a system of laws which undergirds contracts. By this token, civil society does not stand in opposition to strong government, as long as the latter's power is channeled by the rule of law.

Under communism, Eastern Europe states had become increasingly rule-bound. Legality was strengthened, and new constitutions guaranteed certain freedoms and rights. The Polish Constitution of 1976 required police to obtain a court order before making an arrest, and specified that people could not be detained without charge for more than 48 hours.[42] Yet these guarantees had no solid foundation in political and social pluralism, or in the rule of law and an independent judiciary. They remained privileges, and could always be withdrawn. They also concealed a sinister and wide-ranging surveillance.

Developing the *Rechtsstaat* in Eastern Europe requires laws, practices, and attitudes, all of which will take time to develop. Serious problems remain in this realm. Letowska declared in 1992 of Poland that "The law is still treated in an expedient way, as a tool of the existing politics or policies.... The subordination of law to politics still exists although it has been officially rejected."[43] The distrust in governmental institutions which was characteristic of the communist era infects the workings of the new institutions of the democratic political system and of the market.

It is not just the continued arbitrariness of the political system which retards development of a plural and tolerant civil society. The market, too, holds danger as well as promise. In Eastern Europe, it is remote from the legal, moral and social restraints that attend it in developed market societies (even if they don't always work there). It is in the context of the fluid, and somewhat abstract social content of civil society that we encounter the competing claims of nationalism.

6. Nationalism and civil society

In economic, material, and environmental areas, the destruction wrought by communism is obvious. But its social legacy is even more devastating. As Schöpflin put it, "Communist rule was a kind of desertification. It atomized society—it destroyed the institutions and bonds of pluralism—sweeping away ideas, values, solidarities and people and preserving only a few of these, often in distorted form, from the pre-communist part."[44]

At first sight, and especially given this legacy, there do not seem to be many good reasons why the trust which differentiates commercial transactions from swindling should be forthcoming in Eastern Europe. And the confidence men, and even criminals, encouraged by the emergence of the free market have given substance to this doubt. To the communist legacy of distrust must now be added the distrust of ruthless profiteers. Who, then, can we trust? Nationalism gives us a way of answering this question: only the members of one's nation are trustworthy. This proposition is vastly more popular than it is reliable.

Nationalism and civil society, whatever else they represent, are different models of community: different ways of integrating individuals within a society, and different ways of conceiving the nature of the social cement. At certain points, and especially in the convergence of anti-Soviet and anti-communist feelings, they can be mutually reinforcing. Yet almost as soon as 1989 had occurred, their alliance began to crumble. Where it is strongly held, and of a particular character—exclusivist, irredentist— nationalism is the enemy of civil society. It resiles from the assumption, basic to civil society, that people who are not intimates can have sufficient trust in each other for society to cohere and prosper. Thus, nationalism can see civil society as a type of cosmopolitanism, with an allegiance to civility and tolerance overriding the preferential treatment that should be given to members of the same nation. Popper's classic defense of the "open society" conceded that there were social needs which could not be satisfied in such a society,[45] and here lies an opening for nationalism.

It should not be assumed that nationalism is always, or by its very nature, ugly or narrow. Adam Michnik, I think wrongly, defined nationalism as "the articulation of provincialism and particularism, a basis for xenophobia and intolerance."[46] Certainly, it carries that potential. But the alliance between nationalism and civil society can make a complementary contribution to the nature of social relationships in commercial societies. The latter are mass, anonymous societies, and nationalism can provide an emotional texture to relationships which are mutually self-interested and thus potentially divisive. Both are products of modern societies. But nationalism gives us a sense of a shared framework of language and communication. And it plays a role in identifying a moral community.

The reassertion of national memories in post-communism has created deep problems. If those memories were at first unambiguously turned against the Soviets in the emancipation of 1989, they could subsequently find a ready and diverse employment closer to home. In the early 1990s, for example, Yugoslavia disintegrated into warring states and ethnic cleansing.

The revolutions of 1989 have revealed, once again, that modern nationalism remains a potent force in identifying political communities. In the summer of 1992, Havel conceded that "The sudden outburst of freedom has not only untied the straightjacket made by communism, it has also unveiled the centuries-old, often thorny history of nations.... It is entirely understandable that such a situation becomes a breeding ground for nationalist fanaticism, xenophobia and intolerance."[47] But nationalism was not entirely dormant under communism, though it was politically manipulated;[48] and it need not resort to bolstering identity by separation and exclusion.

Since 1989, many commentators have pointed to the rise of nationalism as the most dangerous portent for future instability in post-communist states, and even as a barrier to liberal democracy.[49] We have already seen it break into armed conflict. Even more importantly, nationalism threatens to undermine civil society, and the hopes for freedom and prosperity that animated the reluctant revolutionaries of 1989.

7. Conclusion

The consequences of 1989 may not yet be the "return to Europe" envisaged by many Eastern Europeans, but societies are not *tabula rasa*; opportunities are always confronted by constraints. Eastern Europe is at last connected to the tensions and problems which confront the whole of Europe. The quality of civil society is the central problem; everywhere it is confronted by the challenges of tribal nationalism, by the problems of unemployment and social "breakdown," by the power of economic giants.

Civil society in Eastern Europe is confronted by its former ally nationalism, feeding on atomisation, poverty and insecurity. Nationalism is a ready source of social identification and solidarity. It is a vehicle of social resentment, which specializes in identifying and punishing the winners in what is seen as a zero-sum game. It has much to feed on. When polled in the early 1990s, most Eastern Europeans thought that their conditions had either not changed, or had worsened.[50]

Civil society, of course, presents its own dangers; it is not an automatic recipe for freedom. In an important sense, freedom consists in the regularity and security within which one may live one's life, or conduct activities without interference. For this, a healthy sense of the privacy allowed by civil society is essential. Yet it can encourage people to choose between private wealth and civic virtue.

In rejecting paternalism, it is important for Eastern Europeans not to retreat into the sphere of non-interference, now increasingly guaranteed by the law. The new freedom of the individual is important, but as Benjamin Constant pointed out almost 200 years ago, modern liberty itself will be endangered if it is not linked with a healthy level of participation in the making of the political and legal rules which determine its boundaries. Without democratic self-government, he insisted, negative liberty may be too easily crushed.[51] But this set of problems is for the moment secondary.

The costs of freedom are becoming apparent to Eastern Europeans. The freedom to work, invest, and own property brings with it not just the potential for wealth, but the insecurities of unemployment, deregulated prices and financial hardship. In the short term—in the transition to the market economy—these costs have been prominent, and many people are nostalgic for the security and entitlements of the past. It will require considerable political skill as well as political will to steer the new democracies through this period of transition, before the material advantages of market societies can predominate.

If I have stressed the "negative" aspects of the events of 1989, it is not to diminish the achievements, or the bravery of those who undertook them, but to give the appropriate attention to the challenges to freedom. The desire for freedom was, at the most basic level, the desire to reassert one's humanity—chiefly by being able to enjoy a sphere of privacy. The demand for civil society in Eastern Europe gave expression to this desire, while its nationalist partner threatens to smother it. Ultimately, freedom relies on hard work and tolerance; it is chiefly mundane, incremental, constructive work. 1989 has taken the romanticism out of the quest for freedom. Perhaps its prospects of success are the better for its want of extravagance, but its contest with nationalism makes any optimism in this regard a cautious optimism.

Notes

[1] Victor Kravchenko, *I Chose Freedom: The Personal and Political Life of a Soviet Official*. London: Robert Hale, 1947.

[2] R.J. Crampton, *Eastern Europe in the Twentieth Century*. London: Routledge, 1994, pp. 391–495.

[3] Eric Hobsbawm, *Age of Extremes: The Short Twentieth Century 1914–1991*. London: Abacus, 1995, p. 487.

[4] Crampton, p. 407.

[5] Timothy Garton Ash, *The Uses of Adversity: Essays on the Fate of Central Europe*. New York: Random House, 1989.

[6] David Close, "The Meaning of Revolution." *Revolution: A History of the Idea*. Ed. David Close and Carl Bridge. London: Croom Helm, 1985, pp. 1–14.

[7] Hobsbawm, p. 399.

[8] Ralf Dahrendorf, *Reflections on the Revolution in Europe, in a letter intended to have been sent to a gentleman in Warsaw, 1990*. London: Chatto and Windus, 1990.

[9] V.I. Lenin, "'Left-Wing Communism'—An Infantile Disorder." *Selected Works*. 3 vols. Moscow: Progress Publishers, 1976, vol. 3, pp. 293–374, at p. 347.

[10] Crampton, p. 411.

[11] Ivan T. Berend, *Central and Eastern Europe, 1944–1993: Detour from the Periphery to the Periphery*. Cambridge: Cambridge UP, 1996, p. 252.

[12] Hobsbawm, p. 374.

[13] Berend, p. 230.

[14] Ibid., p. 231.

[15] Ibid., pp. 231–32.

[16] Ernest Gellner, *Conditions of Liberty: Civil Society and Its Rivals*. Harmondsworth: Penguin, 1994, p. 38.

[17] Klaus von Beyme, *Transition to Democracy in Eastern Europe*. Basingstoke: Macmillan, 1996, pp. 74, 77.

[18] Leslie Holmes, *The End of Communist Power: Anti-Corruption Campaigns and Legitimation Crisis*. Melbourne: Melbourne UP, 1993.

[19] Joseph S. Berliner, "Conclusion: Reflections on the Social Legacy of Communism." *The Social Legacy of Communism*. Ed. James R. Millar and Sharon L. Wolchik. Cambridge: Cambridge UP, 1994, pp. 379–85, at p. 281; White, Stephen. "Eastern Europe after Communism." *Developments in East European Politics*. Ed. Stephen White, Judy Batt, and Paul G. Lewis. Basingstoke: Macmillan, 1993, pp. 2–15, at p. 8.

[20] Ben Fowkes, *The Rise and Fall of Communism in Eastern Europe*. Basingstoke: Macmillan, 1993, p. 2.

[21] David W. Lovell, "Memory and the Transformation of Eastern Europe." *Memory, History and Critique. European Identity at the Millennium. Proceedings of the 6th International ISSEI Conference at the University for Humanist Studies,*

Utrecht, The Netherlands, August 1996. Ed. Frank Brinkhuis and Sascha Talmor. CDROM, 1997.

[22] Cited Crampton, p. 409.

[23] J.F. Brown, *Surge to Freedom: The End of Communist Rule in Eastern Europe*, 2nd. Durham: Duke University Press, 1991, p. 25.

[24] Piotr S. Wandycz, *The Price of Freedom: A history of East Central Europe from the Middle Ages to the present*. London: Routledge, 1992, p. 10.

[25] Wandycz, p. 11.

[26] Dahrendorf, p. 79.

[27] Leszek Kolakowski, "The Myth of Human Self-Identity: Unity of Civil and Political Society in Socialist Thought." *The Transition from Socialism: State and Civil Society in the USSR*. Ed. Chandran Kukathas, David W. Lovell, and William Maley. Melbourne: Longman Cheshire, 1991, pp. 41–58, at p. 57.

[28] John Locke, *Two Treatises of Government*. 1690. Ed. Peter Laslett. Cambridge: Cambridge UP, 1988, pp. 347–48.

[29] John Dunn, *Political Obligation in its Historical Context: Essays in Political Theory*. Cambridge: Cambridge UP, 1980, pp. 29–52.

[30] Vaclav Havel, et al., *The Power of the Powerless: Citizens against the State in Central-Eastern Europe*. Ed. John Keane. Armonk, New York: M.E. Sharpe, 1985, p. 28.

[31] Alexander Zinoviev, *The Yawning Heights*. Harmondsworth: Penguin, 1979.

[32] Cited Hobsbawm, p. 478.

[33] John Gray, *Liberalisms: Essays in Political Philosophy*. London: Routledge, 1989, pp. 239–66.

[34] David W. Lovell, *Marx's Proletariat: The Making of a Myth*. London: Routledge, 1988, pp. 42–56.

[35] Eugene Kamenka, *The Ethical Foundations of Marxism*. 2nd ed. London: Routledge and Kegan Paul, 1972, pp. 26–31.

[36] Jan Kavan, "Charter 77 and Other Independent Movements." *Debates on the Future of Communism*. Ed. Vladimir Tismaneanu and Judith Shapiro. New York: St Martin's Press, 1991. 116–28, at p. 116.

[37] Havel, p. 45.

[38] James R. Millar, and Sharon L. Wolchik. "Introduction: The Social Legacies and the Aftermath of Communism." *The Social Legacy of Communism*. Ed. James R. Millar and Sharon L. Wolchik. Cambridge: Cambridge UP, 1994, pp. 1–28.

[39] Berend, pp. 341–43.

[40] Zdenek Strmiska, "Political Power and Social Inequality." *Equality and Inequality in Eastern Europe*. Pierre Kende and Zdenek Strmiska. Trans. Françoise Read. Leamington Spa: Berg, 1987, pp. 342–78.

[41] Chandran Kukathas, and David W. Lovell. "The Significance of Civil Society." *The Transition from Socialism: State and Civil Society in the USSR*. Ed. Chandran Kukathas, David W. Lovell, and William Maley. Melbourne: Longman Cheshire, 1991, pp. 18–40.

[42] Berend, p. 159.

[43] Cited ibid., pp. 313–14.

[44] George Schöpflin, "Post-Communism: Constructing New Democracies in Central Europe." *International Affairs* 67 (1991), pp. 235–50, at p. 235.

[45] Karl Popper, *The Open Society and Its Enemies*. 5th ed. 2 vols. London: Routledge and Kegan Paul, 1966.

[46] Cited David S. Mason, *Revolution and Transition in East-Central Europe*, 2nd ed. Boulder: Westview Press, 1996, p. 144.

[47] Cited Mathew Horsman, and Andrew Marshall. *After the Nation-State: Citizens, Tribalism and the New World Disorder*. London: HarperCollins, 1994, p. 81.

[48] Leszek Kolakowski, "Amidst Moving Ruins." *Daedalus* 121.2 (1992), pp. 43–56, at pp. 51–55.

[49] Peter A. Heltai, and Zbigniew Rau. "From Nationalism to Civil Society and Tolerance." *The Reemergence of Civil Society in Eastern Europe and the Soviet Union*. Ed. Zbigniew Rau. Boulder: Westview, 1991, pp. 129–44, at p. 130.

[50] Paul G. Lewis, "History, Europe and the Politics of the East." *Developments in East European Politics*. Ed. Stephen White, Judy Batt, and Paul G. Lewis. Basingstoke: Macmillan, 1993, pp. 262–79, at p. 266.

[51] Benjamin Constant, "The Liberty of the Ancients Compared with That of the Moderns." *Political Writings*. Ed. and trans. Biancamaria Fontana. Cambridge: Cambridge UP, 1988, pp. 307–28.

The Center Still Will Not Hold: European Violence in the 1990s and Beyond

Katherine Maynard

> ... twenty centuries of stony sleep
> Were vexed to nightmare by a rocking cradle
> And what rough beast, its hour come round at last,
> Slouches toward Bethlehem to be born?
> William Butler Yeats, "The Second Coming"

A millennium may be a mere period or anniversary of 1000 years, or it may be a splendid new era in human existence: "a period of prevailing virtue or great happiness or perfect government or freedom from [the] familiar ills and imperfections of human existence."[1] But there is also the far more pessimistic vision of the millennium expressed by William Butler Yeats in his poem, "The Second Coming," where he warns that when the Second Coming does occur 2000 years of "stony sleep" will be replaced by a new era of violence and chaos when "mere anarchy" will be "loosed upon the world" as "The best lack all conviction, while the worst/ Are full of passionate intensity."

As Europe slouches toward its second millennium, the optimism generated by the collapse of communism and the improved prospects for peace and unification have been replaced, in many cases, by pessimistic fears regarding certain recent social, political, and economic changes and developments. In nations and societies as otherwise different as Scotland and Germany, there are disturbingly similar symptoms of social pathology: disenfranchised young people, industrial decline, structural unemployment, violence, extremist or racist politics, and drug and/or alcohol abuse. In both societies, these symptoms can be considered evidence that, as Europe approaches the millennium, the euphoria created by the end of the Cold War may be replaced by new anxieties about the continent's future involving xenophobia, neo-fascism, and various kinds of destructive (or self-destructive) behavior primarily by young people.

During the sanguine days of the late 1980s and the early 1990s when communism was being abandoned first by eastern Europeans and then by the Soviet Union itself, the English periodical *Granta* celebrated those events with its Winter 1990 issue entitled "New Europe!" with an image of Mikhal Gorbachev on its cover holding a bottle of champagne to celebrate the new decade. Behind Gorbachev are a caricature of Lenin and an heroic propaganda image of a young Soviet worker striding boldly toward the future—two pieces of agit-prop that had become suddenly and ironically passé, relegated to the dustbin of history. On the back cover *Granta's* editors proclaimed that 1989 was an "annus mirabilis .... After 1989 Europe will not—it cannot be—the same Europe it was before." Inside that issue of *Granta*, a mail order company offered Russian army belts and buckles and 2" pieces of the Berlin Wall for sale; Isaiah Berlin said that his reactions to European events in 1989 were "similar to those of virtually everyone I know ... astonishment, exhilaration, happiness" (148); and Stephen Spender specifically invoked the millennium, noting that it had come ten years earlier than expected: "I [feel] that I am witnessing apocalyptic events out of the Book of Revelations... the collapse of the totalitarian regimes ... is something I had given up hope of witnessing in my lifetime," since he had believed that it "would be perpetually postponed to the next century, after the millennium" (168). Suddenly it seemed possible that a continent troubled by centuries of violence and misery, as well as by great triumphs and glories, might enjoy the kind of millennium, by the year 2000, described as "freedom from [the] familiar ills and imperfections of human existence."

This optimism has faded with remarkable rapidity as Europeans quickly discovered that the Cold War could be replaced as a source of anxiety and concern by both new and recurrent dilemmas and difficulties—social, cultural, and political problems which would have to be solved by the Europeans themselves if they wished to have a genuinely better society rather than yet another millennium in which Yeats' pessimism might be all too appropriate.

To analyze some of the most important sources of this pessimism, I have focused this essay on two texts from the early 1990s which—though they have significant differences—also have some important, salient similarities: Irvine Welsh's 1993 novel *Trainspotting* and *Granta*'s Winter 1992 issue on Germany which was bluntly entitled, "KRAUTS!" with an image of swastika graffiti on its cover. Trainspotting and this particular issue of Granta can be seen as a kind of diptych, as separate but thematically related texts, because I believe that even though Welsh's novel is about Scotland and the Winter 1992 issue of *Granta* is about Germany, they describe nations that are confronting some disconcertingly similar hazards during the 1990s. Moreover, much of what *Granta*'s journalists and cultural commentators state in relatively abstract, general terms about Germany, Welsh's Scots characters enact in fictional terms.

Both of these texts have a jagged, fragmentary, de-centered quality. Though Welsh's *Trainspotting* has a main character—a twenty-five-year-old Edinburgh heroin addict named Mark Renton—it is an episodic novel with rapidly changing viewpoints and narrative perspectives shared mostly among Renton's male friends (plus a few of the women he knows), so that it often seems more like a series of vivid short stories and anecdotes than a novel with a central consciousness and a consistent, identifiable protagonist. In addition, perhaps to make the novel even more challenging to non-Scots readers, much of *Trainspotting* is written in slang so thick that when the film version was shown in the United States, subtitles were added to a few scenes. (The American edition of the novel has a glossary.) The "KRAUTS!" issue of *Granta* is ostensibly more unified since it has been translated into standard English and virtually all of it is about Germany, but it too has shifting perspectives as assorted foreigners and German authors, essayists, novelists, journalists, and poets from both the Federal Republic and the former GDR (Günter Grass, Hans Magnus Enzensberger, Monika Maron, Wolf Biermann) reminisce about the end of World War Two, interview other Germans, and analyze or comment on current conditions in the recently-unified Germany of the early 1990s. Granta's graphics also seem to be a melange: 1945 photographs of refugees and holocaust victims are mixed with images of Gay bars, young Neo-Nazis at meetings, skinheads throwing rocks at hostels or attacking Asians on the Berlin subway, and bleak documentary pictures of dreary Eastern German workers' housing flats and industrial cityscapes.

However, both texts come into focus quickly when one applies the metaphor of disease to them: both deal with pathologies, with epidemics, and many of their seemingly fragmentary perspectives are thematically united by the ways in which both texts are focused on symptoms or epicenters of these pathologies. In *Trainspotting* the main pathology is drugs and HIV with alcoholism running a close second. As Renton's father informs the family, after his son nearly dies from an overdose of heroin, in the mid-1980s Scotland had eight percent of the UK's population but sixteen percent of its HIV cases, and Edinburgh had eight per cent of the Scottish population but over sixty percent of its HIV infections, "by far the highest rate in Britain" (193). In Granta the main pathology is Neo-Nazism and violence against foreign immigrants, *Gastarbeiter*, and refugees, a kind of social epidemic whose most virulent outbreaks were occurring in the former GDR.

Within both texts similar causes of—or influences upon—these pathologies can be glimpsed. Both Scotland and the former GDR have large numbers of what Enzensberger calls "superfluous" people—chiefly blue-collar workers who might have been employed in heavy industries like ship-building or steel-making a few decades earlier in Scotland or only a few years earlier in the GDR. The threats and oppressions of communism may be gone, he implies, but now they have been replaced by the more diffuse insecurities of post-welfare-state capitalism. Thus one of the most "virulent" features of the contemporary world, Enzensberger says

> is the overarching [power] of "the world market." It declares ever larger sections of mankind to be superfluous, not through political persecution … or party resolution, but spontaneously, as it were, by its own logic. The result is no less murderous, but the guilty can never be brought to book. In the language of economics that means: an enormously increasing supply of human beings is faced by a clearly declining demand. Even in wealthy societies people are daily rendered superfluous. What should be done with them? (26)

During the early 1990s, immediately after unification, some eastern German states had under- and unemployment rates as high as fifty percent, and though these rates declined fairly rapidly, by 1994 the unemployment rate was still hovering around fifteen percent and younger workers between the ages of eighteen and twenty-five had some of the highest rates of unemployment.[2] A German family whose son was a skinhead and appeared in an interview reprinted in *Granta*, can be interpreted as *Granta*'s illustration of what Enzensberger meant by "superfluous" people. The parents both work for EKO, a steel mill in the former GDR, where the blast furnaces are being demolished, and the mother thinks she may lose her job in a few months. When asked to describe an "average day," the son replies that he often stays "in bed till eleven or twelve"; then he goes over to a friend's house, where they "chat, have a beer, and mooch around" for the afternoon; then he and his friends meet again in the evening, "stick around together .... Sit in the garage, listen to records," and sometimes go to a disco (Mehr, Sylvester 142).

Welsh's blue-collar Scots in *Trainspotting* have a similar way of life. Between 1979 and 1982 after Margaret Thatcher's Conservatives came to power, Fintan O'Toole has reported, "Scotland lost more than one-fifth of its manufacturing jobs and a tenth of its industrial output. In 1979 there were 600,000 people working in Scottish manufacturing industries. In 1994 there were only 350,000, and they were much more likely to be assembling computers" than working in heavy industries like shipbuilding (69–70). By the 1990s this change has meant that Scotland has not one but two generations of unskilled, largely unemployed, blue-collar workers. Renton respects his unemployed father, since after "being made redundant ... he's punted [sold] gear [clothes] in the markets at Ingliston n East Fortune instead ay sitten in Strathie's bar moanin his fuckin box [head] oaf aboot everything" (190), and Renton himself believes that he's grown up in what he calls "an era ay mass unemployment" (191). Consequently he and his generation have had more opportunities to hone their talents at being "superfluous" and redundant, and therefore they have developed a wider range of ways to "mooch" their ways through life than the Germans in *Granta* have done.

Renton's older brother Billy and his mates, men in their late twenties and early thirties, are all unemployed, sleep until noon, except when they have to show up to register for the dole on some mornings, then drink and smoke for the rest of the afternoon while they gamble with their football club's treasury money. Two of the group have been in prison for, respectively, assault and housebreaking (97). Billy demonstrates more initiative by enlisting in the British army, only to be killed by the IRA in Ulster, since—as Renton sardonically observes—"Anybody will tell you; the Scots make good soldiers" (190). Renton's generation is no improvement. They sneer at low-pay, service-sector job opportunities to become hotel porters, or, in Renton's case, he turns down an "exciting career opportunity to work in the Burger King in Notting Hill Gate" (146). Instead, Renton and his mates are all full-time alcoholics or drug addicts and include a petty thief and shoplifter (Spud), a pimp (Sick Boy), a washed-up soccer player (Second Prize), a drug dealer

(Johnny Swan), and Begbie who has already been in jail for an unspecified felony and does assaults and burglaries until (in the film version) he graduates to armed robbery. Renton, the most intelligent of the lot, supports himself by doing "giro drops," filling out fraudulent applications for unemployment payments at five addresses in Scotland and London, cashing the checks, and showing up for interviews (which he tries to sabotage) for unskilled jobs when required to do so by the unemployment authorities. ("Rents never seemed to work, but always had money," as one of his friends comments [43].) Gav, one of Renton's cousins, has gone to the University and graduated with a degree in English; unfortunately he and most of his fellow graduates are on the dole, but he still recommends higher education because, "It's a good social life" (38).

One of the most powerful, implied "messages" one gains from reading *Granta's* "KRAUTS!" and *Trainspotting* (or seeing the film version) is that "superfluous" people are also very destructive people. During the Cold War, the great threat to western Europe's future and security was external, dozens of divisions of Soviet infantry and tanks stationed in the GDR, Poland, and Hungary, and hundreds of missiles with nuclear warheads poised to launch an attack that would have obliterated most of Europe's cities and population. In the 1990s the threats have become more local, smaller in scale, and more internal—but they can still be rather nasty. Instead of the agit-prop Cold War Soviet worker on the cover of *Granta's* "New Europe!" issue striding toward a socialist future and presumably about to trample over Europe on his way there, *Trainspotting* (in its film version) showed Edinburgh addicts mainlining drugs, stealing anything not nailed down to support their habits, and—in one publicity still—the actor (Ewan McGregor) playing the main character, Renton, is lying on a railroad roadbed with his head on one track and his feet on the other, presumably waiting to spot the train that will put him out of his misery. Many of the images in the Winter 1992 *Granta* are, if anything, even more pessimistic since they are documentary, journalistic ones: Berlin skinheads attacking Asian immigrants, the funeral of three Turkish women who were killed when their hostel was burned down, and thuggish young neo- Nazis throwing rocks and glowering in beer halls.

For the drug addicts of Trainspotting, their behavior is chiefly self-destructive, a way of evading consciousness of how dismal their lives are by narrowing their needs to a single addiction. As Renton, the novel's main and most self-reflective character, explains to his friend Tommy, "Life's boring and futile. We start oaf wi high hopes, then we bottle [lose] it. We realise that we're aw gaunnae die, withoot really findin out the big answers… we live a short, disappointing life; and then we die. Smack's an honest drug, because it strips away … delusions" (89). And Tommy himself, high on speed, cocaine, and booze at an Iggy Pop concert has his own nihilistic epiphany when Iggy is playing "Neon Forest" and, says Tommy: Iggy "looks right at me as he sings the line: 'America takes drugs in psychic defense'; only he changes 'America' for 'Scatlin', and defines us mair accurately than all the others have ever done" (75).

But drugs and self-destruction are only one of the "psychic defense[s]" and roads to ruin in *Trainspotting*. Another path is represented by an important character in the novel, Francis Begbie. Begbie, a second-generation alcoholic, is addicted to violence.[3] As Renton sums him up in the film version of the text, just as Begbie is starting a riot in a bar, "the guy's a psycho, but it's true, he's a mate as well, so what can you do? … Begbie didn't do drugs either, he just did people. That's what he got off on: his own sensory addiction" (Hodge 27). Renton, Tommy, Spud, and the other drug addicts in *Trainspotting* risk destroying themselves when they "do" heroin; Begbie gets his thrills when he "does" people by attacking them, and someday, Renton prophecizes, Begbie will go on "one ay his periodic drink and angst fuelled wars against the local populace" and "git his one day. Nothing wis surer. Ah jist didnae want tae be aroond whin he did" (82). In the meantime, Begbie rules and bullies his mates by a combination of fear and camaraderie so that he has become "like junk … a habit … a dangerous one" (83, 134) that they cannot escape, even though some of them, like Renton and Spud, hate and fear him (78, 155). In *Granta*, one can see Begbie's German equivalents in action as they attack Asians in the Berlin subway or fuel their rage against Poles, Turks, gypsies, and other "outsiders" by drinking beer and attending neo-Nazi meetings. These are not the kind of people who will be invited to drink champagne with Mikhal Gorbachev to celebrate a "New Europe!" Instead they will be drinking cheap lagers and bad bocks in their beer halls in Berlin and Leipzig; but this does not mean that it may be safe to ignore them—after all, Adolf Hitler's rise to power began with a *Putsch* attempt organized in a beer hall in 1923.

Though it may sometimes masquerade as patriotism and nationalism, this violence really represents a kind of tribalism that has two important features in common. First, the people doing it seem to gain a feeling of strength by preying on persons who are "different" and preferably weaker than they are. The young thugs who seemed to "spring from the paving stones" of German cities in the early 1990s and resembled Hitler's Brown shirts, Martha Gellhorn wrote scornfully, "attacked, in the accepted style, the helpless and the weak: refugees. Not Turkish men, who are tough and know how to defend themselves"(208). This kind of violence began with attacks on individuals or small groups of refugees, escalated to attacks on refugee hostels by mobs of stone-throwing right-wing youths shouting, "*Ausländer raus!*" ("Foreigners Out!"), and were sometimes tacitly tolerated by the German police. These attacks escalated even further to attacks with Molotov cocktails against refugee hostels in the summer and fall of 1992— until three Turkish women in the North German town of Mölln were burned alive in their own home in November 1992 by Neo-Nazi skinheads who deliberately threw their Molotov cocktails so that the house's doors would be blocked. This event gave Germany so much bad publicity that the police finally began to enforce their nation's laws more strenuously and make more arrests (Hasselbach 48, 53. Grass 100).

In *Trainspotting*, Renton says he hates people "like Begbie … that are intae baseball-batting every fucker that's different: pakis [Pakistanis], poofs [homosexuals], n what huv ye" (78), and in two episodes from his novel Welsh shows the same combination of racism and cowardice that Gellhorn emphasized in her condemnation of Germany's "young thugs." In the first of these scenes, a minor character, Stevie, goes to a soccer game between the Hibbies (Hibernians) and the Hearts (of Midlothian) before meeting his girl friend at a train station. The Hibs are considered Edinburgh's "Catholic" team, because many of their fans are Irish immigrants, and the Hearts are the town's Protestant team. Loyalty to these tribal/religious values is shown by the color of one's scarf: Green and white for the Hibs fans, red for the Hearts. As he nears the station walking alone, Stevie meets a band of Hearts fans who see his scarf and begin taunting and attacking him. But Stevie is, after all, a sturdy young Scots male who might fight back, and so the Hearts turn their attention to abusing an Asian woman and her two small children.

—Fuckin Paki slag [bastard]!

—Fuck off back tae yir ain country.

They made a chorus of ape noises and gestures as they left the station. (49–50)

Stevie tries to sympathize with the Asian woman until he realizes that she is almost as frightened of him as she was of the Hearts fans: "She saw another white youth with slurred speech, bleeding and smelling of alcohol. Above all, she saw another football scarf, like the one worn by the youths who abused her. There was no colour difference as far as she was concerned [between a green or a red scarf], and she was probably right" (50).

In another incident in the novel, Spud recounts an incident involving his uncle Dode. Spud's grandmother had many husbands and lovers, and Dode's father was a West Indian sailor. ("There's a strong tea-leaf tradition in ma family, likesay," Spud acknowledges [124].) In a pub where Dode and Spud are having a friendly pint, they encounter a mixed gang of Ulstermen and skinheads who begin taunting them, first by singing, "Ain't no black in the union jack," and calling Dode "nigger" (128). Someone in the pub says that the gang is not "real Orangemen, thir Nazis n that," but the Ulstermen are encouraging the skinheads, and Dode and Spud are heavily outnumbered. Dode, who is no coward, returns his enemy's insults in kind:

—Fuck you, Dode sneers. It's a route the cat's travelled down before.... They aw start singing:—You black bastard! You black bastard!" (128) until Dode retaliates by attacking one of the skinheads. In the melee that follows Dode and Spud are rescued by Billy Renton and his father who happen to be in the same pub, but Dode is stabbed and ends up in the hospital. After he's been "patched up," Spud tries to console him, but Dode replies that

—S awright .... Ah've hud a loat worse n the past, and ah'll have a loat worse in the future.

—Dinnae [don't] say that man. Dinnae say that, ken?

He looks at us like ah'll never really understand, n ah ken that he's probably right. (129)

The fact that Dode's tormentors in this scene are described as "Nazis" suggests the disturbing possibility that even in places like Scotland, as well as in Germany, some parts of the population may not be heading toward a "New Europe," as so many people assumed in the late 1980s, but rather that they may be trying to return to the old Europe of the 1930s by mimicking the fascist mentality and behavior that was supposedly demolished by World War Two. Though the actual political support that overtly neo-fascist or neo-Nazi political groups receive at the polls may be minuscule in Germany and non-existent in Scotland, this fact is small comfort to any Black people, Asian immigrants, or unwary homosexuals who get in the way of rampaging skinheads or drunken Scots soccer fans.

As *Granta*'s "KRAUTS!" reveals this wish to return to fascism is explicit in Germany. As shocked German and foreign journalists reported in the early 1990s, Neo-Nazis and skinheads were painting their swastika graffiti by night (since such emblems are illegal) and by day they were wearing t-shirts and flaunting banners with nationalistic emblems like the older imperial German eagle. The violence and extreme right-wing politics of these young men, Grass commented sardonically in Granta, made "those assurances of [the] unification- happy days" seem hollow. For just as the newspapers were trumpeting "the end of the post-war era" and the "beginning of a new chapter in our history ... the past has tapped us on the shoulder" (100–1). One of the heavier ironies in the Granta interview with the skinhead, who was accosted by his mother while throwing rocks at a refugee hostel, occurs when the mother complains that when she and her family visited countries like Poland, Czechoslovakia, and Hungary, people would shout, "Nazis go home!" and that this was unfair, because "They should let bygones be bygones. Can't they let us forget that we lost the war?" and the boy's father agrees with her, because "it's history" (Mehr, Sylvester 138). But then a few minutes later their son reminds the reader of one of the reasons why Germans *began* the war. "The German territories in the east should be returned," he says,"… The Poles have settled on our patch…. Once Germany's re-established we can develop the eastern territories. Then we'd be a bigger country" (141). Suddenly, as Grass says, "the past has tapped us on the shoulder," since the young skinhead is repeating exactly the same demand for *Lebensraum* that the Nazis used to justify invading Poland and other nations at the beginning of World War Two. Suddenly what the boy's father had dismissed as "history" has returned to haunt them. In fact, the Neo-Nazis themselves have flaunted their relationship to the darkest days of Germany's past by adopting, as one of their favorite slogans, "*Wir sind wieder da*!" ("We're back!"), as if they want to assure foreigners and their nervous fellow Germans that they are the same Brown Shirts who terrorized first their own nation and then the rest of Europe in the 1930s and the 1940s (See Hasselbach 47).

In Welsh's *Trainspotting*, this identification of the characters' violence with fascism is made metaphorically and more obliquely through the nickname Welsh has given to the most violent character in the novel, Francis Begbie. Begbie could be called Frank or Frankie, but instead his mates have chosen to call him "Franco," presumably in honor of Europe's most successful and long-lived fascist dictator. In one passage in the novel, Renton refers to Begbie as "General Franco," and Spud often calls him both "Franco" and even "Generalissimo Franco" (156). Like the other characters in *Trainspotting* (with the partial exception of Renton), Begbie has virtually no political awareness, but in one passage he reacts to the sight of Renton reading a book with a chilling recapitulation of the kind of ferocious anti-intellectualism that characterized many 1930s fascists: "See if it wis up tae me, ah'd git ivray fuckin book n pit thum on a great big fuckin pile and burn the fuckin loat. Aw books ur fir is fir smart cunts tae show oaf aboot how much shite thuv fuckin read.... Ah'll gie them fuckin books ..." (116). In the rather unlikely event that Scotland or England ever did have a political movement like the ones led by a General Franco, a Mussolini, or a Hitler, the novel implies, Begbie would be an eager recruit—not because his personal politics are particularly right-wing, but because such a movement would give him the opportunities he craves to bash heads and burn books.

Conclusion

When the waning years of the Cold War are reconsidered in the contexts established by these texts, the 1980s no longer seem like the prelude to a millenarian future in which all of Europe will become happy, virtuous, and enjoy "perfect government." Instead those years can be considered more of a distraction in two ways. First, they enabled Europeans to ignore or underestimate many of the early warnings and significance of the pathologies described in this essay. Drug abuse and youth violence (like Begbie's) were serious problems in the United Kingdom well before *Trainspotting* was published in 1993, and skinheads and Neo-Nazis had begun to flourish and to attack immigrants in the German Federal Republic before their ranks were swelled by enthusiastic recruits from the former GDR. But the significance of these problems could be ignored or underestimated because it was so easy for the media, politicians, and intellectuals to focus their fears and criticisms on the bad things like martial law that were happening in places like Poland or on the exciting events that were taking place in the Soviet Union during Gorbachev's regime. Second, the 1980s were also a distraction because they made Europeans far too optimistic about capitalism and democracy— made free markets and free elections seem panaceas for their continent's problems merely because they were the opposites of soviet-style socialism and repression. Capitalism, freed from any sense of responsibility for the welfare of the nations and communities in which it now flourishes, produces the kind of "superfluous" people that Enzensberger and Welsh described: young people too alienated from mainstream society and its values to be employable in the kinds of menial jobs that are available for them in a "global" economy. Democracy, unattached to any serious commitment to the values of a genuinely civil society, can degenerate into the freedom to get high as long as one does not get caught by the DS (Drug Squad) or to bash immigrants and Black people after soccer games. Or democracy can degenerate into the virulent tribal politics of the German skinheads and Neo-Nazis whose definitions of a "political action" include throwing rocks and Molotov cocktails at refugee hostels.

Thus, as these texts show, in the early 1990s Europe's intellectuals, journalists, and politicians, as well as its ordinary citizens, had scarcely finished celebrating the fall of communism before they were forced to relinquish the millenarian "triumphalism" that accompanied that celebration. Now as the 1990s end and they approach the millennium, they must confront the kinds of problems and dangers that are described in Irvine Welsh's fiction and *Granta*'s journalism, and this will be difficult since these are problems, threats, and dangers that are endemic to Europe's own past and recent history—not ones that were imposed on them like the Berlin Wall or aimed at them by outsiders like Brezhnev's rockets were during the Cold War.

Notes

[1] *Webster's Third New International Dictionary* (1986). The main source for these optimistic visions of the millennium is the Bible: Rev. 20, but also see Mat. 24.

[2] Lewis 28. See also Kite, 115–24. For similar or analogous developments in Scotland, see Harvie 34, 159–60.

[3] Heavy drug dependency may be a recent development in Scotland, but alcoholism is not. According to Harvie (156), Scots spending on alcohol per capita was only 89% of the UK level in 1955, but by 1970 Scots were spending 9% more than other residents of the UK on alcohol. A 1975 Report had recommended longer pub hours on the grounds that "drink could now become a civilized accompaniment to life"; however, "by then there [already] were doubts. Scots alcoholism ran at five times the UK rate; the Scots late-night reveller or football [soccer] supporter was scarcely a civilized accompaniment to anything; the connection of alcohol with violence, vandalism, and road accidents was all too clear… drink took a frightening toll, until it seemed almost a collective escape from the grim and stressful present, like the similar behavior of old European industrial areas when confronted in the nineteenth century with their own obsolescence."

Works Cited

Berlin, Isiah. "The State of Europe." *Granta* 30 (1990): 148–50.

Enzensberger, Hans Magnus. "The Great Migration." *Granta* 42 (1992): 15–54.

Gellhorn, Martha. "Ohne Mich: Why I shall never return to Germany." *Granta* 42 (1992): 199–208.

Grass, Günter. "Losses." *Granta* 42 (1992): 95–108.

Harvie, Christopher. *No Gods and Precious Few Heroes: Scotland 1914–1980.* Toronto: U of Toronto P, 1981.

Hasselbach, Ingo, and Tom Reiss. "How Nazis are Made." *New Yorker* 8 Jan. 1996: 36–57.

Hodge, John. *Trainspotting: A Screenplay*. New York: Hyperion, 1996.

Kite, Ulla. "Political, Economic, and Social Changes and Developments since Unification." *German Monitor: Germany in the 1990s*. Ed. H.J. Hahn. Amsterdam, Atlanta: Rodopi, 1995: 115–124.

Lewis, Rand. *The Neo-Nazis and German Unification*. London, Westport: Praeger, 1996.

Mehr, Max, and Regine Sylvester. "The Stone-thrower from Eisenhuttenstadt." *Granta* 42 (1992): 133–44.

O'Toole, Fintran. "Imagining Scotland." *Granta* 56 (1996): 59–76.

Spender, Stephen. "The State of Europe." *Granta* 30 (1990): 168–70.

Welsh, Irvine. *Trainspotting*. London: Secker and Warburg, 1993; New York: W.W. Norton, 1996.

European Postmodernist Influences on British Figurative Painting

Peter McCarthy

Postmodernism was marked in the area of Painting by a return to figuration as the preferred mode of expression. A new type of expressionism started to be seen in Europe that had its roots within Modernism but that differed fundamentally from the US based formalistic abstraction of late Modernism. This new type of figuration was seen by some curators and critics as representing an opportunity to reestablish European dominance in Painting since it championed practices of figuration that had always been strong in Europe even during the heyday of Modernism. This essay will examine the assumptions that underlie the relationship between the European figurative survivors of Modernism and some British figurative innovators who are working in the wake of Postmodernism. By discussing examples of artists' work represented in three hallmark exhibitions I will compare the differing ideologies and terms of reference of these merging streams and will attempt to identify the forces that are beginning to pull them apart.

The full impact of postmodernism on the practice of painting was not felt in Britain until in 1981 the Royal Academy mounted its milestone exhibition *A New Spirit in Painting*. The exhibition had a clear purpose, never admitted in the catalogue but understood fully elsewhere, which was to restore painting to its customary position at the forefront of contemporary art practice. The Royal Academy is a deeply conservative Institution. It has never been comfortable with the ephemeral nature of contemporary art practice. In the seventies its chief discomfiture seemed to stem from the difficulty, shared by many other art institutions, of establishing a yardstick for measuring the quality of the abstruse practices of the then avant-garde. Beuys and Duchamp could be seen clearly as precursors of the type of esoteric informalism that was in vogue then as now, but their strategic dependence on irony and negation seemed to debar their practice from any role that it might otherwise have had as a defining tendency. The Academy was only too eager therefore to champion the revival of interest in painting and to bring this resurgence of interest to the attention of the British Public at the earliest opportunity.

The exhibition set out to establish Europe as the center for the revival of figurative Painting within a postmodernist context. Of the thirty-eight artists in the exhibition twenty-eight were European. The ten American artists were all household names, the likes of Warhol, De Kooning, Stella, Guston etc., but many of the Europeans were anything but familiar. The exhibition served to promote them through association with these distinguished and uncontroversial American contemporary masters. There was a disingenuous refusal to acknowledge discrepancies in the approaches to figuration that had been identified by the organizers as incontrovertibly new. In the altogether inadequate introduction to the catalogue Frank Auerbach's work for instance was placed, along with Anselm Kiefer's, in a context that also embraced the figurative excursions of Malcolm Morley and the gaudy generalities of David Hockney.[1]

Useful comparisons between the work of different artists could have been made but the catalogue ignored altogether the discrepancy between the modernist roots and credentials of the older artists and the much broader postmodernist tendencies of the newly emerging ones, seeing instead their figurative commonality as a sufficient basis for their inclusion under the show's thematic umbrella. The catalogue went on to offer the conjecture that Auerbach must have been deeply impressed with Bacon and De Kooning.[2] This truism evades the deeper question of why Auerbach stayed loyal to the tradition of working from observation whilst admiring the work of two artists who clearly did not. Auerbach was in fact virtually alone among the thirty or so exhibitors in working from observation. Improvising an image of the subject through independent means from within the process itself seemed to be the more favored approach and one that fitted more easily into the liberal framework of postmodernism.

Auerbach exhibited no desire to escape from the constraints of observational discipline — and this in spite of an emphasis on process that was so extreme as to be justifiable only within the parameters of expressionism. He demonstrated instead a romantic belief in the observational link as the only way of achieving the authenticity that his mentor David Bomberg referred to as the "spirit in the mass." It is more rewarding to think of the gestural nature of this manifestation as coincidental with abstract expressionism rather than derivative of its familiar stylistic signature. In classic abstract expressionism the gesture was used as a formal device to liberate the artist from the more utilitarian aspects of image-making so as to freely express the psyche. Auerbach's extravagant worrying of the surface is used for the opposite purpose. It is a procedure that seeks to focus on the subject with such observational intensity as to unlock the inner meaning. In so far as it maintains the integrity of this approach it is traditional, but in so far as it emotionally charges the procedure it is entirely modern in its strategy and radical in its effect.

Neither Bacon, nor Auerbach, nor De Kooning can be said to have gone on from this exhibition to achieve greater things, but Lucien Freud, the other figurative master included in the Show, certainly did. Like Auerbach he was fiercely loyal to the observational tradition of figurative painting. His approach is liberated by modernism only to the extent that the surface becomes fractured and textured in a self-conscious manner. Otherwise Freud does the same thing over and over again. Unlike Auerbach however, who would make the same claim, this is within an observational framework that is at odds with the experimental nature of modernism.

According to Lawrence Gowing "...Trying to do the same thing must have meant determining on the enduring sense of painting, deciding that painting should always be in its entirety and in every part identified as something physical and alive without the slightest doubt or escape, to the exclusion of non-sense, the cherished airs and graces and the concomitant mumbo-jumbo."[3] The note of approval that is struck here for the enduring sense of what painting should be about, of what is in other words of central concern to the activity, represents a deeply conservative position. It is one that might have been more difficult to maintain before the New Spirit show than afterwards. But even then the self-righteous tone of this passage is at odds with the many contradictory definitions of true purpose that were represented by the other exhibitors. It was round about this time that the word pluralism began to appear in the art-press as a way of embracing the plethora of activity that was going on. Pluralism however implies tolerance, liberalism, and diversity. Gowing's much narrower position is one that has been associated with English figurative painting particularly through the Slade School of Fine Art. It values exactitude in the exercise of powers of observation, control in the demonstration of skills of representation, and accountability in the pursuit of authentic statement, and seems to distrust all else.

Gowing's assertion that sense had triumphed over nonsense, and that the natural order of things had been restored after the alienating influence of modernism, is not supportable. Lucien Freud's stylistic reference point is only coincidental with figuration's traditional alignment with the real world. It represents instead a deliberate act of defiance in the face of a narrow cultural imperative. Much has been made of the care that Freud takes in choosing his subjects. This and his habit of concentrating on the fleshiness of his nude sitters is seen as the defining characteristic of his work — his postmodernist foible one might even say, but this would be wrong. Anselm Kiefer or Gerhardt Richter are much more typically postmodern in that they exploit the freedoms that postmodernism allows. They use the deconstructed framework of modernist obsessions and procedures to their own advantage. Their use of figurative conventions matured and blossomed in the context of postmodernism, where borrowing and ironic reference were valued as creative strategies. Lucien Freud's work on the other hand grew and blossomed in isolated circumstances that eschewed both modernism and postmodernism. In spite of this isolation the work steadily improved after 1982 when Gowing wrote the eulogizing text for his monograph. The audience for his work also grew exponentially, not because he held to truer values, but because post-modernist liberalism allowed a revisitation and re- evaluation of the nature of his obsession without the need to seek a modernist purpose. His use of a familiar paradigm no longer required polemic justification but could be seen instead as the exercise of the right to define painting in whatever way one might choose. That this definition might be at odds with the figurative mainstream was seen as a virtue rather than a disadvantage. This blossoming mainstream was in any case otherwise well represented in the show.

Two of its greatest exponents Kiefer and Richter both appeared in *A New Spirit in Painting*, but Richter was inexplicably excluded from the much larger and more influential show *Zeitgeist* that was mounted in Berlin in the subsequent year under virtually the same curatorship.[4] More significantly however and more understandably in view of Nicholas Serota's lack of involvement in the second show, all the British "old masters" and Picasso, De Kooning, Guston, Brice Marden and Matta were also excluded. This culling of some of the greatest names in painting who were active at the time denuded the exhibition of its weightier participants, but it made for a much more focused and didactic exhibition that concentrated on the work of artists that had already been named as Neo-Expressionists. In his catalogue essay Hilton Kramer claims that "Neo- Expressionism's first task was to restore to painting its capacity to encompass the kind of poetry and fantasy that had long been denied it, and toward that end it was obliged to mount an attack — sometimes it seemed literally — on the picture surface."[5] He qualifies this by saying "For a hundred years or more, the vitality of painting had seemed to depend on stripping it of its conventions and resources in order to isolate some irreducible core or essence. By placing itself in open opposition to this tendency the Neo- Expressionist movement did something more than offer itself as a new style. It put into question the very practice of identifying the vitality of art with this process of progressive degeneration."[6]

The newness implied in the title of the first exhibition which was compromised to some extent by the inclusion of artists who were anything but new, was therefore built into the very fabric of the second show and reinforced by the inclusion of such extremists as the German artist Salome, the American David Salle and the Italian Francesco Clemente. Salle has survived as the most significant and influential artist of this trio. His apparent indifference to the implicitly violent and sexually evocative nature of his imagery is matched only by his indifference to the aesthetics of pictorial organization and the traditional obligations of pictorial representation. Essential aspects of both modernist abstract painting and traditional figurative painting are virtually ignored as imagery is strewn across the picture plane in a mixture of random styles. (Gowing may well have had this type of painting in mind as an example of the non-sense that was in such contrast to Lucien Freud's good sense.) Much has been made of the cinematic and media origins of this strategy. His paintings seem to be in tune with the seamless web of visual information that we are subjected to through television commercials in particular. His isolation of random moments in this flow of information to create a "composition" is intrinsically arbitrary and the resultant object, because the paintings are invariably large, is palpably absurd when measured against modernist parameters.

There is however another aesthetic against which we might judge the work of the artists who were launched by *Zeitgeist* and *A New Spirit in Painting*. It is one that eschews elegance and abstract refinement in favor of a more anarchic engagement with the processes of painting. This extends as much to the choice of subject as it does to the style and method of application. The style is predominantly expressionistic with a vigor of application that gained some of its accelerated momentum from the influence of Abstract Expressionism. The roots of the style can be seen clearly in German Expressionism and the work of such French artists as Soutine and the Fauves, but the ingredient that was inherited from Abstract Expressionism was the all-important one of scale. Part of the reaction against the French Academy that motivated the Impressionists was a rejection of the vast scale of many of its otherwise vacuous prize-winning paintings. This rejection of scale as pompous and dishonest carried over into Post-Impressionism and German Expressionism. It was also an important consideration within modernism where the natural scale of the easel painting seemed to represent an appropriately modest means for exploring the new languages of painting. (Braque and Picasso's analytic cubist period for instance.) With the Abstract Expressionists large scale became an important ingredient once again. The objecthood of the canvas was seen as a significant extension of the legitimate concerns of abstraction. Non-referential art undoubtedly profited from the introduction of real scale as a tangible alternative to the mere illusion of scale.

With the Postmodernist figurative artists this is almost universally the case. The actuality of large scale abstraction is coopted into the service of a new form of figuration. One that is conscious of its ambitions but comfortable with its limitations. I mentioned Francis Bacon in relation to British figuration. Bacon was striving after scale at a time when it was not fashionable to do so within the figurative idiom. He achieved scale by employing the antiquated device of the tryptich and building his way towards it in order to maintain intensity. The sincerity of Bacon's struggles with the profoundest questions of human existence should not be doubted. His work has to be measured against it. It would be a mistake however to use the same yardstick to measure the work of the Postmodernist figurative expressionists. Clemente would like to pretend to be doing something as profound, but Salome's work should not be read in this way, even though it seems to express the same intensity of purpose. Salome's courting of decadence and triviality is no accident. An extravagance of scale is used to glorify the hedonism and decadence of the life-style that he represents on canvas. Large scale is common to nearly all the artists in the show where as Robert Rosenblum informs us in his essay, "eight of them will display (in the two-storeyed atrium) gigantic canvases, (3 x 4 meters) executed specifically for this space and this occasion. Such opportunities recall the heroic efforts made by both conservative and radical mid-19th-century artists to muster together their full strength in enormous paintings that were to arrest the attention of the visitor if only by sheer size."[7]

Scale has continued to be an important factor in the work of successive generations of figurative artists since the Zeitgeist show. The emerging generation of British figurative artists seen recently in the survey show *About Vision* at the Museum of Modern Art, Oxford, were generally represented by large works. The legacy of Zeitgeist however seemed to stop there. The recidivist aspects of postmodernist practice where quotation from historical sources could stretch back even to myth and the Bible has been replaced by more immediate references to junk culture. The unaffected nature of this imagery rules out any pretensions to the heroic or profound. Indeed this seems to be part of its appeal to this generation of artists. The self-conscious poetics and titanic struggles of that previous generation are neither valued nor imitated. Cynicism has replaced irony, with the sometimes audacious visual pun as the only discernible ingredient within the work. Angela Dimitrakaki points out in her review of the Show in Third Text that the catalogue introduction tries hard to justify this position by "advancing the legitimation of a user-friendly autonomy of painting, this time an autonomy based on a playful interaction among materials, aesthetic traditions and cultural codes."[8] She also characterizes the artists as "talking dirty in the museum"[9] which is no more than the familiar avant-garde ploy of shocking the bourgeoisie — except as she points out, the audience is no longer provoked and the artist no longer reprimanded.

Marcus Harvey's work is the most blatant example in the exhibition of this strategy at work. Sarah Kent writing in the Saatchi Collection catalogue says of this artist — "Marcus Harvey manages to have his cake and eat it. On the one hand, his paintings are an orgy of unrestrained sensuality, on the other, an indirect indictment of the illustrious history of the nude. His polymorphous perversity of infancy, in which all tactile impulses are equal — his work equates eating, excreting, art-making and love-making — provokes some basic questions."[10] She goes on to claim that studies of the (female) nude have often carried a sexual undercurrent and that Harvey simply takes this to its logical conclusion. This can be justified by selective reference to particular paintings by particular artists. Her own example is the Rockeby Venus by Velasquez. Manet's Olympia is also often cited. More frequently however the nude figure was mannerist in its treatment. Both male and female nakedness was generally neutralized and idealized by its alignment with the classical origins of mythological subjects. As a result the pre-modern treatment of the nude was on the whole anodyne, safely located within a Health and Beauty context. In the twentieth century things have been different. The study of the nude has become self-conscious. Stripped of its mythical associations it has been exposed to post-Freudian scrutiny and conjecture. It has also had its context broadened by the proliferation of soft porn imagery which has never pretended to hide the specific nature of its interest in the female body. Harvey is drawing on this in a bold gesture that subverts the means of art production that one associates with abstract expressionism to yield the unlikely and slightly sordid image of the reader's naked wife. One is tempted to interpret this as a metaphor but one would be better advised to see it as an expression of attitude.[11] The word belongs to Brit-Pop culture and now permeates the ambitions and determines the styles, subjects, and working methods of this new generation of artists. Ephemerality, which is virtually the trade mark of Pop music, does not sit happily within a tradition where permanence has been built into the very means of production. The wild antics of the younger exhibitors of *Zeitgeist* could be brash and crude, but at least they had a serious purpose. They undoubtedly benefitted from the simple parameters that defined postmodernism. They were able to quote, they were able to make historical references, they were able to evoke subject matter that was challenging and that in other circumstances might have seemed pretentious. None of these strategies has survived in the intervening period. Although there is a refreshing iconoclasm about the new figuration, its disavowal of direct engagement will surely guarantee its impermanence and leave the door open for something truly new.

Conclusion

What this new trend or persuasion might be is more difficult to say. I have pointed out in the main text that implicit within modernist practice was the assumption of a type of succession that depended on invention. It was not in any sense a progression. The relationship with preceding styles tended instead to be antithetical and destructive. This combative approach has largely disappeared, but it has not been replaced with anything more stable. The retroactive aspects of postmodernism suited European artists and they took full advantage during the eighties. *A New Spirit in Painting* attempted to illustrate this. In the succeeding period Lucien Freud emerged as a key figure. I claim that this is not because of any radical shift in his style or subject matter but because of a shift of attitude in his audience. He is unmistakably traditional in his aspirations, his methodologies and his subject-matter, yet his work has contemporary appeal. The Postmodernists that surrounded him and whose strategies he ignored were not ashamed to take on subject matter that would have been invalid within both traditional and modernist practice. I try to show that a new iconoclasm has emerged subsequently, particularly in Britain where Damien Hirst's generation reject the refinements of postmodernist ideologies and theories, and favor instead a raw and brazen celebration of the artist's ego. In the final section of the paper, I contend that the future cannot lie this way, and that the great richness of the European tradition must surely be capable of delivering more.

Notes

[1] Christos M. Joachimedes, 1981, A New Spirit in Painting, Royal Academy of Arts, London. p. 16.

[2] ibid., p. 16.

[3] Laurence Gowing, 1982, Lucian Freud, Thames and Hudson, London. p. 132.

[4] The curators for A New Spirit in Painting were Christos M. Joachimedes, Norman Rosenthal, and Nicholas Serota. Zeitgeist was curated by Christos M. Joachimedes and Norman Rosenthal.

[5] Hilton Kramer, 1983, Signs of Passion, Zeitgeist, Weidenfeld and Nicholson, London. p. 17.

[6] ibid., p. 17.

[7] Robert Rosenblum, 1983, Thoughts on the Origins of "Zeitgeist." Zeitgeist, Weidenfeld and Nicholson, London. p. 11.

[8] Angela Dimitrakaki, 1997, About Di/vision/s, Third Text No 38 Spring 1997, p. 101.

[9] ibid., p. 99.

[10] Sarah Kent, 1994, Shark Infested Waters, the Saatchi Collection, Zwemmer, London, p. 33.

[11] for a fuller discussion of this issue see Angela Dimitrakaki, ibid., p. 103.

Cross-Cultural Understanding and Ethics

James R. Mensch

With the end of the cold war, ideological conflicts have faded. In their stead, we have witnessed the rise of cultural strife. On the borders of the great civilizations conflicts involving basic cultural values have arisen. These have given increased emphasis to the ethical imperative of cross-cultural understanding. How do we go about understanding different cultures? What are the grounds and premises of such understanding? How does such understanding tie into the basic ethical theories that have marked the West? The premise of this essay is that such understanding requires a new paradigm, one fundamentally different from that animating Western, scientific rationality. What is required is a rethinking of what constitutes our ethical selfhood. After proposing a concept of such selfhood, this essay shows that it is an implicit premise of Plato's, Kant's, Freud's, and Darwin's thoughts about ethics. It makes some practical suggestions for increasing cross- cultural understanding and then concludes with a brief description of the normative, ethical ideal of such understanding.

The Two Cultures: The Sciences and the Humanities

When we speak about cross-cultural understanding, we are at once confronted by two different types of understanding. They are exemplified by the sciences and the humanities. The understanding fostered by the sciences is global. Scientists all over the world share their results, collaborate, and make progress together. The universal understanding that science embodies thus crosses cultural boundaries without any difficulty. It is "cross-cultural" in the sense that it is a collective enterprise. It is open to anyone independent of his or her cultural background.

The reasons for this character are easy to specify. They stem in large part from the modern, scientific project of mathematizing nature. The project originally arose from skepticism regarding our senses. As Descartes observes, our sense perceptions are *not* given to us to provide accurate information about the inherent qualities of objects. Their purpose is our bodily preservation rather than truth. They are given, he writes, "only to indicate to my mind which objects are useful or harmful" (Descartes 1990, p. 79). To move beyond this pragmatic concern, we have to attend to the numerable aspects of what we perceive, that is to the bodies' extensions, sizes, weights, and so on. Grasping these, we apprehend what pertains to the objects in themselves. This grasp is, of course, an abstraction. Abstracting from the so-called "secondary qualities" of bodies, that is, their tastes, smells, colors, and so on, we abstract from those things given to us by nature for our preservation. This is also an abstraction from our embodiment, that is, from our physical selfhood as a sensing subject. Only the "I" of the "I think"—the "I" that grasps the primary, numerable qualities of bodies—is taken into account. This "I," Descartes assures us, can be considered apart from the body. The gain here is in the universality of our understanding. Since selfhood is reduced to the status of a disembodied, pure observer, each observer is substitutable for any other. Each can perform the same crucial experiments and observe the same results, since each limits himself to the selfhood that is a correlate of these abstract and measurable aspects of reality.

When we turn to the humanities, we find a very different view of the understanding. The focus of the humanities is on the qualia of nature, its sensed existence. Colors, tastes, sights, and sounds are all crucially important. A person's appearance can affect his role in history. A historian can legitimately ask, for example, about Joan of Arc: How charismatic was she? Did she have a penetrating voice and manner? How was she able, through her visions, to move both king and commoner? As these questions indicate, the focus here is on Joan's embodiment, both physical and cultural. It is on her embodied presence as it reflects a specific cultural environment.

With this, we have the question of how we grasp another culture. In the sciences, cross-cultural understanding is possible by virtue of an *abstraction* from specific national cultures. What is understood is, in fact, *not* culture, but rather what *transcends* its boundaries. No such abstraction, however, is possible in the humanities. If they abstract from culture and more generally from embodied selfhood, they lose their objects entirely. They must focus on such items. Given this, how is cross-cultural understanding possible for them?

Understanding as Embodiment

A good example of understanding in the humanities is provided by reading a foreign novel. Reading Kawabata's *The Sound of a Mountain*, a North American becomes immersed in the world of its chief character Shingo (Kawabata 1970). The skill and intensity of Kawabata's description is such that the reader identifies with Shingo, an older man living in a Tokyo suburb in the 1950s. The reader sees the world through his eyes, tastes what he tastes, feels the kimono he wears on his skin. All of this gives the peculiarity of humanistic understanding. At its most immediate and direct, it is a living *as* another by a living *in* the other. It is a sharing of the other's embodiment. It is "empathy" in the sense of *feeling* or experiencing *in* the other's body. To ask how cross-cultural understanding is possible is to ask how such empathy is possible. What is its basis?

Are there, as some suggest, "universal" features of mankind, features that make possible cross-cultural understanding? This cannot be true if "universal" means what is grasped through an abstraction from the particularities of our nature. The selfhood grasped by disregarding such particulars would be no different from the abstract disembodied one presupposed by the sciences. That the selfhood in question is not such is shown by the peculiar universality of cultural artifacts. These artifacts, like Kawabata's novel, work through their particularity. The more particular the understanding they manifest, the greater, often enough, is their appeal. It is not his sharing in universal features that makes Shingo appeal to us. It is rather his uniqueness, his rootedness in a particular culture and time.

What then is the basis for our understanding Shingo's particularity? If an appeal to universal or common features washes out the uniqueness that is the special object of cross-cultural understanding, to what should we appeal? How can our understanding work if it is denied its abstract universal objects? The dilemma, I believe, can only be resolved by broadening the notion of understanding. What is required is a shift in our paradigms. We must move from the scientific model of *understanding through observing and abstracting* to one of *understanding through embodying and particularizing*. A corresponding shift is required in the notion of the self that respects and tries to understand. The observing self distinguishes itself from its object, which it regards at a distance. In Descartes's scientific paradigm, this self is autonomous and disembodied. It grasps its objects, not through the senses but through the understanding that abstracts, counts, and measures. The embodying self, by contrast, understands through overcoming the distance between itself and its object. Its understanding is through its own states. Its paradigmatic mode of expression is not "I observe," as in "I observe heat," but rather "I am," as in "I am hot."

In a general sense, the condition for the possibility of this second type of understanding is the "transparency" of subjectivity. Rather than having any given features, the subject is transparent to such features. It lets them appear through itself. This may be expressed in term of Aristotle's position that "the actuality of the sensible object *qua* sensible is in the sensing subject" (*De Anima*, III, ii, 426a10). Each of our five senses provides examples of what he means: The actual taste is in the tongue, the actual odor is in the nose, and so on. By *act*ual is meant the *act*ing taste, odor, etc. Aristotle's corresponding term is *energeia*, signifying not just actuality, but also being-in-act, being-at-work. Thus, to say that the actuality of the odor is in the nose is to say that it is at work there. The nose manifests the odor's presence. It lets it appear through itself. The same holds for each of our senses. It also holds for our selfhood insofar as it is a sensing self. Such a self is the place of sensuous presence. *As such a place, it takes on its features from its environment.* The contents it manifests spring from the nature of the objects it perceives. Insofar as we judge and understand on the basis of what we perceive, the self that understands is also shaped by its environment. It becomes the place where its intelligible relations can be present, in Aristotle's words, the "place of the forms" that specify *this* environment (III, iv, 429a 27). These forms can be "universal" or common features; but they are such as features of a particular, sensuously embodied environment. Their basis is not abstraction, but rather embodiment.

The same point can be made in a contemporary, non-Aristotelian context, by noting the effect sexual difference has on the understanding. In the paradigm we are investigating, our first, most immediately shaping environment is the body. We experience the world in and through our bodies. Our bodily senses are the place of the world's sensuous presence. The nature of this presence shapes the self that experiences through embodying. Given this, the different bodies men and women have shape different selfhoods. This difference affects their self- understanding. Men and women can, of course, understand each other by abstracting from these bodily differences, which in any case are hardly total. But when they do so, they fail to grasp each other in their specificity. Men are not grasped as men, nor women as women. To actually grasp them as such is, of course, more complicated than crossing the biological, bodily divide of sex. Cultural considerations also come in. Different cultures have different interpretations of the body. They have different body images. These often affect the body as a place of presence, affecting the self-understanding that is based on this presence.

Yet in spite of this, a good novel does allow us to cross biological and cultural barriers. In particular, it shows that cultural empathy is possible. To hazard a definition of such empathy, I would say that the possibility a good novel realizes is that of myself as another. It symbolically presents through its prose the tastes, smells, textures, sounds, and sights of a different cultural environment. When I use my imagination to fulfill or make vivid the intentions given in its text, not just an environment is represented. As I imaginatively enter into the life of a character in the novel, my own subjectivity undergoes a doubling. In this, the novel represents the subject to itself as another by providing him with an alternate environment. In other words, the subject's transparency is such *that it can undergo a double shaping*. It is both itself, defined by its given environment, and it is another, insofar as it makes vivid this second environment. The identity that allows me to see myself as another is, thus, not based on an empty universalization. I do not abstract from the distinguishing features of the two selves to regard what is the same. Its basis is rather a self-transformation. It is a representing oneself as another by imaginatively placing oneself in the other's defining world. The same thing can happen when another person is actually present to me. Genuine empathy, in taking up the other's standpoint, enters into the other's environment. As such, it disrupts self-presence. It makes it dual by including the other.

The notion of this disruption is impossible on the paradigm that takes the self as an objective observer. Such a self never encounters another. As Merleau-Ponty remarks, "The existence of other people is a difficulty and an outrage for objective thought" (Merleau-Ponty 1967, p. 349). For such thought, they stand as objects. They appear over and against the observer, who distinguishes himself from them as an abstract subject, that is, as a disembodied self. There is, then, in Merleau-Ponty's words, "a contradictory operation" required for objective thought to grasp another. Confronting another person, "I ought to both distinguish him from myself, and therefore place him in the world of objects, *and* think of him as a consciousness, that is, the sort of being that has no outside and no parts…" (italics added). In other words, I have to conceive him both as an object and as a conscious subject like myself. But a consciousness that has "no outside" cannot be made objective.

A solution to this impasse is possible only by redefining what counts as a self. Selfhood must be taken as embodied. For Merleau-Ponty, the self's embodiment places it within the perceptual world, making it graspable by another self (p. 351). I would add that such embodiment also defines it. It gives it its sense as a unique place where the world that situates it can come to presence in all its sensory richness. So regarded, selfhood should not be thought as inhabiting a body as something placed in a box. On the level of what Aristotle called the "passive intellect," selfhood is particularized through its bodily senses. When it acts, its agency becomes personal by being situated (Sartre 1966, pp. 423, 428). This does not mean that its unity is given by its body taken as an objective physical structure. In the paradigm I am advancing, the self's agency does not flow from any *pregiven* unity. The self is not pregiven as a Cartesian "thinking substance." Still less can it be conceived as a Kantian "transcendental unity of apperception." Its unity is a function of its situating environment. This is why it can encounter another person by attuning itself in empathy to the other's situation.

Given that the self is defined by its situation, empathy always involves a certain self-disruption. It is not as if the distance between self and other is closed by a fusing of two distinct unities. One is rather overlaid on the other. There is, as I said, a certain doubling of selfhood. This doubling can be highly disturbing. The disruption it causes is part of the risk of genuinely encountering another. The attraction of abstract thought may well be tied to this. Engaging in this thought, we avoid such disruption. Situated by an environment composed of abstract, measurable quantities, our selfhood, as long as we engage in scientific pursuits, becomes a self like every other. Everyone, at least in theory, can replicate the experiments another scientist performs. Everyone can make the same observations. As a disembodied Cartesian spectator, we can, for a time, avoid the risks of encountering differently situated selves. There is, of course, a price to be paid. When we abstract from our embodiment, we abstract from the kind of situatedness that yields the duality of our self-presence. Remaining within the scientific attitude, we do not see the necessities imposed on us by our being shaped by others. Such necessities may determine our practice. They may be part of the life-world experience that make it possible. Yet, they escape our notice.

Selfhood and the Duality of Self-Presence

Since we have to live with others, the duality of self-presence is a fundamental phenomenological given. It follows from the situational character of the self. Encountering others, I am drawn out of myself. My situatedness and, hence, my selfhood, becomes overlaid with that of others. The result gives my self-presence its characteristic ambiguity. My self-presence is in part a function of my organic being. I am present to myself in my pleasures and pains. My agency is particularized by the appetites and fears that flow from my embodied state. Yet, because I do not live alone, I am always being resituated in terms of others. Functioning as both an organic and social being, I regard the world both from my own and others' standpoints. I take into account what is "true for me" and what is "true for others." Concretely regarded, such truths point to a task, that of arriving at agreements I can share with others. This happens whenever I attempt to mediate between my own self-knowledge and what others say about me. This mediation is actually a "negotiation" of my self-presence. In the back and forth that this term implies, I attempt to find an acceptable solution to often competing claims.

We should not think of such negotiation as involving self and others as given units. The ambiguity of self-presence is also that of the functioning self. Such a self maintains its unity through such negotiation. *It is its result rather than its cause.* Thus, the failure of the negotiation signifies its inability to function as whole both organically and socially. Given this, the primary task of the self is that of managing the dualities of self-presence involved in its being with others. It maintains itself as a functioning self through negotiating the differences involved.

This notion of selfhood is, I believe, implicit in much of Western thought about ethics. The object of the various ethical systems that have been proposed is not just that of sorting out the obligations one has to oneself and to others. It has to do with the presence underlying these obligations. Its goal is that of coming to terms with the duality of our self-presence. The systems are attempts to negotiate this duality. In this view, the answer to the question, "why be ethical?" concerns the selfhood that is the result of such negotiation. Being ethical is its preservation. The ultimate sanction of morality is that ethical failure involves its progressive loss. It results in the self's increasing inability to function both organically and socially.

A few examples will demonstrate this point. In Plato's *Gorgias*, the self that is defined by its bodily appetites appears in the person of Callicles. Socrates represents the self that is defined by reason. This is the self that is concerned with others As Socrates makes clear, what is at issue in their debate is Callicles's selfhood. Failure to engage in dialogue with Socrates means that Callicles "will remain at variance with himself his whole life long" (Plato 1971, p. 76). Limited to his appetites, he cannot acknowledge others. In fact, "he is incapable of social life" (p. 117). Kant takes up the same theme when he proposes his dichotomy of the intelligible and sensible worlds. Acting in terms of the intelligible world, I act according to my conception of others. I ask: "What would happen if everyone, in similar circumstances, engaged in what I am doing? Could everyone, for example, make false promises to get out of difficulties? Would such promises be believed?" Such thoughts do not occur to me insofar as I am a member of the sensible world. In Kant's words, "if I were solely a part of the world of sense, my actions would have to be taken as in complete conformity with the natural law of desires and inclinations" (Kant 1955, p. 453). I would act only according to my appetites. But

I belong to both worlds. I am both a rational and a sensing, desiring self. Because of this, I have the sense of ethical obligation. To cite Kant again, "when we think of ourselves as obligated, we consider ourselves as belonging to the world of sense and yet at the same time to the intelligible world" (p. 454). This duality of self-presence is responsible for the "ought." Working out the "ought" in a concrete situation is my negotiation between my self-presence as sensuously embodied and as a member of a rational community. The members of this community ask, "What would happen if others acted as I do." My ethical selfhood—the selfhood that experiences the "ought"—arises in the process of considering both perspectives. For Freud, this community of others becomes concrete in what he calls the "super ego." It includes the influence of our parents, of our "family, racial and national traditions handed on through them, as well as the demands of the immediate social milieu which they represent" (Freud 1969, p. 3). Opposing it is the "id"—the term that designates our instinctually based, bodily appetites. It is the task of the "ego" to balance the competing demands of id and superego. That this balance involves our very selfhood is clear from the neuroses Freud traces to its failure. A complete elimination of either the id or superego results in the self's collapse into psychosis.

Plato, Kant, and Freud, of course, are very different in the ethics they propose. Yet they all agree that we live in and through competing demands. We are embodied beings living with others. Both forms of self-presence have their imperatives. That such demands are real, that they touch us in our very selfhood, points to the fact that the duality they express is that of our own selfhood, our own self-presence. My point is that the attempt to negotiate this duality, in whatever form it appears, works out our concrete response to the ethical "ought." This response is our ethical action in its most immediate form.

Outsiders

The few examples I have given could be multiplied. Were I to extend this description and fill in its details, a phenomenological account of the history of ethics would arise. It would devote itself to describing how the different forms of ethical theorizing arise from the fundamental fact of the division in our self-presence. Rather than further engaging in this history, I would like to note a little regarded fact about the origins of ethics in the West. The initiators of the three major streams of Western ethical thinking, the Jewish, the Christian, and the Greek, were all outsiders. Moses, to whom we owe the Mosaic law, was a murderer. Having killed an Egyptian overseer, he fled to Midian. The people to whom he gives this law were themselves outsiders. As he frequently reminds the Jews, they were "strangers in a strange land" before he led them out of Egypt. Christ was also an outsider. Apparently an illegitimate child, he was associated with the least regarded elements of his society. Ultimately, he was crucified by the local religious and political authorities. For mediaeval philosophers his death recalled that of Socrates, who was also executed for not following the norms of his society.

Being outsiders, all three represented a disruption of the self-understanding of their milieu. As they came to prominence, their presence disrupted its self- presence. When, through their disciples they ultimately prevailed, their success added another dimension to this self-presence, one whose negotiation became an ongoing, culturally defining task. The nature of their accomplishment can be put in terms of the fact that the self maintains itself through an ongoing process of negotiation, one where it accommodates our different self-presences. Adding another dimension, they enriched this process. Both through their actual presence and their teachings, these figures made others present in a new way. The result was not just a new sense of the ought, a new tension between my embodied self and others. It was a richer sense of self. Phenomenologically, these figures were involved in our self-constitution. This follows because our ethical selfhood, experienced as the "ought," arises in the very process of this negotiation. As such, it is dependent on the duality of our self-presence. To eliminate the duality is to eliminate this selfhood. It is, in Freudian terms, to lapse into the psychosis that marks the victory of either the id or the super ego. As long as there is a duality, there is an ethical tension. There is also the negotiation between the competing presences that is ethics in its most concrete form. Given this dependence of our selfhood, ethics in this sense is constitutive of the functioning self and, thus, prior to it.

The Understanding of Other Cultures

How, then, do we go about understanding different cultures? Can we draw some practical answers from this analysis? Such answers require taking "culture" in a sense that is appropriate to the analysis. This means understanding it in terms of the mutual definition of self and environment. On the one hand, the self is the place where this environment comes to presence. As such, it is informed by its body as well as by the things and people it encounters. All of this, in defining the self, makes its agency personal. On the other hand, the action of the self shapes this environment. Thus, the self is not just informed by other persons, it also informs them. The same holds for the things that make up its physical milieu. It arranges and shapes them according to its needs. It does so through its body. Its body is both itself, being its most intimate, situating environment, and a means for its agency. At the latter, the body does not just determine the self. It is determined by it. Situated by its body, the self, as an agent, situates its body. It determines its bodily location in the world. The self, then, determines the environment that determines itself. This reciprocal determination of self and environment never occurs in isolation. Every self engages in it and, in so doing, affects the environments that situate its others and their agency. When selves determine environments, which in turn determine selves, there is no first cause, no set of final determinants. Since the resulting whole is not a systematic structure with clear principles or beginnings, it cannot be subjected to a foundational analysis. It has no independent ground or foundation outside of itself, which is to say that its "ground" or cause is nothing but itself. The whole, then, is simply a non-foundational, self-determining totality of actors, actions, things and events, each of which functions both as cause and caused. *Culture*, in the broad sense, *is this whole*. Viewed from the perspective of the selves that are its human component, a culture designates the ongoing relationships that determine a group in its selfhood. Such relationships can exhibit definite patterns. They can be conceptualized. But since the whole is non-foundational, these concepts cannot be deduced. They rather form a mutually defining set.

The consequence is that we have to participate in this whole in order to grasp its dynamics. Such participation is essential for understanding another culture. This means that the data that form the basis for the concepts of this understanding must be drawn from a first person experience of the particular "surrounding world" of a given culture. These concepts have their universality only as designating the common features of *this* world. In a certain sense, the understanding I am advocating is similar to that practiced by field anthropologists, who base their studies on the actual experience of living in a particular culture. Often, however, their work is undermined by their attachment, as social scientists, to a different paradigm. The result is the loss of the empathy that comes through the immersion in a given environment. Such empathy does not arise from the external analysis and observation that characterizes the foundationist paradigm of modern science. To describe a cultural environment objectively, i.e., to statistically describe and formulate the laws of its development, I must stand outside of it. I cannot be a situated participant. This, however, is precisely what is required for empathy. The paradigm for empathetic understanding is that of incarnation. Its basis is the experience of a particular world coming to presence in oneself. On the most basic level, this is an experience of how one's bodily being and functioning is particularized by a given world.

This paradigm is the opposite of that assumed by many states in their attempts to understand each other on an official level. Diplomatic services normally change diplomatic postings on a regular basis. They do so because they fear that a career diplomat will lose objectivity if the same remains in a country beyond a certain period. The paradigm of understanding underlying this practice is that of the detached observer. In rotating their diplomats, states attempt to prevent this detachment from being undermined. Behind this practice is the fact that relations between states are seen as involving external powers. This relationship demands an understanding that is external to the standpoint of the observed. This necessity may be put in terms of the normal use of state power, which is that of determining circumstances to suit its interest. Insofar as this interest is external, the understanding which serves it must maintain its detachment.

The misunderstandings which this attitude has fostered are present throughout the history of diplomatic relations. They are more or less inevitable as long as we equate culture and nation. The difficulty here is not just that nations may have divided cultures—as the Canadians do with their French and English speaking inhabitants—or that different nations may share the same basic culture. It is that, when we take culture and nation as equivalent, the understanding of different cultures occurs in the context of distinct nations with distinct interests and powers. As such, it involves the subordination of understanding to the power employed to advance these different national interests. Such subordination distorts our grasp of the otherness of the other. This follows because the determination of circumstances to suit an external power is, by definition, a limitation of such otherness. It is a limitation of what can appear through such circumstance. Thus, the employee reacts to the power of his supervisors by telling them what they want to hear. He or she appears in the role or persona demanded by the circumstances they have determined. Given the unequal powers of nations, the same sort of limitations are at work in their attempts to understand each other through their diplomatic representatives.

To apply the paradigm of respect and empathetic understanding to international relations, states would have to change the training of their diplomatic corps. Their education would have to include the practice of taking up the standpoint of a different culture by living like its inhabitants. Doing so, they would not be shielded by the importation of a lifestyle that generally accompanies a diplomatic mission. Rather than being representatives of a foreign power, they would enter into the environment that determines a cultural group in its specific selfhood. Having experienced both their own and another culture, they would be better equipped to provide the type of understanding and foster respect that state power obscures. Their experience of the disruption of self-presence that comes through being shaped by another culture would be particularly valuable in the negotiations between states of very different cultures. This is because they would already have experienced the general pattern of such negotiations within themselves. Their own self-presence would be a result of the balancing of the standpoints of their own and the foreign culture. The same experience would uniquely qualify them to deal with questions of immigration and asylum. Their serving in the responsible agencies would be a corrective to the powerlessness of the groups that form their clientele. In dealing with officials, the asylum seeker often has the feeling of being "invisible," of not being seen or understood in the particulars of his or her situation. One way to overcome this invisibility is through the empathetic understanding that comes from the official having lived in a different culture.

Conclusion

All of these suggestions may seem to be an unwelcome intrusion of ethics into politics. Since Machiavelli's time, their separation has been part of the *Staatsräson*, which views states only in terms of their interests. The European disasters that have followed from this amoral stance are well known. Reflecting on them, we have to ask whether or not morality itself should be included among the abiding interests of states. Currently, this is done through a certain emphasis on "human rights."

Often such rights are conceived in abstract, universal terms and are opposed to "economic rights," also conceived abstractly. In such debates, the self that is the subject of such rights is rarely examined. The purpose of this essay has been to raise the question of this self in terms of the presences that constitute it. Its suggestions are attempts to introduce ethics into politics on this basic level. Thus, their goal is not just a greater practical understanding. It is, in general, a richer sense of self, a more complex understanding of the others that underpin our self-presence. The consequence is a deeper sense of the ought, a greater depth to the ethical dimension of life. In fact, in their attempt to understand each other, different cultures may be seen as taking up an ethical stance. This is because the imperative of cross-cultural understanding is, at bottom, an ethical imperative. It is a call to the negotiation of differences, a negotiation that is the very process of our ethical selfhood.

To speak of normativity in this context is to consider the demands of such selfhood. Both within and across cultures, richness of self-presence may be taken as a normative, ethical ideal. Those actions and attitudes which diminish this presence count as a departure from this ideal. This includes every expression of power that forces the other into a limited role. Such expressions may be necessary for maintaining our current economic and social structures. Yet, to the point that they prevent the others from stepping out of the role assigned to their groups, they come at an ethical price. Limiting their presence, they limit our own. This follows because self-presence always involves others. As involving a *balance* between self and others, the ideal of richness of self-presence does not demand our being overwhelmed by others. It, rather, forbids an excessive focus on self or others, on one's own or on other cultures. It also forbids their collapse into an undifferentiated unity. In this, it respects the alterity that is implicit in empathy. This does not mean that in taking up another's standpoint, one cannot find it lacking. There are standpoints that are genuinely disbalanced. There are practices, both individual and national, that undermine selfhood. The judgment that they are such, however, is the prerogative of empathy. Only by our admitting others into our self-presence can we have the possibility of being admitted into theirs. Stepping out of the roles we assign to each other, there is the possibility of an encounter that can genuinely change our self-presence. This task is difficult and not without risks. It is, however, inherent in the back and forth of every successful negotiation, be it personal or between nations.

References

Aristotle (1964). De Anima (my own translation). Greek text taken from *On the Soul, Parva Naturalia, On Breath*, tr. W.S. Hett. Cambridge: Harvard University Press.

Darwin, C. (1967). The Descent of Man. In *The Origin of Species and the Descent of Man*. New York: Random House.

Descartes, R. (1990). *Meditations on First Philosophy*, tr. L. LaFleur. New York: Macmillan.

Freud, S. (1969). *An Outline of Psycho-Analysis*, tr. James Strachey. New York: W. W. Norton and Company.

Kant I. (1955). "Grundlegung zur Metaphysik der Sitten." in *Kants Gesammelte Schriften*, IV. Berlin: Georg Meiner.

Kawabata, Y. (1970). *The Sound of a Mountain*, tr. E.M. Seidensticker. New York: Perigee Books.

Merleau-Ponty, M. (1967). *Phenomenology of Perception*, tr. C. Smith. London: Routledge & Kegan Paul.

Plato. (1971). *Gorgias*, tr. W. Hamilton. London: Penguin Books.

Sartre, J.P. (1966). *Being and Nothingness*, tr. Hazel Barnes. New York: Washington Square Press.

The Practical Relationship of Consciousness and Performance: An Intercultural Approach

Daniel Meyer-Dinkgräfe

Several important European theater artists encountered experiences of desirable altered states of consciousness (ASC) in their practice. They conceptualized them in terms of bodies of knowledge at their disposal, and sought, unsuccessfully, to develop (training) techniques to systematically re-create such experiences. On the basis of the model of consciousness proposed by Vedic Psychology, the relation of theater and consciousness is reassessed, leading to hypotheses on the potential of this model for enabling transformative change of consciousness through theater practice.

Theater and Consciousness

Despite current emphasis on the importance of the body for theater performance, consciousness, although more elusive and intangible, is at least as important for any performance to take place and be successful. Just one example to demonstrate this: a few years ago I had the opportunity of interviewing British actor Timothy West, who has made a name over the last two decades or so with portrayals of historically well known characters, both on television and on stage, such as conductor Sir Thomas Beecham, politician Churchill, and, in David Pownall's *Master Class*, Stalin. During the interview West pointed out that for playing Stalin, he had watched a lot of film footage on him and had realized that one of Stalin's arms was paralyzed and how Stalin managed to hide that fact. To demonstrate, he took on the body posture which had been characteristic of his portrayal of Stalin in the production of *Master Class* a few years before my interview with West took place. Immediately the atmosphere of threat and menace so characteristic of the production was present in West's study. It is open to debate whether the body posture triggered the correlating mind set, parameters of consciousness, or whether the mental attitude led to the body posture. Beyond doubt, however, was that body posture alone could not have created this strong effect, West's *presence*.

The actor's presence is at the center of Eugenio Barba's theater anthropology. All his research originated from the question: "Why, when I see two actors doing the same thing, I get fascinated by one and not by the other."[1] Barba tends to focus his research on the body, because it is more tangible, but poetically talks about the third organ of the body of theater as "the irrational and secret temperature which renders our actions incandescent." It is "our personal destiny. If we don't have it, no one can teach it to us."[2] Barba's description almost suggests an altered, non-ordinary state of consciousness, which is an appropriate term to describe Grotowski's concept of *translumination*, in which the mind-body split is overcome: "the division between thought and feeling, body and soul, consciousness and the unconscious, seeing and instinct, sex and brain then disappear."[3] The actor in the state of translumination has achieved totality, "a certain quality of attention, or consciousness, characterized by a full presence in, and recognition of, the moment."[4] The actor who has attained this state is also free from "the time-lapse between inner impulse and outer reaction in such a way that the impulse is already an outer expression. Impulse and expression are concurrent."[5] On more traditional levels of understanding is the issue of the actor's emotional involvement with the feelings the character is supposed to be experiencing. Diderot suggested that the actor should maintain a distance from those emotions, should not get involved, should keenly observe behavior and reproduce its outward manifestations on stage during performance. Only in rehearsal was the actor allowed to identify with the character's emotions. Stanislavsky, on the other hand, clearly advocates the actor's emotional involvement, as deeply as possible, during each and every performance. However, Stanislavsky is aware of the danger of getting lost in the emotions. He seeks to provide psycho-techniques allowing the actor to intentionally access the level of the subconscious to gain access to stimulate deep emotions, and requires the actor to simultaneously watch over all those processes. A kind of dual consciousness is thus at the center of Stanislavsky's ideas. The ancient Indian treatise on drama and theater, the *Natyashastra* appears to be contradictory on the issue of the actor's emotional involvement: in one passage it first states that the actor needs full concentration, suggesting involvement, and a few lines later advises that the actor playing an angry character should not be angry him/herself, or that an actor playing a character who has to weep should not feel sad him/herself.

Many of the ideas about the relationship between theater and consciousness go back to direct experiences of theater artists which they found desirable for themselves and for others, and which they then tried to talk and write about. They also tried to re-create and if possible, systematize, such desirable experiences. In doing so, they went back to all the bodies and sets of knowledge at their disposal, freely combining, for example, concepts (for talking about) and techniques (for re-creating the experiences) found in psychology, psychoanalysis, and especially non-Western traditions of psycho-philosophy, theater aesthetics and meditation under the term of yoga. I have shown elsewhere in detail[6] that such fascinating aspects of the theater, all related to consciousness, require a cogent model of consciousness which can explain and account for the relationship of theater and consciousness. Such a model has been lacking in the theater artists' attempts to deal with their experiences and aspirations. The model of consciousness is based on traditional Indian philosophy, especially Samkhya, Yoga, and Vedanta systems. The model was originally conceptualized by Maharishi Mahesh Yogi as Vedic Psychology. Maharishi is a disciple of the late Swami Brahmananda Saraswati (1869–1953), who held the position of Shankaracharya of Jyotir Math for the last 13 years of his life. This one of four monasteries in India founded by the sage and philosopher Shankara to safeguard the tradition of his Advaita Vedanta philosophy. As Brahmananda Saraswati's disciple, Maharishi Mahesh Yogi is in the direct line of Shankara's Advaita Vedanta philosophy.

Vedic Psychology's Model of Consciousness

Vedic Psychology proposes "an architecture of increasingly abstract, functionally integrated faculties or levels of mind."[7] This hierarchy ranges from gross to subtle, from highly active to settled, from concrete to abstract, and from diversified to unified. The senses constitute the grossest, most highly active, most concrete and most diversified level of the mind, followed by desire, the thinking mind, the discriminating intellect, feeling and intuition, and the individual ego. Vedic psychology uses the term "mind" in two ways: "It refers to the overall multi-level functioning of consciousness as well as to the specific level of thinking (apprehending and comparing) within that overall structure." Underlying the subtlest level, that of the individual ego, and transcendental to it, is the Self, "an abstract, silent, completely unified field of consciousness." Each subtler level is able to "observe and monitor the more expressed levels."[8]

Vedic Psychology not only describes distinct levels of the mind, but also proposes higher stages of the development of consciousness, stages that go beyond the ordinary states of waking, dreaming, and sleeping. The development is characterized initially by glimpses of a simultaneity of experience of transcendental consciousness together with either waking, or dreaming, or sleeping. When transcendental consciousness is permanently experienced together with any of the other three, this state is called cosmic consciousness. Cosmic consciousness is followed by refined cosmic consciousness, characterized by the refinement of sensory perception. Finally, in unity consciousness, a person is able to perceive everything in terms of his own transcendental Self.[9]

Theater and Consciousness Reassessed

Vedic Psychology offers an opportunity to explain the actors' consciousness-related experiences from its model of the mind. Diderot's theory of the emotional stimulation of the spectators through an emotionally uninvolved actor is paradoxical on the level of an ordinary waking state of consciousness as described by Vedic Psychology. On this level of consciousness, the Self as the basis of the mind is not open to direct experience. It is overshadowed by the (sensory) objects of experience. The Self identifies with the objects of sensory perception, or with the emotions and feelings. In such a state, detachment from one's own experiences and actions is difficult, and ordinarily considered as undesirable. According to Vedic psychology, in the state of cosmic consciousness the Self is by definition experienced as separate from the manifest levels of the mind (ego, feelings, mind, intellect, senses). This liberated Self could be associated with Diderot's "disinterested onlooker" whom the actor must have in himself. The Self is fully developed in cosmic consciousness, and the actor's development towards that stage is characterized by his increasing ability to perform with growing realization of the Self. This growth will be experienced both in time quantity, as well as in quality, i.e., depth. Initially, the experience of "witnessing," characteristic of cosmic consciousness, will be experienced for short periods during a performance, the length of experience will increase, and ultimately the experience of the Self will be maintained throughout activity, no longer limited to acting on stage. Simultaneously, the functioning of the expressed levels of the mind will be improved, so that the actor can meet Diderot's demand for penetration, an intellectual quality. Moreover, the actor's ability to observe nature as a source for imitation will be enhanced by heightened sensory functioning.

The proposed solution to Diderot's paradox from the perspective of Vedic Psychology also applies to Stanislavsky. Whereas Diderot proposed unemotional acting stimulating emotions in the spectator, Stanislavsky described the actor's art of being both deeply emotionally involved while acting and yet in conscious control of acting through watching himself. Vedic Psychology would argue that the actor's deep emotional involvement is facilitated through the actor's development of consciousness. This development goes along with the growing ability to experience the Self as a witnessing agency of consciousness together with the witnessed objects of (sensory) perception, together, that is, with any activity.

Grotowski aims for a state of consciousness and body where the actor transcends incompleteness and the mind-body-split, where he achieves totality, full presence, where he becomes a *holy actor*. Such *translumination* is clearly an experience of not only cosmic consciousness, characterized by a separation of Self and activity, but an experience of unity consciousness as defined by Vedic psychology: knower and known are experienced as a unity, the striking duality of Self and expressed levels of consciousness, characteristic of cosmic consciousness, disappears. For the duration of the experience of cosmic consciousness or unity consciousness, all action, performative or other, is fully spontaneous, there is no longer a time-lapse between inner impulse and outer action. At the same time, all activity in those states of consciousness will be fully disciplined in the sense that there will be no entropy, no waste of energy, actions will lead to the intended result following the principle of least action. Barba's concept of *incoherent coherence* is thus rendered obsolete. The coexistence of spontaneity and discipline is characteristic of higher states of consciousness.

The Future Potential of Theater

The model of consciousness proposed by Vedic Psychology allows to explain and understand experiences by several major theater artists who have influenced theater practice world-wide. However, as indicated earlier, those theater artists fall short of systematically re-creating the desirable experiences of altered, higher states of consciousness in and through their theater practice. I would argue that it should be possible to develop systematic training and acting techniques appropriate for individual cultural conditions which allow the development of higher states of consciousness for those involved in theater, including, of course, the spectators. It will not be helpful to merely try to go back in time and history to what we may assume some earlier cultures, such as the ancient Vedic culture, in whose oral tradition the *Natyashastra* has its origin, to have achieved already. We can understand the *Natyashastra* both as a description of what a performer who has reached at least a level of cosmic consciousness will automatically, spontaneously do to create specific effects in a given audience, and as a manual of how to achieve such higher states in the first place (the combinations of physical movements serving as techniques to allow the mind to develop such higher states). It should be possible to adapt the material and the techniques provided in the *Natyashastra* to our present time, and add whatever else is suitable for the purpose from the vast reservoir of meditation techniques, breathing techniques and other techniques for the development of consciousness available in India. To avoid the kind of eclecticism characteristic of Grotowski or Barba and many other theater artists who are currently attracted to non-Western theater aesthetics, it will be necessary to have constant input in the debate from experts not only in Indian performing arts, but also from experts in the development of consciousness, Vedic masters, such as Maharishi Mahesh Yogi, or Shri Shri Ravi Shankar, people who not only talk about higher states of consciousness but live them, and know which of the available techniques and methods will be suitable for the specific purpose of developing higher states of consciousness through theater.

Conclusion

The model of consciousness proposed by Vedic Psychology is able to cogently explain various experiences of desirable altered states of consciousness described by various European theater artists. The model also allows to develop plausible and testable hypotheses as to the systematic re-creation of those initial experiences in performers and spectators.

Notes

[1] Eugenio Barba, "Interview with Gautam Dasgupta," *Performing Arts Journal* January 1985, 10.

[2] Eugenio Barba, "The Way of Refusal: the Theater's Body-in-Life." *NTQ* 4,16 (1988): 291.

[3] Jennifer Kumiega, *The Theater of Grotowski.* (London, New York: Methuen, 1977), 128–29.

[4] Kumiega, 139.

[5] Jerzy Grotowski, J. *Towards a Poor Theater*, ed. Eugenio Barba with a preface by Peter Brook (London: Methuen, 1969, 16).

[6] Daniel Meyer-Dinkgräfe, *Consciousness and the Actor: A Reassessment of Western and Indian Approaches to the Actor's Emotional Involvement from the Perspective of Vedic Psychology*. (Frankfurt/Main: Peter Lang, 1996).

[7] Charles N. Alexander et al., "Growth of Higher Stages of Consciousness: Maharishi's Vedic Psychology of Human Development," in C.N. Alexander, and Ellen J. Langer (eds.) *Higher Stages of Human Development. Perspectives on Human Growth*. New York, Oxford: Oxford University Press, 1990), 290.

[8] Charles N. Alexander, et al., "Transcendental Consciousness: A Fourth State of Consciousness beyond Sleep, Dream, and Waking," in J. Gackenbach, (ed.), *Sleep and Dream. A Sourcebook*. (New York, London: Garland, 1986), 291.

[9] Charles N. Alexander et al., "Growth of Higher Stages of Consciousness: Maharishi's Vedic Psychology of Human Development," in C.N. Alexander, and Ellen J. Langer (eds.) *Higher Stages of Human Development. Perspectives on Human Growth* (New York, Oxford: Oxford University Press, 1990), 290.

Nietzsche's Vision of Europe: On the Thousand and One Goal(s)

Uschi Nussbaumer-Benz

In this article, I would like to demonstrate that Nietzsche's insights into the cultural and political processes of his time have not yet been fully understood, and that his texts provide us with new perspectives in respect to Europe's classical heritage. In the course of European unification these insights could help us avoid getting trapped once again in the life-denying cultural and political systems that our century has already experienced to excess.

"Von tausend und Einem Ziele." (on the thousand and one goal[s]): this is the title of a subchapter in the first part of Nietzsche's *Thus Spoke Zarathustra*. "Thousand" stands for the variety of countries and peoples that all had once created their own values, virtues, and vices to preserve and to distinguish themselves from their neighbors. First, so we are told, the peoples were the creators, and only later individuals - the individual himself being the most recent creation. Only the one goal of humanity, the "yoke for the thousand necks," is lacking up to now, says Zarathustra harshly. The English translations of this title in the editions of both Oscar Levy and Walter Kaufmann use the word "goal" in the plural: they speak of "the Thousand and One Goals," which reminds us, like the German version, of those famous exotic tales, *A Thousand and One Arabian Nights*. But unlike the German version, the English title with "goals" unambiguously plural does not reflect the implied relationship between the many and the — potentially — one.

In 1884, having completed the first three parts of *Zarathustra*, Nietzsche expected that in about fifty years time, i.e. in the 1930s, some people would become aware of what his writings had accomplished, namely that they had paved the way for mankind towards a new synthesis. According to Nietzsche, the "good Europeans" walking ahead, having already realized that Europe wished to become united and that a Herculean task awaited them.[1]

Having recognized early on what was happening during his lifetime, Nietzsche presents Zarathustra (Part II) as startled at the sight he perceives in the mirror: his teachings have already been perverted. On the one hand, Nietzsche clearly dissociated himself from the kind of heroism fostered, among others, by the well-known historian and Nietzsche's antipode, Wilamowitz. In conformity with the German *Reich*, Wilamowitz perceived the hero Hercules as a symbol of a "Gospel of actions," allegedly characterized by Christian modesty; Wilamowitz's conception of heroism thus combined the qualities of a Greek hero and Jesus. Even worse for Nietzsche was the fact that Richard Wagner, who had moved from

Tribschen in Switzerland to Bayreuth, seemed increasingly to value the age-old metaphysical or even esoterical concept of the *Reich*. To this concept Wagner added a special note, not only with his compositions, *Parzifal* and the *Ring of the Nibelungen*, but with his own version of Buddhism. His uncompleted music drama, *Die Sieger* (The Victorious), was to have presented Gautama, the Buddha, on stage! In 1885, after the completion of the fourth and last part of *Zarathustra* and under the impact of what was going on in Germany, Nietzsche revised his original expectation: It would not take fifty, but a hundred years before he and his work would be properly understood. Perhaps we need to recalculate this number today…

There is strong evidence that Nietzsche knew a lot more about the metaphysical or esoterical ideas behind the conception of the *Reich*[2] than we have known up to now. He most certainly learned through classical texts about age-old concepts concerning the progression of time through the astronomical/astrological constellations.[3] Indeed, several allusions to this subject matter can be found in Nietzsche's texts. Probably the most obvious one, previously overlooked by academic Nietzsche specialists, is to be found in one of his *Dionysos Dithyrambs*: "Ich sehe ein Zeichen -,/ aus fernsten Fernen/ sinkt langsam funkelnd ein Sternbild gegen mich…/ Höchstes Gestirn des Seins!/ Ewiger Bildwerke Tafel!/ *Du* kommst zu mir?/ Was keiner erschaut hat, deine stumme Schönheit, -/ wie? sie flieht vor meinen Blicken nicht?"[4]

As far as the Herculean task of unifying Europe is concerned, Nietzsche introduces his perception with the following words: "I find pleasure in hearing that our sun is moving quickly towards the constellation called *Heracles* [= Hercules]:" he adds that he hopes that men upon this planet will equal, that is to say, live up to the sun in this respect. In 1783, the former military musician, Friedrich Wilhelm Herschel (1738–1822), stated that our sun is moving together with its planets through space in the direction of the constellation called Hercules; two years earlier, in March 1781, Herschel had discovered Uranus - the planet that is assigned to the constellation of Aquarius.[5]

In fact, in the light of the newly translated and published historical sources of his time, Nietzsche transvaluates the still virulent (but not well known) archetypical myth of a thousand brilliantly glittering lights. This myth was presented by Dante in the *Divine Comedy* and taken up in the conception of the *Reich*. It is shared by our traditional "yoke," namely by the three major monotheistic or monologic cultures that accord priority to unity and have been decisive for the destiny of Europe, and not only of Europe.

In his concept of world rulership Hitler combined Wagnerian ideas with the sacral world emperorship of the Hohenstaufer Friedrich II: the concept of the Kingdom of David was understood as an empire of peace and justice, which embodied Jewish eschatological and Oriental Islamic ideas. This archetype of the sacral world ruler can also be found in Dante's *De Monarchia* as well as in Buddhism in the Sanscrit tradition of the prophesied Buddha Maitreya who will incarnate in order to initiate a new age. This tradition was already fairly well known throughout Europe in Wagner's and Nietzsche's time.

In my view there is strong evidence that Nietzsche had learned about the English translation and publication of the Ceylonese Buddhist Canonic texts written in Pali, probably through one of the editors and his colleague of many years, Ernst Windisch. In the *Dighanikaya*, a part of these Ceylonese texts, the pre-Buddhist and even pre-Aryan myth of a perfected great man is taken up. This man holds a vessel in his left hand, and with his right hand he sprinkles a wheel that has appeared in the sky as a result of his acquired perfection. He bids it to roll to all four corners of the world and, with his more than thousand chivalrous sons, wins the world. He does so, however, *without violence*, by instituting justice, thus restoring stability and welfare in each country and ruling as far as the four ends of the world.

Ironically, it is precisely because Nietzsche wished to keep his distance from the *Zeitgeist* that he revealed this background of his writings only in a very hidden manner and only to a few, but at least two, of his alleged friends: to the Wagnerian Heinrich von Stein and to Lou Salomé, whom he tried to win for his cause, abeit in vain. And it was largely because of his silence about this background that Nietzsche became heavily identified with the *Reich*.

Nietzsche-Zarathustra finally calls upon his adherents to "roll out of themselves" like the wheel of the perfected great man in the *Dighanikaya*, to invent a thousand kinds of living,[6] and not to follow him, but their own ways, because "the way" — the monotheistic and monologic way or "yoke" — does not exist. Thus Nietzsche virtually manages to initiate a biophile (life-centered) movement from Alexander the Great to counter-Alexanders, from the universal to the particular, from the general to the individual, from the global to the regional.

In order to fulfill this purpose, Nietzsche composed his texts in a manner which undermines all certainties, attacks established views by means of innumerable unforeseen and intertwined perspectives, and exposes the recipient (provided that he/she is ready to become intellectually and emotionally involved to such an extent) to the experience of total disintegration. Although only in the realm of theory, Nietzsche quite existentially confronts his readers with different sorts of abysses, throwing the recipient back on himself/herself, namely upon the "society building" of countless intelligences or wills to power, which constitute and direct his/her body.

Thus, with his/her evaluations, such a true individual will contribute to an agonal game played by diverse identities. Similar to the culture of Athens in the 4th century BCE, this complex, multi-leveled, and more or less noble contest finally allows for the development of different moralities. Its specific boundaries, however, having been torn apart, the culture envisaged by Nietzsche gives way to tragic feelings comparable to those of the Greeks in the 5th or 6th centuries BCE.

Today, however, it has become more and more difficult, for a Western philosopher, to keep one's distance to words, expressions, and ideas, all of which stem from our tradition or seem to have been misused in the course of that tradition. Nazism, for example, not only seemed to have a sense for tragedy as well, but also intended to train "new German blood" in order to build up a modern political system modeled on Hellenistic city states. The statement to this effect of an SS leader was, however, followed by the remark: municipal states, with their broad economic basis of Helots, a form of slaves.[7]

Nietzsche foresaw such a development resulting from the contemporary concepts of democracy within an industrial civilization, without necessarily fostering it (compare *Twilight of the Idols*: the German *Reich* as a form of decay of the state[8]). And he dismisses visions of a simple return of the virtues of the formerly ideal polis (like the dreams of any other simple return) as merely reactionary.[9] All too often are there only nuances in his texts that reveal Nietzsche's basically different point of view. These nuances are even more difficult to grasp without knowledge of Nietzsche's hidden Pali source.

In any case, Nietzsche's individuals are supposed to pay in their own currency: far from rejecting refined intellectuals — as dictatorships quite generally have done — and being rich and noble enough to experience gratefulness, they keep in mind and feel enriched by what has been raised by the so-called Judaic-Christian heritage.[10] This heritage includes the historical sense[11] and the shifting away from world rule in the image of Alexander towards the transformation of individuals into counter-Alexanders with tragical wisdom, which was missing, even in those two centuries before Socrates.[12]

Now, I would like to suggest the following: It is, to some degree, in accordance with the widespread reservation against the European Union in the United Kingdom, France, and Switzerland today that Nietzsche opposed the contemporary conception of the "United States of Europe." Nietzsche offered his own specific vision of a "Hyperborean,"[13] one of the children of Hercules traditionally identified with the Celts.

The Celts and their culture are associated by Nietzsche, in an extremely hidden manner, with Jewish henotheism (belief in one god among a number of existing gods) or perhaps panhenotheism of an intermediate time, the time after the Jews' exodus from Egypt.[14] Nietzsche makes this association of Celts with Jews because of their common conception of the One waking over or underlying the disparate and different — despite appearances to the contrary.

The connection between the Celts and the Jews is intimated by Nietzsche in his pun upon the word "Sela" in one of his *Dionysos Dithyrambs* (*Among Daughters of the Desert*). He thereby mocked Wagner as well as "his" Germany, especially through the use of the word in juxtaposition to the appearance of this name in the Old Testament. Sela was the Celtic name of the part of the river Inn (one of the tributaries of the Danube) near its source in the Engadine, Nietzsche-Zarathustra's landscape high above the *Reich*. Herodotus, for example, whose work Nietzsche knew quite well, had already assumed that the Swiss have Celtic origins and had mentioned that the Danube has its source in the land of the Celts. Today, however, this name of the upper part of the Inn, Sela, is remembered by only a few of the older inhabitants and, in fact, it has not been associated with Jewish culture to date.

After all that has been said, it would be somewhat naive to assume that Nietzsche identified totally with the Celts and their culture: this would have seemed to him simply outdated and therefore reactionary. Nietzsche used the example of the Celts to hint at another strand of our history: a once mighty, but obviously benevolent, sympathetic, and caring culture characterized, as it were, by Dionysian dynamism and the competition for excellence and perfection. Although the Celts had a priestly culture, were notorious for their quarrels as well as belligerence, and participated, for example, in Alexander the Great's world-conquering military campaign, they seem never to have striven for world empire, nor even for a truly and thoroughly organized state. On the contrary, an old prophecy of Druids (a priestly class among the Celts) in Asia Minor called for them to sacrifice themselves, when the time will have come, for the new age of Pisces. This obviously they did, for example, when they stood up to fight against Hannibal on his march across the Alps against Rome, for at that time, one part of the Druids already saw in the Romans the representatives of the new age.[15]

Conclusion

The experience of fragmentation in our modern world having become quite common, Nietzsche provides us, as I hope I have shown, with a synthesizing narrative which renders our traditional ones — Jewish, Christian, and Islamic — obsolete. The Nietzschean narrative corresponds to our modern existence, where the monologic no longer holds, and at the same time it proves to be more biophile. For on the one hand, the Nietzschean narrative assumes that men and women are natural beings and likely to respect and honor their natural/cultural environment to a much greater extent than heretofore. On the other hand, it dissolves the framework of an exclusively sexual determination of men and women.

Finally, I would like to emphasize that it is precisely the radical cultivation of the historical sense we owe to our much-deplored so-called Judaic-Christian scientific tradition that can give new impulses and could contribute greatly to Europe's changing direction at the crossroads, towards a "U.S.E." of a thousand and one goal(s) in the coming age.

Notes

[1] *Beyond Good and Evil*, 8, aph. 243, 256, in: *Friedrich Nietzsche, Sämtliche Werke, Kritische Studienausgabe* (KSA), Vol. 5 (Berlin/New York: dtv de Gruyter, 1980), pp. 183, 201.

[2] See, for example, Joachim Köhler, *Wagners Hitler. Der Prophet und sein Vollstrecker* (München: Karl Blessing Verlag, 1997); E.R. Carmin, *Das schwarze Reich. Geheimgesellschaften und Politik im 20. Jahrhundert* (München: Wilhelm Heyne Verlag, 1997; 1st ed. Verlag Ralph Tegtmeier, 1994).

[3] Nietzsche may also have heard about the prophecy of Nostradamus, perhaps from Richard Wagner. Wagner had spent some time in Paris, where originals of Nostradamus' works are to be found in the library, and Nietzsche also intended to visit Paris. Later on, it was Hitler who consulted Nostradamus' prophecies and the Swiss astrologer Karl E. Krafft; but finally he brushed aside Krafft's warnings regarding the military campaign against Russia.

[4] *Dionysos-Dithyramben. Ruhm und Ewigkeit*, KSA 6, p. 404. "I see a sign -,/ from remotest distances/ slowly, sparkling, a constellation of stars is sinking towards me…/ Highest constellation of being!/ Tablet of eternal patterns of art!/ *You* are coming to me?/ What nobody has beheld, your mute beauty, -/ what? it doesn't flee from my glance?" (My translation).

[5] The planet Uranus is associated by astrologers with the French Revolution. In autumn 1885 Nietzsche met the astronomer Ernst Wilhelm Tempel (1821–1889) in his observatory in Florence. See Curt Paul Janz, *Friedrich Nietzsche. Biographie*, Vol. 2 (München: dtv wissenschaft, 1981), pp. 411ff. Tempel, who proved to be an enthusiastic reader of his writings, probably informed Nietzsche about those astronomical findings.

[6] KSA 10, p. 181; Nachgelassene Fragmente, November 1882 – February 1883 4[256].

[7] See Joachim Köhler, *Wagners Hitler* (München: Karl Blessing Verlag, 1997), pp. 477ff; the citation is from Eugen Kogon, *Der SS-Staat* (München, 1988), p. 42.

[8] KSA 6, pp.140 ff.

[9] KSA 13, p. 168; Nachgelassene Fragmente, November 1887 – März 1888, 11[375].

[10] Cf. KSA 11, p. 173, Sommer-Herbst 1884, 26[90]: "Was *erreicht* worden ist in der Erkenntniß, ist Sache des Philosophen, festzustellen; und nicht nur darin, sondern überhaupt! Die Geschichte als die große *Versuchs-Anstalt*: die bewußte Weisheit *vorzubereiten*, welche zur Erd-Regierung noththut. Das Zusammen-denken des Erlebten -". See also KSA 12, p. 536, Herbst 1887, 10[143]: "Nichts fällt uns leichter als weise, geduldig, überlegen, voll Nachsicht, Geduld und Mitgefühl zu sein; wir sind auf eine absurde Weise in Allem und Jedem unmenschlich-gerecht, wir verzeihen Alles. Verzeihen, das gerade ist

unser Element. Ebendarum sollten wir uns etwas strenger halten und an uns wenigstens von Zeit zu Zeit einen kleinen Affekt, ein kleines Laster von Affekt, heraufzüchten. Es mag uns sauer angehen - und, unter uns, wir lachen über den Aspekt, den wir dabei geben -: aber was hilft es! wir haben keine andere Art mehr von Selbstüberwindung…"

[11] Whereas Hitler tried to force an anti-historical order: "Ich als Politiker brauche einen Begriff, der es erlaubt, die bisher auf geschichtliche Zusammenhänge beruhende Ordnung aufzulösen und eine ganz neue, antihistorische Ordnung zu erzwingen und gedanklich zu unterstützen. Ich muß die Welt von ihrer historischen Vergangenheit befreien." Cited in Hermann Rauschning, *Gespräche mit Hitler* (Zürich, 1940), p. 218.

[12] *Ecce homo*, The Birth of Tragedy, aph. 3; KSA 6, p. 312.

[13] As to the conception of the Hyperboreans in the Third Reich, compare Carmin, *Das schwarze Reich.*

[14] In this context it is of special interest that the Celts counted 29 "Egyptian weeks;" see Michael Vescoli, *Keltischer Baumkreis* (Zürich: Edition M, 1988), p. 13. They also believed in the transmigration of souls; see *Lexikon der Alten Welt* (Zürich/Stuttgart: Artemis, 1965), p.1515, and Vescoli, pp. 15ff.

[15] And the Swiss Guard in the Vatican is still in charge of the security of the Pope.

The Ludic Politics of Vaclav Havel

Mary I. O'Reilly

Vaclav Havel is a key figure in "The New Europe at the Crossroads." Respected by Western intellectuals since the 1960s when his plays began to appear in the U.S., Canada, and Europe and the 1970s when his essays began to be published in *Encounter* and the *New York Review*, his accession to the presidency of, first Czechoslovakia, then the Czech Republic, delighted those who remember the samizdat legends of the playwright's days in the brewery and the prison laundry. In *Audience* (1978), for example, the protagonist Vanek is a playwright who has been assigned a job as assistant to a Brewmaster, who is supposed to inform on him. The recent, acclaimed film *Kolya* culminated with a view of the key-shaking crowds in Wenceslas Square welcoming "Havel to the Castle" and bidding farewell to the totalitarian regime which had ruled the Czech lands and Slovakia since 1948. In this article, I examine the impact of Havel's unorthodox training as playwright and dramaturge upon his political philosophy: I argue that such training, relying as it does upon Europe's classical literary heritage and cultural traditions, may actually be superior to academic political science as grounding for leaders of "the New Europe."

At first glance, Havel's background as playwright, actor, dramaturge, and stagehand does not ideally fit him for political office: as he said to the crowd two years ago when accepting an honorary degree at Harvard on June 8, 1995, "I don't know if my mother is looking down at me from heaven, but if she is I can guess what she's probably thinking: she's thinking that I'm sticking my nose into matters that only people who have properly studied political science at Harvard have the right to stick their noses into."[1] Yet an older tradition, echoed recently by Sir Isaiah Berlin, suggests that theatrical training, especially that requiring improvisation, can be especially valuable for an emerging statesman. That training, particularly Havel's exposure to the little theaters of the 1960s, to the rock bands, and to the improv clubs of Prague—together with his study of Patocka, Heidegger, Popper, and his great personal hero Franz Kafka, has enabled him to develop a seamless world view and approach to politics in which playfulness, expectancy, and hope merge to enable him to become a consummate spokesman for a country at the "crossroads of Europe" and for a new vision of Europe as a whole.

As a dramatist (and, one may say, as a Czech), Havel has a highly developed sense of cosmic play. The political value of his ludic apprenticeship in Prague's little theaters has long been apparent to him; as he told an interviewer in 1986: "We didn't try to explain the world; we weren't interested in theses, and we had no intention of instructing anybody. It was more like a game—except that the 'game' somehow mysteriously touched the deepest nerves of human existence."[2] In these theaters, Havel discovered "the experience of absurdity."[3] "There is," he says, "no philosophizing in these plays as there is in Sartre, for example. In their meaning, however, they are always philosophical."[4] Yet this philosophical undertone does not undermine the "game": "They tend," he continues, "to be decadently joking in tone. They know the phenomenon of endless embarrassment."[5] These remarks remind us of excruciating moments in the plays, in *Unveiling*, for example, when the yuppie husband Michael boasts of his wife's carefully-tended figure: "'Of course, Vera is still just as attractive as always—I'd even say that now...she has ripened even more...well, judge for yourself!' (Michael undoes Vera's clothes, uncovering her breasts)."[6]

This well-honed sense of the absurd leads to "performances" in the political realm that would scarcely be believable from another world-stage politician: accepting an honorary degree from Hebrew University some four months after being elected President of Czechoslovakia, Havel identified Franz Kafka as a profound influence, as almost a double: "I sometimes feel that I'm the only one who really understands Kafka...I don't need to read and re-read Kafka because I already know what's there. I'm even secretly persuaded that, if Kafka did not exist, and if I were a better writer than I am, I would have written his works myself."[7] He then goes on to confess his own profound feelings of unworthiness and to reveal his conviction that "the real reason I am always creating something, organizing something, it would seem, is to defend my permanently questionable right to exist."[8] "You may well ask," he continues, "how someone who thinks of himself this way can be the president of a country. It's a paradox, but I must admit that, if I am a better president than others, it is precisely because somewhere in the deepest substratum of my work lies this constant doubt about myself and my right to hold office. I am the kind of person who would not be in the least surprised if, in the very middle of my presidency, I were summoned and led off to stand trial before some shadowy tribunal, or taken straight to a quarry to break rocks."[9] One can hardly imagine Bill Clinton or Tony Blair putting, as Havel says later in the same speech, "so many cards on the table," yet this internalized sense of personal absurdity seems to have served Havel well first as dissident and prisoner, later as statesman.

This is a playfulness that barely masks high seriousness—as Havel says, "the deeper the experience of an absence of meaning...the more energetically meaning is sought."[10] In *Largo Desolato,* the protagonist Leopold finds his meaning in his constant awareness that "They" will come, eventually, to take him away to "There." When "They" finally arrive, Leopold learns that all he need do to escape "There" is to disown an offensive article by claiming to be a different "Leopold Nettles" from the author. "They" return the next day and Leopold announces triumphantly: "I'm not going to sign that statement. I'd rather die than give up my human identity—it's the only thing I've got!"[11] The First Chap replies, "You don't have to sign anything! Your case has been adjourned indefinitely."[12] And Leopold, imagining life without the constant threat of "There," shouts, "I don't want an adjournment! I want to go there!"[13] In the last scene, Leopold is again alone on the stage, again beginning his trips to peer through the front door peep-hole. The lights come up; he goes to the footlights and bows.[14]

Parallel to Absurdism in Havel's development is a slightly different but even more "playful" theatrical tradition, that of improvisation, which has contributed to Havel's political finesse as well as, more profoundly, to his vision of the good society. He remarks in *Disturbing the Peace* that small theaters and cabarets "had once had a rich tradition in [Czechoslovakia], with theaters like Dada, the Liberated Theatre, the Red Seven, and others like them, but after 1948 they vanished from our theatrical culture."[15] Among their successors in a world of censorship were the music clubs of the 1960s and rock bands of the 1970s: of the former, Havel writes:

> [Their program was] just a series of songs, one after another, and the songs themselves were about nothing in particular, but it was the delight in performance, the rhythm, the pure fun, that seemed to make all these learned ideological debates seem fundamentally inappropriate, without much in common with real life. It was a manifestation of uncensored life, life that spits out all ideology...Suddenly, against the world of appearance and interpretation, here stood truth—the truth of young people who couldn't care less about any of that, who wanted only to live in their own way, to dance the way they wanted to dance.[16]

Such performances came alive again during the Velvet Revolution when, at one meeting at the Slovak National Theatre called to discuss the difficult question of "the degree of self-government to be enjoyed by the two nation (alities) s within the federal state," a group of students came on stage, dressed comically as young pioneers: white blouses, red bows, the girls' hair in pigtails. It is the Committee for a More Joyful Present."[17] In addition to giving an ironic Central European spin to solemn revolutionary councils, such a performance locates us in a world in which Michael Jackson's appearance in Prague has the trappings of a state visit, and where, a generation ago, censorship of the Plastic People of the Universe set off the movement that culminated in Charter 77. Watching these grungy young folks, Havel became clear about his own political goal: "Suddenly I realized that, regardless of how many vulgar words these people used or how long their hair was, truth was on their side."[18] Although, for Havel, Charter 77 resulted in a prison term, it also led the way to the dismantling, twelve years later, of the old regime.

In addition to keeping Havel from taking himself too seriously, his contact with this stage tradition of improvisation and wit contributes to his "readiness" in confronting novel political challenges. The notion that theatrical training nurtures wisdom and mental agility goes back at least to the sixteenth century when humanist schoolmasters had their students—most of whom were destined to careers as statesmen—perform both Latin and vernacular drama. Thomas More describes in *Utopia* the exercises set by Cardinal Morton, Archbishop of Canterbury, in whose household More served his "apprenticeship" as a page. At dinner, he said, the Cardinal would challenge the young and ambitious courtiers attendant upon him to respond spontaneously to a problem: "Should we have a standing army?" "What is the cause of poverty?" The cardinal would thus encourage the "readiness" of these fledgling statesmen, sharpen their mental and verbal agility and would also use these occasions to judge whom to promote:

> He took great delight many times in rough speech to his suitors, to prove, though without harm, what prompt wit and what bold spirit were in every man; in which, as in a virtue much agreeing with his nature...he took great delectation. And the same person, as apt and well suited to have an office in the commonwealth, he would lovingly accept.[19] More himself figures in a legend related in Roper's biography,[20] that, a group of mummers, having arrived at the Cardinal's hall to perform a play, he "stepped-in" and improvised his own lines to general acclaim, an event also memorialized in the Elizabethan *Play of Sir Thomas More* (c. 1595–1596; 1600–1601). Such onstage agility served Havel and his comrades in the Civic Forum well during the Velvet Revolution, as Garton Ash relates:

> Seven-thirty p.m. the press conference. Answers delivered with great assurance to questions they had only asked themselves, in this same room, a few minutes before. No matter. Make it up as you go along. It's all right on the night.[21]

And, lest this agility seem appropriate only to a revolutionary in the crush of events, we hear from Berlin in the recent past that such ability to create fresh solutions rather than follow as if by rote the paradigm of a dusty ideology is the most desirable quality in a statesman of the New Europe: "The excellence of cooks and gardeners still depends today most largely upon their artistic endowment and, like that of politicians, upon their ability to improvise."[22]

Yet Havel himself is sensitive to the charge that his politics is frivolously "theatrical," more a product of flair than of deep thought. Addressing Prague's Academy of the Performing Arts last year, he insisted that training and practice as a dramatist, concern with the logic of dramatic structure, were a valuable background for his work as a politician:

> Politics without a beginning, a middle, and an end, without exposition and catharsis, without gradation and suggestiveness; politics lacking in the kind of transcendence that develops a real drama, using real people, into

a testimony about the world as a whole, that politics is, in my opinion, a castrated, one-legged, toothless politics."[23]

In the same speech, he also remarks on the necessity for the politician to deploy symbols and engage in actual performance:

Inevitably, politics is theater…theater as a system of symbols addressing us as individuals and as members of a community; testifying, through the specific event in which it is embodied, to the great happening of life and the world; and enhancing our imagination and sensibilities."[24]

In his plays, particularly in those written after 1968 when Havel became progressively less acceptable to the authorities, we find continuing reenactment of a ludic politics, a determination to place the most devastating life experiences into the framework of a high-level game. This is a game that is ruled by transcendence: in *Audience*, for example, the Brewmaster, railing against Vanek for visits from his fancy friends such as the pop star Karel Gott, protests: "Well, you know I ain't no pop star like Gott or nothing! I'm just your everyday brewery hick—" And Vanek replies, "You're a professional at what you do just like Gott is at what he does."[25] Gott is, actually, a "post-modern" pop singer who is, according to Milan Kundera, an "exponent of music minus memory, the music in which the bones of Beethoven and Ellington, the dust of Palestrina and Schonberg, lie buried" (*The Book of Laughter and Forgetting* [New York: Knopf, 1981], 181)[26] Gott is a historical figure, yet Havel is glad to avail himself of the pun on Gott's name, to insert him into his post-modern dialectic of absurdity and transcendence.

The essential playfulness of this and other dialectical oppositions that one finds in Havel's work suggests the degree to which he maintains an attitude of constant expectancy. In this respect, he finds congenial the indeterminist philosophy of the Austrian emigre Karl Popper. (I am not sure when Havel first became familiar with Popper's work. Havel frequently apologizes for the sporadic nature of his education, but he has read hungrily in contemporary philosophy since his high school days and adopted the Czech philosopher Jan Potocka as his informal tutor during the fifteen years of their friendship before Potocka died a martyr to Charter 77. Havel was greatly moved when the nonagenarian Popper visited him in Prague shortly before Popper's death.) Speaking to an audience at Victoria University of Wellington, New Zealand, Havel says,

I can confirm that Sir Karl Popper was right [in his attack on "holistic social engineering"]. In the beginning was an alleged scientific theory of historical laws; that Marxist theory subsequently gave rise to the communist utopia, the vision of a paradise on earth that eventually

> produced the gulags… needless to say, life, with its unfathomable diversity and unpredictability, never allowed itself to be squeezed into the crude Marxist cage.[27]

This emphasis on life's unpredictability suggests Havel's dual allegiance to the ludic in drama and to indeterminism in Popper's thought. "Indeterminism" in Popper means, first of all, "the doctrine that human actions, though influenced somewhat by preexisting psychological and other conditions, are not entirely governed by them but retain a certain freedom and spontaneity."[28] Popper, however, extends this "freedom, and spontaneity" to historical events as well. He derived this conviction, writes Brian Magee, from his study of quantum physics which led him to believe that it is "logically impossible to give a scientific prediction of the future course of history."[29] Such indeterminism accommodates an element of play in the universe, thus preventing the doctrinaire rigidities both Popper and Havel despise: Havel's first published play *The Garden Party* (1963) skewers with equal glee the inflexibility of middle-class family life and the stupidities of government apparatchiks: Hugo, the promising young son of the Pludek family, goes to a garden party given to bolster the morale of the employees of the Office of Liquidation; there, he learns that the agency is seriously threatened by "dadaistic joksterism," adapts himself brilliantly to its bureaucratic language and culture, dons a false nose, and returns to his family who, fooled by his witty disguise, do not recognize him. Soon, however, they are thrilled by the news that Hugo has taken his first step up in the government career they have dreamed of: he has been chosen to liquidate the Office of Liquidation. As Paul I. Trensky notes, "The most outstanding feature of Hugo is his ability to adapt to his surroundings, through which he is able to outclass others in the complex bureaucratic world."[30] Trensky also sees that Havel's language in this play "points up not only the impossibility of communication by people but the very corruption of intellect by language."[31]

Havel's anti-ideological stance, which he has maintained throughout his dramatic and political careers, was first seen in the 1960s as "containing important ethical implications that might have a significant long-range impact on the country's political course as well"[32] (Trensky 105) and may also owe something to Popper's distaste for "utopians" as such; at least, it finds much in common with this distaste: as Douglas E. Williams writes: "Popper distinguishes utopians who 'dream about distant ideals' and those people like himself, 'who believe in man as he is, and who… have not given up hope of defeating violence and unreason, [and who] must demand that every man should be given the right to arrange his life himself so far as this is compatible with the equal rights of others.'"[33] Havel's defense of the Plastic People of the Universe partakes of this conviction that privacy and the right to do as one likes are primary political rights. In line with this willingness to wait to see how the diversity of human choices will play themselves out, both Popper and Havel espouse a "gradualism" in political life that is related to Havel's aesthetic notion of politics as a matter of "gradation," "suggestiveness," "civility," "good taste" and "decorum": "Improvements must be made," Havel says, "according to whatever has proven to be good, practical, desirable, and meaningful, without the arrogant presumption that we have understood everything about this world, and thus already know everything there is to know about how to ameliorate it."[34] Yet Havel warns in the same speech about the fatalism he sees among some Czechs who have given up on amelioration in favor of fatalism and apathy: he sees these as falling, paradoxically, into the same error as the utopians—they are equally arrogant about their own hopelessness.[35] Instead, he recommends an approach that sounds to transatlantic ears similar to those of such American philosophers as John Dewey and Harry Truman: In the words of the latter, "Well, we'll try it, and if it doesn't work, we'll try something else."

This modest pragmatism is one with the philosophy of hope that Havel maintains: if the world is essentially indeterminate, if God does, in fact, play dice with the universe, is, perhaps, an Absurdist playwright, then despair is presumptuous and betrays a sad want of curiosity. (Havel says that he does not fear death but would be sorry to die prematurely, before seeing "how everything comes out.") This hope is, Havel says, the opposite of optimism: it is independent of "prognostication" as the Czech language denotes statistical "forecasting"; it is rather "a state of mind...an existential phenomenon which has nothing to do with predicting the future."[36] Speaking to the French Academy of Humanities and Political Sciences, he discourages "waiting for Godot," if, by Godot, one means universal salvation, but rather encourages the dissidents' stance of creative waiting informed by the skill of a dramatist who understands that "the world, Being, and history have their own time."[37] He himself was impatient, he says, when he first became president, for all to be well in Czechoslovakia, once communism was over. But, he says, "I wanted to nudge history forward in the way a child would when wishing to make a flower grow more quickly: by tugging at it...[but], just as we cannot fool a plant, we cannot fool history. But we must water history as well, patiently and every day. This kind of waiting is more than just waiting. It is life."[38] Havel's horticultural metaphor must have put his French audience in mind of Voltaire, yet this waiting is not one of withdrawal from public life but of continuing contributions to it.

This commitment to play, to expectancy, to hope seems to create the radical integrity of this playwright/politician and to be the secret of his success. And, in addition, he can always surprise us: in his own spirit of fun, we can take pleasure in anticipating what he will do—or say—next. As his friend and collaborator Pavel Kohout writes, "Both Havel and his fictional twin brother Vanek have everything that makes a man a man, but they have retained the soul of a child."[39] And, like a child, Havel, even when engaging in so adult an activity as politics, retains the essential qualities of play, expectancy, and hope that his theatrical background has largely bestowed.

Conclusion

This examination suggests that Vaclav Havel's unorthodox training as a man of the theater has endowed him with a rich sense of humanity deriving from Europe's cultural heritage. His understanding of politics as structured in the manner of classical drama, along with his nimble wit and flair for improvisation nurtured in the little theaters and clubs of Prague, has lent him the skills needed to lead a country newly emerging from the totalitarian past. Havel's example suggests that Europe should look to heirs of its humanistic tradition rather than to bureaucrats and technocrats to provide the leadership it needs in this difficult time of transition.

Notes

[1] Vaclav Havel, *The Art of the Impossible* (New York: Random House, 1997), 53.

[2] *Disturbing the Peace* (New York: Vintage, 1991), 52.

[3] Ibid., 53.

[4] Ibid., 53.

[5] Ibid., 54.

[6] Marketa Goetz-Stankiewicz, ed., *The Vanek Plays. Four Authors. One Character* (Vancouver: UCBP, 1987), 41.

[7] *The Art of the Impossible*, 29.

[8] Ibid., 31.

[9] Ibid.

[10] *Disturbing the Peace,* 201.

[11] Vaclav Havel, *Largo Desolato* in *Selected Plays*: 1984–87 (London and Boston: Faber and Faber, 1994), 59.

[12] Ibid.

[13] Ibid.

[14] Ibid., 60.

[15] 42.

[16] *Disturbing the Peace*, 49.

[17] Timothy Garton Ash, *The Magic Lantern: The Revolution of '89 Witnessed in Warsaw, Budapest, Berlin, and Prague* (New York: Random House, 1990), 112.

[18] *Disturbing the Peace,* 127.

[19] Thomas More, *The Utopia of Sir Thomas More, Including Roper's Life of More and Letters of More and His Daughter Margaret* (New York: Van Nostrand, 1947), 27.

[20] Ibid., 57.

[21] 108–109.

[22] "On Political Judgment." *New York Review of Books*. 3 Oct. 1996, 30.

[23] *The Art of the Impossible,* 251.

[24] Ibid., 253.

[25] Goetz-Stankiewicz, 12.

[26] Quoted in Goetz-Stankiewicz n. 3, 26.

[27] *The Art of the Impossible,* 204.

[28] Brian Magee, *Popper*. Fontana Modern Masters. Ed. Frank Kermode (London: Collins, 1973), 15.

[29] Ibid., 16.

[30] *Czech Drama Since World War II* (New York: Sharpe, 1968), 107–108.

[31] Ibid., 109.

[32] Ibid., 105.

[33] *Truth, Hope, and Power: The Thought of Karl Popper* (Toronto: University of Toronto Press, 1989), 363.

[34] *The Art of the Impossible*, 204.

[35] Ibid., 205.

[36] Ibid., 236–237.

[37] Ibid., 106.

[38] Ibid., 107–108.

[39] Goetz-Stankiewicz, 243.

The Legacy of the Cold War: Dispute of the German P.E.N. Clubs

Rado Pribic

The history of the P.E.N. movement and more specifically the case study of the German P.E.N. dispute, i.e. the difficulty and complexity of unification, parallels quite closely the trends and developments of European cultural and political developments in the twentieth century. The lessons that could be learned from this analysis should help to understand the difficulties that a Europe intent to unify economically and politically is and will be facing for quite a while. Every nation honors its best creative writers by including them in its P.E.N. Club (The World Association of Writers).[1] Normally, every nation has also only one National P.E.N. Association. But this is not necessarily always the case. The United States of America, due to the large size of the country, has several P.E.N. branches, located in Boston, Chicago, New Orleans, Portland, and San Francisco, which are coordinated by the P.E.N. American Center in New York City. Altogether there are about 130 P.E.N. Centers worldwide with more than 10,000 members. Germany presently has three internationally recognized P.E.N. Centers.

While the German Exile P.E.N. Club is nowadays insignificant, the inability of the P.E.N. Center West and the P.E.N. Center East to unify as one German P.E.N. Club has caused a significant amount of attention, especially in the press. It seems that eight years after the German unification, the two literary groups constitute the most visible segment of the German society that has not been assimilated and in many ways continues the split that was caused by the Cold War.

The Creation of the International P.E.N.

When John Galsworthy and other literary leaders decided in 1921 to create an International P.E.N. movement in London "to foster understanding among men and women of letters in all countries," they clearly reacted to the horrors of the "Great War," or the First World War. They wanted the cultural and the literary world to unite behind the traditional idealistic and humanistic values found in European classical heritage. Throughout the centuries, but especially during the 19th century, writers in many parts of Europe were given the status of "sages" and the readers had high expectations to find answers to their everyday problems in, e.g. the philosophical writings of Leo Tolstoy or the sociocritical works of Charles Dickens. With the drastic increase in literacy among the masses and the technological advances in mass communication, the role of the writer, reporter, or artist after the First World War became even more critical. Books, newspapers, films, illustrations, radio broadcasts, etc. became more and more powerful in disseminating information, providing entertainment, and influencing political and social movements. Often they contributed to the corruption of public taste, but they also added significantly to education and the enhancement of values.

The First World War drastically changed the geography of Europe. Four major empires ceased to exist and a number of new independent countries formally came into existence. The feelings of complacency and security disappeared, which caused a wave of vigorous intellectual activity. Technological and scientific advances influenced and broadened the scope of all other traditional endeavors. The writers became more concerned with the average man, the collective behavior of the masses, and with ideologies. Unfortunately, this sense of insecurity was enhanced by political and economic disasters. Most new democracies were replaced by right or left wing totalitarian systems. The staggering inflation rates and the stock market crash further underlined the economic interdependency of nations. As usual, the wars, revolutions, and "solutions to the hardships" created at least as many new problems as they solved. The national and international problem-solvers failed miserably. The idealistic and pan-humanistic European values promoted by classical thinkers fell prey to pragmatic, selfish, and chauvinistic policies. However, there were undoubtedly many well-meaning attempts to create harmony among men.

One can look at the International P.E.N. Center as a reflection of the European ideals and problems. The members of P.E.N. viewed themselves just as much spiritual and intellectual leaders, if not necessarily powerbrokers, as some political, economic, and religious leaders did. They promoted the traditional humanitarian, democratic European heritage as is reflected in the P.E.N. Charter:

> LITERATURE, national though it be in origin, knows no frontiers and should remain common currency among nations in spite of political or international upheavals.
> IN ALL CIRCUMSTANCES, and particularly in time of war, works of art and libraries, the heritage of humanity at large, should be left untouched by national or political passion.
> MEMBERS OF PEN should at all times use what influence they have in favor of good understanding and mutual respect among nations; they pledge themselves to do their utmost to dispel race-, class- and national-hatreds and to champion the ideal of one humanity living in peace in the world.
> PEN STANDS FOR the principle of unhampered transmission of thought within each nation and among all nations, and members pledge

themselves to oppose any form of suppression of freedom of expression in their country or their community.
PEN DECLARES for a free press and opposed arbitrary censorship in time of peace. It believes that the necessary advance of the world toward a more highly organized political and economic order renders free criticism of governments, administrations, and institutions imperative. And since freedom implies voluntary restraint, members pledge themselves to oppose such evils of a free press as mendacious publication, deliberate falsehood, and distortion of facts for political and personal ends.[2]

Case Study: The Dispute of German P.E.N. Clubs

In order to understand fully the dispute between the P.E.N. Clubs, one needs to look back into German history. After Hitler's takeover in 1933 and the establishment of the Third Reich, the German P.E.N. Center was forced to break off all its ties to the International P.E.N. Association. In November 1933, it *de facto* voted itself out of existence. However, in 1934 the International Association of Writers (P.E.N.) decided to recognize a German Exile Writers' Association based in London. The members of that Exile P.E.N. Club, known as the "Deutsche Gruppe des Internationalen P.E.N.-Clubs in London," had to flee Nazi Germany and attempted to direct a new German cultural center for German language writers in a politically free environment. The most prominent members of the London Center were Lion Feuchtwanger, Heinrich Mann, Johannes R. Becher, Walter A. Berendsohn, Hermann Friedmann, Wilhelm Sternfeld, and Wilhelm Unger. This Exile P.E.N. Club, which is still in existence today and known as the "Center for German-Speaking Writers Abroad," was instrumental in re-establishing a new P.E.N. Center in Germany free of Nazi ideology and legacy after the Second World War. Also, the exiled Nobel Laureate Thomas Mann used his influence to advocate a re-establishment of the German P.E.N. Center on German soil.

Concretely, the Exile P.E.N. Club approached Hermon Ould, general secretary of the International P.E.N. since 1926 (until his death in 1951), asking him to set in motion the reactivation of the German P.E.N. Club. Mr. Ould supported the request, and the issue was discussed in June 1946 at the 18th International P.E.N. Convention, the first after the Second World War, in Stockholm. The next year, at the 19th International P.E.N. Convention in Zürich, he invited the German writers J.R. Becher, Ernst Wiechert, and Erich Kästner as observers. Also in 1947, in October, the first German Writers Congress convened in Berlin. Finally, on April 2, 1948, Hermann Friedmann, member of the Exile P.E.N., announced the formation of a "German P.E.N. Club on German Soil," which was later recognized at the 20th International P.E.N. Convention in Copenhagen. The names of the twenty writers (minimum number for a P.E.N. Club) who became the founding members of the newly formed German P.E.N. were picked by an international P.E.N. commission but certainly not without controversy. The Cold War was already initiated and the capitalist-communist rivalry was in full swing.

At its first convention, on November 19, 1948, in Göttingen, the German P.E.N. Center elected Hermann Friedmann, J.R. Becher, and Ernst Penzoldt as co-presidents and Erich Kästner and Rudolf Schneider-Schelde as secretaries. The other founding members were Ludwig Renn, Theodor Plivier, Anna Seghers, Hermann Kasack, Herbert Eulenberg, Elisabeth Langgässer, Johannes Tralow, Hanns Henny Jahnn, Günther Birkenfeld, Axel Eggebrecht, Dolf Sternberger, Paul Wiegler, Reinhold Schneider, Friedrich Wolf, and Günther Weisenborn.[3] The members affirmed the statutes of the International P.E.N. Charter, emphasizing particularly Article Three, i.e., pledging "to champion the ideals of humanity living in peace in one world."

They also agreed that no writer who was "serving the Nazi-propaganda" could be elected into the German P.E.N. The convention closed with great hope for an intellectually free and peaceful life for all Germans and an independent P.E.N. Center that would bridge the political divisions in an occupied Germany.

However, this hope was never realized. In the next five years, a series of meetings made the ideological differences between the writers residing in the Western occupied zones and those in the Soviet occupied zone obvious. Nasty personal attacks and political editorials became common place. The propaganda apparatus of both, the Federal Republic of Germany and the German Democratic Republic, became fully involved. Especially effective was a pamphlet produced by the West German Ministry for Questions of the Whole of Germany (Bundesministerium für gesamtdeutsche Fragen) that appeared in May of 1951. This pamphlet, "Freedom Demands Clear Decisions. Johannes R. Becher and the P.E.N. Club"[4] attacked the East German president of the P.E.N. Center, J.R. Becher, a convinced communist who later became the minister of culture in the GDR. The pamphlet raises the issue of Becher's support for the didactic communist dogma in his capacity as a member of the Central Committee of the East German Communist Party (SED), which conflicts with the freedom of speech concept of the P.E.N. Charter.

In October 1951 a group of West German P.E.N. members sent a political essay, "About Tolerance and Freedom of Expression" to the International P.E.N. leadership, in order to inform all P.E.N. members "of the situation of freedom of speech under the Soviet Communist regime." In response, Becher challenged the writers of the essay to take a close look at the sites of the former concentration camp Buchenwald so that they could fully understand what intolerance and capitalism mean.[5]

Eventually, several West German writers — the majority of the newly-elected P.E.N. members obviously came from the much larger West Germany — canceled their P.E.N. memberships, citing the fact that a number of their colleagues, due to their "totalitarian ideology," were not in compliance with the statutes of the P.E.N. Charter. These dissidents established a new "Deutscher P.E.N. Club (Bundesrepublik)" on December 4 and 5, 1951 in Darmstadt. Eventually all the West German members left the German P.E.N. Center, which was founded in 1948, and the 25th International P.E.N. Convention in Dublin officially recognized two German (three counting the Exile Club) P.E.N. Centers: The "German P.E.N. Center East and West" which later became "only" P.E.N. Center East, and the "German P.E.N. Center (Federal Republic of Germany)," later to become P.E.N. Center West.

Since German unification in 1989, the P.E.N. Center East (during the GDR times referred to as GDR P.E.N. Club), with its 150 or so original and more recent members, attempted on several occasions to start a dialogue leading to a fusion of the two centers. Every time, however, it was rebuffed by the P.E.N. Center West, which was heavily influenced by several of its members who were formerly citizens of the GDR. These writers were expelled from the GDR Writers Association, often persecuted for "activities hostile to the state," and eventually sent to the West. These ex-GDR writers, the best known being Sarah Kirsch, Günter Kunert, Reiner Kunze, Monika Maron, and Hans-Joachim Schädlich, represented a small minority inside the P.E.N. Club West, but they threatened to resign from the PEN Club if writers who belonged to the GDR Club in 1989, at the time of unification, were accepted in a unified German P.E.N. Club. The threat of resignation by its members made the leadership of the West P.E.N. shy away from any unification discussion for several years.

The P.E.N. Center East continued to pursue a unification policy, and formed an internal "honorary council" (Ehrenrat) that investigated all its members for activities against the spirit of the P.E.N. Statutes (Charter), resulting in several resignations by members guilty of collaboration with the "Stasi," the GDR secret police agency. But even this failed to pacify some members of the P.E.N. Club West. Some extremists demanded that "all Stasi-skeletons" needed to be removed. This meant that the removal of perpetrators was not enough but that those who "tolerated" the GDR regime, i.e., all writers who opted to remain in the GDR, should be categorically excluded from membership in P.E.N..

The climax to the unification debate within the P.E.N. Center West came at its annual meeting in May 1995 in the city of Mainz. At the poorly attended meeting, 51 West P.E.N. members voted for a "Mainzer Abgrenzungsbeschluß" (Mainz Resolution of Limitations) effectively prohibiting any official contacts between the P.E.N. Clubs and thereby terminating any unification negotiations. Thirty of the members present voted against the resolution and thirteen abstained. The newly-elected hard-line president of the P.E.N. Center West, Ingrid Bacher, emphasized repeatedly in interviews, such as in the *Berliner Zeitung* of January 18, 1996, that the past record and activities of the P.E.N. Center East and its members needed to be thoroughly investigated before any talks about unifying the two centers could begin. This type of thinking appears to the East P.E.N. members as another example of "Wessi" (West German) arrogance by looking at the Easterners as the perpetrators and the Westerners as judges. After all, a P.E.N. member is internationally recognized and honored and one member of the GDR P.E.N. Center, Stephan Hermlin, was even elected to the vice presidency of the International P.E.N.

The general secretary of the PEN Center East, Joochen Laabs, viewed the "Mainz Resolution" as unfortunate, bordering on defamation. He suspected that some people were projecting a cruel picture in which "the GDR, shrunk to the size of the East German P.E.N., has survived as some kind of a black hole in which all the evil forces are concentrated" (interview in *Berliner Zeitung*).[6] This interpretation is probably also in reference to a number of defamatory statements made by exiled ex-GDR P.E.N. members, now activists in the West P.E.N. The best known of the belligerent verbal attacks is Günter Kunert's, who argues that everyone who has remained in the GDR until its dissolution is "damaged beyond any possibility of repair." This of course outrages the East P.E.N. members. "Enough was enough," as Steffen Meusching explained in an interview in *Frankfurter Rundschau*, "We had a tendency for too long to apologize for having lived in the GDR."[7]

The reaction to the "Mainz Resolution" was quick and vocal. Of the ca. 500 members of the P.E.N. Center West, 81 to show solidarity also decided to join the P.E.N. Center East, effectively becoming members of both P.E.N. Clubs, (illegal by the international statutes). What made the "Mainz Resolution" even more controversial is the fact that the majority of the 150 members of the P.E.N. Center East, including its current president, Dieter Schlenstedt, who is a professor of German literature at the prestigious Alexander von Humboldt University in Berlin, have been voted into the P.E.N. Association since unification in 1989. With the "double members," the East P.E.N. membership today has grown to around 230.

The most prominent member of the P.E.N. Center West who demonstratively also became a member of the P.E.N. Center East is undoubtedly Günter Grass, the author of numerous internationally successful novels, such as *The Tin Drum*. In an interview with the left-wing newspaper *Neues Deutschland* of January 22, 1996, he commented: "My dual membership is a reaction to the 'Mainz Resolution,' which tried to prohibit contact." He continued: "Why does the West, which also has its own history, think that it can play the role of a judge?" Grass attended the January 1996 P.E.N. Center East Convention in Berlin and complimented its participants for the ability to listen with patience to lengthier speeches, for the intellectual depth of discussion, and especially for a climate in which even controversial arguments are presented and received with respect, void of any "defaming tone" as is often the case in the West. Parenthetically, one should point out that the percentage of belletristic writers in the P.E.N. Center East is higher than that in the P.E.N. Center West, where many of its members are journalists and literary critics. Some prominent West German authors, such as Hans Magnus Enzenberger, chose not to belong to the P.E.N. at all.

The state of the unification debate drastically changed a few months later. At its annual meeting in May 1996 in Heidelberg, the P.E.N. Center West decided to conduct an opinion poll of its members by mail. The question asked was whether the members advocated a unification of the two P.E.N. Centers. The overwhelming majority of 232 advocated establishing a commission to prepare unification. Ninety-seven members opposed the formation of a commission and thereby voted for separate P.E.N. centers. The old leadership of the West P.E.N., led by its president, Ingrid Bachér, had to resign since it was elected a year earlier on a platform of separation. Interestingly and ideologically significant is the fact that most members of the previous leadership politically supported the conservative Christian Democratic Party (CDU) or its Bavarian affiliate, the Christian Socialist Union (CSU). In contrast, the new P.E.N. Center West leadership, elected on November 24, 1996, sympathizes with the opposition liberal Social Democratic Party (SPD). Both the new president, the literary historian Karl Otto Conradi and the general secretary, Johano Strasser, are active members of the SPD. The connection between political ideology and the approach to the German P.E.N. unification question is obvious. In protest to the new developments and the new direction of the West P.E.N., about twenty to thirty of its members left the P.E.N. association altogether. About a dozen of them are former GDR citizens. The former president, Ingrid Bachér, understandably also gave up her membership.

Finally, nine years after the political unification of Germany, a unification of its P.E.N. Clubs seems to be in sight. In the spring of 1997, the two P.E.N. Clubs established a joint committee to discuss concretely issues and steps that will lead to their unification. After all, Article One of the International PEN Charter states: "Literature, national though it be in origin, knows no frontiers and should remain common currency between nations in spite of political or international upheavals."[8]

Conclusion

Looking at the history and especially the charter of the International P.E.N. Club, it is obvious that the organization is founded on principles of European enlightenment and humanism that should be relevant also in a unified and democratic Europe. To some extent, writers and other publicists continue to shape public opinions and tastes. Also nowadays, the P.E.N. members continue to defend all forms of freedom of expression and individualism. They also promote international understanding through international congresses and by sponsoring translations of works written in obscure or neglected languages.

The case study of the German P.E.N. situation, i.e., unification, should not only be interesting due to Germany's often tragic role in shaping the events of the twentieth century, and most recently, its important leadership role in the push towards a politically and economically unified Europe. It can be said that the unification process of Europe can and should learn from the recent German unification. As seen in the P.E.N. Club dispute, a unification can be quite complex and difficult. Europe needs to work in overcoming such divisiveness created in part by the legacy of the Cold War.

What lessons can be learned? Every observer should be free to draw his or her own conclusion. However, here are a few suggestive questions: Can we easily generalize the understanding of such complex terms as freedom, respect, or opposition? Since people are conditioned by their environment, connotations of a word or expression can vary radically. Do we have to have winners and losers? Exclusion of any group can lead to disruption. How far can we go to accept any forms of individualism? Some forms can be very destructive. It would probably be wise to look at Jean-Jacques Rousseau's *Social Contract* one more time and modify it to the political, economic, and cultural changes that have occurred since 1762.

Europe in its unification process is likely to experience significant and often painful changes. To minimize the pain, one should adhere closely to universal humanistic values expressed eloquently in various forms by many thinkers. If the members of P.E.N. faithfully promote the ideals expressed in their charter, without becoming too narrow in their interpretation, they could have a chance to contribute to the harmony of a unified Europe.

Notes

[1] The acronym P.E.N. stands for "poets, playwrights, editors, essayists, and novelists."

[2] http://www.pen.org./general.html

[3] Christine Malende, "Die Wiedererrichtung und Trennung des PEN-Zentrums Deutschland 1946/48 bis 1951/53." *Zeitschrift für Germanistik, Neue Folge* (1995), p. 85.

[4] *Die Freiheit fordert klare Entscheidungen. Johannes R. Becher und der PEN-Clubs*. Bundesministerium für gesamtdeutsche Fragen. Bonn, 1951.

[5] For further details see Leonore Krenslin, "Dialogbemühungen mitten im kalten Krieg. Johannes R. Becher und der PEN-Club im Jahre 1950." *Weimarer Beiträge*, 34, 10 (1988), pp. 1749–1753.

[6] "Vor der Jahrestagung des Deutschen PEN-Zentrums (Ost)." *Berliner Zeitung*. January 18, 1996, p. 15.

[7] "Neues vom Familienkrieg. Die Jahrestagung des PEN-Zentrums (Ost)." *Frankfurter Rundschau*. January 22, 1996, p.11.

[8] For another interpretation of the German P.E.N. dispute, see also Friedrich Dieckmann, "Deutsche PEN - Geschichten. Eine Akten-Lese." *Aus Politik und Geschichte*, 13–14 (1996), pp. 42–54.

"Assimilation" or "désagrégation"? Reconstructing the Body Politic in France

G.G. Raymond

Assimilation, the French notion of civic integration, expressed an ambition at the heart of French political culture that was traditionally held to make it quite distinct from Anglo-Saxon political culture. This article investigates that distinction and argues that it has now given way to a convergence between the two traditions, and that this change, particularly in France, is powerfully symptomatic of the way Europe as a whole is having to rethink the classical assumptions that have mediated the relationship between the governing and the governed. One of the most frequent, and justifiable, points that preface Anglo-French comparisons with regard to the political culture of the two societies, relates to the very different assumptions that have shaped the perception of the relationship between the citizen and the state, the freedoms and obligations that define that relationship, and the way this has determined the identity of the individual as a civil and a civic person. What I propose to do during the course of this article is to outline the assumptions that anchor the divergent perceptions of the relationship in question, then look at the pressures in Britain and France that have led to a reappraisal of their classically divergent models, leading to increasingly convergent prescriptions for the redefinition of the relationship which must endure at the heart of a properly functioning polity.[1]

The Anglo-Saxon Tradition

In the English tradition the state is the arbiter of freedom, not the architect of it. In Hobbsian terms, having entered a covenant with the sovereign in which the natural and unlimited right to freedom is exchanged for security, the sphere in which the new kind of liberty afforded by civil society is enjoyed, is defined by the silence of the sovereign, i.e., those aspects of life in civil society over which the sovereign has no sway.[2] It is parallel to the civic sphere in which the sovereign exercises his prerogatives, it is coterminous with it, it is underwritten by it, but it is not fundamentally and unavoidably realized through it. Ironically, Hobbes was criticized in some quarters for being too European in his approach, by trying to produce a complete and systematic exposition of statecraft, and, furthermore, not one based on what would become the classical English assumption of human reasonableness and niceness, but on the assumption that human affairs have a natural tendency to degenerate into a condition of war.

Forty years after the publication of *Leviathan*, and proceeding from rather less bleakly pessimistic assumptions, in his *Second Treatise on Government*, Locke nonetheless evokes a political society where the institutions in which authority is vested act, as he calls it, as an "umpire," according to "settled standing rules, indifferent and the same to all parties,"[3] restating the notion of the separate spheres, the one in which the citizen defers to the collective will in order to preserve the security of all (including him or herself), and the private sphere which lends itself to the pursuit of individual fulfillment. A century and a half later, with civil war and regicide a very distant memory and a mere hiccup on the road to a felicitous constitutional monarchy, J.S. Mill could posit a role for the state that, in his essay *On Liberty*, reduced it to a "central depository, an active circulator and diffusor,"[4] disseminating the best practice devised by individuals in the management of localized interests, who can almost always be relied on to do things better than the state.

This is not to assume that the English tradition has not been vigorously challenged in England. Historians like E.P. Thompson and Eric Hobsbawn have illustrated that there was no such thing as a national consensus underwriting the philosophy of the nightwatchman state. On the contrary, peasant, artisan, and working-class movements punctuate the evolution of English society and challenge the idea that the state should not be defined by a vocation to shape civil society so as to assure its citizens a just and equal right to fulfillment, as social and economic persons. And it is certainly the case that the consensus that characterized British political life for most of the years after 1945 bore a more notable resemblance to the Rawlsian notion of a preferential state, actively enhancing the prospects of the least advantaged, than the virtuous indifference envisaged by Mill. In the light of Thatcherism and its enduring legacy, and in view of the timid role being proposed for the state by New Labour, one may wonder whether that consensus was not in fact an aberration. Though contested, and sometimes out of fashion, the assumption that has nonetheless endured and shaped the thinking of the English political establishment is the notion of two spheres, the distinction between the civil and the civic: the civil denoting that private, market-driven and inegalitarian realm in which the individual can freely pursue his interest; and the civic denoting that community of collective rights and obligations to which the individual must adapt for the greater good.

The absence of an explicit commitment governing the actions of those elected to discharge the legislative functions of the state, to define the citizen as a global being within a broad social context which it is the vocation of the state to create, is what in Britain lies at the root of the reliance on ceremony, mystery, or what in Pierre Bourdieu's brand of sociology might be called "social magic."[5] Walter Bagehot's[6] still classic definition of the English constitution evokes a ceremonial function represented by the crown, the key to the continuity of which, as an effective counterbalance to the legislative and executive powers of the state, lay in its mystery. No one who has seen the queen inaugurating the beginning of a parliamentary session could find a more appropriate ceremonial for the analysis of the exercise of symbolic power. Her articulation of the government's program, on the one hand, underlines the democratization of the power that was once solely the monarch's, but on the other hand, symbolizes the act of delegation which transfers, in classical terms, the skeptron to the government, enabling it to articulate the interests of the commonwealth from which it derives its legitimacy. The term, "her majesty's government," encapsulates the mystery which, if it is to allow the English polity to function, must persuade the citizen of the disinterested nature of a government whose vocation may not have been historically determined by a popular desire for liberty, equality, and fraternity but, conversely, whose vocation prevents it from encroaching on that sphere of civil society which is the domain of the private individual or individuals.

The French Republican Tradition

What a contrast then to the model established by the French Revolution, where, proceeding from assumptions antithetical to those distinctions that characterize the English tradition, what occurs is a great process of uniformisation through the operation of the state. The citizen who emerges in the declaration of the rights of man and the citizen is an abstract conjoining of the person in his/her civil guise as a private individual, together with his or her persona as a civic entity, part of a community of rights underscored by principles of intervention, egalitarianism, and solidarity. Furthermore, this loss of particularity is exacerbated by the conflation of the new citizen with the even more abstract notion of Man, in the sense of universal fraternity. This, allied to the transfer of sovereignty to the Nation, whose will, in theory, was expressed by the unitary voice of the state, meant that the citizen was defined primarily in relation to the national state, making the process of "assimilation" the key criterion for success, both for the individual with regard to his or her social ascent and for the state in the assumption of its republican vocation.

This, of course, was not an unproblematic or unchallenged process. The ostensibly liberating, underlying notion of "assimilation" engendered a discourse on citizenship which revealed, from the outset, the real limits placed on egalitarian integration by political and economic factors. With the advent of 1789, the eighteenth-century notion of *l'homme universel*, identifiable everywhere and across all cultures, underwent a radical transformation driven by a determination to overturn absolute historical distinctions in the pursuit of a *citoyen universel*, or universal citizen. More than the stamp bestowed by a new set of legal rights and obligations, the attribution of citizenship expressed the desire by revolutionary France to defeat the kind of anthropological determinisms that had hitherto divided the nation against itself, by replacing them with a will to unity embodied in the notion of citizenship and the new value system it would engender. This act of radical voluntarism was of fundamental importance in the invention of modern France,[7] and laid down a foundation myth for the emerging *République*. However, the disparity between the myth and the reality became an almost immediate bone of contention as the citizens of France began to encounter the constraints on their revolutionary *raison d'être*; i.e., their freedom to act on an ostensibly new and universally level playing field.

The step taken by the National Assembly on 29 October 1789 when it passed the decree introducing the category of "active citizens" was a step forward in underlining that in future in France, power was to emanate from below. It is noteworthy, however, that what the term implied in practice was immediately challenged. The right to vote accorded to active citizens was hedged about with conditions that were quite at odds with the principles of civil equality that had been proclaimed on 26 August 1789 in the Declaration of the Rights of Man and the Citizen. Although in 1790 the franchise was extended to those approximately 4.3 million active citizens who were male, and who paid the equivalent of three days unskilled labor in taxes, the obstacles to genuine participation were in fact greater than they had been for the elections to the Estates-General under the *ancien régime*. Although the Deputies of the National Assembly in 1789 were glad of the mass support that had brought them to power, they had no wish to be controlled by it. When Camille Desmoulins commented bitterly, "But what is this much repeated word *active citizen* supposed to mean? The active citizens are the ones who took the Bastille,"[8] it expressed frustration at a form of participation offered to the citizenry that lacked genuinely democratic substance. And in the years that followed, serious debate about 1789 and its consequences did not center on the validity of the principle of "assimilation," embodied in a citizenry that was defined by its active participation in the political process, but on the extent to which this principle had been fulfilled or frustrated.

In the historical perspective defined by Alexis de Tocqueville, revolutionary radicalism ultimately proved to be the atavistic reflex of the absolute state: the despotism of the *ancien régime* was replaced by the despotism of the omnipresent and intrusive state which, although it had broken the ties which once yoked men unequally, proceeded to make them equally unfree as dependent and servile subjects. For Edgar Quinet, the civil equality that followed 1789 was transient, failed to materialize in institutional terms and was ended by what Quinet judged to be the restoration of a traditional form of absolute power by the Jacobins. By way of contrast, for Michelet, writing his narrative of the Revolution in the aftermath of 1848, the aspirations of 1789 marked the advent of a secular faith in equality and fraternity that had been betrayed but that would triumph again.

In spite of the divergent analyses of the reasons for the failures that followed 1789, the central importance of the citizen, actively assimilated to the body politic, was evoked in all of them. Michelet identified the citizen, conscious of his mission, as the driving force behind the progress of the revolutionary credo.[9]

Once the initiative to participate actively was withdrawn from the citizens, according to Quinet, revolutionary democracy was destined to fail. Underlying Tocqueville's analysis of the failure of democracy is a sense that this is preceded by an abdication of moral responsibility on the part of the citizen which leads to a contempt for public life and the social fabric it sustains, engendering its consequent and inevitable deterioration.[10] From whichever perspective it was viewed therefore, a polity could only be robust through the assimilation of a citizenry socialized and energized by that union.

The conflation of the civil and the civic, of the nation and the state, of Man, as a universal concept, and the citizen, resulted in a political culture where, to paraphrase Michel Wievorka,[11] the national state came to act as an overarching means for condensing and regulating social and political questions, and questions concerning the private and public individual. The classic assumption determining the agenda of French governing elites has therefore been that the aim of all political combat is the conquest of the state, because the state is the incarnation of the indivisible nation and the sole legitimate instrument of social transformation.

The supposition that there is a rigid and widespread fidelity to the republican paradigm for assimilating private to public concerns in the pursuit of change, has been in question even at times when that paradigm should have been most fêted. The bicentenary celebration of the French revolution revealed a surprising and widespread ignorance among France's citizens about the events and actors of 1789. A series of polls conducted among a representative cross-section of French society revealed that one-third of those interviewed did not know the nationality of Marie-Antoinette; almost half were unaware of how Danton died, the role of Saint-Just in the Revolution and whether Robespierre was Montagnard or Girondin.[12]

Findings of the foregoing nature have served to fuel speculation that the paradigm of assimilation established by the Revolution is now undermined by the kind of atavism that unpicks the nexus of common interest which binds the citizen to the Republic, leading to a prospective "désagrégation" of the polity. Alain Minc, for example, argues that in France today the traditional boundaries determined by the state, society, family, and the related freedoms and obligations they engender, are occluded by "gray zones" no longer susceptible to the authority of the foregoing institutions and which reverse the integrating, politically modernizing impetus of 1789, thereby drawing France into a kind of new "middle age."[13]

It is as true of France as of post-industrial western democracies in general that as the influence of normative systems of belief like religion and ideology have waned, and as individuals have become more distant from their social origins, the imperative of fulfillment has become powerfully and personally differentiated.[14] And it may be argued that this process of personalization has permeated the disciplined structures that order the world of politics, appropriating the prerogatives that were once exercised in the collective pursuit of social well-being. The conception of liberty by Rousseau, Saint-Just and others as a social project, is now challenged by what has been called a "parasitic" notion of liberty, that is liberty as a niche or individual space to be hollowed out of the body politic; a process accelerated by what is perceived by an increasing number of French citizens as the redundancy of the political cleavages created by 1789, such as the distinction between left and right.[15] The manifest implausibility of left-wing messianism and the inappropriateness of conservative social and moral assumptions about a pluralistic society like France have left a growing number of citizens unwilling to commit the pursuit of their objectives to the political structures emanating form the traditional foregoing cleavages.

One of the ironies endured by the Socialists under Mitterrand was their rejection by the constituency which had traditionally been most ardent in its support for the millenarist visions of the left. For the 18–24 year-olds who entered the political fray for the first time during the 1980s, the existence of a government of the left did not represent a historic opportunity as it would have done for their counterparts twenty years before. Instead, it represented, for many, just another face of the established order. Those *soixante-huitards* who had gained access to power had become locked in its embrace and indistinguishable from the establishment they had once aspired to change. They had learned to combine their Keynesian, collectivist, and statist vision with a strong measure of economic orthodoxy in order to manage French capitalism.[16] While the stunning reversal of fortune for the center-right in the legislative elections of spring 1997 brought the Socialists back to government, forcing Gaullist president Jacques Chirac to cohabit with Socialist prime minister Lionel Jospin. The latter, like his British counterpart Tony Blair, is most notable for the way his socialist beliefs have adapted to the contours of an opposition once anathematized in left-wing ideology: the division between private and public. Whereas once the provision of well-being, private and corporate, was to be pursued through the assimilation of those ambitions into the public sphere, now there is an increasingly overt acknowledgment that the private sphere is the most propitious to the fulfillment of the desire for change in individual, and even collective destinies.

The identification with the Republican state as the mirror image of the individual self is no longer underwritten by the traditional discourse of social transformation. The vote for Jospin's Socialists in France, like the vote for Blair's new model Labour Party in Britain, was the result of the judgment inflicted on administrations perceived by the electorate as discredited by their venality and obsessive deference to free-market shibboleths. The vote for the "new labour" or "socialist" ticket was not an endorsement for the traditional teleology of the left and the all-encompassing change that envisaged, but for labels that, ideologically, carried little or no performative resonance. The irony was that while the majority of voters in both countries might have hoped for administrations inclined to protect those areas where civil interest and civic obligation cohere, such as where the private individual may expect, as a taxpayer, the state to guarantee a certain degree of well-being, that expectation has been punctured. Thus while Blair has preserved the status quo ante in fields like education and health, even reinforcing the notion that private and personal provision is ineluctable as well as more efficient, Jospin has persevered with the more dramatic U-turn in the political culture of France undertaken by his predecessor, Alain Juppé.

Juppé's determination to make France meet the economic convergence criteria that would enable it to join the European single currency in 1999, not only laid the ghost of the Jacobin nationalism of the Revolution, but also sharply circumscribed the purview of state responsibility vis-à-vis its employees, and citizens as a whole. The wave of strikes which paralyzed France in the autumn of 1995 was a reaction to the pursuit of a policy aimed at releasing the state from the fiscal bonds of life-long employment protection for those in state industries, and substantially diminishing the cradle-to-grave protection that made the French welfare state one of the most generous in the world. But while ostensibly an alternative to Juppé, Jospin has continued the policies which undermine the vocation of the state as the guarantor of egalitarian norms of social well-being. Thus the policy of dismantling state ownership of key national industries has continued, and in the budget of September 1997 Jospin's government increased the tax take on the nation's income by ff14 billion, crucially reversing a century of pro-natalist policies by cutting back on the tax breaks allowed for the purchase of child care.

One could argue that Jospin is the product of a divorce that has been occurring for some time and to which one of the partners, in this case the political establishment, has only recently woken up. The recent introduction of quantitative criteria in France to measure the performance of the state's schools has indicated the extent to which one of the nation's great uniformizing institutions, *l'école républicaine*, has become distanced from the role that Jules Ferry and his colleagues had envisaged for it as a monopoly supplier of a progressive republican identity. The notion of the state school setting the benchmark in the pursuit of upward social self-definition is no longer a sure value, as surveys show that of the top 16 *lycées* in France which enable 100 percent of their students to pass the *baccalauréat*, 14 are private.[17] This has come against the general background of a quiet revolution signified by an ever-growing number of attempts to elaborate new structures with new approaches for defining the citizen's relationship to his or her society in an active way, but one which departs from the traditional party-oriented paradigm. One such attempt was signaled by the growth of *associations* during the 1980s and 1990s, determined to exercise influence on the public sphere, while resolutely rooted in the private sphere. *La vie associative* and the organizations through which it operates are well-established factors in ensuring the smooth functioning of French civil society. In the fields of cultural production, youth work, training, and myriad other activities, *associations* have for many years been delegated the responsibilities and corresponding funds which governments have deemed them most competent to handle, or have received subsidies from Paris and local authorities to underwrite their own initiatives. The new *associations* which sprang up added a new dimension to their activities, staking a clear claim on the battleground for values around which the citizens of France can rally and which allow them to construct a civil identity that is separate from, but which enables them to engage actively with, what they perceive as their civic obligations.

Charente première, *Association des citoyens*, *Mouvement national citoyens citoyennes* are three such associations which emerged in the early 1990s and assumed a high profile. For these associations, the talk was not full of pessimistic allusions to "désagrégation," but rather a positive form of "désolidarisation" from the institutional apparatus for integration that had come to embody a sense of crushing homogenization. Alain Schmit, guiding the future of *Charente première*, summed up its ambition as being to provide a forum for those citizens who wish to decide for themselves what their convictions will be. *Associations des citoyens*, founded in 1990 by Jean-François Chantaraud, drew attention to itself through the organization of public debates and other activities dealing with issues like unemployment, social justice, education, Europe and the environment because of what it judged to be the failure of the parties to address these pressing problems effectively. As for *Mouvement national citoyens citoyennes*, founded in June 1990 and particularly successful in recruiting higher civil servants, its avowed intention is to make the commitment to accountability the indispensable precondition for the exercise of all forms of political power.

On one level, there is much truth in the argument that the high moral ground taken by the *associations* in France is a response to what has been perceived as the moral vacuum at the heart of the establishment, in the light of the successive scandals during the 1980s and early 1990s concerning the illegal funding of political parties and the corrupt relations between government ministers, of both left and right, and clandestine financial interests. However, on a more profound level, the disjunct between the ethical expectations of French citizens vis-à-vis the Republic and their understanding of their obligations towards it in its institutional emanations, is symptomatic of what has been described as "le crépuscule du devoir," or "the twilight of duty." Paradoxically, the rebuttal of the "sacrificial" values that assimilated the individual to the family, church or polity, rather than leading to a decline of ethical preoccupations has in reality led to their proliferation, as norms become increasingly individualized and ethics subjectivized.[18]

The activities of many independent associations and Anglo-American style interest groups may be regarded as reflecting a phenomenon which has been termed "universalized poujadism"[19] in that they were spawned by a crisis of representation, attracting constituencies which feel alienated by the traditional political families and threatened, especially, by economic and social change. However, in contrast to the artisans and shopkeepers who rallied to Pierre Poujade in the mid-1950s to express their discontent at what they perceived to be their exclusion from the growing prosperity of the French Fourth Republic, the demand for different kinds of representation and empowerment implied by the growth in associations does not stem from clearly identifiable professional or geographical constituencies. It is, instead, multiform and diffuse.

What is currently occurring in France is in a sense a new revolution, a transition from the *citoyen universel* to the *citoyen particulier* whose identity is not mediated by a state-led political culture but is one made to measure by the wearer; a postmodern convulsion but one with a particularly Gallic resonance in view of France's contribution to the intellectual legacy of the eighteenth-century. The *citoyen universel* was the fruit of the union between the individual subject and an enlightenment rationalism that envisaged progress as the elimination of the obstacles to the reign of Reason. The disintegration of classic ideologies and universalized concepts has fractured the homology between the individual subject and society as the collective subject. The postmodern individual, being neither the citizen of an enlightenment society or a creature of God, now answers solely to, and identifies only with, his or her project.[20]

Conflicting Traditions and Converging Realities

As Alain Touraine implies in the weighty study cited above, the challenge now is to redefine the vocation of the Republic so that the individual can identify once more with it, perhaps, as we approach the twenty-first century, as the provider of a collective sanctuary against the atomizing depredations of uninhibited market forces. As some critics have remarked, in a sense Touraine is serving up old wine in new bottles, by looking for a way of reversing the much discussed phenomenon of depoliticization and restoring the credibility and centrality of the essentially jacobin republican state. But underlying Touraine's project is a concern voiced across Europe and the rest of the developed world, that by passively accepting the demise of the notion of political community, we may be paving the way for a potentially dangerous dualization of society: that is, a division of society into those who are citizens by virtue of their ability to compete in the market, and those individuals disenfranchised and denied effective participation in society because of their inability to compete.

Whether from within France or from *outre-Manche*, there is a growing consensus that what separated the Anglo-Saxon from the French Republican model for the relation between the civil and the civic, and the repercussions for the elaboration of an identity in relation to the polity, has been superseded by the convergence determined by the realities to which both traditions must adjust in two, comparable post-industrial societies. In particular, the perceptible ideological exhaustion of the revolutionary impetus in France[21] has transformed a uniformizing body politic into one of increasingly independent articulations. The challenge therefore, particularly acute for France in view of its traditions, will be to find a way of managing the divergent interests[22] serving plural identities, if the polity is to continue to serve its very vital function in an increasingly anti-political age.

Conclusion

The challenge to the classical republican model of the relationship between the civil and the civic, the individual and the collectivity, the citizen and the state, is particularly acute in France because of the very distinct political culture that has evolved in that society over the two centuries since the revolution of 1789. However, as the authors of the revolution made clear in manifestos like the Declaration of the Rights of Man and the Citizen, the French revolution was universalist in its ambition for humanity, and as the first of the great modern revolutions destined for export it played a significant part in shaping the discourse of contemporary political life, even in the most elementary terms such as "left" and "right." The pressure emanating from the base of society on the traditional representative institutions of the French republic, added to the pressure from above generated by the construction of the supra-national European Union, make the developments in France, the first modern nation-state on the European mainland, a powerful indicator of the way the classical relationship between the nation-state and its subjects has reached a crossroads on the journey to the creation of a common European home for the peoples of the continent.

Notes

[1] By "polity" I mean a society organized through the operation of civil government and the institutions of the state.

[2] "In cases where the Sovereign has prescribed no rule, there the Subject hath the Liberty to do, or forbeare, according to his own discretion." T. Hobbes, *Leviathan*. London: Dent, 1975, 115.

[3] J. Locke, *The Second Treatise of Government*. Indianapolis: Bobbs-Merrill, 49.

[4] J.S. Mill, *Utilitarianism, On Liberty, and Considerations on Representative Government*. London: Dent, 1972, 165.

[5] P. Bourdieu, *Language and Symbolic Power*. Cambridge: Polity Press, 208.

[6] W. Bagehot, *The English Constitution*. London: Fontana Library edition, 1963.

[7] This is the thesis developed by H. Le Bras, and E. Todd, in *L'Invention de la France*. Paris: Pluriel, 1981.

[8] Quoted in Wickham Legg, L.G. *Select Documents Illustrative of the History of the French Revolution: The Constituent Assembly*, 2 vols. Oxford: Clarendon Press, 1905, I, 173–4.

[9] J. Michelet, *Histoire de la Révolution française*. Paris: Gallimard, 1952, I, 328.

[10] A. De Tocqueville, "L'Ancien régime et la Révolution, fragments et notes inédites." *Oeuvres Complètes*. Paris: Calmann-Lévy, 1953, tome II, 2, 275.

[11] M. Wievorka, "L'Etat et ses sujets." *Projet* no. 233 (spring 1993): 17–25.

[12] The findings of these polls are summarized by O. Duhamel, in "La révolution française est terminée." *Pouvoirs* 50 (1989): 121–25.

[13] A. Minc, *Le nouveau moyen âge*. Paris: Gallimard, 1993.

[14] G. Lipovetsky, *L'Ere du vide: essais sur l'individualisme contemporain*. Paris: Gallimard, 1983, 14.

[15] N. Tenzer, *La société dépolitisée*. Paris: PUF, 1990, 216.

[16] P. Ory, *L'Aventure culturelle française 1945–1989*. Paris: Flammarion, 1989, 224.

[17] C. Baudelot, & R. Establet, "Les meilleurs lycées ne sont pas ceux qu'on croit." *Le Nouvel Observateur*, 27 March – 2 April 1997, 8–9.

[18] G. Lipovetsky, *Le crépuscule du devoir. L'éthique indolore des nouveaux temps démocratiques*. Paris: Gallimard, 1992, 14.

[19] P. Rosanvallon, "Malaise dans la représentation." In F. Furet, J. Julliard, and P. Rosanvallon, (eds) *La République du centre*. Paris: Calmann-Lévy, 1988, 150.

[20] A. Touraine, *Critique de la modernité*. Paris: Fayard, 1992, 410.

[21] J. Hayward, "Ideological change: the exhaustion of the revolutionary impetus." In P. Hall, J. Hayward, and H. Machin, (eds.) *Developments in French Politics*. London: MacMillan, 1990, 32.

[22] This is the challenge identified by Geoff Mulgan in, *Politics in an Antipolitical Age*. Cambridge: Polity Press, 1994, 24.

Identity and Difference in Multicultural Communities

Cristiana Senigaglia

Unlike traditional communities, which were characterized by a relatively homogeneous and restricted self-understanding, modern society has claimed to have universal validity and applicability of its founding principles. Its views have often vouched for equality, but that has been understood in an abstract and generic sense, which wasn't able to give an adequate account of the qualitatively different aspects concerning each person or group. This procedure has been based on logic centered on identity, which considered difference as a simply derived aspect (different "from" something).

A pattern of understanding more attentive to differences and qualities has the task of seeking new forms of interactive relation between identity and difference, rather than being centered generally on identity. This change of perspective is important because it entails a different way of understanding the relationship between the self and the other person too, and in the more extended sphere of the intercultural exchanges it can add to greater interest and recognition for the other as an entity co-operating with the constitution of the identity of the self.

I

In traditional, closed and relatively homogeneous communities, the differences in mental attitude and the concept of life could be seen as an internal differentiation, which was nevertheless related to a certain unity of intention and a shared reference to common values. The radically different was conceived as something extraneous, not really belonging to the conceptual framework of that particular society, and it was either interpreted by means of the normally used categories or not experienced at all.

A good example are the cities of ancient Greece, which in spite of continuous conflicts and rivalries against one another, still showed a certain unity of culture, values and understanding. Although they were societies based on commerce, navigation and contacts with other countries, the common ground of their culture was not affected by their being brought into close contact with other cultures or views on life, which they considered barbaric.

If a background unity in the fundamental and commonly shared values of a community is there, the possibility of dramatic conflicts wasn't excluded in any way. Antigone's tragedy, which represents, according to Hegel,[1] the conflict

between the familiar piety and the laws of the State, and furthermore between a religious morality and a politically outlined "State-reason", is the typical example of conflicting points of view, which cannot be thrown together as a synthesis. Otherwise the Sophists' disputes about the conflicting relation between nature and law, *phýsis* and *nómos*, attest that conflicts were all but removed from the level of the philosophical arena.
Nevertheless, there are some basic mental attitudes which are commonly shared: for instance the idea that an argumentative discussion, based on rational grounds, is able to discover the right path toward the truth, or the conviction that there is a substantial identity between authentic knowledge and the moral ideals of goodness and virtue.

This common background, which is extended to concrete perspectives about several aspects of the social, political, and even religious life too, are not really questioned, even if the realm of the most wide-spread opinions is refuted or criticized. In this sense there is no appreciable difference between Socrates and Plato on the one hand, and Aristotle on the other hand. It is well known that Socrates and Plato distance their philosophical research from the supposed certitudes of the common opinion (*dóxa*). True knowledge is acquired by means of a radical call into question of shared convictions, and a systematic criticism of common judgement. Nevertheless, this critical procedure is performed by taking into consideration both the common people's opinions and the cultural or literary wisdom, conveyed by philosophers and poets. Furthermore, the new level of research consists of an incessant dialogue, which aims to create, on a new and "true" basis, a general consensus among the participants.[2] That is to say, the new method and its performance are concerned with a commonly shared patrimony of beliefs, traditions and cognitions, even if they are refuted and assumed by others as only a basis for upsetting that perspective. Furthermore, Plato tries to establish a consensual unity again, as he outlines the way to truth as the logical, coherent result of a discussion held on an argumentative basis, which aims for the reconstitution of a rational agreement. The real science is only one, and the convergence of the view-points as well as the general acceptance of the resulting conclusions are taken to be a guarantee of the progressive elevation to the realm of ideas and truth.

In Aristotle the reference to tradition and to the common values of the *pólis* is even clearer and more unequivocal; he describes a set of concrete virtues to be practiced in everyday social life and generally recognizes attitudes and patterns that exist.[3] His ethics, which aim to the foundation of a new science, are nevertheless deeply rooted in some common perspectives of the age: the primacy of the contemplative life, the intrinsic social nature of man, the high significance of citizenship and participation in political activity. The meaning of common values and tradition are mirrored in Aristotle's specific methodical approach: both the poets' opinions and the popular points of view are seriously taken into account, discussed and if possible integrated into a more analytical exposition of the problem. Aristotle doesn't shape his philosophical works in the form of dialogues, like Plato; he gives his preference to the genre of the treatise. Nevertheless, he creates the premises for an ideal dialogue, as he discusses other instances and seeks a consensus on the basis of rational argumentation. In addition, the different positions taken into consideration are the product of a relatively homogeneous background, from which foreigners are completely exempt. This excludes *a priori* the possibility of a profitable comparison with alternative sets of values extrapolated by different cultures.

Also the medieval world, which was lacerated by grave conflicts within, was nevertheless dominated by a central function of religion and by a hierarchical representation of reality, which were commonly accepted. The most relevant attempt to structure a philosophical system was performed by St. Thomas, who sought a conciliation between Christian religion and ancient philosophy (especially Aristotle). As MacIntyre clearly pointed out, philosophical systems of that age were inspired by a concrete and traditional notion of goodness, influenced by theological conceptions and expressed by a firm and hierarchical set of values.[4]

II

At the beginning of the modern age, exploration and travel caused a radical change of perspective and points of view. The discovery of other continents, inhabited by populations with very different habits and ways of life, brought for the first time actual diverse realities and systems of values into contact. The gradual dissolution of the social and political structures supporting the hierarchical organization of the medieval world contributed to formulating new conceptions and patterns of life. The leading tendency consisted of a refusal of authority and tradition and of the search for a new normative criteria based especially on empirical knowledge and reason. This new attitude, supported by the increasing results of a science founded upon quantity concepts and mathematical laws, contributed to the prevalence of a method seeking universal principles and rules.

It is a wide-spread tendency of many contemporaneous philosophers (I think for example of Foucault,[5] Arendt,[6] MacIntyre, although they belong to very different schools of thought) to criticize the basic ideas of modernity. One of the fundamental objections relates to the universalizing principles and laws, which don't give an account of qualities, differences, specificity.

This kind of criticism, which is connected to the remark pointing out the excessive stress on subjectivity, often leads to a devaluation of modernity as such. Neither should it be forgotten, that this way of conceiving reality had a radically upsetting and emancipatory effect. The political theory especially, pointing out the natural, that is to say the fundamental rights of the individuals, set quite apart from differences of birth, class and belongings and stressed the equality of each person in the eyes of the law. But this meant at the same time, undermining the old system of privileges and asserting a new conception of justice.

As Charles Taylor pointed out,[7] there are two main tendencies in the political thought of the modern age, both of which stress the aspect of equality. The first one encloses the theories of *natural right*. The second one emphasizes the moment of *participation* and decision about public affairs.

1) The first kind of theories, beyond their different statements, excludes the old system of hierarchy and legitimizes a political system based on the equality of rights for its members. The reference to nature is a device to prove the existence of some fundamental rights which are equally assigned and are not to be injured by the political order. These rights are not dependent on the position of individuals in the society, and they guarantee the legal equality of citizens. According to these theories, the respect due to one's private sphere is strictly related to the status of the individual and to his or her dignity. In other words, the person is first of all worthy as an individual.

With respect to the historical situation, this means a revolutionary conception of the political and social reality. This in turn means that people's consideration should be based on human dignity and not in relation to the specific function ascribed to in the society. On the other hand, the stress on individuals entails an atomized vision of the society, and individuals are therefore considered as particles not qualitatively differentiated one from another. That is to say, the new political systems are very respectful about individuals' private spheres and their particular interests, but they don't prescribe any rules taking these differences into consideration. Self-realization is a matter for the individual, he or she can develop his or her potentiality in all directions consented by law, but there is no support for the preservation of specificity. The individual is equated with an atom, and all other elements constituting his or her identity (language, family, tradition, culture, way of life) are left out of the account.

2) The second tendency of political modern thought emphasizes the moment of *participation* and *decision* about public affairs. This perspective finds its first relevant theoretical justification in Rousseau's political philosophy and its historical expression during the French Revolution. Like the theories of natural right, this conception refuses to recognize the distinction between persons, based on classes, functions, privileges, etc. The founding idea is that all individuals are equal and equally recognized as citizens, and thanks to this qualification they all have the right of participating in public life and in political decisions. The basic issue is the right to vote and moreover the principle: "one person, one vote."

This conception, which found its concrete expression in democracy, has gained remarkable historical relevance in the process of emancipation set in motion in the modern age. Its principles also entail that persons are essentially considered as individuals (or, more exactly, citizens) apart from any qualitative difference or distinction. Membership to a political community ascribes them a dignity, that as a matter of fact is of equal worth and the same for all citizens. The political rights are concerned with the dignity of persons belonging to a particular society, and not with their concrete personal identity.

The two principles described by Charles Taylor differ in the shaping of the relationships between private and public, individual and State. While the theories of natural right aim to preserve a sphere ascribed to the individual which the society cannot invade, the democratic theories are more centered on the active participation of the members of the community to political life. Both prescribe, although to a different extent and meaning, a field of action pertaining to the individual, inside of which he or she, without damaging other people's freedom, can seek his or her self-realization. But specificity is left, at least as a matter of principle, out of the account.

III

The two main tendencies of political thought in the modern age strove by different means for the same result: a society founded on equality, in which people are considered with the same dignity and worth. Notwithstanding the improvement in the sphere of individual and political rights that this process was able to attain, there were some negative aspects which are not to be overlooked. The prevailing of mass societies in this century has especially contributed to an increase in the spirit of conformity and to the devaluation of personal identity; this tendency has found no counterbalance.

On the other hand, people have been confronted with radically different societies and systems of values, which have either made their own convictions dubious or provoked conflicts and tensions. Our modern system of communication has been responsible for a radical change of our perspective and coordinates: it has immediately put different societies in touch with completely different ways of life, without providing them with the suitable instruments of knowledge and comprehension. Every day we are informed about world-wide events; we can physically reach a place in just a few hours and by means of the Internet or the Telefax we can immediately be put into contact with others, without knowing anything about the persons with whom we are communicating.

Besides, the economic and social situation has contributed to bringing these separate worlds immediately in touch. And this happens not only through the largely discussed process of globalization, but also in our everyday life. At every corner we meet persons belonging to other cultures, religions, countries, who don't share our habits and rules.

The result is that we live in a condition of permanent tension and contradiction. On the one hand, the politically prevailing conceptions stress our individual being and the defense of the rights concerning the person. On the other hand, these rights are conceived as being something totally abstract and impersonal, applying to anyone happening to be in the same situation, and the situations themselves being imagined in a too highly theoretical and formal way.

Otherwise, this contradiction can be related to the most relevant political results, our democratic systems were able to attain. The long fight against privileges has led to the elimination of differences, which were merely considered as an obstacle to the performance of the equality of rights. But this attitude has contributed to omitting specificity and differences, which have turned out to be essential to the constitution of personal identity. The individual becomes aware that his or her recognition guaranteed by law, mainly or exclusively concerns his or her human being and overlooks the concrete personal qualities and directions of development. The term "self-realization" is often a question of theoretical utterance, which doesn't correspond to the true state of things.

This sense of indefinite dissatisfaction takes shape by means of an obstinate although implicit refusal of unity and homogeneity, often accompanied by an exaggerated will or desire to distinguish from the other. It testifies to the inability of dealing with identity and difference, similarity and distinction. But as these categories are first of all logical instruments of comprehension, we need therefore a different logical scheme, in order to make them in a new way accessible and understandable.

IV

In our system of logic we are used to thinking first of all in terms of identity. Identity is the first and fundamental principle which has to be maintained, and it represents something tendentially eternal, always equal to itself, not changing or modifying its status at all. Categories such as time and change are normally excluded from our basic logical system. To the contrary, difference is always something dependent on and related to something else; that is to say, we usually perceive the "difference" as something secondary, deriving its status from an external principle, not deserving the same solid, stable structure as identity does.

The dialectical method of thinking has made partial changes in this perspective. It has introduced a dynamic movement internal to logic and it has made possible the comprehension of such categories as time and change (relating the distinct moments to each other, so that they are no longer rigidly opposed, but the one is engendered by the other and exerts an influence over the first generating principle, too). This involves a dynamic understanding of identity, which originates from itself its opposite and is actively modified by it.[8] But the dialectical movement has an innate tendency to maintain identity as well. As a matter of fact, it's true that identity is no longer as stable and static as in the traditional way of thinking, but the dialectical dynamics is a dynamics of the *coming back*: identity changes, becomes alienated, but its (more or less) secret aim is to make the different own, to set a process of appropriation in motion, which is performed by the synthesis.[9] The identity in this case is something more and something less: something more than a stiff substance, and something less than a true openness to the other.

A logical system which would abolish the priority of identity, should maybe displace the center of gravity, which is usually focused on identity as the original starting-point, and find a new fulcrum in the interstice between identity and difference, swinging between the two poles. A possibility could be found in the development of a logical pattern which considers identity and difference as founded in parallel and therefore so intimately related to each other, that identity can be defined only by taking into account the difference (from something or someone else) and on the other hand, that difference can be ascertained only in relation to identity.

This scheme can have a first immediate phenomenological application in relation to the process of the constitution of personal identity. This process has been usually understood by the philosophical tradition either as an act of self-affirmation of the subject[10] or as a movement of dialectical alienation and reintegration. These different interpretations have given rise to alternative ways to articulate the notion and understanding of personal identity. Nevertheless, they all had one aspect in common: they were centered on the moment of identity, of synthesis understood as a coming back to the self. Identity was conceived as a steady substance, principle or function, around which the whole process revolved. Especially the process of constitution of the other was considered both from a logical and a phenomenological[11] standpoint as something subsequent and derivated. The other was logically deduced or constituted by means of an analogy to the self.

An innovation in this sense has been introduced by so-called postmodern thinking, which has stressed the difference, the instability and change dissolving every form of unity and identity called a "subject." By pointing out the structures or processes individuals are inscribed within, the "subject" has been reduced to a fiction, a mask, the mere cover of an emptiness or an interstice. But as MacIntyre has pointed out referring to Foucault,[12] it is impossible to imagine to the last consequences a similar loss of identity, because it would entail the impossibility of memory, communication and thinking. MacIntyre's sound argument is: in order to think or to communicate, we must suppose something persisting from the beginning to the end of the process as well as someone else listening to us and turning out to be stable and addressable. Were we submitted to a continuous modification and change, we'd be unable to bring our thoughts, speeches, etc. with a certain coherence to an end, and we couldn't expect to make ourselves understandable to anybody else. We are supposed to be in some way steady and persistent, and our way of thinking, acting, speaking shows us that it is really so.

This objection excludes a complete elimination of identity, but doesn't entail the necessity of a self-centered subject. A displacement of the center of gravity in the process of the constitution of identity could give reason for a change of perspective, without involving an annihilation of the self. Indeed, although we often deny this point, our process of constitution of the self is not an operation which takes place quite apart from external reality. Even if we are used to abstracting from reality and reflecting on the conditions concerning the self and its existence, the experience we repeatedly have in our life shows us another way.

V

The experience of the self is an experience we originally have as a being in the world. We live in a particular environment, we come into contact with objects and persons, we are embedded in a social reality which determines in one way or another the directions of our thinking and acting. The analysis of the self can be an operation of consciousness and introspection, but it cannot represent the originating moment of the experience of the self.

This experience takes place in the world, it is not the result of a specific event, but it occurs in the two-fold moment of *meeting face to face* and *collision* with the other. The sudden encounter doesn't perforce involve a conflict:[13] what it does entail, though, is the rise of a relation. We can supposedly ignore the presence of the other, but even this seemingly indifferent attitude would be a form of an answer which we cannot refrain from giving. But besides that, it is at the occasion of this encounter-collision with the other, that we experience our self as a being of different make, of "something" separate from the other yet simultaneously relating to them. And the more impressive this encounter is, the better we experience our self.

This displacement doesn't mean an improvement of the taking into consideration of the other. It nevertheless entails the necessity of paying attention to the way the other appears and the taking of them into account. It entails a basic change of perspective in the utterance of judgements too: instead of taking our point of view as a paradigm to judge the other, we are in one way or another compelled to use a more dynamic and modifiable way of reasoning. The basic constitution of the self through relation prevent from the consideration of the self as an unchangeable entity and from deriving the other from the self.

There are more levels of constituting the relationship between the self and the other, which build an ascending scale: each level is more intensive than the former one, but each of them is the result of a free choice.[14]

The first level is *solicitation*. The encounter with the other causes a reaction, but the way of reacting has not been previously ascribed to: you can answer, or not, and you can answer in rather different ways. The solicitation involves the consideration of the other as being someone of worth, who is able to convey a significant message and an incentive to the self. Through the solicitation, the self perceives the significant existence of someone else, and at the same time constitutes him- or herself as a separate but correlative unity.

The second level is *comparison*. Relating him- or herself to the encounter, the self seriously takes the qualitative nature of the other into account and evaluates similarities and differences. This level involves analysis and a knowledge based on understanding, and entails a comprehensive consideration of the environment, in which the other is embedded. The comparison allows for a more exact definition of the specificity with respect to the self and to the other and allows for the differences to be studied. Nevertheless, this is in some respect an intellectual way of relating to the other.

The third level is *dialogue*. In the dialogue a more practical way of getting into contact with the other takes place. The request to speak, involves not only an intellectual consideration of the other, but also the will to let the other express him- or herself and to confront in the immediate dialogue arena the different points of view. Every level entails a form of active recognition of the other, but only in the dialogue is there place for an active cooperation of the other with the self.

This scale could be transferred to the sphere of the relationships between communities too, seeing them as groups of persons characterized by a commonly shared language, commonly shared customs, traditions and history. Of course, there is a difference between the interpersonal relationships and the inter-communitarian ones. Whereas the interpersonal relations can be thought of as simultaneously constituting the identity of the self and of the other, the identity of a community is something already in existence, a "body" of traditions and language which are structured in a system of values, in a cultural patrimony and in some specific patterns of life.[15] Therefore it is not correct, strictly speaking, to speak of a community as originally building its identity in relation to other communities. Nevertheless, we can argue that a community is not to be thought of as a stiff, invariable entity: the willingness to come into contact with other communities and other ways of thought can signify a spiritual growth for the community itself. A community which seeks interaction with other communities, without imposing its views upon them, turns out to be an intrinsically *dynamic* structure, which doesn't fear the encounter with different realities and is *receptive* to their meanings and messages. A community open to the external, demonstrates a certain internal stability and nevertheless a sensibility to the "different," which is judged worthy of being taken into consideration and possibly counted as an *enrichment* to its own identity too.

Also in this case, the first level of relationship could be *solicitation*, which means a paying attention to the other, an exigence to take the other into account, yet without deepening its qualitative and specific aspect. A community which perceives the solicitation as originating from an external reality (being that a person, a group or a community), is a community which doesn't insist on its own closed ideas and views. It shows an interest in something different too, which can be considered and potentially called into question.

The second level could be *comparison*, which can be effectuated within a community, when this one is confronted with other ways of life and thought. The comparison is normally carried out by intellectuals and experts, but if there is a sane system of communication within the society, the analysis of the characters and the peculiarity of another culture can be conveyed to all members (for example, by means of communication). This procedure ensures a wide-spread knowledge, which contributes to undermining prejudices and creating the requisites for a mutual understanding.

The third level could be *dialogue*, which can be accomplished only on the basis of a mutual recognition founded on respect, worthiness, and dignity. The dimension of the dialogue implies that a community recognizes another community as worthy of being considered and especially of being listened to. The dialogue between communities cannot take place, if one community disregards the other or considers it to be inferior; the dialogue necessitates an openness to the message communicated by the other, which includes a receptive attitude, a desire of deep understanding and the acceptance of the free expression of the other in turn.[16]

Such an understanding of interpersonal or intercommunitarian relations should contemplate an adequate solution in politics too. The criticism of a too simplified conception of equality, which tends to lead to the canceling of differences and specificity, is not to be understood as a refusal of democracy, but as a necessary integration to prevent the alienating mass effects. The next task and challenge for democracy could then be to find an adequate system to cater to originality and difference, without prejudicing the principle of equality of rights. In this respect, the constitutive relation between identity and difference could be transformed into a political unity and equality, which respect differences. The moment of equal respect and consideration should be guaranteed by the subsisting of fundamental rights for all persons, heedless of their social condition or their membership to particular groups (communities, nationalities, religions, etc.). On the other hand, it would be necessary to find new laws and rules, which would increase the possibilities of development for everyone, taking his or her personal desires, capacities, and needs into account. This entails not only a formal guarantee of the rights of self-realization, but also concrete measures aiming to supply people with adequate means, education, economic resources and, particularly, moral support. Moreover, from the point of view of communities, such a perspective should involve at least two things: 1) a strengthening of all measures promoting the existence of cultural communities, helped by a specific legislation preserving the language, customs, memory, and tradition; 2) a political system, structured according to the principles of federalism and inspired by a will to decentralize many offices and tasks: this namely would contribute to creating a stronger contact between citizens and institutions and to characterizing political sub-systems in accord with local habits and needs.

Conclusion

A change of perspective in the relationships among different cultures and communities cannot be considered as an immediate result, as it depends on the specificity of local conditions. To the contrary, it has to be sustained by a different approach to reality, which is deeply rooted even in the logical and reflexive structures of thinking and understanding.

Political proposals and solutions have therefore to be considered under this perspective. That is to say, if multicultural communities are to be seriously taken into account, we have first of all to face the question of how structures of thinking normally act and what kind of consequences are to be expected. Political measures need a correspondence to the prevailing mentality, attitude and understanding. But it cannot be ignored that on principle, by means of far-reaching processes of analysis and understanding, new forms of sensibility and attention can be put into effect.

Notes

[1] See G.W.F. Hegel, *Phänomenologie des Geistes*, ed. E. Moldenhauer and K.M. Michel (Frankfurt/Main: Suhrkamp, 1986), 327–354.

[2] See C. Rowe, *An Introduction to Greek Ethics* (London: Hutchinson, 1976), 41.

[3] See A. MacIntyre's interpretation of Aristotle in his book *After Virtue. A Study in Moral Theory* (Notre Dame, Indiana: University of Notre Dame Press, 1981).

[4] See A. MacIntyre, *Three Rival Versions of Moral Enquiry. Encyclopaedia, Genealogy and Tradition* (Notre Dame, Indiana: University of Notre Dame Press, 1990), especially chapter 6.

[5] See M. Foucault, *Histoire de la folie à l'âge classique* (Paris: Gallimard, 1961) and *A verdade e as formas juridicas*, "Cadernos da P.U.C.," 16, 1974, 5–133.

[6] See H. Arendt, *The Human Condition* (Garden City: Doubleday, 1959).

[7] See especially Ch. Taylor, *Des avenirs possibles: la légitimité, l'identité et l'aliénation au Canada à la fin du XXe siècle* (1986), in: Ch. Taylor, *Rapprocher les solitudes* (Sainte-Foy, Quebec: Les Presses de l'Université Laval, 1992).

[8] This dialectical movement has been precisely described by Hegel in his *Phänomenologie des Geistes*, especially in the chapter about self-conscience, in the part concerning the relation between master and slave.

[9] This way of thinking characterizes the dynamics of Hegel's Absolute Spirit, as it is described in the final pages of his *Enzyklopädie der philosophischen Wissenschaften.*

[10] The most relevant example is Fichte's conception of "Ich," but Descartes' affirmation "Cogito, ergo sum" can also be understood in this way.

[11] Husserl's theory of intersubjectivity is here concerned as well, but the phenomenological method has also been used by Fichte in his *Wissenschaftslehre nova methodo.*

[12] See A. MacIntyre, *Three Rival Versions of Moral Enquiry*, chapter 9.

[13] The experience of the other is therefore not necessarily accompanied by that sensation of hostility and uneasiness, which has been described by Sartre in his book *L'être et le néant.*

[14] In this sense, no level is directly derivable from the former one or automatically dependent on any particular conditions.

[15] I refer here to the communitarian conceptions of social life, based on shared values and history (see especially MacIntyre's and Charles Taylor's idea of community, supported by a commonly shared language).

[16] About the conditions of a real and effective dialogue between different traditions and communities, see especially A. MacIntyre, *Whose Justice? Which Rationality?* (Notre Dame, Indiana: University of Notre Dame Press, 1988), chapter 19.

Richard Coudenhove-Kalergi and The Pan-Europa Movement: Precursors to a United Europe

Guy Stern

Not uncommonly a great personality is defined both by the adherents he gains and the enemies he makes. To begin with the latter, as early as 1931 Count Richard Coudenhove-Kalergi, the founder of the Pan-Europe Movement, was excoriated in a book by a National Socialist publication, part of a series of the infamous Eher Verlag. Hans Krebs, then a member of the Sudetendeutsche Party, devoted large passages of his *Paneuropa oder Mitteleuropa* to the Count and accused him of being a co-conspirator with the French government in a bid to dominate Europe:

> Clearly and distinctly the Pan-Europe Plan now stands in full view as a tool for a renewed enslavement of Germany … They [the world financiers and their cohorts] had very neatly contrived that first Count Coudenhove Kalergi was to make the German brains receptive for a Pan-Europe Plan. His book *Pan Europe* was spread by means of countless editions; the "leading press," in overheated articles, paid tribute to him as the savior of Europe … And thousands of good German philistines enthusiastically championed Pan-Europe.[1]

The tirade of Hans Krebs was prelude to the inevitable fate of the Count and his books when the Nazis came to power. On May 10, 1933, his books were burnt during the Berlin bibliocaust and he and his wife had to seek refuge in the United States.[2] This grisly recognition was accorded him despite the fact that the inspired originator and promulgator of the concept of a United Europe never held an official post and often had to finance his ideas and publications himself.

To turn around now and speak of his followers: he could at various times draw for support on statesmen from Aristide Briand and Winston Churchill to Count Sforza, Eduard Beneš and Harry Truman and intellectuals ranging from Albert Einstein to two generations of the Mann family, to Sigmund Freud to André Gide, Aldous Huxley, H.G. Wells and Nicolaus Murray Butler, to name a few at random.[3]

His full name was Count Richard Nicholaus Coudenhove-Kalergi and in that very name cosmopolitanism reverberates. He was predestined by antecedents and birth to become the advocate of internationalism. *Nomen est omen:* sometimes in the nineteenth century the great-grandparents of the count united by their marriage two strains of European nobility: the Dutch Coudenhoves and the Greek Kalergis — not exactly European neighbors. Going back one more generation one of the first Countesses Coudenhoven, a woman of spectacular beauty, was a contemporary of Goethe. She met him during the Campaign in France. According to Goethe's account of the meeting she was seeking refuge in a neighboring state during those troubled times, anticipating, *kat exochen*, the exile fate of her descendant. Thoroughly worried, she asked Goethe, "How do I become a citizen of the City of Frankfurt?" "Nothing easier," Goethe replied. "Marry me."[4] As not infrequently in such matters, Goethe was not entirely serious, or else there might have been a direct lineage from Goethe to the founder of the Pan-European movement.

But even without embellishing through speculations of "what might have been," the geographical scope of the Coudenhove-Kalergis dramatically widened in the following generations. At a relatively young age the father of Richard Coudenhove-Kalergi, at that time a bachelor but with a tragic liaison behind him, entered the Austrian diplomatic service. His first four postings were Athens, Rio de Janeiro, Constantinople, and Buenos Aires. But the most fateful posting was his appointment as chargé d'affaires in Tokyo in 1890. He very soon became an admirer of Japanese culture and language, the thirteenth language he acquired, and of Buddhism. And not only of them. Two years later his admiration began to extend to Mitsuko Ayuama, the daughter of an aristocratic Tokyo family. Franz Coudenhove-Kalergi was then 33, Mitsuko 18. Against all obstacles, foreign, domestic, and of the Austrian Foreign Service, they managed to get married. Richard Coudenhove-Kalergi, their second child, was born in Tokyo in 1894 and was raised in the Castle Ronsperg in Bohemia, where Hungary, Germany and the future states of Czechoslovakia and Yugoslavia were well within the reach of frequent family travels. It was equally accessible to visits by members of the far-flung family and by acquaintances from around the globe. Environment joined heredity in the making of an internationalist.

His principal tutors were his parents. His father, in part because of the negative reactions to his unconventional marriage, had retired from the diplomatic service.[5] From him Richard Coudenhove-Kalergi absorbed a thorough knowledge of world history, geopolitics, philosophy, much of it pacifist, tolerance for other nations and a spirit of noblesse oblige. It is no accident that he would in later years write an addendum to his father's 1905 analysis and refutation of anti-Semitism[6] and that he would author a socio-historical book on the demise of inherited nobility in favor of an intellectual meritocracy.[7]

These views, acquired at home, did not change during his years at the aristocratic Theresianum high school in Vienna where the precocious young man wrote a book, *Objectivity as a Basic Principle of Morality*, nor did he change as a student of philosophy at the University of Vienna. Remarkably enough his treatise of his high school years was accepted as his doctoral dissertation.[8] Withal he still found time, in that false spring before the outbreak of World War

I, to fall totally in love with one of Europe's leading actresses, Ida Roland, then a leading star at the Burgtheater. He was not the only one to admire her. Rilke, who also saw her perform recorded that she was effervescent "like a fountain."[9] Like his father he moved heaven and earth to hurdle all obstacles against such a misalliance — objections voiced by his mother, his guardian and most of his relatives. And so he married Ida Roland in 1919 who would some years later, at the pinnacle of her career, retire from the stage to help her husband in his single-minded, seemingly utopian quest to unite Europe. Until her death 37 years later she was constantly at his side in the quest for Pan-Europa.

When World War I ended — the pacifist Coudenhove-Kalergi escaped service because of a lung disorder — he found himself with a doctorate, a wife, and no position. Imbued with Wilson's internationalism and repelled by Lenin's plans for world revolution, he decided to freelance on the subject of politics and philosophy. Through analyzing global geopolitics and the political and economic success of the U.S., Coudenhove's thoughts began to crystallize around a United States of Europe, with a European economic union and a European parliament its cornerstones. Richard Coudenhove-Kalergi was at that time 24 years old. In 1923 the 29-year-old, having spelled out his vision, found himself the author of an international best-seller entitled *Pan-Europa*. It was published by his own Paneuropa publishing house, but launched with the active advice of his friend, the publisher Paul Zsolnay.[10]

The global success of the book was, of course, predicated on many factors. To paraphrase Lord Byron, "Europe repentant of her fratricide" feared its recurrence. A United Europe, minus the Soviet Union, held an appeal to many groups across the political spectrum, from Kurt Hiller's pacifist-activist socialism to the middle-of-the-road statesman Aristide Briand and the aristocratic Joseph Caillaux.[11] Also the League of Nations, even though lacking U.S. membership, held out a promise for international understanding.[12] And Richard Coudenhove-Kalergi steadily advanced his germinating ideas in the most influential intellectual journals in Germany: the *Neue Merkur*, the *Neue Rundschau*, and Maximilian Harden's *Die Zukunft*.[13]

For many Germans and Austrians these ideas represented a fresh, easily comprehensible and promising approach during bleak times. In the editorial correspondence of the *Neue Merkur*, miraculously preserved and now in the archives of the N.Y. Leo Baeck Institute, there are several encouraging letters by its editor, Efraim Frisch, who had an unerring feeling for quality and fresh ideas. Long before "Pan Europa" had been fully conceptualized, he sought out contributions from Coudenhove-Kalergi, for example in a letter of 26 July 1921: "I certainly need not reassure you, that your suggestions about future contributions are always welcome."[14] Thus Frisch accepted, as early as 1922, an article, *Europa's technologische Weltmission* in which the thought of European unity is already implicit. While arguing that problems such as poverty, substandard housing and the growth of a deprived underclass could be solved by the advance of technology, Coudenhove consistently defined technological advances as a common European task. And even here, in an important aside, he warned that European internecine wars must for all future be avoided: "But in this era every war is a civil war, because it is turning against one's own comrades-in-arms and destroys the common front of our work."[15]

Many of these preliminary ideas jelled in *Pan-Europa*. Coudenhove offered a four-point rationale for such a confederation, some of them viable even today:

1. A union of the 26 European democracies would be able to break with the past and convert past armed conflicts into peaceful cooperation.

2. A common European market would elevate Europe's standard of living and solve some of the social inequities. Having looked closely at the United States, whose wealth sprang from mass production and mass consumerism, high wages and relatively low prices, he identified the lack of customs barriers as one of the bases for America's economic health. Europe must have a customs union, he concluded.

3. He foresaw that such a union might effectively forestall the dynamism of a Soviet-led communist revolution: "Only the alliance of 300 million [West] Europeans in a common defensive alliance can assure peace with the 150 million citizens of the Soviet Union and bring about multilateral disarmament."

4. "Until Britain will shed its insularity and colonial empire, we ought to structure Pan Europe in such a way that Great Britain, without joining the Union, can affiliate with it and share in the customs union." Coudenhove-Kalergi correctly foresaw the reservations the British would have; he wanted to prevent a scuttling of his idea by British opposition.[16] And these British reservations, not entirely dispelled even today, were certainly in evidence, when Winston Churchill, whom Coudenhove-Kalergi had won over in principle, hedged his bet in 1945 in his otherwise commendatory preface to Coudenhove's translated autobiography. Though expressing doubt about the practicality of the Pan European idea, he did not deny its potential:

> When the idea of the United States of Europe drifted upon the wind and came in contact with the immense accumulation of muddle, waste, particularities and prejudice which had long lain piled up in the European garden, it became quite evident that a new series of events had opened.
>
> The resuscitation of the Pan-European idea is largely identified with Count Coudenhove-Kalergi. The form of his theme may be crude, impracticable but the impulse and the inspiration are true.

> The movement towards European solidarity which has now begun will not stop until it has effected tremendous and possibly decisive changes in the whole life, thought and structure of Europe.[17]

But we have rushed ahead to the post-war period. Most initial responses were overwhelmingly favorable even at the time of conception. Of particular value to him was the endorsement of Eduard Beneš. Under the provisions of the peace treaty of St. Germain, Coudenhove, as an inhabitant of Bohemia, had become a Czech citizen. Armed with Beneš's letter he gained powerful political allies in all the 23 countries he wished to unite and even found supporters in Fascist Italy among the opponents to Mussolini. Racing from capital to capital, from conference to conference — some organized by himself — he attracted a core of supporters, many of whom became his permanent disciples. He himself describes these hectic activities as follows:

> During the next few months our journeys took us to Brussels, Budapest and Warsaw. National groups of our movement were constituted in Belgium, Hungary, Poland, Spain, Bulgaria, Roumania, Yugoslavia, Estonia, Latvia and Lithuania.
>
> Within eighteen months of our travels the movement had struck firm roots all over Europe. Among its active supporters we counted not only the leading politicians of many nations and various political parties but also the intellectual elite of the Continent: poets and authors such as Paul Claudel, Paul Valéry, Jules Romains, Heinrich and Thomas Mann, Gerhart Hauptmann, Stefan Zweig, Rainer Maria Rilke, Franz Werfel, Fritz von Unruh, Emil Ludwig, Arthur Schnitzler, Sigmund Freud, Selma Lagerlöf, and Albert Einstein; and philosophers such as Ortega y Gasset and Miguel de Unamuno. Many famous artists had also identified themselves with the movement, chief among them the brilliant violinist Bronislav Huberman, who canvassed the cause of Pan-Europe by lectures and in his writings wherever his journeys took him.
>
> Thanks to the political and intellectual support which we received from these and other quarters, a powerful body of opinion soon emerged in favor of the United States of Europe.[18]

If we add to these impressive results of Coudenhove's missionary work his feat of meeting with virtually every head of state in the Western World, from Mussolini to Herbert Hoover, the question arises, of course, how a private person could accomplish so much with so little. Of course he did the obvious: Through the years Richard Coudenhove-Kalergi followed up his first manifestos with countless mass-mailed brochures and position papers.[19] Beyond his writing he carried the weapon of a faith that could move mountains and of a charisma that was nearly irresistible. Hilde Spiel speaks of it in her autobiography.[20] And when I met him in October, 1963, he had lost none of his tenacity nor his persuasiveness founded on a combination of reason, logic, charm, and urbanity.

He remains in my mind as one of the most remarkable personalities I have ever encountered. We had agreed to meet at the Hotel Dolder in Zürich. It was late in the afternoon, the lights garlanding the hotel terrace illuminated the profile of a man whose Eurasian features immediately identified him. As he walked up to me he portrayed serenity and exuded optimism, the latter immediately apparent in his misplaced confidence in me. In my letter to him I had introduced myself as *Germanistischer Philologe.* He started addressing me, in consequence, in classical Greek. My German response fell short of his expectations.

I had come to see him about his contributions to the *Neue Merkur* and his and Ida Roland's cordial relationship with its editor, Efraim Frisch and his wife Fega. But when answering my questions he drew analogies, time and again, to the Pan Europa movement. Here is an example:

I: "Dr. Coudenhove-Kalergi, were you upset at Frisch when your article on the blessings of European technology brought forth, in the very next issue, a sharp rebuttal from Leo Matthias?"[21]

Dr. Coudenhove-Kalergi: "Not at all. Matthias took an entirely reasonable point of view.… I wish Pan Europa had engendered such an intelligent clash of ideas. One of the reasons for its earlier lack of success may have been a lack of thoughtful but clamorous opposition."

I: "Dr. Coudenhove-Kalergi, did you also meet Wilhelm Hausenstein, at that time the *Neue Merkur's* co-editor?"

Dr. Coudenhove-Kalergi: "Not until much later, when he became Germany's first post-war ambassador to France, an inspired choice of Adenauer's. I've always held that the cornerstone of a United States of Europe was a cordial relationship between France and Germany."

After the formal interview he invited us for cocktails. Of course we spoke of Pan-Europa. His animated face and disciplined gestures accompanied once more his confident hope. He had an audience of two, neither with any influence to speak of. Yet I'm willing to swear that he argued as wholeheartedly as though he were facing DeGaulle or Adenauer. And, frankly, it was thrilling But he could also lace his remarks with humor. We came to speak of Munich and I recalled a chapter in his autobiography, his description how Ida Roland had saved his life during the Spartacus uprising in Munich.[22] "Yes," he said, "but Ida didn't only tell the revolutionaries that I did not use my title [count] as a writer and that I admired Tolstoy, she also said, in her best stage Bajuvarian: "Ach wissen's, der is doch ka richtger Graf net, das ist doch en armes Luder wie ihr. Der lebt doch von meinm Gehalt bei de Bühne." ("Oh, let me tell you, he's no real count. He's a poor devil just like you. Why, he's living off my theater income.")

And then we talked of the Western world of those days thirty years ago. From the episodes he related, it was easy to see that he had become an important behind-the-scenes player on the European chessboard. Political leaders such as Robert Schuman and Konrad Adenauer, the latter already an admirer of him while mayor of Cologne in the Weimar Republic, called on him as advisor. They and others used him as an unofficial ambassador for delicate diplomatic missions designed to draw countries closer to one another in the aftermath of World War II.[23]

Perhaps this brief glimpse of the father of Pan-Europe may in a limited way explain his partial success. It may also explain why his ideas did not have even more of an impact during his lifetime. They did not lead to a crusade of the masses, of the common people who had most to lose by cutthroat economic competition and by new wars. To my mind the initiator of an inspired idea lacked, at least at one critical point, the craft and craftiness to push it towards realization. For example, his passionate appeals contained a pledge card, accepting membership in the United Europe movement. Several thousands of Europeans joined. Yet Coudenhove-Kalergi failed to ask for membership fees or contributors. Lack of funds soon forced Coudenhove to seek large subsidies. He was an inordinately good fund raiser, but his donors were large banks and industrial concerns.[24] Many donors were often motivated by less than altruistic goals: a United Europe, they felt, could dam in the Soviet Union and it could expand their own markets. Some early supporters therefore came to see Pan-Europa as an elitist and German-dominated organization. Heinrich Mann, one of the first to join the Pan Europa movement and a formidable activist of French-German friendship via the meetings at Pontigny, was also one of the first to sense the danger of this one-sided financial support. He would write in 1929, in an essay entitled "Pan-Europa — Traum und Wirklichkeit": "Once the dream of idealists, Pan-Europa now stands in danger of becoming a movement of business people and of the powerful." He warned that it could also become the instrument of imperialists and warmongers. But he conceded that perhaps the goals of the idealists and the pragmatists might for once be walking in tandem. And despite his fears he concluded: "Despite all the foreseeable negatives we must wish for Pan-Europa."[25] And he was not alone in weighing both the merits and the demerits of Coudenhove's approach. Kurt Hiller, one of the most dedicated advocates of pacifism and international socialism — not communism — was convinced that capitalism was far too rapacious — "eine von Raffern beherrschte Welt" — to bring about Coudenhove's utopia. In his now nearly inaccessible book, written in his Paris exile, Hiller conceded that Coudenhove-Kalergi had a high sense of social justice, but that he trusted the capitalist system far too much, ignored socialism, and devalued and demonized the accomplishments of Lenin and Stalin. And yet, with all of his objections, some of them untenable from today's perspective, he found words of admiration for the promulgator of Pan-Europe:

> But on the other hand the clarity and grandeur of his vision of history up to the present, his constructive élan with which he rushes towards the future, his universal abilities at a time of a triumphant narrow specialization or bold pretentious diletantism, his productive drawing of connections of disparate fields, ranging from economics to the most refined, yet nonetheless real irrationalities: all these do elicit admiration, even enthusiasm.

Hiller also advocated that the European idea become a cause of the masses. In that he did not greatly differ from Coudenhove, at least in theory. He, too, wished for a mass movement carried by Europe's younger generation. "Each European," he wrote, "holds a part of the world's fate in his/her hand."[26]

Kurt Hiller, given his reservations, ultimately disaffiliated from the Pan Europa movement. Yet his disclaimers were relatively restrained, as Michael Lützeler has shown in his riveting, well-researched and scrupulously balanced study *Die Schriftsteller und Europa*,[27] Coudenhove was attacked or criticized by three camps.

1. By the rightists who, like the book burners of a few years later, derogated the advocacy of Pan-Europe as "cosmopolitan European decadence," termed them "devalued words" ["entwertete Worte"] and, as did Georg Friedrich Jünger, worthy brother of Ernst, criticized Thomas Mann, who had praised Pan Europa, as a spokesman for the "European bourgeoisie of high finance."

2. By the forces of the left. As Klaus Mann recalled: "When the bankers, cardinals and industrialists made the count their patron saint, his liberal friends began to become suspicious and to gradually withdraw from him. What was his intention? To launch the unification of the continent or a crusade against Soviet Russia?"[28]

But it could be counter-argued, in response to Klaus Mann's second argument, that Coudenhove-Kalergi had an early apprehension of Stalinism, incipient in the first moves of then new Party Secretary Stalin. And Klaus Mann was utterly wrong when he drew parallels between Coudenhove-Kalergi's plans and those of Adolf Hitler. As Paul Michael Lützeler put it: "In saying that, he completely misjudges the founder of the Pan-European Union, who remained at all times an uncompromising opponent of Hitler." Also I was able to find resounding endorsements by political exiles of *all* political stripes when Coudenhove-Kalergi in 1935 reissued, once more with his further condemnations added, his father's earlier denunciation of anti-Semitism.[29]

3. And finally Lützeler identified critics who thought that Coudenhove-Kalergi's ideas were naive and utopian. Among these was Carl von Ossietzky,

who also mistakenly suspected Coudenhove's ally, Aristide Briand, the French Foreign Minister, of using the cause of Pan-Europe as a guise to further French national interests. But Ossietzky was not alone to find Coundehove-Kalergi naive. The Alsatian writer René Schickele spoke of "...the prophet Coudenhove-Kalergi, a man of simple, almost childlike faith."[30] Several of Coudenhove-Kalergi's critics also felt that his assumption that Europe could maintain its colonies — and profit from them — would prove erroneous.

With Hitler's accession to power, the movement went into involuntary hibernation. Hitler had his own plans for uniting Europe. As noted above, on May 10, 1933, Coudenhove-Kalergi's books were burnt on the Opernplatz in Berlin. For him, as for so many of Europe's finest minds and spirits, a flight began across many countries and ended in the United States. He was, to be sure, more fortunate than most. When Ida Roland and he became stateless after Hitler's invasion of Czechoslovakia, the French Prime Minister Paul Reynaud secured French citizenship for them. U.S. friends helped the couple to get to Lisbon after the fall of France and to receive early passage on the Yankee Clipper. In New York, Coudenhove very soon was appointed professor for European history at New York University.[31]

Space will only permit a brief survey of his successful post-war resurrection of Pan Europa through his headquarters in Switzerland. There were setbacks and triumphs. Younger, more powerful men tried to arrogate his achievements unto themselves, one of them Duncan Sandys, Churchill's son-in-law. Churchill himself would ultimately give higher priority to close ties to the U.S. than to the Continent. But Coudenhove's greatest loss came when his fellow Pan European, Ida Roland, died in 1950.

The triumphs, however, predominated. Coudenhove was able to enlist new allies, Harry Truman, George Marshall, Robert Schuman, Konrad Adenauer. He was nominated for the Nobel Peace Prize and was the first recipient of the Charlemagne Prize of the City of Aachen.[32] And when the European parliament opened in Strasbourg, his friend and rival Duncan Sandys, now chairman of the European movement, sent him a letter of appreciation:

> My dear Richard,
>
> I am writing to tell you how much I am rejoicing with you on this great day of the opening of the first session of the Council of Europe. Those of us who have joined your crusade in its later stages pay our tribute to its founder and leader.
>
> I know I am speaking not only in my own name but in that of all my colleagues in the European Movement when I say that Europe owes you a great debt of gratitude for all your faith and inspiration in the past and will continue as much as ever to need your vision and leadership in the future.[33]

Finally when the Schuman plan, also nourished by latter-day ideas of the Pan-Europa movement, became reality, Coudenhove-Kalergi was justified in writing, "The utopia of yesterday has at last become a reality."[34]

Of course we know that only a half-way mark has been reached, that old national and ethnic differences have surfaced that as often divide as they unite. But that does not diminish Coudenhove's enormous achievements. In the words of Thomas Mann, who got to know him in the time of the Weimar Republic:

> His conduct and utterances testify to his unshakable belief in a political idea, of whose unerring wisdom I am not convinced, but which he knows how to disseminate and advocate among the public with most discernible energy.
>
> After all, what is to impress us, if it is not this pioneering and nobly democratic and outstanding representative of a new society. — a representative instinctively used to think in terms of continents and willing to undertake on his own to shape the world according to the dictates of its own intelligence.[35]

It was given to Coudenhove, who died in 1970, to see the partial fulfillment of his impossible dream. Occasionally he traveled a false road towards its fulfillment, "ein Erleuchteter auf falschem Wege," [an enlightened person on a wrong road][36] Kurt Hiller said at one time. We, of course, do not know whether the future will vindicate his vision. In a recent book the vision was downplayed by a colleague from Warwick College who called it one of several "idealistic schemes."[37] But one of the exiles from Nazi Germany, writing as early as 1943 from far-away Chile, may have seen the place of visionaries more clearly: "Those skeptics [in regard to Pan-Europe], aren't they anything more than diligent gravediggers of the 'declining West?' They think of themselves as Realpolitiker and therefore much smarter than the 'dreamers.'"[38] But Coudenhove himself supplied the best answer in advance to all skeptics when he concluded our interview by saying: "Let our thoughts be somber, our actions bright."[39] But we do know that he was, at a crucial time, the catalyst that galvanized the debate about a United Europe, which though suppressed at times, would never cease again. If, as we hope, Europe pursues its present vision of integration, let us salute one of its pacemakers as we pass him.

Notes

[1] Hans Krebs, *Pan-Europa oder Mitteleuropa?* (Munich: Franz Eher Nachf., 1931), p. 26.

[2] For a rather comprehensive, if compact, biography of Coudenhove-Kalergi see Werner Roeder and Herbert Strauss, eds., *Biographisches Handbuch der deutschprachigen Emigration nach 1933* (Munich, New York, London, Paris: K.G. Saur, 1980), I, 117.

[3] These and the following biographical details were culled from the English and German editions of Coudenhove-Kalergi's autobiography. See his *Crusade for Pan-Europe. Autobiography of a Man and a Movement* (New York: C.G. Putnam's Sons, 1943) and *Ein Leben für Europa. Meine Lebenserinnerungen* (Cologne: Kiepenheuer und Wietsch, 1966). This is a revised and enlarged edition of *Eine Idee erobert Europa* (Munich: Desch, 1958).

[4] See Goethe, *Kampagne in Frankreich 1792* in *Gedenkausgabe der Werke, Briefe und Gespräche*, ed. Ernst Beutler (Zürich: Artemis, 1949), 12, 377f.: "Frau von Coudenhove, eine schöne geistreiche Dame, sonst die Zierde des Mainzer Hofes, hatte sich auch hierher [d.h. nach Düsseldorf] geflüchtet.... Frau von Coudenhoven, in dem Enthusiasmus, der sie sehr gut kleidete, rief aus: sie gäbe viel darum eine Frankfurter Bürgerin zu sein. Ich erwiderte: das sei etwas Leichtes, ich wisse ein Mittel, werde es aber als Geheimnis für mich behalten. Da man nun heftig und heftiger in mich drang, erklärte ich zuletzt, die treffliche Dame dürfe mich nur heiraten, wodurch sie augenblicklich zur Frankfurter Bürgerin umgeschaffen werde. Allgemeines Galächter!"

[5] See n. 3.

[6] The original treatise by Coudenhove's father, Heinrich, appeared under the title *Das Wesen des Antisemitismus* (Berlin: S. Calvary & Co., 1901). His son updated his father's book in 1929 and added his own essay *Antisemitismus nach dem Weltkrieg* (Vienna: Paneuropa-Verlag, 1929). For the further publishing history, see n. 29.

[7] See his *Praktischer Idealismus* (Paris, Vienna, Zurich: Pan-Europa Verlag, 1925).

[8] The title of both his high school paper and of his dissertation was "Objektivität als Grundprinzip der Moral." See Rolf Italiaander, *Richard N. Coudenhove-Kalergi, Begründer* der *Pan-Europa Bewegung*, "Persönlichkeiten der europäischen Integration" (Freudenstadt: Eurobuch-Verlag, 1969), p. 20.

[9] Coudenhove-Kalergi, *Crusade*, p. 50. He attributes the remark to a posthumously published letter by Rilke. Despite a diligent search I was unable to locate the original.

[10] Italiaander, p. 29 and *passim* describes Zsolnay's helpfulness.

[11] A good summary of the book's impact appears in Paul Michael Lützeler, *Die Schriftsteller und Europa. Von der Romantik bis zur Gegenwart* (Munich and Zurich: Piper, 1992), p. 313: "Ohne das Buch *Pan-Europa* von 1923 ist die

Europa-Diskussion der zwanziger Jahre unvorstellbar. Es erregte Aufsehen in fast allen europäischen Ländern und provozierte zahllose Stellungsnahmen." Also see p. 315 for a summary of initial supporters of the Pan-Europe concept.

[12] In his *From War to Peace* (London: Jonathan Cape, 1959), transl. Constantine Fitzgibbon), pp. 142–148, Coudenhove-Kalergi devotes a sub-chapter to the initial "hopes [that] were dashed" when the League of Nations failed to become an instrument for peace and European unity.

[13] For Coudenhove-Kalergi's significant role as a contributor to the *Neue Merkur* see my *War, Weimar and Literature. The Story of the "Neue Merkur"* (University Park and London: Penn State Univ. Press, 1971), 33, 37, 57, 69–75, 88, 115f and 120.

[14] The editorial correspondence contains about 15 letters or telegrams by Coudenhove-Kalergi and an equal number by Frisch.

[15] See his "Europas technische Weltmission," *Neuer Merkur* 6 (1922), 331–344.

[16] Coudenhove-Kalergi, while modifying his concept in subsequent books, essentially held on to these early premises. For the shifts in the light of developments during and after World War II, see his *Weltmacht Europa* (Stuttgart: Seewald, 1971).

[17] Winston Churchill, "Preface" in Coudenhove-Kalergi, *An Idea Conquers the World* (New York: Roy Publishers, 1954), p. ix–x.

[18] Coudenhove-Kalergi, *Crusade*, p. 112.

[19] In an interview with Itaaliander, p. 17, Coudenhove-Kalergi states this his main concern was the propagation of his idea, never the organization of the movement.

[20] See Hilde Spiel, "Das Sternbild Europa" in Thilo Koch, ed., *Europa persönlich, Erlebnisse und Betrachtungen* (Tübingen and Basel: Erdmann, 1973), p. 281. Reference to this resemblance in 316.

[21] Coudenhove-Kalergi, see n. 15. For Matthias' rebuttal see his "Zur Philosophie der Technik," *Neuer Merkur* 6 (1922), 580–587.

[22] See his *Crusade*, 72–74, for his and Ida Roland's confrontation with Spartacus insurrectionists.

[23] See Arnold J. Zurcher, *The Struggle to Unite Europe 1940–1958* (New York: NYU Press, 1958), 27.

[24] Ibid., p. 5: "Rarely was there any serious concerted effort [on Coudenhove's part] to influence the broad masses of the public."

[25] Heinrich Mann, "Pan-Europa, Traum und Wirklichkeif" in his *Sieben Jahre. Chronik der Gedanken und Vorgänge* (Berlin, Vienna, Leipzig: Zsolnay, 1929), 381.

[26] Kurt Hiller, "Coudenhofe" in his *Profile. Prosa aus einem Jahrzehnt* (Paris: Edition Nouvelles Internationales, 1938), 151–157.

[27] See n. 11.

[28] Klaus Mann, "Glossen: Coudenhove-Kalergi, *Europa erwacht!*" (Paneuropa-Verlag: Zürich, Wien) in *Die Sammlung*, 2 (1935), 442–444.

[29] Coudenhove-Kalergi updated his earlier essay on anti-Semitism once more in 1935 under the title of *Judenhaß heute*, again with his father's earlier book (see n. 6): Vienna: Paneuropa Verlag, 1935. The new edition also appeared in English translation. See Heinrich Johann Coudenhove-Kalergi *Anti-Semitism throughout the Ages*, edited and brought up to date by Count Richard Coudenhove-Kalergi. Authorized English translation by Dr. Angelo S. Rappoport. London's Hutchinson & Co., Ltd., 1935). A full-page appreciation appeared in *Neuer Vorwärts*, 1935, no. 136, Beilage, p. 3.

[30] See René Schickele, "Europäisch reden" in his *Werke*, ed. Hermann Kesten (Cologne: Kiepenheuer und Wietsch), 3, 932.

[31] As late as 1953 the title page of his book *Die europäische Nation* (Stuttgart: Deutsche Verlagsanstalt) identifies him as a professor of history at NYU. It may also be evidence of his continued affiliation, perhaps as an adjunct professor, that NYU Press published Arnold J. Zurcher's study, *The Struggle to Unite Europe* of 1958, which in its first part, supplies a very positive appreciation of Pan-Europe and its founder.

[32] Virtually all press accounts after 1950 mention Coudenhove-Kalergi as recipient of the *Karlspreis* of that year. See for example Jürgen Schmädeke, "Der Traum vom einigen Europa. Zum 75. Geburtstag von Richard Graf Coudenhove-Kalergi." *Tagesspiegel*, 16 Nov. 1969, 18.

[33] Duncan's letter is reprinted in Coudenhove, *An Idea Conquers the World*, p. 297.

[34] Ibid., p. 309–310.

[35] Thomas Mann, "Pariser Rechenschaft" in his *Reden und Aufsätze* 3, *Gesammelte Werke* (Frankfurt: S. Fischer, 1990), 11, 46–47.

[36] Hiller, "Coudenhofe," 151.

[37] See Robert Stidelsky, "Great Britain and the New Europe" in David P. Calleo and Philip H. Gordon, eds., *From the Atlantic to the Urals. National Perspectives on the New Europe* (Arlington, VA: Seven Locks Press, 1992), 150.

[38] Frederick Hausmann, "Coudenhove's Kreuzzug für Pan-Europa. Kreuzzug oder Real politik? *Deutsche Blätter*, 2 nos.(1944), 14–17.

[39] It was a view that Coudenhove upheld his entire life, exemplified by one of his enjoinders during the Cold War: "The study of philosophy and history shows no grounds for optimism.... In the midst of such dangers and in the shadow of the atomic bomb, it is now more than ever worth fighting for the conclusion of the Great Peace." See his *From War to Peace*, 223 f.

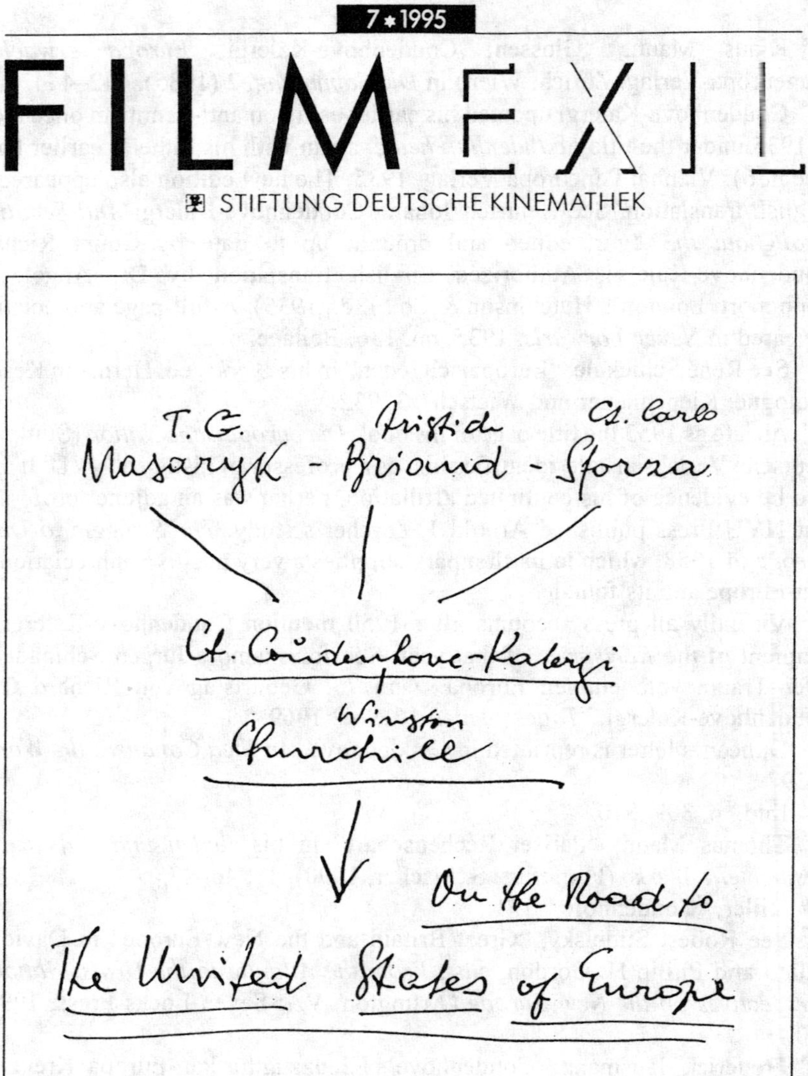

The above sketch, found among the papers of Hans Janowitz, famous film director (*The Cabinet of Dr. Caligari*), illustrates the hold Coudenhove-Klergi's ideas had even on persons outside of politics It is reproduced here from the title page of the magazine *Film Exil.*

To The Nation's Bottom: A Theory of Contemporary Lithuanian National Identities and Identifications

Arturas Tereskinas

As a global lexicon of images comes to dominate the world scene of consumption and unsettles the established norms of national signs and identifications, it becomes increasingly difficult to affirm any kind of monolithic local identities with their peculiar ethnocentric and cultural flavors. This difficulty derives not only from the global transit of the world, its constant translation and transvaluation, and the movement of cultures outside the spaces of any specific language. It also stems from the conflict between the sublimity of national identities and the banality of everyday life, making national promises for justice and well-being seem utopian. In the face of the living world, profane and multiform — government corruption, economic impoverishment and pauperization, Mafia crimes and the formation of new classes,[1] — the chasm between the imagined national community and its reality widens every day.

After the dissolution of the Soviet Empire and a short period of national re-fashioning and euphoria during 1988–1991, which resulted in an independent Lithuania, an ontology and ideology of Lithuanian nationness became more problematic. The Lithuanian nation liberated from foreign domination and Soviet ideological pressures dissipated into a jumble of historical and everyday modalities, a space in which everyday temporality plays a much more significant role than national fictions. The increasing complexity of the social world and diversified sites of national memories and utopias in the 1990s challenge the ideal national imaginings as they were summarized by the canonical nineteenth- and twentieth-century nationalist texts (Lithuania as a land of heroes, the heroic past as a source of spiritual strength, Lithuanians as a people of the highest integrity, working together for their homeland and humanity's good; Lithuania as a source of enlightenment, truth and justice). Such imaginings have lost their power to unite Lithuanians into a new patriotic performance.

In 1993–1997 Lithuanian society shifted towards a public apathy. It appears, as most Lithuanians have personally experienced, that to live the dailiness of national identity is more difficult than to extol its sublimity. In other words, imagining one's own community as a system of cultural and political representation is easier than to enact this imagining.[2] Everyday life and Lithuanian mass media flooded with the picturesque scenarios of crimes, corrupt officials, bankrupt banks, unconcerned entertainment and international celebrity gossip have pushed the slogans of national unity and sublimity into the margins. This is why it is no longer enough to discuss the mythologies of Lithuanian national identity; a look into the everyday workings of nationness is now needed.

In my essay, I will theorize the above outlined complex relationship between the sublimity of Lithuanian national identity and its everyday happenings by analyzing a wide array of texts produced in the last decades of the nineteenth century and the twentieth century. I will interpret mass media and the everyday as spaces of a new nationness in practice demonstrating how the national imaginary is constructed and deconstructed through the circulation of televisual and print media images. Drawing on the ideas of Benedict Anderson about imagined communities created by the press, my essay will touch upon the various kinds of media producing, in Anderson's words, a "league of anonymous equals."[3] How do media help the Lithuanian people think the nation? How do the people negotiate their desire for belonging and solidarity through their everyday acts and experiences of the national imaginary?

1. "Lithuania, Our Fatherland, Land Of Heroes"

In order to establish the norms and canons of a sublime Lithuanian nationality (Lithuania as a theoretical idea), I will first examine the imagined community as created by the nineteenth-century Lithuanian nationalist texts and recycled by the recent Lithuanian national reconstruction and its vehicle *Sajudis,* the Lithuanian popular front founded in the 1988 summer. I define the sublime or theoretical nation after Homi Bhabha as the "medium of a naturalistic continuity of Community or Tradition"[4] and as the large-scale solidarity policed by a gathering of cultural experiences, myths, and fantasies. The sublimity of a nation excludes national temporality and the uncertainty of national boundaries focusing instead on the nation's historicity and the stability of its cultural significations.

The Lithuanian anthem, perhaps the most important nineteenth-century national text, evokes an August Lithuanian past as the source for guiding future actions and as a primal shelter from the everyday wrongs and pitfalls: "Lithuania, our fatherland,/ Land of heroes,/ May your sons draw strength/ From your past" The common denominators of nationness in the anthem are national origins and the heroic deeds of the forebears. The Lithuanian nationness produced by the Lithuanian anthem includes the call for the moral and spiritual chastity of each individual Lithuanian: "May the sun of Lithuania/ Banish all darkness,/ May light and truth/ Guide our steps." The repertoire of a shared experience and popular memory which mobilize the national populace into an imagined community also embraces the summons to unite by a token of love for Lithuania and to work for the nation and humanity's good: "May your children walk/ Only on the paths of righteousness/ May they work for your sake/ And the good of all people.// May love of Lithuania/ Burn in our hearts,/ In the name of that Lithuania/ May unity flourish."[5]

Another national text, the song entitled *We are born Lithuanian* (Lietuvninkai mes esam gime), no less important to the self-creation of modern Lithuania, reiterates a similar outline of nationness. It enacts an image of the origins that assigns an individual biological identity and a linguistic, social, political, and historical place.[6] This text presents the fecundity of the Lithuanian land as a guarantee of national survival: "Notwithstanding that someone attempted to destroy us, the fecund Lithuanian land will be bearing Lithuanians..."[7] According to the song, national identity can be authenticated only within the production of a closed ethnic space (a motherland bearing Lithuanians). The identity politics of native space include the majestic rhetoric of origins, boundary-making and ethnic purity.

The second Lithuanian national re-fashioning of the late 1980s which brought about Lithuanian state sovereignty, revitalized, recycled, and often hyperbolized metaphors of the nineteenth-century national texts. The pedagogy of patriotic performance and national competence professed in numerous demonstrations and mass rallies expressed itself through the phrases of eternal memory, ethnic purity, and past glory.[8] National knowledge was organized around and within the spatial metaphors of the native landscape and enunciated through the inevitable relation between the national and the spatial, the national and the native. The de-sovietized local land was fetishized as the site of national identity and transformed into a symbol of national mobilization.

As one of the leaders of *Sajudis,* Vytautas Landsbergis, put it: "Destiny, history or God — as you may wish — gave us this small bit of land with a beautiful name: *Lietuva* (Lithuania)."[9] According to Landsbergis, identifications and attachments to a local space, inescapably assigned to a national subject, are the basis of a stable national identity: "A native land is our fatherland, in which one can live the best life. Life here is best not because our fatherland pays high salaries, but because its sky is pleasant, its nature is beautiful, and everyone lying in its graveyards is one of us."[10] The nation here is the natural destiny of Lithuanians rooted in the native soil. National responsibilities are naturalized through the concepts of historicized, destined, and divined native space. Through the metaphor of space, erosions and revivals of national identities are expressed: native or inside space articulates a geography of belonging and identification, whereas foreign or outside space speaks of a flow of threatening differentiation and difference.

During 1988–1993, the politics of national mapping also included national pride and national morals. An exaggerated moralism marked the whole fabric of the second national reconstruction. A belief in the collective moral superiority both over the Stalinized Russians and the "degenerate" West was predominant. The theory of Lithuanian (and Baltic in general) genetic goodness is still widespread in Lithuania despite an increasing criminalization of the society and the proliferation of social pathologies:

> Morality (*dora*) is the core of self-consciousness of the Baltic man. It is one of those untranslatable and thus essential words. For a Lithuanian, morality is more than a moral value. Morality is a mark of the divine order and the godly imperative goodness in a man.[11]

Public enactments of moral "purity" and demands for former Communists to repent in 1988–1993 went hand in hand with the reflection on how to shield Lithuanian souls from the "degenerate" West.

The last prescriptive norm of Lithuanian nationness or Lithuania as a theoretical ideality worth emphasizing was visualized by a woman during the tragic confrontation between the mass population and the Soviet Army in January 13, 1991 (13 people killed and more than 500 injured). A woman from the crowd which was attacked by tanks and heavy artillery near the TV station in Vilnius confessed:

> I kneeled by the murdered young man as if he were my son and started to cry ….; I kissed his hands and suddenly I realized that all the killed and wounded have united all the Lithuanian people of a good will with sacred, unseverable blood ties. The innocent blood of the heroes, scattered as the millions of stars, has enlightened our souls wrapped by the gloomy dusk with a new DAWN OF RESURRECTION and it is preparing our hearts to the example of the Pilenai sacrifice[12] if the aggression continues. Our Parliament, its militia and the people guarding the Parliament building are ready for this Sacrifice…[13]

In this catastrophic vision of national emergency, a woman repeats the familiar image of the nation as a ritual community of people tied by blood, sacrifice, and heroism. She couples the being a national subject and suffering in an intensely heroic mode. In her vision, death signifies national rebirth; death purifies people's minds and hearts and transforms the nation into a community in which the dead are more real and substantial than the living.

2. "Hate Me And Continue Your Wild Party, Oh My Screaming Motherland, Turned Into A Café" (From Gintaras Patackas's Poem *Hello, Alexander Blok*)

The perfidious everyday tests and unsettles the canons and norms of national sublimity. It demonstrates the uncertainty and instability of cultural significations and symbolic formulations of the nation. An interminable flow of trivia, gossip, banality — the whole lexicon of images dominating the Lithuanian scene of consumption and popular entertainment — encounters, defies, ironizes, inverts and "desecrates" the sublimity of Lithuanianness. Instead of generating national memory or national knowledge, mass media, consumption and entertainment undermine the issues of national specificity. They are fraught, however, with the problems of national representations and patriotism. In this part of my essay, I will focus on the ways in which media, consumption and entertainment invading the everyday of Lithuanian people not only generate the amnesia of national memory but also produce new sites for national identifications.

Freed from ideological pressures, mass media, particularly television, became instrumental in defining a new collective experience. TV has annexed, although not entirely, older forms of national self-identification and cultural literacy embodied by high literature and art, folkloric festivals and celebrations. By playfully commenting on the public events and everyday happenings, mass media make people think differently about both ordinary everyday and national experiences.

Television (besides cable and satellite TV, there are six national TV channels of which only one is state-controlled and state-funded) occupies a privileged place in the empire of mass communication which both manifests and sabotages national knowledge. Lithuanian TV is saturated with and dominated by international entertainment commodities and locally produced imitations of popular American and European shows. The most memorable TV programs of 1997 included political discussion shows entitled "Debate," and "Crossroads," the show of cultural news "Signs," the "Battle of Words" which resembles the American game show "Wheel of Fortune," the TV game "Millionaire," "Style: Journal of Fashion and Lifestyle," the variety show "Show Boulevard," "News from Hollywood," "Government's Program" and "Scandals of the Week."

Popular Lithuanian talk shows, mirroring the American ones, are essential to the discussion of the norms signifying nationness. In the talk shows, both violently public and shamelessly intimate things flash in Lithuanians' faces: corruption, criminal subcultures, drug addiction, sexual minorities, sexual abuse, and pornography. Displaying the media spectacle as an endless narrative of discomfort which upsets theoretical national norms, talk shows present vulgar, voyeuristic, and sensationalist exchanges of "national" knowledge. The invasion of television into the sensitive domains of religious democracy, sex, crime, corruption, and drugs which were for a long time national taboos indicates the changing norms of Lithuanian nationness: now Lithuanians are represented not only as an ideal and unified preindustrial community with roots in folkloric traditions but as a diverse society whose social preoccupations and conflicts can be found in any other society.

"Will Lithuania remain a Catholic country?" asks a show entitled "The Last Crossroads." Should religious sects and minorities such as Krishna's followers be tolerated? The participants of the show discuss whether the Lithuanian government should finance only traditional religions such as Catholicism or Orthodoxy or should it also support non-traditional religious communities (from the March 28, 1997, show). The Lithuanian erotic show entitled "Vision," almost impossible to imagine five years ago, tastefully presents the art of Kama Sutra and discusses the psychological problems of love relationships.

Discourses of nation, sexuality, and citizenship overlap in the divergent readings of the televised experience creating new norms of what we might call "mass nationality"[14]: non-prescriptive yet public identifications and belongings. The media affirm Lithuanians' cravings for new objects of desire embodied in sexual ads, soap operas, and consumer commodities. Unconcerned entertainment provokes new meanings and pleasures which citizens incorporate into their everyday culture: popular culture becomes a space within and by which new mass subjectivities are constituted. In a popular show "Hollywood News," for instance, the host playfully mingles Lithuanian national events with the happenings of Hollywood glamour. He jokes that on the 16th of February Hollywood gathered to celebrate not Lithuanian Independence Day but Elizabeth Taylor's birthday (the irony lies in the fact that both milestones are on the same day). Unexpected juxtaposition makes the nationally important day merely an ordinary event in the chain of media happenings. Another no less significant and symbolic juxtaposition took place when the hero of the most popular American soap opera in Lithuania *Santa Barbara*, performed in the Lithuanian capital on the 11th of March, the Day of the Restoration of Lithuanian Independence. In a sold-out show in Vilnius, the actor Lane Davies performed some Lithuanian folk songs. The fictional soap hero participated in the national celebration transforming it into a surreal media fantasy.

For the first time, Lithuanians have become concerned with the notion of lifestyle, self-image and self-representation. The Lithuanian dailies run articles about the image of Lithuania in various countries, TV and radio shows discuss how to improve or change the image of Lithuania in the world.[15] There has emerged a variety of TV shows on lifestyle and fashion, and entire sections of Lithuanian dailies are devoted to lifestyle issues. In most cases, "Lifestyles" focus not only on the lives of rich and famous but also on some brutal and sensational Lithuanian news (as in a headline of the "Lifestyle" section, "A Pregnant Woman is Beaten by her Husband's Lover," *Lietuvos rytas* [Lithuanian Morning], No. 78, April 5, 1997). An ordinary "Lifestyle" section covers fashion, personals, a celebrity watch, sexual conduct, medical news, advice how to find Mr. or Ms. Right, horoscopes and travel.

Both "Lifestyle" sections and TV shows include the "invisible" communities of the socially and sexually underrepresented and marginal (the homeless, homosexuals and criminal subculture) which, for the first time, come to be unveiled and un-demonized. By including the invisible as well as marginal, the media present citizens with multiple communities and multiple interests and with a promise of an inclusive and agentive nationality. By creating public and national spheres in which the dailiness of people's behavior participates in the business of making nationality as much as their utopian and patriotic intentions, the media replace uncritical representations of fetishistic nationness (blood, sacrifice, morality and spirituality, purified and virtuous nation) with multi-dimensional national identifications. Mass media interpellate national subjects in multiple ways bringing forth the multiplicity of interpretations and experiences.

As the spectacles of popular entertainment and mass media demonstrate, mass nationality is not afraid of foreign products, models of behavior and cultural practices (note the prevalence of "global" and "universal" modes of narrating (post)modern human experience: talk shows, serials, soap operas, gossip, and sensational news). Notably, quite a few television programs do not simplistically contrast tradition and modernity, Lithuanian vs. Western, virtuousness vs. degradation, but open sites for more complex questions about the nature of patriotism, dishonesty, greed and "wild capitalism." Significantly, no opposition is set between "authentic" and "inauthentic" Lithuanianness.

New parallels, albeit frequently trivial and ironic ones, between being Lithuanian and being European have been drawn. For instance, the DJ of a popular radio station M1 advertises the European chart of pop music by claiming that both "every genuine European listens to Eurochart" and "every Lithuanian listens to Eurochart." One could conclude from the above parallel that either Lithuanians are genuine Europeans or they may become such by listening to Eurochart.

Playful, performative and at times critical responses of mass nationality to the ideal modes of national existence attempt to deconstruct the paradigm of nationhood based on the image of a preindustrial folkloric community. That is why the formation of mass nationality mediated by TV, radio, the trashy press and cheap fiction is seen as the destruction of an ideal imagined nation by most of the literary elite and conservative politicians who still live the stereotypes of the closed, purified, and sanctified Lithuanian nation. In this rhetoric of an archaic nationness, being a national citizen means pledging an unconditional allegiance to the unified national rituals and adhering faithfully to the homogenized theoretical nationality. This "patriotic" view of national identity seeks to use identification with the ideal nation to devaluate all other identifications; it promotes the return to the simpler and better times of "unproblematic" community with its monolithic and exclusionary identity. Lithuanian intellectuals and right-wing politicians still use the discursive conventions of the virtuous unity of the national public sphere which has already become obsolete.

Bemoaning the loss of community and deriding an aversion to patriotism in the Lithuanian society, the Lithuanian intellectuals and conservatives fill the pages of dailies and weeklies with conspiracy theories. The search for enemies becomes definitive of their ideal imagined community. According to one of the most prominent conspiracy theories, both American liberals and Hollywood are responsible for the destruction of the virtuous Lithuanian nation. As one writer puts it:

> And all this "literature," the splashing of excrement, the plastering of slop, fucking, sex, served as a desert after a nutritious dinner or offered by force as a obscene toilet graffiti, all this "art" disfigured and laid on the floor, walls and windows; the rock music which resembles a heavy bombardment and which moves legs, lacerates throats and parasitically evacuates from a person all human thoughts about obligation, responsibility, decency and sacrifice — all this comes from the West, from Dulles, from Hollywood, from the citadel of world democracy.[16]

In order to assert the security of the Lithuanian national identity, threats to that identity are necessarily projected as external: the Other is seen and represented as both an object of desire and abjection, of envy and contempt. Hoping to suppress the conflicts and contradictions within oneself, one assigns them to others, the strangers. The price of the self's coherence is the consistent humiliation of the Other. Abjection is, in Judith Butler's words, "the mode by which others become shit."[17] The feared Other has become a convenient scapegoat upon which the "defenders" of the pure and virtuous Lithuanian nation displace their own responsibilities. It can be argued that the exclusionist and archaic character of Lithuanian identity professed mostly by literary figures and right-wing politicians destroys itself by its hyperbolized significations (purity of language and origins, chastity and spirituality of a Lithuanian, an individual's sacrifice for the mythologized collective; national identity as a compulsory performance or an inescapable destiny). Nationality made into a ritual and burlesque ostentation of exaggerated gestures and permanent appearances satirizes itself. Confronting the reality of "wild" postcommunist capitalism, terrorism, bombs exploding in the editorial offices and the strangest prophesies of Lithuanian psychics concerning economics and banking, the sublimity of Lithuanian nationness becomes merely a self-parody: national norms are continually haunted by their own inefficacy (thus, the search for enemies and complaints about waning patriotism).

It is truly paradoxical that TV and non-governmental radio and print media often accused of irresponsibility and demoralization aim to invent new modes of national and mass cultural memory by constantly manipulating the power of national signs and resistance to them, civic discipline and non-discipline, national order, and disorder. The media provide an insight into the disjunctive forms of representation that signify the nation; it demonstrates that the distance between individuals and collective identities both as a place to be filled up by mass and individual fantasies and as a space where the various logics of identity that circulate through the culture enter into relations of contradiction and not simply analogy. In the descriptions and broadcasts of serial killers, Mafia dealings, intricate prison stories, and dinners for the poor, mass media masquerade the romantic illusions of sublime nationness and folkloric community united by collective dignity and strong customs in a ritual time. Is there any trace of collective dignity left when one is hungry? Can the inquiries into the character of a genuine Lithuanian still be relevant when at the blink of an eye one might lose one's entire life savings?

The mass media ridicule such questions. Newspaper articles and talk shows mock the Lithuanian historical icons and political figures and allegedly "important" questions which trouble post-Soviet national rhetoric. A satire written by a writer turned media figure Juozas Erlickas, for instance, uses references to the repertoire of sacred Lithuanian historical and literary figures and works. The main character of the satire Vytautas (the name of the medieval Grand Prince whose rule made the Grand Duchy of Lithuania one of the biggest and strongest empires in Europe) is depicted as a handicapped person who spends all his time watching TV. Overwhelmed by the flow of TV commercials, Vytautas, together with his wife, constantly cries out the names of foreign commodities, mostly the brands of chewing gum. He proclaims that for him "TV is the only window to Europe" (ironic reference to the well-known Soviet Lithuanian saying that Lithuania was Russia's window to Europe). But Vytautas also scolds TV. "Television!"— he shouts. "Is it possible to preserve one's sanity while watching such broadcasts? And what about Lithuanianness?"

Vytautas's wife abhors him because of the misery and poverty of their life. Annoyed by his wife's swearing, Vytautas goes for a walk. He buys a pack of chewing gum, the same brand he has just seen on TV, and knocks at the door of total strangers. After coming inside, he bewilders the couple who does not recognize him. Vytautas asks absurd and incoherent questions about the fate of some very national literary characters: "I wonder how Biliunas's cat is doing? And what has happened to Brisius? Is he still alive?" (a reference to Biliunas, the Lithuanian prose master of the end of the nineteenth — the beginning of the twentieth century, whose short stories focused on helpless victimized animals and individuals). It is absurdly comic that the strangers confused by Vytautas's questions also bear the names of the medieval Lithuanian royalty, Kestutis and Biruta (the father and the mother of the Grand Prince Vytautas).

Finally, Vytautas leaves the stunned Kestutis and Biruta and returns to the street. He asks himself whether he should go to the forest or to Europe (the forest may signify the place of national resistance and may refer to post-war Lithuanian guerrillas). To resolve this puzzle, Vytautas visits the conference room of Ministers. It turns out that they (i.e., Lithuania) are going to leave for Europe in only five years and that all train seats have already been reserved. Saddened, Vytautas squeezes himself into the corner of the room to listen to the discussion of ministers on the "burning" issue: who disseminates and circulates the rumors that Lithuanians can choose nothing but chewing gum. Ministers decide to bomb all institutions that might contribute to this rumor: the University, the Union of Journalists, schools, reading rooms, publishing houses, etc. Having made this decision, the happy Ministers depart from the room singing a Lithuanian military song.[18]

The above satire skillfully exploits nationally reproduced seriousness and authority based on the devout respect of historical, literary, and political canonicity. By means of laughter, it deconstructs the rituals of power and control which can enforce reverential solemnity and designate what is to be taken seriously. Neither base and cynical political realities, nor the once romanticized but now debased and trivialized historical and literary figures must be taken too seriously, according to the satire. Utopically misrepresented history does no good for a citizen's well-being; neither does one's own corrupt government. The satire reverses the relationship between the past and the present: it is not the past that explains the present, but it is the present that humiliates the heroic past. Everyday politics make cultural and literary mythologies lame and invalid (as the ridiculous character of Vytautas). By transforming nationally respected figures, myths and memories into a media spectacle, the mass media offer a new figuration of nationality in which to be a competent subject, one has to be flexible in reading between the lines of utopian national identity and cynical practical reason.

The mass media shift from the terminology of patriotic monumentality to a lexicon of postmodern national dynamism and change dislocating people's experiences of being national and revealing the national sites which so far were not considered public or national. Now one can relive one's sense of being a citizen not only by reading literary classics and by participating in folkloric festivals but also by watching the American soap opera *Santa Barbara*; not only by reciting the deeds of historical heroes and mythological figures but also by composing new territories of identification through rap music and Internet surfing. Signs of identification codes are changing and with them claims for belongings and exclusions.

The new global economy of culture presents the Lithuanian public with the mobility of texts and contexts and allows the Lithuanians, although often only in the realm of the imagination, to emulate certain aspects of the lifestyles of the bold and the beautiful (allusion to the widely watched soap *The Bold and the Beautiful* translated into Lithuanian as *Chameleons*). Global traffic in images, fashions, and ideas interacts with and contests the nationally produced styles and products; it threatens a world where ancestry and locality sanctioned a national identity. Nowadays Lithuanian consumers of electronic media can experience a common heritage with people they have never seen.

Mass media filling the everyday of Lithuanians suggests that instead of learning to live nationally without losing faith in nationality we should attempt to reconsider the utopian possibilities of national identity which frequently if not always humiliate Lithuanian citizens, revealing them as incapable of negotiating the semiotic, economic, and political locations of their existence. Blind and nostalgic attachment to the norms of sublime nationality that we might also call "infantile" indeed explains the incompetence of a large part of Lithuanian society to deal with the cynicism of postcommunist politics and with the terrifying liability of a growing market economy. The practical impossibility of utopian nationalism produces grotesque effects in the minds of persons challenged by everyday, not idealized, national knowledge. The constant humiliation of the Lithuanian citizen by the texts of everyday life translates itself into the collective fantasies of *fin du monde* "... time and the world are ruthlessly devouring our world and our times, in other words, our very selves. It's self-deceptive to believe that literature or culture can save us from this *danse macabre*,"[19] writes a young journalist and writer. Ironically, "infantile" nationalism which operates in the sphere of nostalgic "unknowing" and believes in the capacity of the nation to be indeterminably utopian confuses its own inability to face reality with the metaphors and images of national and cultural crises.

3. Conclusion: Bargaining Lithuanianness

> "I am looking for 500 individuals to whom I will reveal my biggest secret. After experiencing it, you will feel powerful, fortunate and happy..." (advertisement in a Lithuanian newspaper)

I have started the last section of my essay with a rather cynical advertisement in the Lithuanian newspaper *Lietuvos aidas* (Echo of Lithuania, government daily). A woman who calls herself the Great Benefactress promises to share with 500 people a secret which will make them rich and happy. There is only one condition: one must fill out a questionnaire and send 39 *litai* (about 10 dollars) to the Great Benefactress. If one's life isn't to change after the revelation, a refund is guaranteed.

Unfortunately, there are no refunds, guarantees or easy ways of being and living Lithuanian. And there is no quick magic way to coordinate a new nationality. The recognition of separate ways of both living and imagining nationness is the first premise of such a project. Resistance to oppressive national iconicity reveals that Lithuanians' relation to their own nationality can be multiple and ambiguous. To challenge the national sublimity based on the image of a stable, hierarchical, and authoritative community which justifies itself through the voice of traditions, mythological collectivity and passively accepted national culture, one needs to recognize difference and diversity of national identifications. There exists a plurality of public and private spheres, each having its own separate logic. In the apparent chaos of the everyday, a Lithuanian must learn to continuously bargain and improvise with the meanings and functions of these spheres.

Not only a shared consciousness, but also a dialogic negotiation of one's place in civic society with its polymorphous pleasures and dangers supplies us with a guide for living nationally. Fluid and multiple identities must be constantly revised in order to achieve maximum instrumentality and efficacy. The phenomenon of "mass nationality" created by mass media, entertainment, and consumption engenders the multiplicity of social and national spaces in which the structures of national identification are both constructed and deconstructed, embodied and disembodied. Culture here figures not only as a site of belonging, but also and first of all as a process of transition and becoming. New collective rituals of watching and interpreting talk shows and soap operas provide us with the resources of new communalities and identifications (as does the monument to Frank Zappa in Vilnius). This is to say, that Lithuanian people are able to construct their allegiances and their identifications at the interface between the norms of sublime nationality and the consumption of the products of globalized cultural industries.

Through the commodities of mass media, individuals experience the collectivity of public desire. Popular culture offers to Lithuanians carnivalesque, evasive, and liberating practices in which the hegemony of national sublimity is weakest and least repressive. Postmodern forms of media and visual technology which coordinate the multiple fields of private desires, self-imaginings and self-knowledge are involved in criticism of patriotic monumentality and represent, in most cases, a counterbalance to the powers whose goal it is to clean and euphemize the Lithuanian language (no foreign words!), to clean the nation (nation equals ethnicity plus virtuousness and honesty!) and to mythologize national memory (Lithuanians as the heroic and chaste saviors of Europe!).

Media events demonstrate that a nation is essentially artificial, a cultural product of the collective imagination, not a body which grows out of natural facts, such as native language, blood, and soil. By parodying the myth of national homogeneity, making national belongings inclusive rather than exclusive and transcending linguistic and cultural differences, mass media (and electronic media particularly) have been restructuring Lithuanians' sense of community and collective identity. As a peculiar incarnation of the global in the most immediate local, the mass media oppose the dichotomies of the local and global and demonstrate that the global operates within and is shaped by the local and vice versa. Without discounting the shallowness and vulgarity of the mass media, one must note that they reflect the changing net of Lithuanian social and cultural identities.

Lithuania is no United States. Nor is it Gilligan's Island. Lithuania as a specific locality is no longer tightly territorialized and closed. Similarly, national identity is being constantly reterritorialized: the landscape of national identity is fluid, permeable and conflictual; it is penetrated by and penetrates what lies outside of its location. National identity is constructed and lived in the realm of a context-dependent creativity based on the transfiguration of a Lithuanian citizen by practical, not idealized, national knowledges in which Lithuania as a theoretical ideality encounters Lithuania as a site of practical politics and everyday practices. As members of discursive not territorialized communities whose locations are multiple and contradictory, both domesticated and internalized, we negotiate our identities in a "discontinuous intertextual temporality of cultural difference."[20]

My essay was an attempt to offer a new style of semiotic resistance to nationally established and sanctified Lithuanian nationality, to the meanings which consciously or unconsciously control our behaviors and words. My objective was to outline not only the idealized but also the pathological and repellent sites and sides of Lithuanian society. Although the invisible bottom of Lithuanian, as of any other, nation cannot be fathomed completely (national mythologists say that nations are bottomless and the national spirit is deep and impenetrable), one may see, if one dares, oneself reflected in the concealed depths of both the national imaginary and the national reality. The double interplay of the hard bottom of reality and the mysteriously infinite and soft bottom of the national imagination make me believe that there are no universal or unchanging attributes of national identification. By deconstructing and reconstructing national subjectivity produced by both the domains of utopian national identity and cynical practical national identification, we resist dominant mythologies that serve to sustain particular systems of power relations.

Notes

[1] On the latest events in Lithuania see *Central Eurasia, Daily Report* (Foreign Broadcast Information Service) for 1995–1998 and the Internet under the rubric "Lithuania."

[2] My construction of national community derives from a number of sources, of which most important are Benedict Anderson, *Imagined Communities* (London: Verso, 1983), Homi Bhabha, ed. *Nation and Narration* (New York: Routledge, 1990) and Lauren Berlant, *The Anatomy of National Fantasy* (Chicago: U of Chicago Press, 1991).

[3] Benedict Anderson, *Imagined Communities* 67–82.

[4] Homi K. Bhabha, "DissemiNation: Time, Narrative, and the Margins of Modern Nation," *Nation and Narration* 302.

[5] Both words and music of the anthem were written by the physician and writer Vincas Kudirka (1858–1899) and they were first published in the newspaper Varpas [The Bell] in 1898. The translation of the anthem is taken from *Encyclopedia Lituanica*, eds. S. Suziedelis and J. Jakstas (Boston, Mass.: Kapocius, 1975) 4: 24.

[6] The first stanza of this text reads as follows: "Lithuanians we are born, Lithuanians we shall be; we desire to be such/ And we must not allow/ the innate honor to be Lithuanian perish…" The text was written by the pro-Lithuanian activist in East Prussia Georg Julius Justus Sauerwein (1831–1904).

[7] Cited from *Lietuviu Poezijos Antologija*, eds. J. Aistis & A. Vaiciulaitis (Chicago: Draugas, 1951) 196–197.

[8] The best political account of the 1988–1990 national "revival" is Alfred Erich Senn's *Lithuania Awakening* (Berkeley: U of California Press, 1990).

[9] Quoted from Vytautas Landsbergis, *Atgave Vilti* (Hope Regained) (Vilnius: Sajudis, 1990) 9.

[10] V. Landsbergis, "Doras Darbas, Seima, Gimtoji Zeme" (Virtuous Work, Family and Native Land), *Lietuvos aidas* [Lithuanian Echo] 17 December 1991: 1–3.

[11] A. Patackas, *Redos ratas* (The Circle of Arrangement) (Kaunas, 1988) 2.

[12] The allusion to the mythologized event of Pilenai castle in the fourteenth century. Realizing that the warriors of the Swordbearers Order would capture his castle, Duke Margiris had himself and his people burned alive. The Pilenai sacrifice can be conceived of as a symbol of the heroic, non-opportunistic, yet self-destructive, "nation."

[13] Jadvyga Beliauskiene's testimony, in *Lietuva 1991. 01. 13: dokumentai, liudijimai, atgarsiai* (Lithuania in 01.13.91: Documents, Testimonies, Echoes) (Vilnius: Spaudos Departamentas, 1991) 145.

[14] I have borrowed this term from Lauren Berlant's article, "The Theory of Infantile Citizenship," *Public Culture* 5 (1993): 395–410. Some other observations in my essay are much indebted to this insightful article.

[15] The headline in Lithuanian daily *Lietuvos Rytas* (Lithuanian Morning) claims that "Only a few months left to improve [Lithuania's] image." *Lietuvos Rytas* 2 April 1997: 2. The most comprehensive series of articles about Lithuania's image was published in the Lithuanian daily *Lietuvos Rytas*.

[16] Jonas Mikelinskas, "Naujas senos doktrinos triumfas" (A New Triumph of the Old Doctrine), *Literatura ir menas* (Literature and Art) 2 March 1996: 3.

[17] Judith Butler, *Gender Trouble: Feminism and the Subversion of Identity* (New York: Routledge, 1990) 134.

[18] Juozas Erlickas, "Jei nieko negali, tai ir nereikia, arba Vytautas pas kryziuocius" (If You Can Do Nothing, Do Not Do It, or Vytautas in the Hands of the Swordbearers), *Lietuvos rytas* 2 December 1995: 8.

[19] Liudvikas Jakimavicius, "Literatura ir visuomene" (Literature and Society), *Metai* (Seasons) 5 (1995): 84–85.

[20] Homi K. Bhabha, "The Commitment to Theory," *New Formations* 5 (Summer 1988): 5–24.

Hybrid Identity or Looking to the Future: Migrant[1] Writing in France

Mair Verthuy

A new Europe is emerging today and, like any other society in that situation, finds itself faced with a number of difficult choices, hesitating as to which path to follow. Burdened with a long, frequently conflictual history, subject to socio-economic and political changes of far-reaching effect, this nascent Europe finds its own mirror image, its own *mise en abyme*, in its component parts. All of these far from new nations, each one the vector of a long cultural tradition, each one separately confronting changes similar to those confronting Europe itself, must find their way through and beyond the apparently simple conflict between the old and the new, the traditional and the original, the latest *Querelle des anciens et des modernes*,[2] in order to build a constructive future.

This essay will examine that *mise en abyme* in the context of France and French culture. A brief section will contextualize the current situation by showing how modern post-Revolutionary France initially achieved the integration of all its citizens, old and new, root and branch. At that point, a survey of the writings of a certain number of recent migrants will reveal their views on the hybridization they believe to be more appropriate for the new millennium than the earlier "steam roller" approach. We hope, in conclusion, to establish that the migrant writers, and other migrant thinkers, will be instrumental in bringing about the birth of this new future. This essay will close with some reflections on the French example.

In her conclusion to a recent article[3] in which she discusses certain ambiguities inherent in Hannah Arendt's position among others, on the Greek *polis*, Françoise Collin, makes the following statement:

> Without the majority or dominant group even realizing what they are doing, they occupy the public sphere with their own private dimensions, their own value system, leaving the Others to internalize theirs. For members of the majority, the public sphere is an extension of their private space, which in turn is validated by the former. Their language is the language of both officialdom and social life; their holidays coincide with their religious holy days; their fantasies cover the hoardings; their smells—or perfumes—fill the air; theirs are the fashions which are to be followed; their accent is the norm. Their specificities are universal because they are one with the public sphere which is declared to be neutral. Other people's differences—and all differences are identified

with Others—are relegated to the private domain, to what remains invisible. (Collin, 119–120. Our translation)

The citizens or inhabitants of most contemporary Western nations are certainly extremely diverse in their origins, and Collin is right to draw attention to the frequently uneasy relationships that exist between the various elements. I should like to suggest, however, that both from a historical and from a contemporary point of view, her perspective is unnecessarily pessimistic. On the one hand, what is seen today to be oppressive has often, until the very recent past, been seen in fact — and with good cause — to be beneficial. On the other, Collin seems to me to neglect the very considerable efforts made, in particular but not only, by migrant writers, to define the *rapport* between the members of a given society in a more creative, inclusive and dynamic manner.

After referring very briefly, therefore, to the conditions governing the value system traditionally associated with the French republic, we shall examine some recent writings of mainly migrant writers in order to show the significant changes in perception which are taking place.

It is true that the whole question of the nature and definition of French citizenship or "Frenchness" has been in the forefront of France's preoccupations since the French Revolution when, for the first time, the population ceased being the *subjects* of a monarch, and their relation to the new state therefore required definition. Such redefinition necessarily included questions of gender, of eligibility (*ius soli* vs *ius sanguinis*, for instance) and of a coherent system of national values intended to replace the former feudal fealty.

Thus it was, in 1870, after some eighty years of social and economic turbulence that included both further uprisings and several restorations of the monarchy, that the Third Republic, fearing yet another return to a monarchical system, moved knowingly and with great determination to unite the very diverse French provinces with their various characteristics and affiliations into a single state that shared a common view of the Republic and could command the loyalty of all its members. This political project was entrusted to and carried out by such national institutions as the compulsory lay schools, the public administration and the army.[4] By extension, this same system served to integrate the foreign born and their children into a national value system and to make of them "true" French citizens.

That French system was not without merit.[5] Hippolyte Taine said of the new Republic that, in a lay state, all religions are free to exist without distinction but in turn all religions are subservient to the lay state. The public sphere is declared to be neutral; all religious belief and practice is relegated to the private domain; the political replaces the religious as the primordial social link. This system was preferred to the American mosaic in which, a hundred or a hundred and fifty years after the arrival of their ancestors, U.S. citizens may still define themselves as Irish or Italian and largely intermarry with descendants of the same «origin» as themselves. Until recent years, if not all immigrants then at least the children of immigrants to France "disappeared," were absorbed into the general population and became perfect (or imperfect!) French citizens.[6]

Many citizens of French origin also found the system advantageous. A lay state in which recognition of citizenship is based not on any "religious" or "ethnic" affiliation but on a community of republican values, for instance, necessarily offered significant protection and opportunities to citizens who were not members of the nominally Catholic majority such as Protestants and Jews. For the first time, it was possible for them to enter public life or national institutions and function within society like any other normal citizen.[7]

A number of mainly migrant French writers describing this earlier period, paint a generally positive portrait of this culture of assimilation. The novelist, Yolande Foldès, for example, writing in Hungarian in *La rue du chat qui pêche* (The Street of the Fishing Cat), published in the thirties, tells the story of an immigrant family in France in the years following the First World War. She stresses the egalitarianism of the French school system and its ability to absorb newcomers: "He was not yet familiar with the absolute democracy so characteristic of the French *lycées* where all the pupils are equal, whatever their origin…" (Foldès, 195)

In *Le Cheval blanc de Lénine* (Lenin's White Steed) a memoir-fiction, Régine Robin, the French-born daughter of Polish-Jewish immigrants tells, not without irony but also with considerable tenderness, of her early education in Belleville, a multicultural, mainly working class neighborhood in Paris during and immediately after the Second World War: "Like the Algerian children and the Blacks from Africa, you will learn that 'two thousand years ago, our country was called Gaul and its inhabitants were the Gauls." You will shed a tear when Vercingetorix is defeated by Cæsar […] and you will vibrate when the events at Valmy give birth to a new era." (Robin, CBL, 21) (Our translation.) French children all.

Many other such writers, either by recounting an assimilated childhood or by merely assuming that like everyone else they are normal French citizens, bear witness to this positive aspect of what has been called the "steamroller" approach: Irène Nemirovsky, Catherine Axelrad, Maya Nahum, to name but a few.[8]

More recently, however, for a variety of reasons too numerous and complex to elaborate on here, the situation has changed. The steamroller seems to have met a number of large obstacles, and it is becoming a commonly held view that French society is disintegrating into the American mold. That view is not supported by migrant writers who, while claiming the right to retain certain of their own characteristics or traditions, show how French society itself can benefit from undergoing its own transformation while integrating not only the immigrants, but also many of the skills and cultural values they bring with them. A new two-way street is in the works.

Whereas in slightly earlier times, it was clearly both the duty and the desire of new arrivals to adapt completely to the requirements of French society, today's new arrivals are proposing that both they and the host society move to make the changes that would allow a fresh and constantly changing hybrid society to emerge. The writers and works we have chosen to support our interpretation include the following: Malika Mokkedem, *L'interdite* (Excluded); Mehdi Chareg, *Le thé au harem d'Archi Ahmed* (Tea in Archi Ahmed's Harem); Calixthe Beyala, *Le Petit Prince de Belleville* (The Little Prince of Belleville); Daniel Picouly, *Nec*[9]; *Zaïr, Zaïr, le Gaulois* (Zaïr the Gaul) *and Régine Robin*, "*Pour sortir de l'ethnicité*[10]" (To Escape from Ethnicity.)

This list includes five novels of different kinds, one autobiography and one philosophical reflection. The tactics chosen by the novelist vary from, in some cases, a realistic portrayal of a successful multicultural society to, in one example, a highly symbolic image of the perfect symbiosis. These images are completed by the other two works.

At the very basic level, one might quote the work of Daniel Picouly, a thriller-writer with a degree in Commerce, born to a Martiniquais father. Picouly describes a world only a few blocks away from the area described above by Robin and which figures also in writings by Beyala, but the few blocks make it certainly much rougher and poorer. The genre of the novels, published by Gallimard's *Série noire,* naturally calls for violence, and Picouly provides it. Through all the torture and killings, however, runs a ray of warmth and hope.

In *Nec*, for instance — in which the plot is based on a painting by Uccello, *The Flood Waters Receding* — the murderer, intent on carrying out retributive justice, is motivated by a desire to avenge the earlier State-authorized murder of a Black activist woman from South Africa and is therefore the object of some sympathy. There is clearly a value system at work, no matter how distorted. Indeed, as in many writings of the *roman noir* or thriller genre, it is frequently difficult to distinguish the righteous from the unrighteous!

The community in which this and other killings take place is composed of individuals of very diverse national origin who retain a significant number of cultural characteristics but nevertheless form a coherent unit that takes race, religion, or ethnicity in its stride. In fact, the narrator takes pains to show, in a very impartial manner, the various religions that are practiced by the characters and the affection that links many of the latter across all differences. The action closes on the adoption of an orphan and pyromaniac Black child by the White policeman with the blessing of the variegated — and largely criminal — neighborhood, and the reader will readily understand that the child, who represents the future, represents also the coming together, the collaboration of diverse streams within the population.

Mehdi Charef, the Beur novelist and film-maker, also strives to portray a multicultural society in which assimilation is no longer the name of the game but in which barriers between the groups that make up the inhabitants of some of the larger public housing complexes need not exist. His protagonists of various origins again have cultural rather than racial characteristics, which can then change as the surroundings change. The title of his first, semi-autobiographical novel, *Le thé au harem d'Archi Ahmed*, is difficult to translate properly, containing as it does a play on the words "théorème" (theorem) and the "thé" plus "harem" (tea and harem) as well as on the confusion between the French pronunciation of Archimedes and the possible Arab name Archi Ahmed. But the title also reveals some of the matter of the book. As the French in the eighteenth century took the English word "riding coat" and turned it into "redingote," making it theirs, so today, at least according to the myth, North African children in France transform the name of the geometry theorem and make that theirs. They simultaneously assert their sameness, since they study geometry just like all their classmates, and their difference, since they "arabise" the exercise not only by punning but also by alluding to the tradition of the harem.

Whereas Picouly portrays a world where traditional ties and bonds have given way to another kind of connection, at the center of this book we find family relationships. They may be somewhat dysfunctional but so is the whole universe of Madjid, a young man of Algerian origin living in a huge public-housing development in the suburbs of Paris. The father is deprived of his reason and the son is somewhat shiftless, in part as a reaction to his environment. It is the mother, Malika, contrary to tradition, who works unveiled outside the home in order to feed her husband and children and permit her daughters to continue their studies. France may not have been overly kind to her, but she has acquired a new strength and a new autonomy that were lacking in her earlier life, and her daughters have opportunities that might also have been denied them.

Again, however, the impact is not one-sided. Most, if not all the families, of French or of other stock, who live in the development are affected by alcoholism, by unemployment, by the brutality even desertion of the men or any combination of the above. It is Malika who acts as arbiter in the family disputes, Malika who helps her French neighbors, protects the women who are beaten by their husbands, feeds the poverty-stricken children. Her contribution to the well-being of the unfortunate in her milieu cannot be over-emphasized.

Madjid also experiences some of the positive aspects of a fusion between the different cultures, although at the official level these are few and far between. It is Madjid and his French friend who are at the core of the action, each one giving up something for the other, each one manifesting complete solidarity with the other in the most difficult situations. The book may end with an arrest, but the last image of the French lad, refusing to turn his back on his Beur friend, taken in conjunction with what we know about the rôle of the mother, can only offer an optimistic perspective on a future in which differences don't disappear nor merely coexist, they collaborate to create something new.

A similar portrayal by Calixthe Beyala, the French writer from Cameroon, is both more optimistic and more specific about the changes needed to advance the concept of a successful multicultural society. In the book which first made her famous, *Le petit prince de Belleville*, she describes a year in the life of a newly arrived family of sub-Saharan origin. The family settles in that same multicultural area of Paris that Robin describes in *Le cheval blanc* and that was quoted earlier.

The story is narrated by Mamadou, a youngster of uncertain age, uncertain because the manner of counting is different in France from that practiced in his native country. At the outset, the conflict between the family members and the host society appears to offer no easy solution, although there are many examples in the neighborhood of peaceful and fruitful co-existence. In spite of being able to read the Q'ran in Arabic, Mamadou is considered to be illiterate by his teacher because he doesn't read French. His family's situation is in complete contradiction to the laws of the country. The father has more than one wife and sees no reason not to pursue his traditional culture of polygamy, in which the husband reigns supreme over several wives who are deprived of all power. Furthermore, although Mamadou has been declared to be the son of M'an, the number one wife, the reader discovers at the same time as Mamadou that none of his father's current wives are in fact his biological mother.

As the novel progresses, a number of changes take place. The teacher and indeed his schoolmates, all make a special effort to help Mamadou learn to read and write French and to acquire the cultural milestones necessary to his progress which, of course, is such that he becomes the author of the book we are reading!

Changes also occur in the home and in his surroundings. His sisters continue their studies and clearly expect to remain at school. The women gradually begin to question the absolute authority of the male; indeed the younger wife Soumana refuses to allow the husband to introduce Mamadou's biological mother into the family when she reappears. Soumana eventually dies, however, and as a result of the ensuing enquiry, the father is condemned to a short prison term for fraud against the social security system. Soumana's death and his absence make it necessary for M'an to become the official breadwinner for the whole family and she does so by starting her own business, making African jewelry to be sold. Her success is such that she even has to hire helpers and finds herself employing a white man. On his release, the father accepts this change and develops a new, more egalitarian and more harmonious relation with the one wife he has left.

Again we see new arrivals shedding some of the more unsatisfactory characteristics of previous behavior (polygamy, extreme patriarchal attitudes, etc.) and adopting fresh, more positive practices. Again we see the contribution that can be made to French society by certain aspects of the African culture they brought with them. Mamadou and a young French girl engage in an amorous friendship to which he brings his experience of a loving family relationship that may help to free her from the constraints of her own cold and distant family experience. The parents use their skill at making jewelry to create a new business in which they collaborate with an old-stock Frenchman to give pleasure to their customers. Although Paradise has not been attained, the conclusion of this novel shows the emergence of a more creative union between the host country and the new arrivals.

Zaïr's autobiographical account also reveals that it is possible to become a real "Gaul" without abandoning one's own roots, even though he is careful to point out that this merging or melding is still somewhat imperfect. He himself (Zaïr Kedadouche) was born in France to immigrant parents and, after his father's death, lived an early life of extreme poverty. His exceptional skill at football allowed him, however, to pursue an initial and successful career as a sportsman. At the time of writing his book, he was a regional councillor in Ile-de-France and acted as advisor to the Minister for the City and Immigration in the Juppé government (1995–1997).

The title of his book is also a political statement, rather like that of Charef. Zaïr le Gaulois. Zaïr the Gaul. Children born to Algerian parents in France, as much as children of any other origin, can become, in theory if not quite in fact, full and equal citizens, heirs to the French traditions, sharing the same ancestors. Where Robin gently pokes fun at the custom of teaching children from across the world to learn: "Nos ancêtres les Gaulois..." (Our ancestors, the Gauls), Zaïr clearly wishes to make that custom his own, transforming it for his own purposes. He shows how the French system served to help him and his siblings achieve their stated goals, whether their intentions were ambitious or not. He lays emphasis on the dual culture of his daughter who, half French/Caucasian, half Algerian/Arab, has no identity problems whatsoever and who unites quite easily the two branches of her family. He also relates with great tenderness the story of his mother removing her very French scarf from her head at her daughter's funeral in order to set an example of freedom to young Algerian Muslim women. A true Gaul.

The French tradition of liberty, equality, and fraternity is very important to him, and if he expects the French to be more generous to the Muslim minority because of that tradition, he also wants the more extreme members of that minority to be aware of the French tradition and respect it: "When the question of the veil is raised, it's disgusting. Young brothers imprison their sisters, prevent them from expressing themselves, don't allow them any friends, girls or boys...The telephone is under surveillance. It's true they are in a minority, but it's unacceptable. These youngsters must learn about Colbert, Jules Ferry, Liberty" (Zaïr, 217. Our translation).

Perhaps the most striking image of what the still virtual new France can be is found in Mokkedem's novel *L'interdite*. The author, a medical doctor of Algerian origin, living in Montpellier, France, sets the bulk of the action in her native land, where a young Algerian woman, an exiled doctor like herself, makes a pilgrimage to her place of birth in order to exorcize some ghosts. She herself is the product of two societies, having in effect been rejected by her birth land. Only her exile in France allows her to become a doctor; in turn she uses her medical skill to serve the citizens of France. A happy partnership, so to speak.

But there is a better example of what Mokkedem has in mind. One of the other main protagonists is a Frenchman recovering from a kidney transplant, and the reader learns very rapidly that the kidney used to save his life was that of another Algerian woman killed in a car crash. We then see the man struggling to come to terms with the fact that his body now contains — and depends upon — an organ taken from a donor of a different sex and race. Far from rejecting this foreign, in more senses than one, organ, because, as the surgeon informs him, the match is unusually perfect, his body accepts it without major difficulty as, in the end, in his mind, he too will learn to live with his new improved self, accept his new commingled lease on life.

The coming together of the man, France and the women representing Algerian immigrants heralds a new life. On the one hand, in order to live, the host country needs the contribution of the new arrivals; on the other, the immigrant's symbolic death is the element that releases a positive contribution to the new society. One might prefer, that the immigrant's life not be sacrificed, but, at the symbolic level, the death represents a jettisoning of perhaps the least useful part of one's previous identity in order to make a positive contribution to the fresh life waiting to be built. Similarly, France is seen to be lacking in those very elements the immigrant can contribute. It must be added that, in this image, there is no "disappearance"; the kidney remains a separate organ while allowing the host body to function. Not assimilation, not integration; Mokkedem proposes quite literally a symbiosis.

A constant in much of this writing, fictitious or otherwise, is the disappearance of paternal authority in the immigrant family.[11] Mokkedem's heroine is raised by an old woman; Mamadou's father is condemned to prison and must undergo transformation in order to function in his new world with his wife as the senior partner. The father in Charef's novel is deprived of reason and spends his days staring aimlessly into space while his wife assumes new responsibility. Zaïr's father dies shortly after the birth of the youngest child. Picouly's families, as typified by the Black orphan, all reflect the shifting relationships that have replaced the older family system. There seems to be general, if not always conscious agreement, that the future must include a better, more egalitarian relationship between men and women, that paternity or maternity are not necessarily linked to blood lines, and that youth must be free to redefine itself without compulsory reference to the traditions or mindless authority of the older generations—whether they are from France or elsewhere.

In the works discusses, we can see the shift away from absolute assimilation but also the move towards a new definition of Frenchness itself. As the various immigrants and their children must slough off some of their cultural baggage, so must the French be prepared to slough off some of theirs, to accept ongoing change, an endless transformation of the collective self, in a manner almost reminiscent of the transmutation of base metal into gold.

In a significant essay entitled "Sortir de l'ethnicité," Régine Robin, who is twice migrant, having left France to make a career in Canada, develops the ideas on identity that run through all her writings. Although she speaks fondly, of her earlier schooling in Belleville, she nevertheless rejects the traditional steamroller approach of French integration. She believes it essential to retain and explore some of the characteristics we all bring to the collectivity, whether we are immigrants or not. Having said that, it must also be stated that she rejects even more vehemently both the American and the Canadian multicultural approaches which lock people into some mythical origin. She also rejects any return to or resurgence of some form of religious essentialism. She calls for what she terms a "nomadic space" in which we can all participate, where identity is never fixed but always in a constant state of flux: "Otherness is not difference, and universality is not domination, but that which allows diversity to take flight and beyond diversity that which encourages open debate, the agora, the friction between ideas. *No longer to ask where you come from, as if where I come from defines who I am, but what do you think about this or that topic or situation*" (Robin, Escaping, 36–37. Our translation, our italics).

Identity for Robin is plural, interstitial, indefinite, infinitely open, a coming together in which we are all enriched by what others offer and are rich enough to bring a significant offering in exchange. Her fiction and non-fiction writings capture what we have seen expressed elsewhere. In novels, in autobiography, in philosophical reflection, all these migrant writers are pointing the way towards a new France and a new Europe. After more than a century of assimilation, they are now suggesting that the new way forward is of a different nature; that, to survive well, France and Europe must transform closure into unending openness, that today and in the future they must in their turn assimilate at least in part what the diverse immigrant cultures have to offer, as these cultures will themselves continue to adopt and absorb the cultures of their host countries. The migrants are perhaps the midwives helping with the birth of a new hybrid identity. The host body must now find the time for nurturing that fresh life.

Conclusion

The situation confronting the burgeoning European community is reminiscent of the situation in France during the nineteenth century. The national territory was composed of different regions, often with their own customs and languages or dialects. New territories such as Savoy or Nice were added as the years went by, a process which created its own integration problems. The very values which underlay the Republic required that full citizenship and rights be at last granted to people who did not share the same religious beliefs as the Catholic majority (Jews, Protestants, atheists, etc.). France was also rapidly attracting more and more immigrants from surrounding countries. In all, they comprised a diverse population with diverse traditions.

In the nineteenth century, a strong central government was able to impose its wishes on all the component parts of the nation and create modern France. Although no situation ever achieves permanent stability (regionalism is once again on the rise, extreme right wing ideas exploit the disarray that accompanies major population shifts), France's achievement remains considerable. Today, the authors discussed show how those earlier ideals may be adapted to fit a changing world. Although the same process, from centralization to hybridization, is perhaps neither possible nor desirable in the case of the new Europe, it must be clear from these writings that every effort should and can be made to establish a common identity which achieves both constant flux and a certain stasis.

Notes

[1] The word “migrant will be used here to describe not only recent immigrants, but also the children of immigrants, who may or may not have already acquired citizenship in the new country, in this case, France. This usage emphasizes the existence of the double (or triple…) cultural affiliation at issue here.

[2] La Querelle des anciens et des modernes (The Quarrel of the Ancients and the Moderns): a literary and philosophical quarrel which took place in seventeenth century France, pitting against each other writers such as Perrault and Fontenelle on one side, in favor of modern writers, and on the other Boileau, Racine, etc., who preached the superiority of the writers of Antiquity.

[3] Collin, Françoise. “Point de vue grec et point de vue juif : Hannah Arendt” *in* Kandel, Liliane Ed. *Féminismes et nazisme*, Paris : Publications de l’Université Paris 7, Denis-Diderot, coll. Les Cahiers de CEDREF, série “Colloques et travaux.” (1977), 109–120.

[4] cf. With some reservations: Schnapper.

[5] Indeed, it might be argued that the French experience constitutes both a *mise en abyme* of the situation confronting Europe today and a possible solution.

[6] Taine, Hippolyte, *Les origines de la France contemporaine*, Paris : R. Laffont, 1986. III, t. 1, p. 278.

[7] It should be noted that this tendency would appear to continue today. According to the results of a two-year survey published by the Institut national des études démographiques (The National Institute of Demographic Studies), young foreign-born males, including those of Algerian origin, continue to integrate and to intermarry or establish long-term relationships with young French women at a remarkably high rate, although young females, from Maghreb in particular, seem to have more difficulty in this area in part, no doubt, because of parental pressure to “keep the faith.”

[8] Such was the positive side of the rather negative image quoted in the introduction to this text. Such was the image of France apparently internalized by most, if not all, citizens — with the tragic exceptions of, for instance, the Dreyfus affair and the period covered by the Nazi occupation of France. None of the contemporary reviews I have found, to name but one writer, of the novels and other writings published by Irène Nemirovsky in the 1930s allude to her either as being of Jewish or Russian birth. And although Nemirovsky may portray characters who are Jewish in *David Golder*, for example, their behavior and values are in no way different from those of their non-Jewish counterparts. One may add that, although the relation of immigrants or members of minority groups to the majority population gradually changed after the Second World War, it would still have been highly unusual to find any reference in a critical review to the “ethnic” or “religious” affiliations of such writers as Hélène Parmelin, Dominique Desanti, Vladimir Pozner, Victor Leduc, etc.

[9] It is true that the French filmmaker of Armenian origin, Henri Verneuil, strikes a somewhat discordant note when describing his first years in France. It should be noted, however, that he spent those early years in a private Catholic school. His «Armenianness» was never an issue in his later years either in the public school system or in his professional career.

[10] Foldès, Yolande, *La rue du chat qui pêche* (The Street of the Fishing Cat), Paris: Albin Michel, 1937.

[11] Robin, Régine. *Le cheval blanc de Lénine ou l'histoire autre*. Bruxelles: Complexe, 1979.

[12] Axelrad, Catherine. *La Varsovienne*. Paris: Gallimard, 1990; Nahum, Maya, *La mal élevée*. Paris: Editions de l'Olivier, 1991; Nemirovsky, Irène. Among Others: *David Golder*. Paris: Grasset, 1929.

[13] Mokkedem, Malika. *L'interdite*. Paris: Grasset, 1993.

[14] Charef, Mehdi. *Le thé au harem d'Archi Ahmed*. Paris: Mercure de France, 1983.

[15] Beyala, Calixthe. *Le petit prince de Belleville*. Paris: Albin Michel, 1992.

[16] Picouly, Daniel. *Nec*. Paris: Gallimard, coll. Série noire, 1992.

[17] Robin, Régine. "Pour sortir de l'ethnicité." Lacroix, Jean-Michel and Caccia, Fulvio Eds. *Métamorphoses d'une utopie*. Paris: Presses de la Sorbonne nouvelle, (1992), 25–41.

[18] The situation has been recently confirmed in a number of sociological studies.

Immigrants and Outgroups in the New Europe: Socio-Economic Implications, Political Choices

Mohamed Yamba

As Europeans move toward closer unity, traditionally individualistic national immigration policies will not suffice in the face of the emerging European identity. In this essay I provide an overview of the European Immigration problem. Focusing on Germany, France, Italy, Netherlands, and the UK, I define the problem by examining the historical causes and consequences of immigration and relate the consequences to European attitudes toward immigrants, all within the context of contemporary tensions arising from progress toward European unity. Analysis of contemporary debates and policies on immigration suggest policy alternatives that favor a harmonization of European immigration policy to address not only internal immigration issues but also the external causes of immigration.

I. Background

European immigration policies have always been driven by economic considerations. This assertion is particularly relevant to the U.K., France, and Germany, the three having the largest groups of immigrant populations. Post-war labor needs for reconstruction resulted in open door immigration policies that facilitated the active recruitment of foreign labor. In the case of the U.K., France, and the Netherlands, the workers were ex-colonial citizens who were encouraged to look up to the colonial capital as "home."[1] In the meantime, policy makers, absorbed with the euphoric imperative of the period, failed to anticipate the political and social implications of labor migration. The era of economic expansion came to an end in the 1970s as part of a global phenomenon. Immigrants' hope of eventual return faded away and many were joined by family members. Those European nations had become de facto multicultural societies with spatially defined concentrations of non-native populations, but official policy continued to ignore their presence. Thus, "immigrants," many of whom are actually European-born, became "outgroups," insular in their lifestyles and identities, easy target for anti-immigrant sentiment, including violence, xenophobia, and racism.

Subsequent events on the European scene have aggravated the immigration issue. On the one hand, a European Union, with free movement of goods and persons, raises the problem of what to do about these "immigrants," both legal and illegal, who would have all of greater Europe to their advantage. On the other hand, the unification of the two Germanys and the disintegration of the Soviet bloc have raised the fear of an influx of unemployable immigrants from Eastern Europe and the former Soviet Union. The immigration issue has consequently become one of how to regulate, control, and deal with unwanted residents and uninvited new comers.

II. Controlling Immigration

Controlling immigration has become a top European domestic priority for several reasons. First, the numbers of non-European community citizens in Europe is on the increase. There are about 14 million foreign residents in the 12 E.U. member states out of a total population of 329 million, excluding illegals.[2] Country differences notwithstanding, the increases are modest overall, representing a rather small proportion of total populations (see Table 1).

Table 1: Percentage of foreign population in selected Western European countries

	1988	1989	1990	1991	1992
Germany	7.3	7.5	8.2	8.1	8.3
France	5.9	6.2	6.4		
Italy	1.1	1.3	1.4	1.2	1.3
Netherlands	4.2	4.3	4.8	4.8	4.9
U.K.	3.2	3.2	3.3	3.4	4.1

Source: SOPEMI. Trends in International Migration. Parts: OECD, 1994

Much more disturbing is the increasing numbers of asylum seekers (see Table 2), which is blamed for the dramatic increases in the numbers of "illegal immigrants." Table 2 shows Germany to have the greatest numbers of asylum seekers, a consequence of liberal asylum laws and geopolitical factors, like proximity to the former communist bloc and Yugoslavia.[3] These increases are in spite of legal and administrative changes that have made it more difficult for those seeking refugee status to gain admission.

Table 2. Asylum seekers into selected OECD countries (thousands) (1982–1992)

	1982	1984	1986	1988	1990	1992
Germany	37.2	35.3	99.9	103.1	193.1	256.1
France	22.5	21.6	26.2	34.3	57.7	50.0
Italy		4.6	6.5	1.4	4.7	27.0
Netherlands	1.2	2.6	5.9	5.9	21.2	21.6
U.K.	4.2	3.9	4.8	5.7	30.0	57.7

Source: SOPEMI. Trends in International Migration. Paris: OECD, 1992

Table 2 does not include the category of "illegals," those who are neither legal entrants nor asylum seekers, and those asylum seekers whose petitions have been rejected but who have failed to leave. The International Labor Organization (ILO) estimated that there were about 2,600,000 illegal residents, comprising about 14 percent of the total foreign population, in Western Europe in 1996. Illegals have been prevalent in Europe. Only now becoming notorious, they are engaged in the underground economy, in vital services that indigenous citizens often find unattractive. The number of illegals certainly exceeds the ILO estimate, the nature of illegal residence being such that it defies numerical definition.

Collinson (1993:3) may have been moved by those facts to conclude that "... the spectacle of large numbers of migrants evading immigration rules provides a dramatic example of the erosion of state sovereignty...."[4] Thus, the presence of undocumented foreigners poses several problems.

First, states like the U.K., France, Germany, and the Netherlands that took in large numbers of immigrants in the past are still struggling to come to terms with the socio-political implications of the presence of those immigrants. Therefore, there is the perception that immigration is a threat which Europe, with its porous borders, is ill-equipped to deal with, and that there is no end in sight. Second, the immigration imperative is related to the politics of change, meaning concern over the rapid changes that have followed the end of the cold war, including the drive to a united Europe. This, amid pressures of budget deficits, unemployment, inflation, questions about the welfare state, a generally traumatic uncertainty in times of change. Third, the immigration issue has entered political conflict in the nature of disagreements over policy. Mainstream political parties are being forced to share power with right wing, nationalistic, racist political parties that are gaining electoral power.[5] Traditional parties have failed to incorporate the concerns of segments of the population who demand more effective regulation of immigration. Finally, it is estimated that the European Union labor force will increase to 180 million by the year 2010. This will be matched by 166 million actual jobs, leaving 14 million unemployed.[6] Large numbers of undocumented immigrants would aggravate the unemployment problems that will confront the E.U. Immigration is consequently of real concern, and this concern affects the attitudes of Europeans toward immigrants and provides the context for public policy debates about immigration and immigrants.

III. European Attitudes toward Immigrants and Outgroups

The presence of insular minority groups and the inflow of more immigrants during a period of increasing unemployment (all within a context of uncertainty raised by changes that are occurring in Europe) have contributed to considerable anti-immigrant feeling, and politicized racial issues in national elections.

Generally, the negative bias against immigration is replete with misinterpretations, stereotypes, and misconceptions. Certainly, there is some cause for alarm, but for the most part European attitudes have not been shaped by realistic appraisal of the issues.

It is assumed that, given the chance, migrants will flock en mass to Europe. King (1993) argues that this is false and that only a minority actually migrate.[7] It is also assumed that migrants, who propose to visit Europe temporarily, will remain as permanent residents, legally or otherwise. However, the advent of easy travel implies that even the permanently settled never sever ties with "home," and that it is actually the limitations on immigration that cause immigrants to settle permanently for fear of not being able to re-enter Europe if they should leave.[8]

European politicians are aware of the rising xenophobia, leading the E.U. to declare 1997 the European "year against racism." Previously, in 1995, an E.U. advisory committee on racism and xenophobia did issue a report calling on European schools to make special effort to meet the needs of minority youth, for the media to make a special effort to combat racism and xenophobia, and for E.U. nations to take steps to ensure that all legal residents have equal access to employment and fair treatment.[9] In the meantime the outcry against the presence of immigrants in Europe has benefitted the far-right political parties who have feasted on the paranoia of immigration, unemployment, crime, and general uncertainty.[10]

In Germany, youth unemployment, the continuing influx of asylum seekers, the steady stream of incoming ethnic Germans from the East at a rate of about 220,000 persons per year since 1993, and the rise of ethnic ghettos have caused great anxiety and provided rich fodder for right-wing parties. In France, National Front's Leader Le Pen's extreme right ideology blames all social ills on immigration: "Everything comes from immigration. Everything goes to immigration."[12] Similar to Germany, behind the ill-will looms national unemployment (about 12 percent in France) which is blamed on immigrants, though the jobless rate among those immigrants is really about three times the national average.[13] The National Front has consequently garnered a consistent 10–15 percent of the national vote, largely by urging "national preference," demanding that immigrants be sent back, and calling a halt to further immigration.[14] According to Franklin (1995), many share Le Pen's views.[15] A *New York Times* article (April 27, 1995), quoted presidential candidate Jacques Chirac as stating: "France must firmly oppose illegal immigration." This was not surprising, it being an obvious attempt to win votes from the extreme right. So it is that traditional European parties are having to accommodate the views of the radical right.

These factors notwithstanding, well organized right wing parties are in the minority,[16] and general public opinion is not supportive of the views of right wing parties. Putting the blame of all social ills on immigrants is not representative of the views of the voting majority. A 1993 statistical analysis of

Eurobarometer survey data (based on a 1991 survey of the attitudes of Europeans towards immigrants and other related social issues) indicated that only an average 5 percent of the national samples drawn from the UK, France, Germany, and the Netherlands expressed support for, or were sympathetic to, right wing views about immigration and immigrants.[17] Sociodemographic variables like education, age, religion, and the feeling of "alienation" were found to be modestly significant, overall, in determining respondents' level of approval of policy proposal to repatriate all immigrants. For the French and German samples only "changes in family income" was found to be significant in determining respondents' level of sympathy with right-wing views on immigration and support for right-wing parties.[18] However, contrary to the survey data cited above, Franklin (1995) has noted that about a 52 percent majority of Europeans (in 1991, 1992, and 1993) feel that there are too many non-E.C. persons in Europe.[19] If Democratic societies generally tend to make policies that do accommodate public opinions, especially when such opinions are characterized by intensity of feelings and saliency of issues, then we should expect that those views discussed above will influence public policies toward immigrants. Political dialogue has consequently focused on "immigrant" issues, as certain groups, those of Pakistani origin in the UK, Muslim and Arab origins in France, and the Turkish in Germany, are singled out for the focus of anti-immigrant sentiment.

Otherwise, there is little cross country consistency that is discernible in the attitudes of Europeans to migrants and minorities in their midst.[20] Two observations are consequently warranted: one is that ill-feeling towards foreigners tends to be suppressed in times of economic prosperity and general well-being, and aggravated when the quality of life is perceived to be under threat; the other is that immigration issues cannot be divorced from the tensions that accompany the progress toward a single Europe.

IV. The "Immigrant Problem"

Why is there an immigrant problem? As suggested in the previous section, the answer can be found in a combination of factors, including the presence of unwanted immigrants, increasing numbers of asylum seekers, an unknown number of illegal residents, and the fear of further immigration from the unstable East and structurally poor South, as well as the uncertainty inherent to the process of European Union, all of which have led to the politicization of immigration and race. The problem finds expression in economic and social dynamics, given the inability of individual states to devise and implement consistent immigration policies. Also, because the mainstream political parties are failing to accommodate the diversity of European concerns in these changing times, they are being rushed into supporting a hodgepodge of short-term, ad hoc solutions to immigration problems.

The economic dimension of the problem revolves around the Single European Act, which calls for freedom of movement of persons and goods. If non-E.C. nationals are restricted, then they will present a large pool of structurally unemployed, further depressing local economies. Rather, immigrants who are opportunistic, will become mobile in search of better opportunity. Immigrants tend to be found in well-paid professional positions if they have a permit to work and have qualifications, or at the bottom of the economic structure if they have none. It is not uncommon to find immigrant doctors and technicians from Eastern Europe and Africa toiling away in underpaid restaurant jobs for which they are grossly overqualified. Therefore, it is not entirely accurate that the immigrants take lucrative jobs away from nationals. The reality is that undocumented immigrants compete for the lowest paid jobs which nationals often avoid.

A second aspect of the Single European Act is the drive toward a European Monetary Union (EMU) which requires member states to converge around 5 economic factors: 1) inflation is to be brought within 1.5 percent of the average of the 3 best performing states; 2) long-term interest rates are to converge around the same standard as above; 3) national budget deficits are not to exceed 3 percent; 4) national public debts are not to exceed 60 percent of Gross Domestic Product (GDP); and member states are to maintain normal margins of the exchange rates for two years. The economic measures needed to achieve this convergence have been unpopular. For example, budget cuts need to be made and social spending reduced at a period of high unemployment. However, in times like these, social spending ought to increase, not decrease as is demanded by the EMU. Nevertheless, these fiscal policy decisions need to be made for member states to qualify for the single monetary union. Short-term unemployment is consequently anticipated to increase.

Much more disturbing is the incidence of long-term unemployment which has increased to a two-decade high. Germany's figures, though lower than others, is said to be the highest since the post-war reconstruction, at a time when contrary to E.U. requirements, deficit spending is an attractive alternative to achieve job creation (see Table 3).

Table 3: Long term unemployment (12 months, in thousands)

	1985	1986	1987	1988	1989	1990	1991	1992	1993	1994
France	1042	1054	1117	1058	986	873	847	861	930	
Germany	890	882	903	823	793	673	634	817	1201	
Italy	1361	1564	1584	1729	1729	1560	1591	1264	1338	
Netherlands	331		293	254	254	233	209	165	202	
UK	1501	1436	1378	801	801	667	683	974	1230	

Source: European Communities. *Eurostat Yearbook '95* Luxembourg: Office for Official Publications, 1995.

As a consequence, budget deficits incurred by the individual governments as a percentage of the Gross Domestic Product (GDP) have increased, with accompanying increases in the gross debts of the general government as a percentage of the GDP. Therefore, newly elected French leader, Lionel Jospin, demanded that the E.C. consider a job creation program as a precondition for France's consent to the next stage of E.U. progress.[21] The reality of poor economic performance militates against the required budget cuts and deficit reduction that the single EMU requires.

When labor markets shrink in Europe, migrant labor suffers exclusion. The results are spatial and social polarization between immigrants and host societies, creating a social underclass of minorities of recent immigrant origin. They live in substandard housing that is overcrowded and unsanitary. For example, Walker (1996) writes about 150,000 immigrants from North and West Africa who live in France's 710 high-rise hostels which are overcrowded, isolated from mainstream society with few jobs or industry, and little opportunity to integrate.[22] The situation is similar in Germany. Illegal immigrants present a different set of problems. Their actual numbers are unknown. They are to be found in cities, living in overcrowded conditions, often as many as 4 to a single flat, working around the clock in underpaid jobs. Great talent goes to waste as immigrants with high levels of technical and social-scientific knowledge, as well as proven capabilities elsewhere, are driven into the informal labor economy. They usually avoid trouble because they must keep out of sight of law enforcement officials. All the same, there is significant loss of revenue to the state and loss of economic capacity that would have been realized from an integrated labor force. Second and third generation immigrants (and guest workers) are excluded from political participation. They complain of ill-treatment and a lack of opportunity due to their perceived ethnicity.[23] Few studies exist on the impact of economic changes on immigrant populations, so the public is informed by journalistic distortions, wherein immigrants are depicted as fostering violence, crime and drugs, further damaging minority relations. Nevertheless, immigration does increase the need for social assistance, promote inequality, and fuel anti-immigrant sentiment. Thus, a poorly integrated immigrant enclave can be a potential source of social tension. In that regard, government policies have failed: they have not been successful in integrating immigrant populations.

The combination of poor economic performance and high levels of unemployment, large numbers of marginalized immigrant and ethnic populations (at a time when fundamental changes are occurring rapidly in the European political social and economic fabric) are proving to be traumatic overall. What is needed is thoughtful policy making and implementation based on innovative leadership on the part of European policy makers.

V. Immigration Policy Choices

The "immigrant problem" is a multifaceted one, but the only consensus among European nations is the agreement that immediate action needs to be taken to halt the unchecked tide of unwanted persons. Traditional practices are consequently of the category that seek to restrict entry and regulate the activities of those already present in Europe. Those practices are mostly related to rising anti-immigrant sentiment, political choices that tend to be short-term and uncoordinated. Beyond that consensus, policy implementation tends to be individualistic, reflecting a mix of individual priorities, capacities, political structures, and geographical location. Overall, the haphazard approach to immigration policies has been unsuccessful: large numbers of asylum seekers continue to arrive; several await processing; many more unknown illegals enter Europe daily; and social tensions continue to mount as minority enclaves emerge in inner cities across Europe.

At the national level, traditional practices have included a two-pronged approach that involve restrictive visa requirements to reduce the number of entrants, accompanied by internal control mechanisms that include measures to integrate minorities, more efficient processing of asylum seekers, and police enforcement of the laws.[24] Brochman (1993) provides a useful model for analyzing these policy approaches.[25] The various measures may be grouped into external and internal categories that find implicit or explicit expression. Thus, according to the Brochman model, explicit external immigration policies include controls like visa schemes, entry restrictions, penalties against carriers of illegal immigrants, and computerized data bases on criminals and other undesirables (a requirement of the Schengen agreement). But these explicit measures may only be minimally effective against documented immigrants. The measures imply a lack of distinction in national needs and permit erratic handling of entry, replete with the possibility of corruption of immigration officials and increasing illegality. On the other hand, internally explicit mechanisms include surveillance and identity card systems, the monitoring of immigrant access to accommodation and social benefits, sanctions against employers who employ undocumented immigrants, as well as integration of immigrants by means of amnesties, citizenship acquisition, and other legalization procedures. However, the implicit dimensions of internal controls contribute to hostility against "immigrants" as the measures deny them access to mainstream society and consign them to economic marginality. The implicit dimension is often concealed, effectively undermining explicit policies. Moreover, those internal control mechanisms do pose a threat to citizenship and civil liberty and may result in social tensions among nationals, because they will be subjected to objectionable security searches, ostensibly to catch a few illegals.

The problem is further aggravated by national inconsistencies in the distinction between nationals and foreigners. In France and the UK, "foreign" looking persons may be nationals and that fact is recognized. Therefore, the preferred term is "minority." In Germany, on the other hand, all immigrants and their descendants are referred to as "foreigners" regardless of their legal status.[26] Another set of inconsistencies relate to approaches to the integration of minority groups. The UK approach is implicitly multicultural with emphasis on race relations, comparable to the approach in the Netherlands. The French favor assimilation. Italian policy makers talk about multiculturalism while taking no policy action in that direction. Germany presumes to be a non-immigrant society while possessing some of the most liberal asylum laws in Europe. At the same time, the increasing politicization of race and immigration issues is causing these governments to distance themselves from any explicit integration measures, or race-specific policies, because they are currently politically unpalatable. By implication, contemporary practices are uncoordinated, haphazard responses in the light of perceived right-wing demands channeled into public opinion. Thus, non-European minorities tend to be the least integrated in Europe, most of them remaining marginalized in inner city ghettos.

The relative geographical location of countries in Europe also causes difficulties in immigration policy implementation. Italy and others on the Mediterranean rim have uncontrollable borders and are an illegal immigrants' conduit to the north. For example, Italy's new immigration bill allows illegal immigrants to be deported, but they are given 15 days to depart and are then set free. Many escape up north, of course. Similarly, Germany's generous asylum laws encourage illegals to use German ports as points of entry from where they gain easy access to other parts of Europe. In reaction, the UK and France have little confidence in the ability and capacity of their neighbors to police their borders and prevent illegal immigration.

Compounding the difficulty is the different administrative approaches to internal control. France's identity card system permits greater internal administrative regulation of immigrants, including official authority to stop, search, and seize immigrants. The UK has no similar control mechanisms, nor are UK citizens willing to tolerate such police powers. This means that illegals who enter the UK have a greater chance of remaining undetected, hence the UK's distrust of others' ability to keep out unwanted immigrants.

Finally, restricted entry and control mechanisms are based on the assumption that would-be immigrants will be deterred by the hostile regulations and the incidence of illegals will decline. Needless to say, this assumption is false. For every illegal immigrant who is interdicted at the border and repatriated, five to ten others gain entry. Illegal migrants are resilient. Many are deported one day only to return a week later. If at first they try and do not succeed to enter the country of their choice, they try again, and again, until they succeed. Potential illegal migrants would endure untold hardships to reach European ports. West African immigrants bound for Europe have trekked across the Sahara, risking life and liberty to reach Algeria, Tunisia, Morocco, or even Libya, because somebody has a "connection," meaning the knowledge of someone who knows another who has the wherewithal to smuggle, guide, or provide documents to gain access to Europe and beyond. Others have gone the circuitous route of either stowing away on ships bound for South American ports en route to Europe, or to some Asian port, then on to Russia, Finland and finally, Western Europe. Yet still others have gone to Liberia or other trouble spots from where they may become legitimate refugees fleeing persecution and war. Once in Europe, these migrants are willing to brave any economic and social deprivation, because those hardships are ultimately to be preferred to conditions in their home environment. Also, the marginal living that they manage to scrape together provides them with enough savings for remittances home to support relatives and family. Therefore, illegal immigration (at least) is guided by estimations of Comparative Deprivation. Because the relative deprivations of Western Europe are preferable to those of immigrants' home countries, the latter will risk it all to enter Western Europe and other western industrial societies.[27] In effect, control mechanisms do not work against illegal immigration. With little internal consensus on appropriate immigration policies, the widely divergent ideological views of immigration, the differential capacity and ability to enforce laws, European nations are only succeeding to encourage illegal immigration, criminalize immigrants, and stigmatize them as social undesirables, thus fueling the fires of widespread xenophobic hostility.

VI. Assessment

Immigration has posed a challenge to traditional notions of European identity and homogeneity, the consequence of one-sided view of immigration that made labor needs imperative and failed to provide opportunities for the integration of immigrants into mainstream society. Some immigrant groups are favored more than others, resulting in sectoral and spatial segregation of minority groups. The marginalization has, in turn, made those immigrants victims of ill feeling in the contemporary context of high unemployment, rising crime, overburdened welfare rolls, and the political uncertainty inherent in Europe's rush to a single polity.

A review of the literature points to the difficulty, but need to harmonize migration policies at the supranational level. Hence, a single European immigration policy that facilitates practices to

* standardized classification of immigrant groups
* harmonize border controls and internal control mechanisms in order to exercise some control over the movement of third country nationals
* harmonize the appraisal of conditions that give rise to asylum seeking
* harmonize naturalization laws

* facilitate the inclusion of immigrants

Some of these ideals are incorporated by the Single European Act, and mandated by the Schengen Accord which seeks (1) to eliminate all internal border checks, (2) to enforce consistent and tighter external border controls, (3) more uniform visa policy, and (4) a coordination of different asylum policies. However, according to Ralf Dahrendorf of Oxford (LA Times, May 26, 1996):

> When you start talking about pulling down political boundaries or becoming part of a greater whole, people have a desire to want to preserve what is unique about themselves.

This statement illustrates the difficulties inherent in the harmonization of 12 national policies (soon to be joined by others in the European Union). Besides internal tensions and mistrusts, total control is impossible, nor is total control desirable. There are hundreds of tiny harbors in Europe, thousands of border crossings, and many open borders that will aggravate the problem of control. Control measures are inward looking. They seek to deal with the problem at the point of entry, but that is only one half of the equation. Migration pressures from outside the European Communities are unlikely to subside. Therefore, South to North and East to West migrations will continue. Western Europe will continue to need cheap labor to sustain its massive welfare system and that cheap labor will be furnished by immigrants. According to the World Almanac and Book of Facts (1997), Europeans are experiencing negative population growth. France has a natural increase of .02 percent. Germany has a natural increase of -.1 percent. Italy has a zero percent natural increase. The Netherlands has a .3 percent increase, and the UK has a .02 percent increase. These growth rates are hardly enough for sustainable labor replenishment. There is consequently a need for the EU to anticipate their future labor needs in the light of a birth deficit and an aging population.[28]

In view of the above demographic projections, reliance on restrictive measures may be unwise. European governments need to plan and seek ways to turn immigration to advantage. European policies need to include external policies designed to take advantage of immigration. Instead of identifying countries that will face strict visa requirements because of their reputation as migrant sources, the EU ought to develop information and training programs in those countries. This, according to Collinson (1993), will serve the dual purpose of an early warning system about immigration conducive conditions, as well as provide worker training at the source.[29] This calls for the targeting of aid, open communication about policy intentions among multinational actors, and the inclusion of non-governmental actors in the process. Such an option is future oriented and outward looking.

Finally, immigration has social and cultural implications that Western Europe have to be willing to deal with in order to realize a future of multicultural children who are capable of operating in multiple cultures. This will not be realized by putting up the shutters, stigmatizing immigration, and getting tough.

VII. Conclusion

Immigrants have always been attracted to Western Europe, for historical, economic, and cultural reasons. They are generally welcome in times of economic prosperity. But contemporary Europe is changing. A dramatic influx of immigrants and refugees is causing economic and social concern. Fiscal policies required as part of European progress toward unity are causing unemployment to increase. A redefinition of the European identity poses questions about what to do about European immigrants. The result is a move toward greater control of immigration and immigrants, creating an atmosphere of anti-immigrant hostility. In the meantime, national policies are individualistic and often work at cross-purposes. There is the need for harmonizing national policies and administrations under one European approach. However, in the push to restrict immigration, care should be taken: immigration is driven by forces not totally within the control of the European polity. Policy must address problems at the source of immigration as well as making provisions for European needs. A well integrated labor force being essential to the emerging European economy, Europe must make active provision for the integration of its immigrant populations.

Notes

[1] See Stephen Castles, *Here for Good: Western Europe's New Ethnic Minorities* (London: Routledge and Kegan, Paul, 1994).

[2] *Eurostat Yearbook. '96* (European Communities, Luxembourg, Office for Special Communications, 1996).

[3] Conflict in the fragmented remnants of Yugoslavia has unleashed a wave of refugees into Germany, Sweden, France, and other European countries. See no. 2 above.

[4] Sara Collinson, *Beyond Borders: Western European Migration Policy towards the 21st Century* (London: Royal Institute of International Affairs, 1993).

[5] P. Weil and J. Crowley, "Integration in Theory and Practice: A Comparison of France and Britain," in M. Baldwin-Edwards and M.A. Schain, eds., *The Politics of Immigration in Western Europe* (London: Frank Cass, 1994).

[6] ANP English News Bulletin, April 4, 1996.

[7] R. King, ed., *The New Geography of European Migration* (London: Belhaven Press, 1993).

[8] Ibid.

[9] The European Union "year against racism" was launched in February, 1997. Also, see European Parliament, Committee of Inquiry into Racism and Xenophobia, Report on the findings of the Committee of Inquiry (Luxembourg: Office of Official Publications, 1997).

[10] Luciano, et al., eds., *The Far Right in Western and Eastern Europe, 2nd ed.* (London: Longman, 1995).

[11] R. Walker, "Feeling Squeezed, Germany Opens Tough Debate on Who Belongs," in *Christian Science Monitor*, 3 April, 1996, p. 13.

[12] M. Vaughan, "The Extreme Right in France: Lepenisme' or the Politics of Fear," in Luciano, et al. *The Far Right* in Western and Eastern Europe, 2nd ed. (London: Longman), p. 226.

[13] The Economist, 27 April, 1996, p. 53.

[14] M. Vaughan, op cit, p. 227.

[15] D. Franklin, Migration: "New Demands and Approaches for Europe," in G. Luciani, ed., *Migration Policies in Europe and the U.S.* (Dordrecht: Kluwer Academic Publishers, 1993) p. 25.

[16] C. Luciano, et al., p. ; M. Curtis, ed., Western European Governments and Politics (New York: Longman, 1997).

[17] M. Yamba, "A Comparative Analysis of Feelings Toward Immigrants and Outgroups in 4 Western European Countries," paper delivered at the 89th Annual Conference of the American Political Science Association, Washington, DC, 1993.

[18] Ibid.

[19] D. Franklin, pp. 26–31.

[20] M. Yamba, p. 29.

[21] The Economist, 9 November 1996, p. 64; For current projections, see UN World Population Prospects, Population and Development Review, 7 December 1997.

[22] R. Walker, p. 13.

[23] A. Sage, "Cracked Dreams Turns Boys into Real Terrorists," *The Observer*, 17 September 1995.

[24] See Baldwin-Edwards and Schain, pp. 6–7; Sara Collinson, p. 3.

[25] G. Brochman, "Control in Immigration Policies: A Closed Europe in the Making," in G. Luciani, p. 105.

[26] Collinson, p. 90.

[27] Author's conversations with several refugees, asylees, and immigrants in America and Europe.

[28] Barry James, "UN Rights Report Flays France for its 'Racist' Immigration Laws," *International Herald Tribune*, 12 April, 1996.

[29] Collinson, p. 91.

Is Cross-Cultural Communication Possible?

Andrzej Zaporowski

The main objective of this article is to discuss one of the most important consequences that result from the concept of multiculturalism, that is, the problem of communication. What I mean by communication are both verbal and nonverbal human actions that allow one to understand the others' behavior. In an integrated society it seems obvious that its members can easily communicate, assuming also that communication allows integration. In case of multiculturalism problems appear:. How can we communicate with the members of other cultures (or subcultures)? What are the grounds for understanding alien behavior? Is there any method of judging such a behavior? And more generally, what is the meaning of the concept of multiculturalism?

To answer these questions I am going to present two approaches to the problem of communication. One is Peter Winch's interpretation based on understanding and the other is Donald Davidson's passing theory rooted in his radical interpretation. They both are directly or indirectly linked with Ludwig Wittgenstein's concepts of language-games and forms of life. I shall investigate whether these approaches succeed in solving the problems in question. When doing this I presuppose that both cultural relativism and ethnocentrism can be dangerous views, for they lead either to a logical contradiction or an unjustified attitude towards the aliens. The results of my investigation can be applied to the study on contemporary condition of European culture. They should then indicate the possible course Europe may take in terms of integration and multiculturalism.

Integration and Multiculturalism

When talking about integration and multiculturalism, one needs to comprehend words "integration" and "multiculturalism" in a particular way. This is an especially essential condition, since talking requires both the speaker and the hearer. There must be something that they share, namely some meaning of an utterance that is being exchanged between the former and the latter. Otherwise there is nothing but silence or senseless sounds. Here we come to the problem of communication: my claim is that to share some meaning with some person means to be able to communicate with this person. It can also be said that an ability of sharing some meaning of an utterance is called understanding. Therefore, when the hearer says he/she understands the utterance, he/she is able to share particular meaning of this utterance with the speaker. They both can communicate with each other. Moreover, as far as I am concerned the communication means not only verbal, but also nonverbal actions.[1]

Now, let us return to the words “integration” and “multiculturalism.” What are their meanings? There can be several ones. However, if I am supposed to be the speaker (or writer), I propose the following definitions: By “integration” I mean a state in which there is a group of people whose members (basically) share the same meanings of both verbal and nonverbal actions. “Basically” only suggests that we do not live in an ideal world, and so some misunderstandings or misinterpretations can occur. On the other hand, “multiculturalism” means a state in which there are several groups of people, and what distinguishes one from another are the different meanings (of the actions in question) applied within each of these groups. I will call a society integrated, if there is (basically) nothing but common meanings present within it. The society will be multicultural, if its members are grouped due to diverse meanings exchanged by them.[2]

When analyzing the integrated societies, one sees no problem. The reason is that the members of such a society can easily communicate. Troubles arise in multicultural society. The point is that this kind of society is composed of various integrated groups among which there is no communication, for the members of each of them understand only their unique meanings, and these meanings can not be exchanged between two different groups. What I want to stress here is that sharing some meanings makes its users form the integrated group. We can see then that the concept of multiculturalism is vague. For to say that some particular society is multicultural amounts to claiming two things: (1) there are several, autonomous groups which actions are accompanied by specific group defined meanings; (2) these groups form some common entity. How can this contradiction be avoided?

One might say that in the multicultural society there are the meanings which are common to all the members of the society, and there are also the meanings which are specific to its particular parts. The best response should provide us with the possibility of having some link between two different groups. This can be called cross-cultural communication. This can be, as I think, an appropriate tool to allow one group to have an access to the meanings shared within the other group. But how is such a communication possible? And what are the grounds for it? To try to answer these questions I propose to examine two seemingly different approaches: Peter Winch's interpretation based on understanding and Donald Davidson's passing theory rooted in his radical interpretation. In fact they are linked together as will be clarified later on.

Winch's Approach

His thoughts are presented in various works (Winch, 1958; 1972; 1987), and are based on Ludwig Wittgenstein's conception of language-games (1958). The crucial category of the first book is what Winch calls understanding.[3] What is understanding? What does it mean to understand an action? Winch suggests that understanding an action means to comprehend it in its own context. In other words, understanding the action amounts to grasping a meaning the action is given by the actors. There are social scientists (E. Durkheim, for example) that often appeal to the concept of explanation which presupposes an objective approach to the societies investigated. The objective approach to the natives' actions is given in terms of the objective laws, which ignore the subjective meanings of the actions. This is unacceptable for Winch. The investigator will have no appropriate knowledge about any human action unless he/she understands it. And how to do this? We need to introduce the concept of rule which Winch borrowed from Wittgenstein. As it is well known, any language-game is based on a rule. To know the rule means to be able to make a proper move in the game.

Winch also states that understanding is closely linked with what we perceive as a human life which in turn is based on what he calls limiting notions (1972). By these he means birth, sexual relations and death. The limiting notions are to be the guidelines of our investigation. Winch suggests that these notions shape the existence of each human society. It seems that the limiting notions allow the investigator to see the common ground with the native being investigated. Whatever meaning the native's action may have, the investigator can finally reveal it. If we want to understand any native's action, we must not treat it independently from the limiting notions, which for Winch are of an ethical nature. Whatever action we deal with, we need to see it as something performed by a human being.

Here we may ask: "What does it mean to interpret a human action?" It means that we deal with the rational action. If both our and the native's actions are rational, then there must be a possibility of understanding what seems strange and unusual to us. Talking about human life and limiting notions amounts to performing a particular verbal action which is accompanied by some meaning(s). Winch says that what we can learn from the natives' behavior is how the human life can be given various meanings. However, we ourselves give the expression "human life" some meaning too. If I want then to take these meanings to be the "objects of comparison" (Wittgenstein's expression), I need to look at them as if they were put before my eyes. How is this possible?

This is possible because I give the expression "human life" the ethical meaning. This in turn allows me to compare several hypothetical meanings several natives are familiar with. Therefore, the ethical meaning has to be of universal nature. In other words, all the human beings form an integrated society. Now we can see that Winch's proposal allows us to communicate with those whom we usually call natives. But is this cross-cultural communication? Not at all, for when communicating the investigator appeals to some background (ethically defined) which is common to all human societies. Therefore, what we call multicultural society or group just vanishes.

Davidson's Approach

It seems then that it is difficult to maintain the concept of what I have called multicultural society. Let us try, however, to discuss another proposal of interpretation,.such as Donald Davidson's passing theory (1984b). It is very good example, for Davidson is one of the prominent philosophers of language (neopragmatists) whose interests are closely linked with the problem of understanding, what Winch would call a primitive society. In the essay Davidson makes a distinction between what he calls the prior theory and the passing theory. One needs to stress that when doing his/her fieldwork, the interpreter has already learned some meanings of the actions. When facing some native's action, he/she may interpret it according to his/her previous knowledge. As long as he/she succeeds, everything may seem okay. And this could be called his/her prior theory. However, the problems appear when he/she fails. The interpreter must then learn a new meaning of the action, a meaning that he/she has not shared before. Still, the interpretation may go both directions, so that the native learns how to follow the interpreter's actions. The process of learning new meaning by any side is called the passing theory. This means that the interpreter and/or the native need to have a theory of how to construct a whole where particular meanings overlap each other.

There are serious consequences of such a view. If the communication means permanent passing to new meanings, then there is "no such thing as a language" (1984b, p. 446), where the language is taken to be a set of stated rules that govern our speech acts. One may appeal to Ferdinand de Saussure's *langue* in this respect (1961). Instead, what takes place is an exchange of the meanings, where the meanings permanently change, which requires our permanent learning.

Is there, however, any passing theory for getting in touch with, say, a stone or wind? Let us focus on what Davidson says about the grounds for understanding a native's meaning of an action. To catch the meaning we need to know the native's beliefs towards an utterance (a proposition, for example). And here he introduces the following concept: the *principle of charity* (1984a). What he means is that the interpreter has to treat the native as a rational creature. The native may, of course, lie, cheat or make fun of the interpreter. Still, this can be revealed. In other words, the native's actions and reactions are possibly understandable or predictable. Why is this so?

Here we come to one of Davidson's essential assumptions. His guess is that the native's beliefs are similar to ours. This is why the passing theory is able to succeed in seeking for a possible (that is, understandable) meaning of any verbal (or even nonverbal) action. One could ask: But what if the native's beliefs were not similar to ours, or were not coherent? Davidson's reply would be: We would have no reason to treat the native as the rational, senseful and belief based creature.[4]

If it is so, then Davidson's position is similar to Winch's one. For he says that despite several meanings there is a common ground that allows the interpreter to catch them. And this is possible due to Davidson's remark that the native's beliefs must match our standards. These two positions remain very similar, even if Davidson appeals to a logical coherence of the native's actions expressing his/her beliefs, whereas Winch focuses on an ethical requirement to respect what all humans have in common.

Trying to Find the Answer

This conclusion makes the answer to the question "Is cross-cultural communication possible?" negative. And it is negative according to how the term "communication" has been defined above. However, let us look at this issue from a slightly different point of view. What we are seeking is a situation where at least two members of two different integrated groups are able to communicate with each other, that is, can share particular meanings. To solve this problem I would propose the following:

If an interpreter wants to understand a native's verbal or nonverbal action, then he/she has to learn the way the action is performed. It is simply because there is no common ground — ethically or logically defined — for understanding any action in question. We need to remember that our talking about common beliefs or limiting notions is just a series of verbal actions whose meanings we share, so that we become — through reading, listening or the like actions — an integrated group. We also must not forget that through the talking just mentioned we appeal to something that is located beyond what we call the verbal actions. It is not my intention to undermine one's beliefs or limiting notions. All I want to say is that nothing but these verbal actions makes the beliefs and the limiting notions come into existence. It is so because we mean something when uttering particular words or phrases. There can be several such series of verbal (or nonverbal) actions accompanied by particular meanings, which allow us to form quite new integrated groups. Now let us assume that there is some series where through a performance of particular actions we say that there is something that we call an integrated society, a multicultural one, and so on. Here I would say that what the members of the integrated society have in common is that they all share particular meanings of the actions performed. If we are not going to appeal to any quality that would seem to govern our ability of understanding the native's actions, then it will be quite right to say that to understand this action means to *learn* to perform it as it has been observed.

Now let us suppose that there are two integrated groups. The one is our interpreter's, the other is our native's. The question is: Can they communicate with each other? Well, the interpreter may learn how to perform the native's actions, so that he/she can understand what is going on. Shall we call this cross-cultural communication? No. The reason is that what has happened in this case is that the interpreter has become a member of the native's group. What is missing is the mutual process. In the case discussed the interpreter can understand the actions that are performed in his/her own group as well as in the native's one. On the other hand, the native can not do this. However, if they both learn from each other, then each of them may become a master in performing recently unintelligible actions. This would result in a situation where they both could belong to two different integrated groups at the same time. This is what I mean by cross-cultural communication. The point is not to think the interpreter and the native would come into some kind of agreement and start to share some common meanings. This would simply mean that they have formed some new integrated group. What we are considering here are the groups which already exist.

My claim is that cross-cultural communication is a mutual process where the interpreter and the native know what is meant by each other's verbal and/or nonverbal actions. It is worth mentioning that what is meant in both cases is by definition completely different. I also claim that the interpreter becomes a native, and the native becomes an interpreter. This is what mutual process of interpretation and learning requires.

Now we can try to define a relation between two terms "integration" and "multiculturalism." I would say that these are not the opposite but the complementary ones. On the one hand, there can be an integrated society in which its members share the meanings of particular verbal and/or nonverbal actions. Still, we can also talk about a multicultural society. We could take it to be a whole composed of several integrated groups which members could communicate with each other through a mutual process of cross-cultural communication described above. Of course, we may face a situation where there are the groups between which one finds no communication at all. In such a case, however, we would call them just separate integrated groups, and would never use an expression "multicultural society." This results in a remark that we must not apply the term "multiculturalism," if it is not accompanied by the phrase "cross-cultural communication." And, to repeat, we are to meet this requirement in our series of verbal actions in which we define what is integrated, multicultural, and so on.

When imagining cross-cultural communication, I presuppose that both actors, A and B, are going to master each other's action, so that they catch its meaning. To master an action so defined means to predict its consequences. Therefore, a successful communication makes A and B recognize a pair of consequences that result from a successful performance of a pair of actions. Of course, the consequences are defined in terms of the action they result from. If it is so, then they become the "objects of comparison" for both A and B. The consequences are likely to go completely different directions. Still, it is possible that they oppose each. We can imagine a situation, where the performance of one action excludes the possibility of performance of other action (one can think of democratic and totalitarian systems in this respect). On the other hand, the consequences of both actions may show lots of resemblances. In such a case the actors may try to adjust their own actions, so that they become identified. There are, of course, many other possibilities of comparing the consequences in question, but they all can be located between these two extreme options I have just mentioned.

On the other hand, we need to remember that cross-cultural communication may not take place at all. The point is that it is given in terms of possibility, and not of necessity. Still, we perceive any action as heard sounds or seen bodily movements. To understand such an action means to catch its meaning properly. Otherwise we produce simple metaphors, when referring to the action. In other words, we look at it in a wrong way.

All this has important consequences for the study on European condition of culture in terms of communication. We can see Europe as a set of integrated societies, groups, organizations or associations. The question arises, whereas it is a multicultural site. As far as I am concerned the response should be given in the form of the following conditional: Europe is the multicultural site if and only if there is cross-cultural communication between any two distinguishable integrated groups living in Europe.

In contemporary Europe one may face both the states of conflict and the processes of reconciliation. The question is, whether they result from cross-cultural communication or from metaphors produced by any side. My guess is that to answer this question we need to introduce the notion of partnership. To accept or reject an action one has to know its consequences in terms of an actor's meaning.

Violence and destruction are especially visible, when noticing that the mutual process of communication is replaced by dominance of any side. One can enumerate lots of conflicts in European history, which have been initiated to destroy or subordinate other peoples. Some of them are still present. Northern Ireland, Corsica, Basque Provinces and Bosnia remind us of a struggle against the invaders to save one's own identity and autonomy. On the other hand, one has to remember that to be at a war means to distinguish between the invader's soldiers and civilians. This distinction is followed by the identification of a fighter and a terrorist by means of completely different characteristics. Do we face the results of communication or of metaphors here?

Reconciliation is the opposite process to conflict. Here one presupposes that one should reach a compromise with one's opponent to redefine future neighborhood. Poland is a good example in this respect. It has been invaded by Germany or Russia, but also has invaded other countries (Ukraine, for example). Poles' reconciliation with Russians and Ukrainians is not the same thing. Another problem is the relation between Poles and Jews. These are the peoples who used to live close to each other for nearly a thousand years. Now they seem to take quite distant positions. One should also look at the relation between East and West Germans or Slovaks and Hungarians. How many metaphors are still present?

As I have already said, any reconciliation or conflict requires cross-cultural communication. Otherwise there is nothing but misleading metaphors. It is individuals, however, who decide whether to reconcile or not. So do the ones who may initiate any conflict. What cross-cultural communication gives us is a choice between one's having metaphors and one's experiencing different cultural realms.

Conclusion

This article started with the question "Is cross-cultural communication possible?." The question is put in terms of integration and multiculturalism. Both the former and the latter are defined by means of the concept of meaning of verbal and nonverbal actions, and are taken to be a tool applied in the studies of culture. As I have tried to show, the answer is positive. It results in a claim that "integration" and "multiculturalism" are complementary terms. As a consequence of this, cross-cultural communication is a mutual process of interpretation performed by the representatives of different integrated communities, which live in a multicultural site.

Cross-cultural communication may become a tool to allow the Europeans to share more ideas with each other rather than impose their own on the others. The Europeans can also try to apply the communication to respect and get in touch with other cultures, so that Europe is no longer associated with colonialism or postcolonialism. A successful performance of cross-cultural communication should replace both states with co-existence and co-operation.

Notes

[1] Let us suppose that some speaker says, "it is raining." If some hearer reacts with words "then you should take an umbrella with you, if you are going to go out," we can say that he/she understands the speaker's message. On the other hand, if a person A sees a person B with the umbrella, then A may suppose that it is raining. If A wants to go out and takes his/her umbrella or raincoat with him/her, then we can say A understands B's message as well. The latter situation can be called nonverbal action. I do not want to distinguish between intentional and, say, reflexive action (or behavior). What is essential here is a remark that both verbal and nonverbal actions are accompanied by some meaning that may (although may not) be grasped. And the process through which one gets acquainted with the meaning of a perceived action (heard sounds or seen bodily movements) can be called an interpretation.

[2] Note that I am now using the words, which have some meanings. If they are to be understood by you (a hearer, a listener or a reader) as they are by me (a speaker or a writer), then we will be called an integrated group. Still, the group may be a part of multicultural society. There can be quite different meanings of words "multiculturalism" and "integration." But what about the meanings of a word "word"? This is very important issue, for the question suggests that the definitions just mentioned are of metalinguistic, and not just linguistic nature. Saying that we (hypothetically) are the integrated group amounts to seeing "us" as a part of some picture before our eyes. The point is that we can talk about several things, and it is possible to have our talking among these things. Here we will operate on a higher level, for our talking about "our talking" suggests that our present talking is metalinguistic as compared to what has been noticed, namely linguistic "our talking." Therefore, if I say that we can be the integrated group, I refer to something that has happened on the level below, and the term "integrated" has now completely new, metalinguistic, meaning. I am saying all this to avoid a contradiction. What does this mean? If I say that words have meanings, I produce some utterance. But it would be incorrect to say that a meaning has some meanings. What I am only allowed to say is that a word "meaning" has some meanings. Here the quotation marks show that some linguistic word has been included in the metalanguage. To conclude: saying that we can be the integrated group means nothing but the fact that we reflect on our verbal (or nonverbal) actions. The present saying (or writing) could also be analyzed in the same way. It would be then reflected on or, say, put before our eyes.

[3] To have a proper picture of it we need to respect a distinction Winch made between philosophy and social sciences. In his opinion the former clarifies the concepts which the latter uses as a tool of investigation. Still, one may talk about particular segments of philosophy like the philosophy of religion or the philosophy of art. They provide a scientist (an investigator) with specific

instructions about particular subject. On the other hand, there is philosophy as such, and here we come to the task it is designed for, that is, epistemology. The term "epistemology" may seem ambiguous here, or even suspicious as seen by Richard Rorty (1979). But Winch provides us with a criterion that clarifies the concept: the criterion is that epistemology is nothing but defining the conditions of understanding the verbal or nonverbal actions the investigator faces. This is not to say that philosophy tells (social) sciences how to understand a specific action. Philosophy is to determine the very possibility of understanding the action. It is then to answer the question, how understanding is possible at all. After the satisfactory response is given, the particular segments mentioned above may play their role successfully.

[4] The argument reflects Davidson's view on a relation between meaning and truth, and truth and belief. It is an essential part of his theory of radical interpretation (1980). To understand it we need to appeal to Alfred Tarski's concept of truth semantically defined (Tarski, 1956). It is well known that according to his convention T the truth-value of a linguistic proposition has to be located outside the language due to the antinomy of a liar (liar paradox) analyzed by J. £ukasiewicz. That is the reason for introducing the metalanguage in which we are able to define the linguistic proposition as true. Any metalinguistic definition is given in the form of: (1) *x* is true if and only if *p*, where *p* means any proposition ("copied" from the language), and *x* means any individual name of this linguistic proposition. It can easily be seen that (1) defines the equivalence between "*x* is true" and "*p*." Still, to define a linguistic proposition as true one needs to know the meaning of the proposition (so that it can be "copied" into metalanguage). This requirement states that the language is to be included into the metalanguage. Otherwise one would deal only with syntax, and would not be able to deal with semantics (See Ajdukiewicz, 1978). However, when doing one's fieldwork, one may not know what a native means by his/her expression (*e*). I need to stress here that Davidson rejects an applicability of reference (due to the inscrutability of reference) during research. It will be impossible, therefore, to define if *e* is true or not. But Davidson claims that what we can reveal here is the native's belief *e* is true. What is essential is that the native's affirmative uttering *e* suggests his/her particular attitude towards *e*. If he/she then takes *e* to be true, he/she shows his/her belief towards *e*. Here we come to a close link between truth and belief, and their relation to meaning. Davidson says that if the interpreter knows the native's belief towards *e*, then he/she knows whether *e* is true, so that can find out what *e* means. He appeals to the "disquotational" nature of truth in this respect. Of course, when interpreting *e* the investigator treats it holistically, that is, takes it to be a part of a homogenous unity logically defined.

References

Ajdukiewicz, K. (1978). "Epistemology and Semiotics." In his: *The Scientific World-Perspective and Other Essays 1931–1963*, ed. by. J. Giedymin. Dordrecht: D. Reidel Publishing Company.

Davidson, D. (1980). *Essays on Actions and Events*. New York: Oxford University Press.

Davidson, D. (1984a). *Inquiries into Truth and Interpretation*. New York: Oxford University Press.

Davidson, D. (1984b). "A Nice Derangement of Epitaphs." In: E. Lepore (Ed.), *Truth and Interpretation: Perspectives on the Philosophy of Donald Davidson*. Oxford: Basil Blackwell.

Rorty, R. (1979). *Philosophy and the Mirror of Nature*. Princeton: Princeton University Press.

Saussure, F. de (1961). *Kurs jêzykoznawstwa ogólnego*. Trans. into Polish by K. Kasprzyk. Warszawa: PWN *(Cours de linguistique générale*. Genéve 1915: Charles Bally, Albert Sechehaye & Albert Riedlinger.)

Tarski, A. (1956). *The Concept of Truth in Formalized Languages*. In his: *Logic, Semantics, Metamathematics*. Oxford: Clarendon Press.

Winch, P. (1958). *The Idea of a Social Science*. London: Routledge and Kegan Paul.

Winch, P. (1972). "Understanding a Primitive Society." In his: *Ethics and Action*. London: Routledge and Kegan Paul.

Winch, P. (1987). *Trying to Make Sense*. Oxford: Basil Blackwell.

Wittgenstein, L. (1958). *Philosophical Investigations*. Oxford: Basil Blackwell.

